T0260408

Computational Intelligence in Image and Video Processing

Computational Intelligence in Image and Video Processing presents introduction, state-of-the-art and adaptations of computational intelligence techniques and their usefulness in image and video enhancement, classification, retrieval, forensics and captioning. It covers an amalgamation of such techniques in diverse applications of image and video processing.

Features:

- A systematic overview of state-of-the-art technology in computational intelligence techniques for image and video processing
- Advanced evolutionary and nature-inspired approaches to solve optimization problems in the image and video processing domain
- Outcomes of recent research and some pointers to future advancements in image and video processing and intelligent solutions using computational intelligence techniques
- Code snippets of the computational intelligence algorithm/techniques used in image and video processing

This book is primarily aimed at advanced undergraduates, graduates and researchers in computer science and information technology. Engineers and industry professionals will also find this book useful.

Chapman & Hall/CRC Computational Intelligence and Its Applications

Series Editor:
Siddhartha Bhattacharyya

For more information about this series please visit: www.crcpress.com/Chapman-HallCRC-Computational-Intelligence-and-Its-Applications/book-series/CIAFOCUS

Computational Intelligence in Image and Video Processing

Edited by Mukesh D Patil,
Gajanan K Birajdar and Sangita S Chaudhari

CRC Press
Taylor & Francis Group
Boca Raton London New York

CRC Press is an imprint of the
Taylor & Francis Group, an **informa** business

A CHAPMAN & HALL BOOK

First edition published 2023
by CRC Press
6000 Broken Sound Parkway NW, Suite 300, Boca Raton, FL 33487–2742

and by CRC Press
4 Park Square, Milton Park, Abingdon, Oxon, OX14 4RN

CRC Press is an imprint of Taylor & Francis Group, LLC

Library of Congress Cataloging-in-Publication Data
Names: Patil, Mukesh D., editor. | Birajdar, Gajanan K, editor. |
  Chaudhari, Sangita S, editor.
Title: Computational intelligence in image and video processing / edited by
  Mukesh D. Patil, Gajanan K. Birajdar, Sangita S. Chaudhari.
Description: First edition. | Boca Raton : Chapman & Hall/CRC Press, 2023. |
  Series: Computational intelligence and its applications series | Includes bibliographical
  references and index. | Summary: "Computational Intelligence in Image and Video
  Processing presents introduction, state-of-the-art and adaptations of computational
  intelligence techniques and their usefulness in image and video enhancement,
  classification, retrieval, forensics and captioning. It covers an amalgamation of such
  techniques in diverse applications of image and video processing"—Provided by publisher.
Identifiers: LCCN 2022037980 (print) | LCCN 2022037981 (ebook) |
  ISBN 9781032110318 (hbk) | ISBN 9781032420769 (pbk) | ISBN 9781003218111 (ebk)
Subjects: LCSH: Image processing—Digital techniques—Data processing. |
  Digital video. | Computational intelligence.
Classification: LCC TA1637.5 .C66 2023 (print) | LCC TA1637.5 (ebook) | DDC 006.3—dc23/eng/20221012
LC record available at https://lccn.loc.gov/2022037980
LC ebook record available at https://lccn.loc.gov/2022037981

ISBN: 978-1-032-11031-8 (hbk)
ISBN: 978-1-032-42076-9 (pbk)
ISBN: 978-1-003-21811-1 (ebk)

DOI: 10.1201/9781003218111

Typeset in Palatino
by Apex CoVantage, LLC

Contents

Preface

Over the years, there has been tremendous growth in the contents of online/offline multimedia. There is a plethora of application domains in which image and video play a dominant role. Some of the problems in these fields are audio/video perception, controlled activity planning through computer vision, medical diagnosis, etc., and they need to be solved by formulating optimal and intelligent solutions. There is vast research and development in the computational intelligence field and its applicability in a wide range of problem domains. In this book, the concepts of neuro-fuzzy system, deep learning, evolutionary algorithms and nature-inspired optimization algorithms are introduced with their applications in image and video processing. The main objective of this book is to provide a common platform for academicians, researchers and practitioners to obtain a deeper insight into the current state-of-the-art techniques/technologies in the computational intelligence domain and their use in the image and video processing domain. This book:

- Covers various aspects of image and video processing and intelligent solutions using computational intelligence techniques
- Discusses the latest evolutionary and nature-inspired approaches to solve optimization problems in the image and video processing domain
- Covers heuristic as well as metaheuristic algorithms to provide intelligent and optimized solutions
- Illustrates key case studies involving intelligent image/video processing from various application domains
- Includes the code snippets/pseudocodes for the algorithm/techniques for intelligent image and video processing

Keywords

Object detection, Classification, Image/video forensics, Pattern recognition, Evolutionary algorithms, Nature-inspired optimization algorithms, Machine learning, Deep learning, Artificial intelligence

Objective

This book aims to present advancement of image/video processing applications using computational intelligence techniques. Mostly, the image/video processing applications are based on conventional approaches, but this book will emphasize extensive utilization of computational intelligence techniques in designing and developing apt image/video processing applications. The readers will be provided with use of fuzzy, neural (shallow and deep learning) networks and other evolutionary and nature-inspired optimization algorithms to enhance performance. The readers will get an in-depth knowledge of applications of computational intelligence techniques and acquire an understanding of the processes involved in the development of image/video processing applications. The book covers a variety of image and video processing applications such as enhancement, segmentation, object detection and classification, multimedia forensics, retrieval, quality assessment, etc. This wide area coverage will help to attract the attention of various researchers working in these areas. This book will be helpful to identify how to integrate computational intelligence algorithms in the image/video processing applications.

Book Organization

The book consists of 17 chapters arranged in three sections illustrating the use of computational intelligence in image and video processing. A brief summary of each section is presented next.

Section I

This section includes computational intelligence techniques (neural network, fuzzy system, machine learning, deep learning, evolutionary algorithms, nature-inspired algorithms) for image processing, and its chapters are based on the following:

- Image enhancement and compression
- Image segmentation and classification
- Image security and forensics
- Image retrieval and captioning
- Medical image processing

Section II

This section includes computational intelligence techniques (neural network, fuzzy system, machine learning, deep learning, evolutionary algorithms, nature-inspired algorithms) for video processing including chapters based on the following themes:

- Video enhancement, noise removal and registration
- Video segmentation and compression
- Video matting, watermarking/fingerprinting and forensics
- Video captioning

Section III

This section covers an overview of computational intelligence techniques used in image and video processing. It highlights the state-of-the-art literature review of computational intelligence approaches and their suitability in various image and video processing applications. It includes chapters based on the following:

- Rudiments of CI approaches in image and video processing
- Recent advancement in computational intelligence and its applicability in image/video processing
- Research challenges in computational intelligence in image and video processing

Target Audience for This Book

This book is geared toward graduate students, academicians, research scholars, working professionals, and academic institutions involved in associated fields. It also targets industry experts and government research agencies working in the field of computational intelligence in image and video processing.

Editors

Dr. Mukesh D Patil is the Principal of Ramrao Adik Institute of Technology, Navi Mumbai, India. He obtained his Master of Technology and doctorate from Systems and Control Engineering, Indian Institute of Technology Bombay, Mumbai, India, in 2002 and 2013. His current research areas include robust control, fractional-order control and signal processing.

He has published over 45 refereed papers and several patents, most in the areas of fractional-order control and signal processing. He is a senior member of Institute of Electrical and Electronics Engineers, Fellow of the Institution of Electronics and Telecommunication Engineers and life member of the International Society for Technology in Education. He has served on the program committees of various conferences/workshops and as a member of several prestigious professional bodies.

Dr. Gajanan K Birajdar obtained his Master of Technology (Electronics and Telecommunication Engineering) from Dr. Babasaheb Ambedkar Technological University, Maharashtra, India, in 2004 and doctorate in blind image forensics from Nagpur University, India, in 2018. He is working in the Department of Electronics Engineering, Ramrao Adik Institute of Technology Nerul, Navi Mumbai, University of Mumbai. He is a member of various professional bodies like International Society for Technology in Education, Institution of Electronics and Telecommunication Engineers, and the Institution of Engineers (India). His current research interests are multimedia security and forensics.

Dr. Sangita S Chaudhari obtained her Master of Engineering (Computer Engineering) from Mumbai University, Maharashtra, India, in 2008 and doctorate in Geographic Information Systems and Remote Sensing from Indian Institute of Technology Bombay, Mumbai, India, in 2016. Currently, she is working as Professor in Department of Computer Engineering, Ramrao Adik Institute of Technology Nerul, Navi Mumbai. She has published several papers in international and national journals, conference proceedings and book chapters. She is an Institute of Electrical and Electronics Engineers (IEEE) senior member and active member of IEEE GRSS and IEEE Women in Engineering. Her research interests include image processing, information security, geographic information systems and remote sensing.

Contributors

Hazrat Ali
Hamad Bin Khalifa University, Qatar
    Foundation
Doha, Qatar

Ujwala Bhangale
K.J. Somaiya College of Engineering
Somaiya Vidyavihar University
Vidyavihar, Mumbai, India

Ujwala Bharambe
Thadomal Shahani Engineering College
Bandra, Mumbai, India

Rakesh P. Borase
Ramrao Adik Institute of Technology
D. Y. Patil Deemed to be University
Nerul, Navi Mumbai, India

Rahul Chakre
MET's Institute of Engineering
Bhujbal Knowledge City, Nashik, India

Archana Chaudhari
Vishwakarma Institute of Technology
Pune, India

Dhivyaa C R
Kongu Engineering College
Tamilnadu, India

Yogesh Dandawate
Vishwakarma Institute of Information
    Technology
Pune, India

Dipnarayan Das
National Institute of Technology Durgapur
Durgapur, West Bengal, India

Narendrakumar R. Dasre
Ramrao Adik Institute of Technology
Nerul, Navi Mumbai, India

Priyadarshan Dhabe
Vishwakarma Institute of Technology
Pune, India

Asha Durafe
Shah & Anchor Kutchhi, Engineering College
Mumbai, India
Sir Padampat Singhania University
Udaipur, India

Jayanand P. Gawande
Ramrao Adik Institute of Technology
D. Y. Patil Deemed to be University
Nerul, Navi Mumbai, India

Christer Grönlund
Umeå University
Umeå, Sweden

Pritam Gujarathi
Ramrao Adik Institute of Technology
Nerul, India

Muhammad Shakaib Iqbal
COMSATS University Islamabad
Abbottabad, Pakistan

Tushar Jadhav
Vishwakarma Institute of Information
    Technology
Pune, India

Nithya K
Kongu Engineering College
Tamilnadu, India

Nasir Khan
COMSATS University Islamabad
Abbottabad, Pakistan

M. U. Kharat
MET's Institute of Engineering
Bhujbal Knowledge City, Nashik, India

Nikita Kotwal
Vishwakarma Institute of Technology
Pune, India

Lakshmi JVN
Sunstone Eduversity
Bangalore, India

Kalamani M
KPR Institute of Engineering and
    Technology
Arasur, Tamilnadu, India

Krishnamoorthi M
Dr. N. G. P. Institute of Technology
Coimbatore, Tamilnadu, India

Paritosh Jitendra Marathe
Vishwakarma Institute of Information
    Technology
Pune, India

Chhaya Narvekar
Xavier Institute of Engineering
Mumbai, India

Mukesh Patel
Uka Tarsadia University
Bardoli, Gujarat, India

Rachna Patel
Uka Tarsadia University
Bardoli, Gujarat, India

Vinod Patidar
Sir Padampat Singhania University
Udaipur, Rajasthan, India

Ashwini Patil
Vishwakarma Institute of Technology
Pune, India

Dipak V. Patil
GES's R. H. Sapat College of Engineering,
    Management Studies and Research
Nasik, India

Nagamma Patil
National Institute of Technology Karnataka
Surathkal, Mangaluru, India

Sunita R. Patil
K. J. Somaiya Institute of Engineering and
    Information Technology
Mumbai, India

Anaya Pawar
Vishwakarma Institute of Technology
Pune, India

Sushant N. Pawar
Ramrao Adik Institute of Technology
D. Y. Patil Deemed to be University
Nerul, Navi Mumbai, India

Kamalraj R
Jain Deemed-to-be University
Bangalore, India

Srivaramangai R
Department of Information Technology
University of Mumbai
Santacruz-East, Mumbai, India

Md. Mijanur Rahman
Jatiya Kabi Kazi Nazrul Islam University
Mymensing, Bangladesh

Mahnuma Rahman Rinty
Southeast University
Dhaka, Bangladesh

Jayanti Runwal
Vishwakarma Institute of Technology
Pune, India

Anbukkarasi S
Kongu Engineering College
Tamilnadu, India

Mythili S
Bannari Amman Institute of Technology
Sathyamangalam, Erode, Tamilnadu, India

Gurdeep Saini
National Institute of Technology Karnataka
Mangaluru, India

Affan Shaikh
Vishwakarma Institute of Technology
Pune, India

Sneha Shinde
Vishwakarma Institute of Technology
Pune, India

Gauri Unnithan
Vishwakarma Institute of Technology
Pune, India

Jyoti G. Wadmare
Pillai HOC College of Engineering and
 Technology
Mumbai, India

K. J. Somaiya Institute of Engineering and
 Information Technology
Mumbai, India

Muhammad Arfat Yameen
COMSATS University Islamabad
Abbottabad, Pakistan

1

Text Information Extraction from Digital Image Documents Using Optical Character Recognition

Md. Mijanur Rahman and Mahnuma Rahman Rinty

CONTENTS

1.1 Introduction 2
1.2 Background Study..3
    1.2.1 Image Processing Systems..3
    1.2.2 Optical Character Recognition in Text Extraction 6
    1.2.3 Text-Extraction Techniques 9
        1.2.3.1 Text Preprocessing.. 10
        1.2.3.2 Text-Extraction Methods.. 10
1.3 Materials and Methodology 11
    1.3.1 Image Acquisition and Preprocessing 12
    1.3.2 Edge Detection 12
        1.3.2.1 Canny Edge Detection 12
    1.3.3 Adaptive Thresholding 14
    1.3.4 Long-Line Detection.. 15
    1.3.5 Morphological Operation 15
    1.3.6 Block Extraction (Text Block Segmentation) 15
    1.3.7 Optical Character Recognition 17
1.4 Results and Discussion.. 17
    1.4.1 System Development.. 17
        1.4.1.1 Input Image and Grayscale Operation 17
        1.4.1.2 Canny Edge Detection Process............................ 18
        1.4.1.3 Adaptive Thresholding Process 18
        1.4.1.4 Long-Line Detection and Removing Process 18
        1.4.1.5 Block Extraction and Extraction of Word Using Optical Character Recognition 18
    1.4.2 Experimental Results 19
    1.4.3 Outcomes and Limitations 19
1.5 Conclusion... 27
References.. 27

DOI: 10.1201/9781003218111-1

1.1 Introduction

The present is the revolutionary era of information and communication technology (ICT) and computer technology. Recent research solely depends on ICT tools and computer applications. Optical character recognition (OCR) is one of the most promising technologies in modern science. This study relates the fields of OCR and text information extraction systems (TIESs) and assists text information extraction from documented images. Thus, the extracted text in these images can give useful information [1]. Recent image processing research has demonstrated the relevance of content extraction from images [2]. The image and text processing approaches include several methods, such as detection [3], localization [4], extraction [5], enhancement [6], binarization [6], segmentation [7], and recognition of text from a digital image [8–12]. Text recognition from images using OCR tools is essential in the text-extraction process [13]. Vamvakas et al. [14] presented a three-phase OCR approach for detecting historical texts, whether written or printed, without knowing the lettering concern. The first two phases include the creation of a database for record training, while the third interests the recognition of incoming document images.

In recent years, there has been an increase in demand for historical documents and books to be preserved and converted into digital format [15]. The texts in photos and videos aid in the study of such images and videos and indexing, archiving, and retrieval. The data abstracted from the content can be used for a variety of reasons. Digitalization is a requirement in today's environment. As a result, duplicating information from publications to data collection is a time-consuming and inefficient procedure. In these cases, text extraction comes in handy [16]. Document analytics is aided by intelligent text extraction and storage in structured documents [17].

This study explores a variety of ways to extract text from images. The most popular methods are connected component based, edge based, region based, mathematical morphology based, computerized image processing, and OCR-based text extraction. Character recognition and document analysis have benefited from the use of morphological feature extraction techniques. This approach is strong enough to function with various image modifications [18]. The Canny edge detection method produces excellent results when applied to a modified image with the best image contrast [19]. Therefore, we decided to use Canny edge detection for suppressing noises. The Tesseract OCR engine is the most accurate and plays an important role in efficient text identification [20]. Artificial intelligence can now access the vast quantity of information that exists in text owing to OCR. A new study handles textual details in photographs captured by low-cost handheld devices, such as digital cameras and mobile devices. Thus, the purpose of this study is to acquire text information using OCR technology, which allows us to search for text information in a document and attempt to develop a way for extracting any information from a printed or scanned page.

The proposed system contributes a conceptual framework for text information extraction in the Ubuntu (Linux) operating system (OS) environment utilizing the Tesseract OCR engine. Furthermore, C++ frameworks will be utilized to create all the necessary algorithms and functions, including the Qt creation tool and its integrated development environment. In addition, before getting the ultimate outcomes, it will create several resultant images of the system's methods, also known as the system's intermediate outputs (such as thresholded picture, edge detected image, text blocks detected image, and so on). Moreover, the proposed method appears to have satisfactorily completed the core objective of text extraction.

This study aims to design a text information system using OCR tools to detect and recognize lettering content from documented images. It can automate extracting written or printed documents from images and insist on the effective usage of image manipulation and enhancement. The suggested system can effectively be used in text-based applications, such as image database retrieval [21]. Various techniques in extracting text information from images and videos [22, 23], such as text segmentation [24], text objects extraction [25], text recognition [2], and content-based picture or video indexing [26], have been reviewed to develop the proposed text information extraction system. Moreover, the proposed approach involves extensive research. When extracting text, there are many possible sources of variations, such as complex background and low-contrast images or variations in text objects (font type, size, style, color, effects, and direction; arrangement) [15]. These variants make it difficult to draw the process automatically with the design approach. Thus, at first, we investigate the previous developed worked on text extraction from images, and then we try to limit all the challenges of the existing system as well as to propose the appropriate method to design a robust text-extraction system.

1.2 Background Study

Before designing the proposed system, we need to know a clear concept of digital image processing [27], character recognition [28], and various aspects of text extraction in digital documents [29], as shown in Figure 1.1. Therefore, digital image processing is a critical task, and this study performs the experiment based on digital image documents. Several methods or operations are performed on a picture document to mine text information and provide the features data in a text format as output.

At first, a colorful photograph is converted to grayscale and black and white (B/W) illustration (referred to binarization). Then the allied objects detection, two-way projection (horizontal and vertical), and reconstruction are performed to extract text from a background image [30]. A crucial solution in extracting text information from pictures or videos includes OCR [31], and the quality of OCR documents has a significant impact on its outcomes. After detecting text in images or videos [32], the approach generates text boxes with a simplified backdrop, and the OCR engine receives this text for character recognition [4]. Once the text has been extracted, it may be transmitted to the repository together with the document. This section presents many approaches for extracting lettering objects from image documents using image processing methods and OCR tools.

1.2.1 Image Processing Systems

Image processing operations are performed on digital photos that enhance image quality and extract useful objects or features from them. Digital image processing (DIP) is a sort of signal processing, where both input and outcome are digital images or image-relevant features. The primary purposes of the DIP include image visualization, sharpening and restoration, retrieval, pattern analysis, and recognition [33]. Furthermore, as most of the acquired images contain noise or signal distortion, the DIP approach focuses on enhancing visual information, image data transmission, and representation for automatic machine perception [34]. Three fundamental objectives make image processing

(a) Title text in a colored image.

Chapter 2

Biological neural networks

How do biological systems solve problems? How does a system of neurons work? How can we understand its functionality? What are different quantities of neurons able to do? Where in the nervous system does information processing occur? A short biological overview of the complexity of simple elements of neural information processing followed by some thoughts about their simplification in order to technically adapt them.

Before we begin to describe the technical side of neural networks, it would be useful to briefly discuss the biology of neural networks and the cognition of living organisms – the reader may skip the following chapter without missing any technical information. On the other hand I recommend to read the said excursus if you want to learn something about the underlying neurophysiology and see that our small approaches, the technical neural networks, are only caricatures of nature – and how powerful their natural counterparts must be when our small approaches are already that effective. Now we want to take a brief look at the nervous system of vertebrates: We will start with a very rough granularity and then proceed with the brain and up to the neural level. For further reading I want to recommend the books [CR00,KSJ00], which helped me a lot during this chapter.

2.1 The vertebrate nervous system

The entire information processing system, i.e. the vertebrate *nervous system*, consists of the central nervous system and the peripheral nervous system, which is only a first and simple subdivision. In reality, such a rigid subdivision does not make sense, but here it is helpful to outline the information processing in a body.

15

(b) Descriptive text in an image.

FIGURE 1.1
Text variations in digital images.

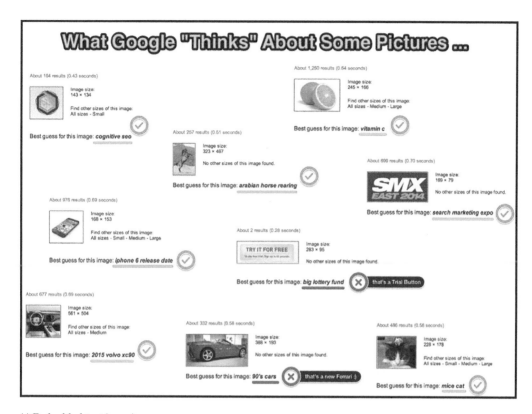

(c) Embedded text in an image.

(d) Written text in an image.

FIGURE 1.1
(Continued)

fruitful [35], including (a) importing images using acquisition tools, (b) examining the images, and (c) achieving outcomes based on image analysis.

Presently, several advanced image processing systems [36] have been reviewed and analyzed to examine further and evaluate recent developments and applications in image processing systems. There are several methods in image processing systems to develop the methodology of image processing systems in various applications. The fundamental steps in digital signal processing performed by image processing systems are described as follows:

- *Image Enhancement*: Image enhancement involves removing obstacles preventing us from comprehending and evaluating an image and altering the image content information (pixels). Some image enhancement techniques include interpolation, density slicing, edge enhancement, noise removal, Otsu's method, etc. [37].
- *Image Restoration*: Image restoration improves the appearance of a digital image [38]. Because there was no criterion for assessing the enhancement outcomes, the process of image enhancement and retrieval of information based on the optimal measure was merely for better perceiving the image by its visual appearance.
- *Image Compression*: The cost of storing and transferring images is expensive. To minimize the cost, we may use "image compression". It is a sort of data compaction used in digital images. "Lossless compression" and "lossy compression" are the two forms of image compaction techniques [39]. Various image compression schemes in image processing, include the JPEG method, the MPEG method, the MPEG 2 method, the MPEG 4 method, etc. [40].
- *Image Zoning*: Image zoning separates image pixels into different zones (based on their brightness, texture, color, or correlation) [41]. An image processing task is required in various applications, such as image therapy, machine vision, image compression, object science, etc.
- *Image Segmentation, Representation, and Description*: Image segmentation partitions a given image into its essential parts or candidate objects [11, 42]. It decides the image data representation (boundary values or regions) that follows the expected segmentation output. Finally, the description involves the mining of useful attributes/features, also known as feature selection.

1.2.2 Optical Character Recognition in Text Extraction

OCR involves the electrical translation of an image's text objects (typed, written, or printed text from a scanned document) into machine-readable content. Vamvakas et al. [14] offered an OCR-based approach for identifying historical texts (printed or handwritten) from scanned document images without having prior knowledge of the content. This approach involves several stages of preprocessing, segmentation, clustering, database creation, and recognition. The preprocessing stage deals with binary image conversion. A top-down segmentation process extracts character objects from the binary image. The next stage annotates character clusters and creates a database using the extracted characters. The recognition stage recognizes text and converts the content into a text file utilizing the database. A block diagram in Figure 1.2 gives the methodology of the OCR-based system. The experimental results of this system are shown in Figure 1.3 to Figure 1.5.

First, the acquired document images (see Figure 1.3) are preprocessed to remove noise and adjust for perspective. The resultant image is then transformed to grayscale and

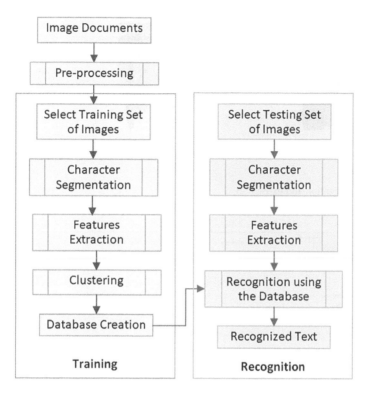

FIGURE 1.2
Flowchart of the OCR-based methodology.

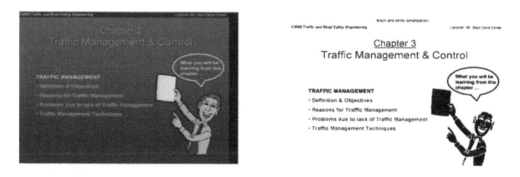

(a) Original document image.   (b) Output of Otsu's segmentation.

FIGURE 1.3
Results of image segmentation.

binarized for further processing using the Otsu thresholding technique. The appropriate segmentation of foreground objects is further confirmed by examining the mean horizontal run of the length of both black and white pixels. For document images with a dark-background and bright-foreground, the binarization output is inverted, resulting in a black-background (defined as 0's) and a white-foreground (defined as 1's). Next, the white pixels in the Otsu segmentation output are calculated. For the image document shown in

  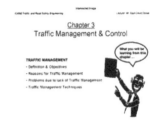

(a) Horizontal projection.   (b) Vertical projection.   (c) Combined image.

FIGURE 1.4
Outcomes of text localization and extraction.

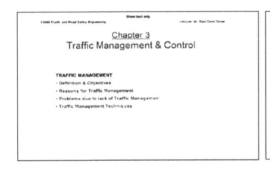

(a) Result for OCR of a binarized frame.   (b) Connected components.

FIGURE 1.5
Text extraction using OCR-based approach.

Figure 1.3, the mean horizontal length of black pixels is 32.3, while it is 6.1 for white pixels. Figure 1.4 shows the results of text localization and extraction using the run-length smoothing algorithm (RLSA) in the image's horizontal, vertical, and combined outputs. A horizontal projection profile analysis is performed first to detect white text on a black-background. Then a vertical projection pattern analysis is performed to eliminate undesirable pixel portions smaller than a threshold value. Figure 1.5 depicts the finished binarized image and its connected components.

As a result, OCR may be used on various documents and can even cope with distinctive characters or ligatures. Nevertheless, the outcomes are significantly dependent on the quality of OCR photographs or manuscripts. The major stages in building an OCR engine are listed as follows, and most researchers followed this approach that provides the intended expectation in character recognition [43].

- *Preprocessing*: It helps to reduce noise from images, makes characters more visible, and essentially improves picture rendering for segmentation. Preprocessing includes tasks such as grayscale conversion, binarization, thinning, skewing, and normalization.

- *Segmentation*: After preprocessing, creates a noise-free, clear character image; the image is split into several subcomponents. The three segmentation stages comprise characters, word (connected characters), and line (connected words) segmentation.

- *Feature Extraction*: The key goal is to abstract significant patterns from characteristics in the image.
- *Training and Recognition*: Template matching, statistical approaches, syntactic or structural techniques, and artificial neural networks can be used to analyze OCR (or pattern recognition).
- *Post-processing*: Activities such as grouping, mistake identification, and repair take place in this last step. However, it is challenging to achieve cent percent accurate character recognition, and only inevitable mistakes may be identified and removed depending on the context.

1.2.3 Text-Extraction Techniques

The content in an image document is categorized into two important groups: perceptual content and semantic content [22]. For example, the color intensity, figure or shape, texture, and temporal characteristics are perceptual content, whereas semantic content includes objects, events, and relations [44]. Several studies used relatively low-level perceptual content for image and video indexing applications. In addition, many studies investigated text, face, vehicle, and human action in the image as their semantic content interest. Among them, we have an attractive appeal in text content in a digital image. It has descriptive properties and easy extraction compared to semantic content.

Moreover, it enables keyword-based image search, automatic video logging, and text-based image indexing applications. The study on text information mining from an image document includes several operations, like detection, localization, tracking, extraction, and recognition [45]. A typical architecture of such a TIES is shown in Figure 1.6 [22]. This TIES can be implemented based on several image and text processing approaches, such as edge detection, connected component analysis, morphological operations, texture analysis, and OCR [46].

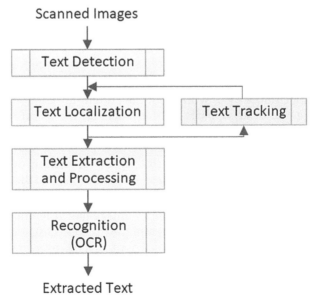

FIGURE 1.6
A typical architecture of a text information extraction system.

1.2.3.1 Text Preprocessing

Preprocessing is the first step in text mining applications. A typical text mining framework consists of preprocessing, feature extraction and selection, clustering, and recognition steps [47, 48]. The preprocessing step has a significant influence on the success of the next phase and, consequently, other stages. For example, preprocessing involves tokenization, filtering, lemmatization, and stemming [49, 50]:

- *Tokenization*: It breaks character sequence into tokens, such as words or phrases. It possibly skips certain symbols like punctuation marks, etc. The list of tokens is then used in the following phases.
- *Filtering*: Filtering is used to remove some words from documents. Standard filtering is a stop-word removal that removes the words having less content information (e.g., prepositions, conjunctions, etc.). Also, it eliminates those words that carry little information or irrelevancy in the documents.
- *Lemmatization*: This task handles the morphological analysis of the words. To lemmatize the text requires indicating the parts of speech (POS) of each word in the text [50].
- *Stemming*: The stemming process is used to obtain stem, also known as the root of derived words. The stemming algorithm is language dependent, and it is widely used in English [51].

1.2.3.2 Text-Extraction Methods

The most widely used methods in extracting text information from digital documents are as follows:

1. *Region-Based Method*: The color (or grayscale) qualities of the text field or the relevant characteristics of the background are used in the region-based approach [52].

   Thus, this approach is employed based on sufficient color variation within the text region and the text's instant background. It is accomplished by thresholding the pixel intensity between the text region and its instant background color. Additionally, this technique is categorized into two groups: connected component (CC)–based method and edge-based method.

   The CC-based techniques [53] work from the bottom-up, combining tiny components into bigger and larger parts until all areas in the picture are recognized. This technique locates text rapidly; however, it fails while the background will be complicated. In contrast, the edge-based method [54] deals with text edges that are consistent regardless of color/intensity, layout, orientation, or other factors. In addition, the edge-based technique focuses on creating a solid distinction between the text and its instant background.

2. *Texture-Based Method*: As the text in a digital image has different textual behavior that differs from its background, this technique utilizes these textual features for extracting text objects [55]. A texture-based approach has been employed based on Gabor filter, wavelet, fast Fourier transform (FFT), and spatial variance to identify the textual features in the image [56]. This technique can identify text against a complicated background.

3. *Morphological-Based Method*: This is an image analysis principle based on topological and geometrical principles [57]. Character recognition and document

analysis have both benefited from morphological feature extraction approaches. This method mines significant text features from the images [58]. These features are invariant upon different geometrical variations like translation, rotation, and scaling in the images [59].

1.3 Materials and Methodology

The prospective methodology is based on efficient algorithms of image color reduction, edge detection, localization, segmentation, and extraction of text with OCR in image documents [4]. After performing image processing and text detection tasks, the proposed approach provides text boxes with a simplified background as outputs. Finally, the OCR tool receives the candidate text boxed outcomes for succeeding character recognition. Thus, the proposed approach is divided into the following steps for text extraction from digital image documents. The overall data flow diagram of these steps is presented in Figure 1.7.

1. Image Acquisition and Preprocessing
2. Edge Detection
3. Adaptive Thresholding
4. Long-Line Detection
5. Morphological Operation
6. Block Extraction (Text Block Segmentation)
7. Character Recognition

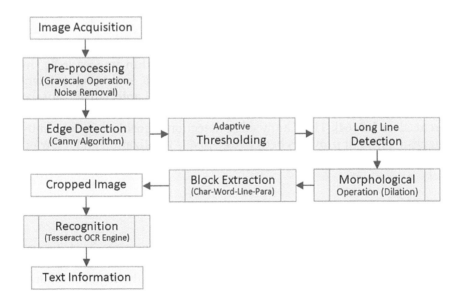

FIGURE 1.7
The overall block diagram of the proposed methodology.

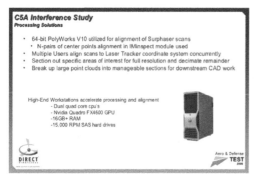
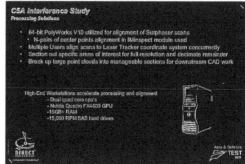

(a) Original image.   (b) Grayscale image.

FIGURE 1.8
Resulting grayscale image after denoising.

1.3.1 Image Acquisition and Preprocessing

This is the initial step in image processing that acquires documented images, attachment-file images, etc. Then it requires adjusting the intensity levels and denoising the input images. It also includes image color reduction, i.e., converting a color image to grayscale, as shown in Figure 1.8. The most widely used image denoising techniques are spatial filtering, transform domain filtering, and wavelet thresholding [60]. Spatial filtering removes noise by calculating the gray value of each pixel based on the correlation of pixels in the image [61]. The resulting image preserves edges and provides a uniform visual appearance of all regions.

1.3.2 Edge Detection

This deals with the detection of regions where text content appears. Edge detection is the process of finding the boundaries of objects within images [62]. This study highlights the gradient and Laplacian-based techniques, including gradient operator, Sobel operator, Robert's operator, Prewitt's operator, Laplacian of Gaussian (LoG), difference of Gaussian (DoG), and Canny operator, for edge detection problems based on different ideas [63, 64]. The Canny edge detection algorithm presented by Canny [65] is suggested here. It provides better edge-pixels localization and a low error rate. The resulting images after applying various edge detection algorithms are shown in Figure 1.9.

1.3.2.1 Canny Edge Detection

The edge detection initially softens the image by suppressing noises. Next, it computes the picture grade using any gradient operator to highlight areas with distinguished spatial derivatives. This method then hides non-maxima pixels in the regions to thin the edge ridges. Two thresholds (a high T1 and a low T2) used by hysteresis further reduce the gradient array. These thresholds track the remaining non-suppressed pixels. It indicates an edge pixel that has a value greater than T1. It also detects connected edge pixels (connected

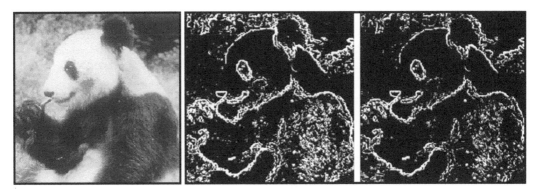

(a) Input image.   (b) Edge image using gradient operator.

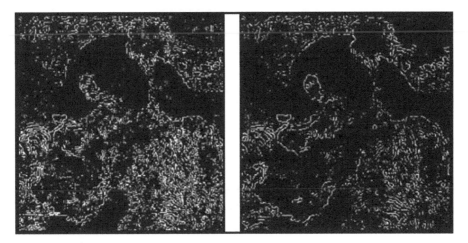

(c) Edge image using LoG and DoG.

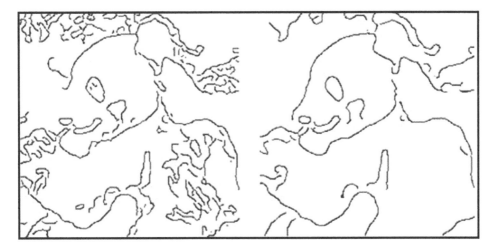

(d) Edge image using the Canny method.

FIGURE 1.9
Resulting images using various edge detection operators.

to any other edge pixel) with a value greater than T2. This algorithm follows the following algorithmic steps [23]:

Step 1: Soften the input image by removing noises with a Gaussian filter:

$$g(m, n) = G\sigma(m, n) * f(m, n) \tag{1.1}$$

and

$$G_\sigma(x, y) = \frac{1}{\sqrt{2\pi\sigma^2}} \exp\left[-\frac{x^2 + y^2}{2\sigma^2}\right] \tag{1.2}$$

Step 2: Calculate the grade of $g(m, n)$ using gradient operators:

$$M(n, n) = \sqrt{g_m^2(m, n + g_n^2(m, n)} \tag{1.3}$$

and

$$\theta(m, n) = \tan^{-1}\left[\frac{g_n(m, n)}{g_m(m, n)}\right] \tag{1.4}$$

Step 3: Set threshold M:

$$M_T(m, n) = \{^{M \text{ if } M(m,n) > T}_{0 \text{ otherwise}} \tag{1.5}$$

Randomly choose threshold value T that suppresses most of the noises.

Step 4: Suppress non-maxima pixels in the edge regions to thin the edge ridges with M_T. To do so, check to see whether each non-zero $M_{T(m,n)}$ is greater than its two neighbors along the gradient direction $\theta_{(m,n)}$. If so, keep $M_{T(m,n)}$ unchanged; otherwise, set it to 0.

Step 5: Thresholding the obtained edge array using two dissimilar thresholds (a high T_1 and a low T_2) to achieve two binary images, one for T_1 and another for T_2.

Step 6: Connect edge pixels in T_2 to bridge the continuous edges. To do so, first find each point in T_2, and then look for its neighbor in T_1 until getting another edge segment in T_2.

1.3.3 Adaptive Thresholding

Thresholding specifies the image areas as candidate text regions or their background. The defined edge zones represent text edges and non-text edges in the image. Adaptive thresholding [66] is employed to compute an appropriate threshold value, T, that is used to eliminate the non-text edges [67]. Removing the non-text edges from the detail content builds a binary image. Figure 1.10 illustrates a sample uniformly enhanced image by binarization using adaptive thresholding. The computation of the threshold T follows the following equations:

$$T = \frac{\sum(es(i, j) \times s(i, j))}{\sum s(i, j)} \tag{1.6}$$

 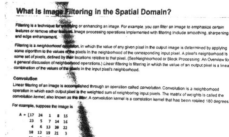

(a) Image suffering from illumination. (b) Applying adaptive thresholding.

FIGURE 1.10
Result of binarization using adaptive thresholding.

$$s(i,j) = Max\left(\left|g_1 ** es(i,j)\right|, \left|g_2 ** es(i,j)\right|\right) \tag{1.7}$$

$$g_1 = \begin{bmatrix} -1 & 0 & 1 \end{bmatrix} \; and \; g_2 = \begin{bmatrix} -1 & 0 & 1 \end{bmatrix}^2 \tag{1.8}$$

Equation 1.7 denotes two-dimensional (2D) linear convolution, and the binary image (I) is computed using the threshold T, as follows:

$$I(i,j) = \begin{cases} 255, if \; es(i,j) > T \\ 0, otherwise \end{cases} \tag{1.9}$$

1.3.4 Long-Line Detection

As the edge detection detects the edge pixels, line detection searches for long lines in the intensity image [68]. A line has a form of $\rho = x\,cos(\theta) + y\,sin(\theta)$, where ρ is line length, and θ is line direction. The mapping of all the edge points from an edge image generates a lot of cosine curse in Hough space. The Hough transform algorithm is used to find log lines with (ρ, θ) pairs and their intersections utilizing a specific threshold value [69]. If two edge pixels place on a line, their equivalent cosine curves will cross a particular (ρ, θ) pair.

1.3.5 Morphological Operation

This probes the small shape or the morphology of features (structuring element) in binary/ grayscale images [70]. A dilation operation is performed here for enhancing the text regions of a binary image. Three kinds of edge dilation operators (horizontal, diagonal, and vertical) help to find the text zones. In very few cases, the selected text zones may hold a few non-text edges. Putting restrictions on the block size overcomes this problem, and the final text regions are obtained.

1.3.6 Block Extraction (Text Block Segmentation)

This step deals with blocking a character, word (sequence of characters), line (a set of words in the same line), and paragraph (few lines) of text content in the documented image. All block seems like a rectangle shape, and the rectangular block decomposition is found first.

It is the final phase of segmentation. This operation is performed by the best-fitting block (BFB) algorithm [71]. It connects all the adjacent text blocks [7]. Initially, the BFB process finds foreground pixels using a top-down scan. Then, another search operation is conducted to find all foreground points adjacent to the previously detected blocks. Finally, all points in the blocks are altered to background pixels. This procedure is also known as text block segmentation or block decomposition [7]. The overall description of this procedure follows the following algorithmic steps:

Step 1: Perform a raster scan to get a foreground pixel (x_0, y_0) such as

$$I(x_0, y_0) = 1$$

Step 2: Locate the opposed vertex (x_{op}, y_{op}) of the BFB at (x_0, y_0).

(a) Set $BlockNum = 1$

(b) Set $XF[1] = x_0$, $XL[1] = x_{op}$, $YF[1] = y_0$, $YL[1] = y_{op}$

(c) Set $I(x, y) = 0 \, \forall \, x \in [XF][1] \ldots XL[1] \wedge y \in [YF[1] \ldots YL[1]]$

Step 3: Set $iter = 1$

Step 4: For every (x, y) belonging to the adjacent line block with opposite vertices at $(XF[iter], YF[iter])$ and $(XL[iter], YL[iter])$ and obeying $I(x_0, y_0) = 1$:

(a) Find the opposed vertex (x_{op}, y_{op}) of the BFB at (x, y).

(b) Set $BlockNum = BlockNum + 1$

(c) Set $XF[BlockNum] = x$, $XL[BlockNum] = x_{op}$, $YF[BlockNum] = y$,
     $YL[BlockNum] = y_{op}$

(d) Set $I(x, y) = 0 \, \forall x \in [XF[BlockNum]] \ldots XL[BlockNum]] \wedge y \in$
     $[YF[BlockNum] \ldots YL[BlockNum]]$

Step 5: If $iter < BlockNum$ then $iter = iter + 1$ and go to Step 4.

The coordinates of the detected blocks with allied text are put into $XF[i]$, $XL[i]$, $YF[i]$, $YL[i]$ (for $i = 1 \ldots$ Blocks). This procedure segments the whole image content into several blocks. Finally, cropping is done to remove the outer zones of the image to enhance blocking, highlight content, or alter the aspect ratio [23]. Figure 1.11 illustrates the image content blocking (into rectangular blocks) in a binary image [71].

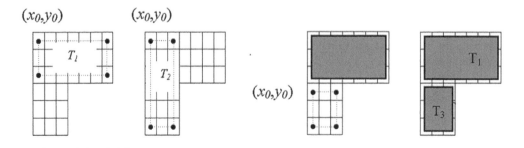

FIGURE 1.11
A simple binary decomposition process.

1.3.7 Optical Character Recognition

This stage deals with translating image content (printed or written or text) into device-readable text. This study employed the Tesseract OCR engine [72] for extracting text content from the image documents. It is an open-source OCR tool [73] in which recognition is done in a two-pass way. The first shot is prepared to recognize each word in a line (text lines were broken into words before). Then, every acceptable word pushes into an adaptive classifier as training data. The adaptive classifier has the potential to recognize text with better accuracy. Finally, the OCR's second pass scans the entire page content to recognize missing words (not identified previously) again.

1.4 Results and Discussion

The proposed design approach has been developed using different software development tools in a suitable platform. The design phase specifies the system requirements, including input data and outcomes, data flow model, and data storage. The developed system has been tested using different types of digital images with text content. The results of these stages will be figured out in this section.

1.4.1 System Development

The development phase describes how to implement the final system and how it works. Thus, it involves the creation and testing of programs and software tools. It determines how the outcome is achieved and meets the user's expectations. The proposed system uses Tesseract with OpenCV to recognize text from document images. Thus, this design approach has been developed using the Tesseract OCR engine in the Ubuntu (Linux) OS environment. The C++ framework (including the Qt creator tool with its IDE) has been used for developing cross-platform software. The methodological steps have been implemented with different methods/functions and parameters to develop the proposed system. The code snippets in the system development are given in the following sections.

1.4.1.1 Input Image and Grayscale Operation

To read the input image (color image) by OpenCV, the "imread()" function is used. The "cvtColor()" function converts it into a grayscale image. The related code modules are as illustrated:

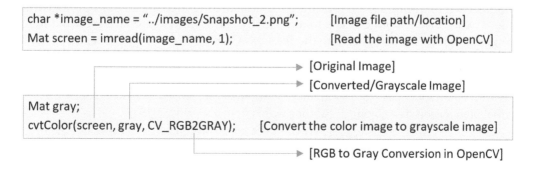

1.4.1.2 Canny Edge Detection Process

OpenCV performs a Canny operation with the "Canny()" function by taking a grayscale image and some true edge values as its parameters. The code statements of the Canny edge detection process are as illustrated:

```
                                              ─────► [Edge Detected Image]
Mat edges;
Canny(gray, edges, 0.66*50, 1.33*50, 3, true);     [Edge detection using Canny algorithm]
                                              ─────► [Grayscale Image]
```

1.4.1.3 Adaptive Thresholding Process

This technique performs some mathematical calculations by OpenCV and checks which values are more appropriate for the text edge than the non-text edge. The code statements of the adaptive thresholding process are as illustrated:

```
# use a hardcoded threshold value for basic thresholding
(T.threshInv) = cv2.threshold(blurred, 230, 255, cv2.THRESH_BINARY_INV)
Cv2.imshow("Simple Thresholding", threshInv)
Cv2.waitKey(0)
```

1.4.1.4 Long-Line Detection and Removing Process

A HighGUI module of OpenCV is used for finding long lines from the grayscale image. Then, a morphological dilation operation is performed using the "dilate()" function that takes the detected long lines as parameters to expand and remove the long lines. The related code statements are as illustrated:

```
Mat lines;
cvgui :: findLongLines(gray, lines);
Mat lines_viz = lines.cole(),
Dilate(lines_viz, lines_viz, Mat :: ones(4, 4, CV_8UC1));
```

1.4.1.5 Block Extraction and Extraction of Word Using Optical Character Recognition

Unit block is extracted for each character by calculating a character's height and width values. After that, a word block is found. Finally, these word blocks are extracted to find the paragraph blocks and passed to the Tesseract OCR to extract text. The related program codes are the following:

```
Vector<OCRWord> get WordsFromImage(const Mat& screen, const Blob& blob) {
Mat blobImage(screen,blob);    [Getting words from a specific region]
                               ["screen" is the image and "blob" is the specific region]
```

```
Mat ocrImage;                    [The image passed to tesseract]
float scale = preprocess_for_ocr(blobImage, ocrImage);

vector<OCRWord> ocr_words;

[Passing the image to the OCR that returns the all words in the specific region]
ocr_words= OCR :: recognize_to_words((unsigned char*)ocrImage.data,
                          ocrImage.cols, ocrImage.rows, 8);
}
```

1.4.2 Experimental Results

In the OCR-based text information extraction experiments, we tested 120 images acquired from different sources, like online images and scanned documents. Most of them were documented or printed images, mostly with text; some were pictured images with few texts, and very few were handwritten text images or bent text. After getting the results, we found that documented scanned images give accurate text-extraction results with little noise. But photos mostly with picture content give text-extraction outputs along with some unwanted noise. A handwritten or bent text image does not give any text result except garbage value or noise. Thus, the developed system is appropriate for text information extraction from documented images or scanned book materials.

The proposed system has been tested by utilizing different image documents with text content. Some intermediate images of different stages have been built before achieving the documented images' text information (see Figure 1.12). These include Canny edge detected image, thresholded image, non-edge removed image, block-extracted image, line block image, paragraph-block image, etc.

The Canny algorithm gives the most accurate result for edge detection. Figure 1.12(b) illustrates text segments of the input image for closed region boundaries using the Canny algorithm. Adaptive thresholding is then applied to discard unwanted pixel regions, the Hough transformation algorithm finds long lines, and then unnecessary long lines are removed from the image. After using the edge detection algorithm, a morphological operation (dilation) is required to eliminate the non-edges from the edge array. Figure 1.12(c) shows the resulting image with only text edges after thresholding and dilation operation.

The blocking step adjusts a rectangular block for each character in the text content. Each character block in a sample text document is illustrated in Figure 1.13(a). The BFB procedure connects all adjacent character blocks in a single-line block, as shown in Figure 1.13(b). All line blocks are then combined to a para-block, and a full-stop or gap count determines the area of the para-block, as shown in Figure 1.13(c). Finally, the extracted text information is given to a text data file (see Figure 1.14). The experiments showed that the final outcome (text information extraction) achieved better accuracy for documented scanned images.

1.4.3 Outcomes and Limitations

The developed OCR-based system offered text information from image content in a text file as output. The text has been extracted from documented images. It generated some resulting images before receiving the final outcomes (such as thresholded image, edge

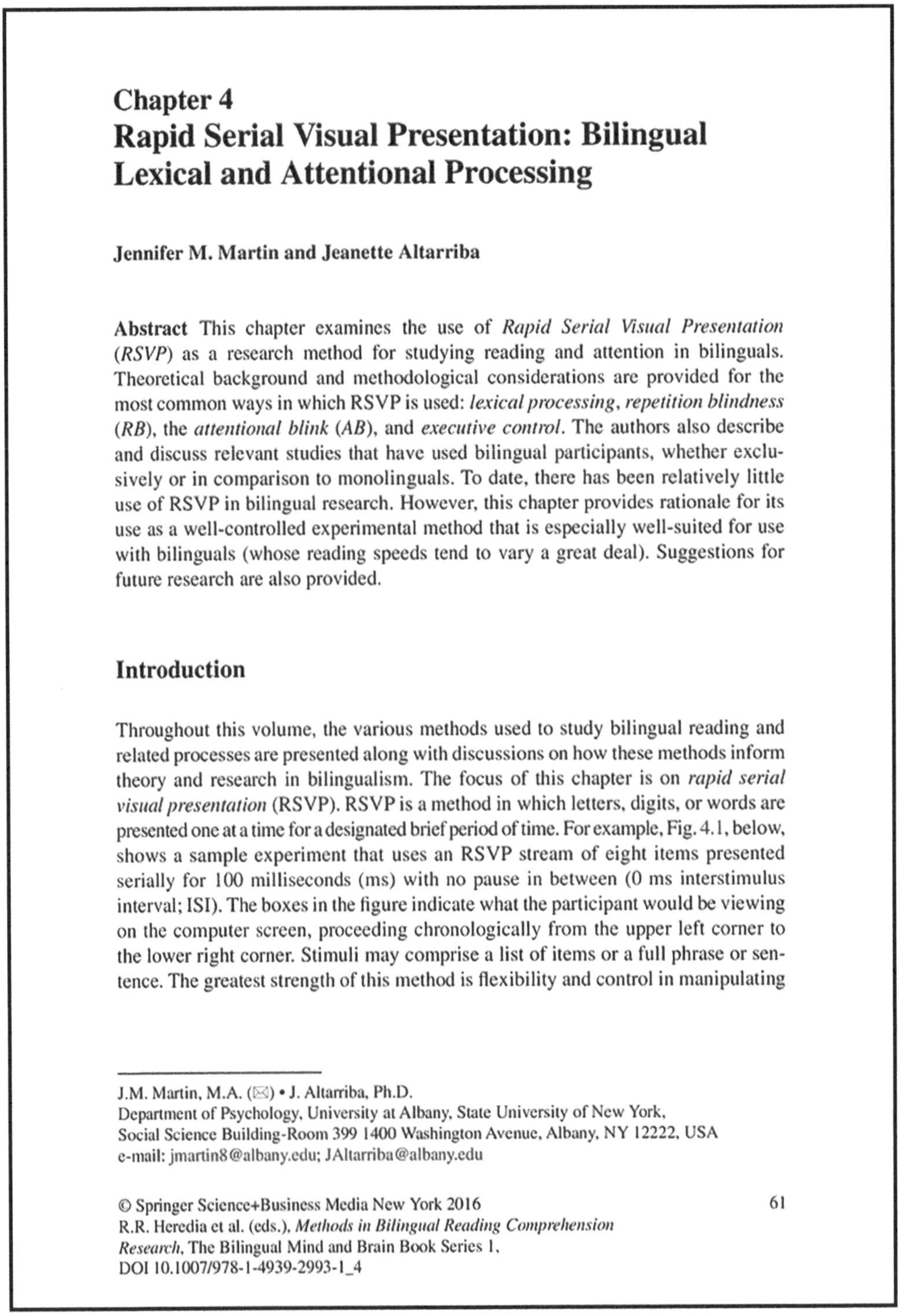

Chapter 4
Rapid Serial Visual Presentation: Bilingual Lexical and Attentional Processing

Jennifer M. Martin and Jeanette Altarriba

Abstract This chapter examines the use of *Rapid Serial Visual Presentation* (*RSVP*) as a research method for studying reading and attention in bilinguals. Theoretical background and methodological considerations are provided for the most common ways in which RSVP is used: *lexical processing*, *repetition blindness* (*RB*), the *attentional blink* (*AB*), and *executive control*. The authors also describe and discuss relevant studies that have used bilingual participants, whether exclusively or in comparison to monolinguals. To date, there has been relatively little use of RSVP in bilingual research. However, this chapter provides rationale for its use as a well-controlled experimental method that is especially well-suited for use with bilinguals (whose reading speeds tend to vary a great deal). Suggestions for future research are also provided.

Introduction

Throughout this volume, the various methods used to study bilingual reading and related processes are presented along with discussions on how these methods inform theory and research in bilingualism. The focus of this chapter is on *rapid serial visual presentation* (RSVP). RSVP is a method in which letters, digits, or words are presented one at a time for a designated brief period of time. For example, Fig. 4.1, below, shows a sample experiment that uses an RSVP stream of eight items presented serially for 100 milliseconds (ms) with no pause in between (0 ms interstimulus interval; ISI). The boxes in the figure indicate what the participant would be viewing on the computer screen, proceeding chronologically from the upper left corner to the lower right corner. Stimuli may comprise a list of items or a full phrase or sentence. The greatest strength of this method is flexibility and control in manipulating

J.M. Martin, M.A. (✉) • J. Altarriba, Ph.D.
Department of Psychology, University at Albany, State University of New York,
Social Science Building-Room 399 1400 Washington Avenue, Albany, NY 12222, USA
e-mail: jmartin8@albany.edu; JAltarriba@albany.edu

© Springer Science+Business Media New York 2016   61
R.R. Heredia et al. (eds.), *Methods in Bilingual Reading Comprehension Research*, The Bilingual Mind and Brain Book Series 1,
DOI 10.1007/978-1-4939-2993-1_4

(a) Input documented image.

FIGURE 1.12
Resulting images after thresholding and edge detection.

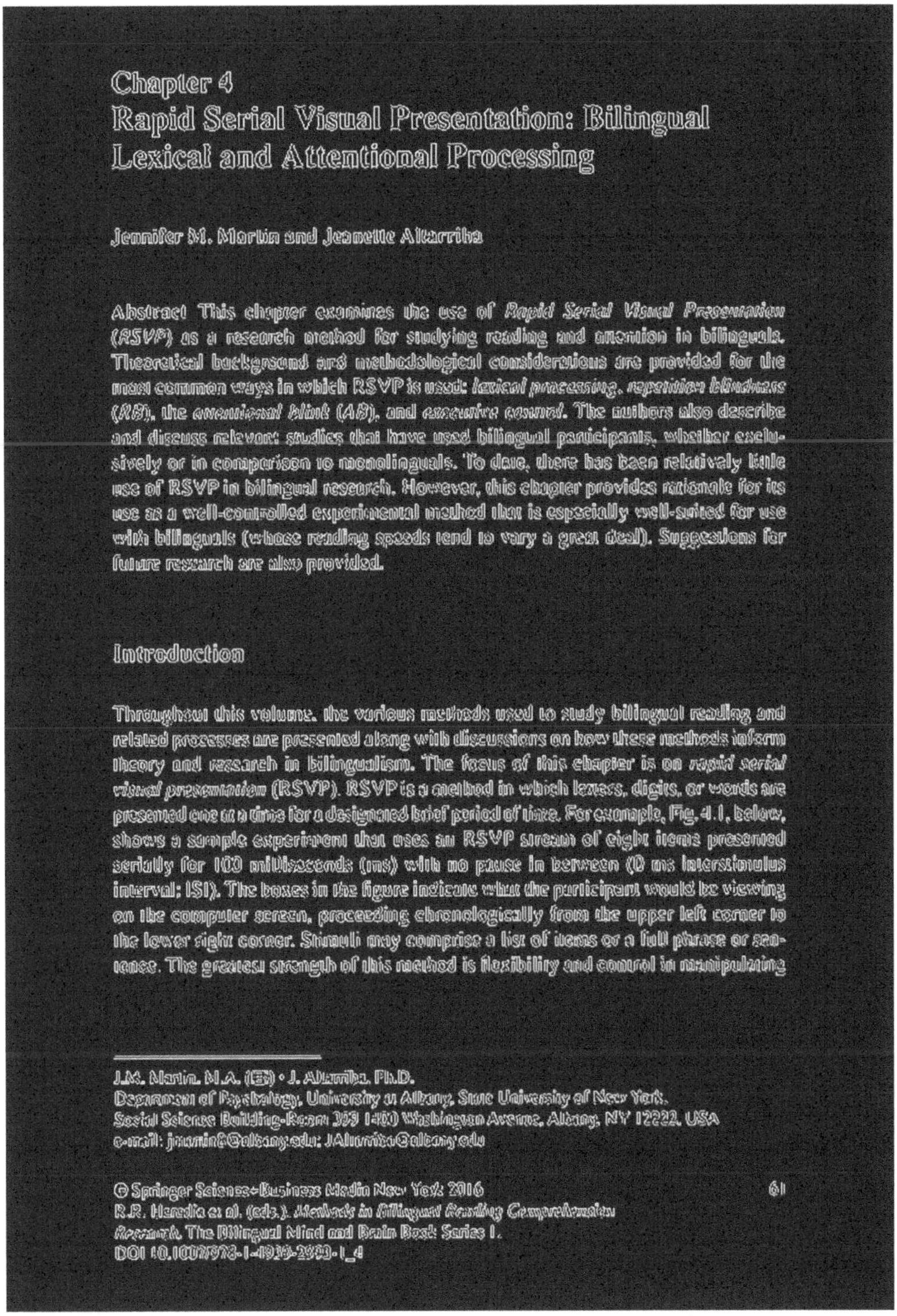

Chapter 4
Rapid Serial Visual Presentation: Bilingual Lexical and Attentional Processing

Jennifer M. Martin and Jeanette Altarriba

Abstract This chapter examines the use of *Rapid Serial Visual Presentation* (RSVP) as a research method for studying reading and attention in bilinguals. Theoretical background and methodological considerations are provided for the most common ways in which RSVP is used: *lexical processing, repetition blindness* (RB), the *attentional blink* (AB), and *executive control*. The authors also describe and discuss relevant studies that have used bilingual participants, whether exclusively or in comparison to monolinguals. To date, there has been relatively little use of RSVP in bilingual research. However, this chapter provides rationale for its use as a well-controlled experimental method that is especially well-suited for use with bilinguals (whose reading speeds tend to vary a great deal). Suggestions for future research are also provided.

Introduction

Throughout this volume, the various methods used to study bilingual reading and related processes are presented along with discussions on how these methods inform theory and research in bilingualism. The focus of this chapter is on *rapid serial visual presentation* (RSVP). RSVP is a method in which letters, digits, or words are presented one at a time for a designated brief period of time. For example, Fig. 4.1, below, shows a sample experiment that uses an RSVP stream of eight items presented serially for 100 milliseconds (ms) with no pause in between (0 ms interstimulus interval; ISI). The boxes in the figure indicate what the participant would be viewing on the computer screen, proceeding chronologically from the upper left corner to the lower right corner. Stimuli may comprise a list of items or a full phrase or sentence. The greatest strength of this method is flexibility and control in manipulating

J.M. Martin, M.A. (✉) • J. Altarriba, Ph.D.
Department of Psychology, University at Albany, State University of New York,
Social Science Building-Room 369 1400 Washington Avenue, Albany, NY 12222, USA
e-mail: jmartin@albany.edu; JAltarriba@albany.edu

© Springer Science+Business Media New York 2016
R.R. Heredia et al. (eds.), *Methods in Bilingual Reading Comprehension Research*, The Bilingual Mind and Brain Book Series 1,
DOI 10.1007/978-1-4939-2993-1_4

61

(b) Canny edge detection.

FIGURE 1.12
(Continued)

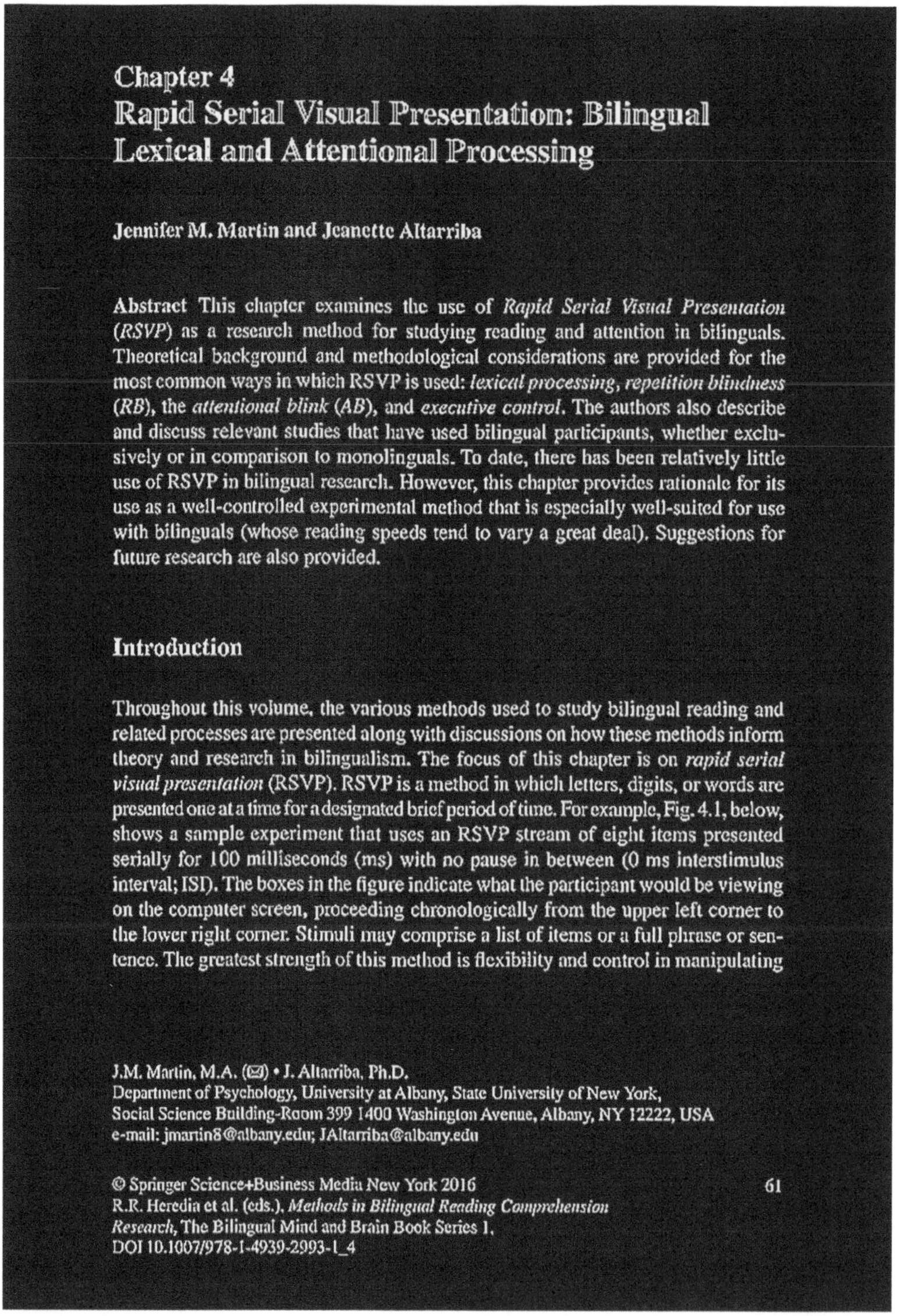

Chapter 4
Rapid Serial Visual Presentation: Bilingual Lexical and Attentional Processing

Jennifer M. Martin and Jeanette Altarriba

Abstract This chapter examines the use of *Rapid Serial Visual Presentation* (*RSVP*) as a research method for studying reading and attention in bilinguals. Theoretical background and methodological considerations are provided for the most common ways in which RSVP is used: *lexical processing, repetition blindness* (*RB*), the *attentional blink* (*AB*), and *executive control*. The authors also describe and discuss relevant studies that have used bilingual participants, whether exclusively or in comparison to monolinguals. To date, there has been relatively little use of RSVP in bilingual research. However, this chapter provides rationale for its use as a well-controlled experimental method that is especially well-suited for use with bilinguals (whose reading speeds tend to vary a great deal). Suggestions for future research are also provided.

Introduction

Throughout this volume, the various methods used to study bilingual reading and related processes are presented along with discussions on how these methods inform theory and research in bilingualism. The focus of this chapter is on *rapid serial visual presentation* (RSVP). RSVP is a method in which letters, digits, or words are presented one at a time for a designated brief period of time. For example, Fig. 4.1, below, shows a sample experiment that uses an RSVP stream of eight items presented serially for 100 milliseconds (ms) with no pause in between (0 ms interstimulus interval; ISI). The boxes in the figure indicate what the participant would be viewing on the computer screen, proceeding chronologically from the upper left corner to the lower right corner. Stimuli may comprise a list of items or a full phrase or sentence. The greatest strength of this method is flexibility and control in manipulating

J.M. Martin, M.A. (✉) • J. Altarriba, Ph.D.
Department of Psychology, University at Albany, State University of New York,
Social Science Building-Room 399 1400 Washington Avenue, Albany, NY 12222, USA
e-mail: jmartin8@albany.edu; JAltarriba@albany.edu

© Springer Science+Business Media New York 2016   61
R.R. Heredia et al. (eds.), *Methods in Bilingual Reading Comprehension
Research*, The Bilingual Mind and Brain Book Series 1,
DOI 10.1007/978-1-4939-2993-1_4

(c) Non-edge removal.

FIGURE 1.12
(Continued)

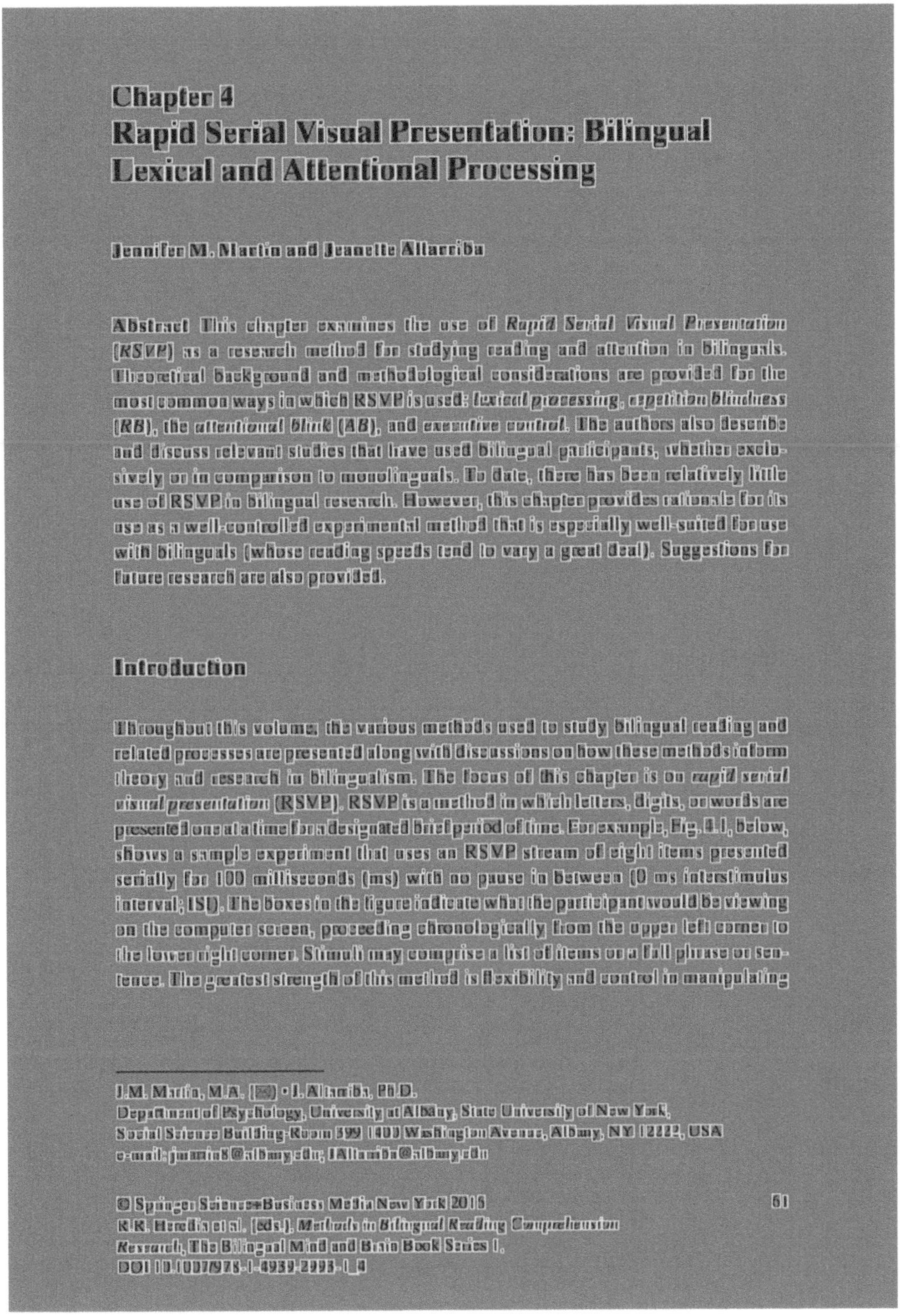

Chapter 4
Rapid Serial Visual Presentation: Bilingual Lexical and Attentional Processing

Jennifer M. Martin and Jeanette Altarriba

Abstract This chapter examines the use of *Rapid Serial Visual Presentation* (RSVP) as a research method for studying reading and attention in bilinguals. Theoretical background and methodological considerations are provided for the most common ways in which RSVP is used: *lexical processing, repetition blindness* (RB), the *attentional blink* (AB), and *executive control.* The authors also describe and discuss relevant studies that have used bilingual participants, whether exclusively or in comparison to monolinguals. To date, there has been relatively little use of RSVP in bilingual research. However, this chapter provides rationale for its use as a well-controlled experimental method that is especially well-suited for use with bilinguals (whose reading speeds tend to vary a great deal). Suggestions for future research are also provided.

Introduction

Throughout this volume, the various methods used to study bilingual reading and related processes are presented along with discussions on how these methods inform theory and research in bilingualism. The focus of this chapter is on *rapid serial visual presentation* (RSVP). RSVP is a method in which letters, digits, or words are presented one at a time for a designated brief period of time. For example, Fig. 4.1, below, shows a sample experiment that uses an RSVP stream of eight items presented serially for 100 milliseconds (ms) with no pause in between (0 ms interstimulus interval; ISI). The boxes in the figure indicate what the participant would be viewing on the computer screen, proceeding chronologically from the upper left corner to the lower right corner. Stimuli may comprise a list of items or a full phrase or sentence. The greatest strength of this method is flexibility and control in manipulating

J.M. Martin, M.A. (✉) • J. Altarriba, Ph.D.
Department of Psychology, University at Albany, State University of New York,
Social Science Building-Room 399 1400 Washington Avenue, Albany, NY 12222, USA
e-mail: jmartin8@albany.edu; JAltarriba@albany.edu

© Springer Science+Business Media New York 2016
R.R. Heredia et al. (eds.), *Methods in Bilingual Reading Comprehension Research*, The Bilingual Mind and Brain Book Series 1,
DOI 10.1007/978-1-4939-2993-1_4

61

(a) Character blocks.

FIGURE 1.13
Resulting images after applying the best-fitting block algorithm.

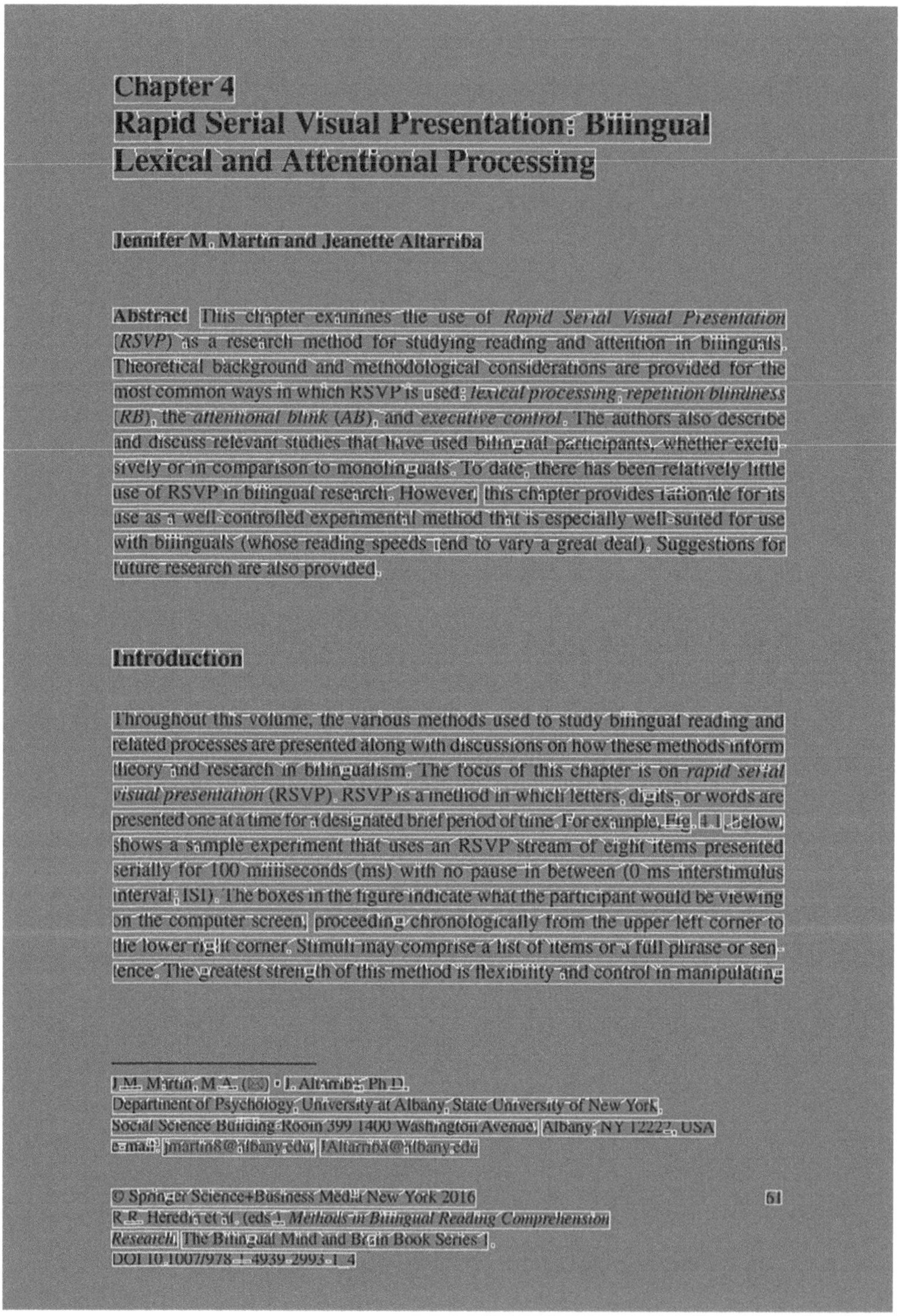

Chapter 4
Rapid Serial Visual Presentation: Bilingual Lexical and Attentional Processing

Jennifer M. Martin and Jeanette Altarriba

Abstract This chapter examines the use of *Rapid Serial Visual Presentation* (RSVP) as a research method for studying reading and attention in bilinguals. Theoretical background and methodological considerations are provided for the most common ways in which RSVP is used: *lexical processing, repetition blindness* (RB), the *attentional blink* (AB), and *executive control*. The authors also describe and discuss relevant studies that have used bilingual participants, whether exclusively or in comparison to monolinguals. To date, there has been relatively little use of RSVP in bilingual research. However, this chapter provides rationale for its use as a well-controlled experimental method that is especially well-suited for use with bilinguals (whose reading speeds tend to vary a great deal). Suggestions for future research are also provided.

Introduction

Throughout this volume, the various methods used to study bilingual reading and related processes are presented along with discussions on how these methods inform theory and research in bilingualism. The focus of this chapter is on *rapid serial visual presentation* (RSVP). RSVP is a method in which letters, digits, or words are presented one at a time for a designated brief period of time. For example, Fig. 4.1 below shows a sample experiment that uses an RSVP stream of eight items presented serially for 100 milliseconds (ms) with no pause in between (0 ms interstimulus interval, ISI). The boxes in the figure indicate what the participant would be viewing on the computer screen, proceeding chronologically from the upper left corner to the lower right corner. Stimuli may comprise a list of items or a full phrase or sentence. The greatest strength of this method is flexibility and control in manipulating

J. M. Martin, M.A. (✉) · J. Altarriba, Ph.D.
Department of Psychology, University at Albany, State University of New York,
Social Science Building Room 399 1400 Washington Avenue, Albany, NY 12222, USA
e-mail: jmartin8@albany.edu; JAltarriba@albany.edu

© Springer Science+Business Media New York 2016   61
R. R. Heredia et al. (eds.), *Methods in Bilingual Reading Comprehension Research*, The Bilingual Mind and Brain Book Series 1,
DOI 10.1007/978-1-4939-2993-1_4

(b) Line blocks.

FIGURE 1.13
(Continued)

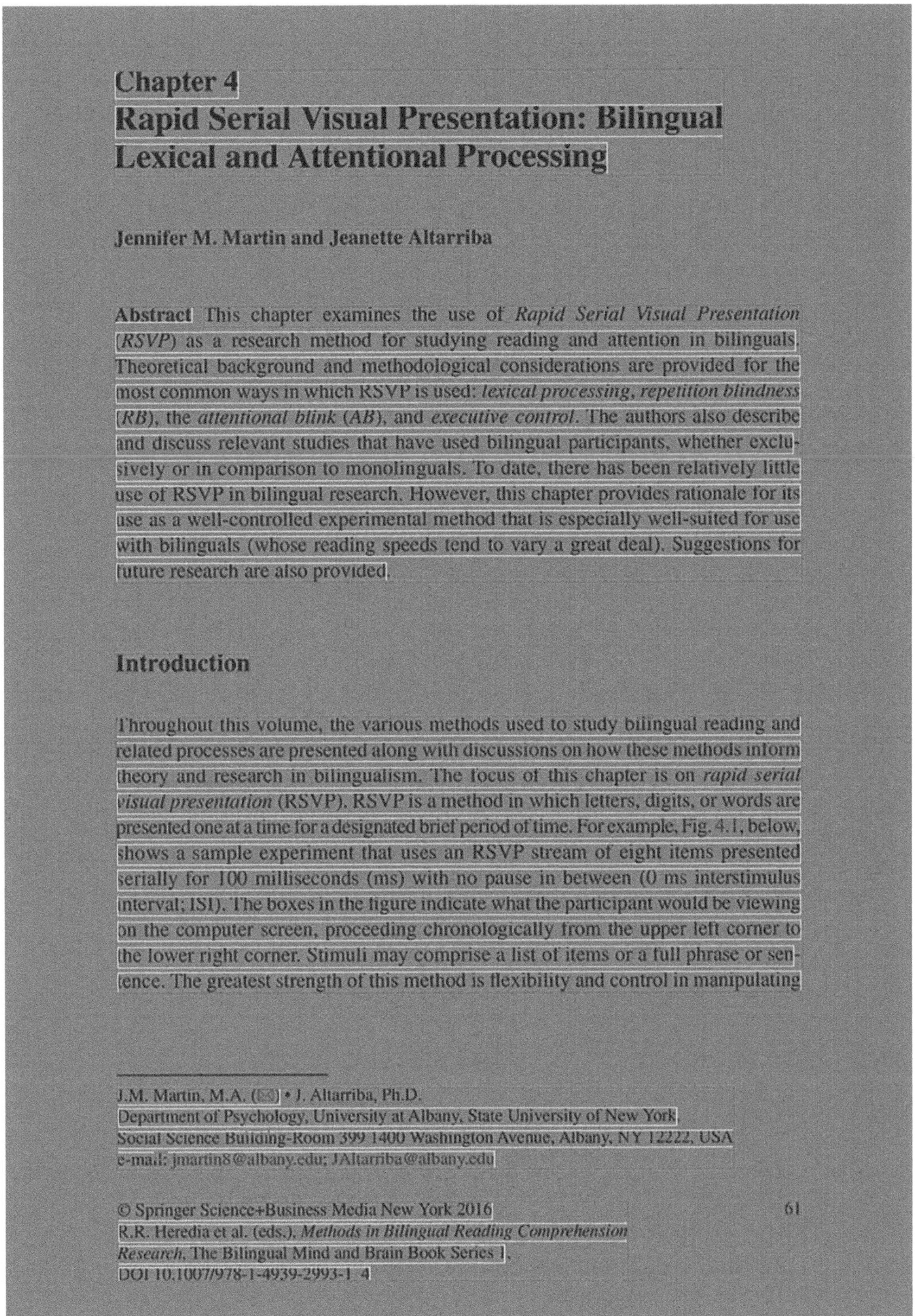

Chapter 4
Rapid Serial Visual Presentation: Bilingual Lexical and Attentional Processing

Jennifer M. Martin and Jeanette Altarriba

Abstract This chapter examines the use of *Rapid Serial Visual Presentation* (*RSVP*) as a research method for studying reading and attention in bilinguals. Theoretical background and methodological considerations are provided for the most common ways in which RSVP is used: *lexical processing, repetition blindness* (*RB*), the *attentional blink* (*AB*), and *executive control*. The authors also describe and discuss relevant studies that have used bilingual participants, whether exclusively or in comparison to monolinguals. To date, there has been relatively little use of RSVP in bilingual research. However, this chapter provides rationale for its use as a well-controlled experimental method that is especially well-suited for use with bilinguals (whose reading speeds tend to vary a great deal). Suggestions for future research are also provided.

Introduction

Throughout this volume, the various methods used to study bilingual reading and related processes are presented along with discussions on how these methods inform theory and research in bilingualism. The focus of this chapter is on *rapid serial visual presentation* (RSVP). RSVP is a method in which letters, digits, or words are presented one at a time for a designated brief period of time. For example, Fig. 4.1, below, shows a sample experiment that uses an RSVP stream of eight items presented serially for 100 milliseconds (ms) with no pause in between (0 ms interstimulus interval; ISI). The boxes in the figure indicate what the participant would be viewing on the computer screen, proceeding chronologically from the upper left corner to the lower right corner. Stimuli may comprise a list of items or a full phrase or sentence. The greatest strength of this method is flexibility and control in manipulating

J.M. Martin, M.A. (✉) • J. Altarriba, Ph.D.
Department of Psychology, University at Albany, State University of New York,
Social Science Building-Room 399 1400 Washington Avenue, Albany, NY 12222, USA
e-mail: jmartin8@albany.edu; JAltarriba@albany.edu

© Springer Science+Business Media New York 2016   61
R.R. Heredia et al. (eds.), *Methods in Bilingual Reading Comprehension Research*, The Bilingual Mind and Brain Book Series 1,
DOI 10.1007/978-1-4939-2993-1_4

(c) Para-blocks.

FIGURE 1.13
(Continued)

Chapter 4
Rapid Serial Visual Presentation: Bilingual
Lexical and Attentional Processing
Jennifer M. Martin and Jeanette Altarrilm

Abstract This chapter examines the use of Rapid Serial Visual Presentation
(RSVP) as a research method for studying reading and attention in bilinguals.
Theoretical background and methodological considerations are provided for the
most common ways in which RSVP is used: lexical pmcessing, repetition blindness
(R8), the attentional blink (AB), and executive control. The authors also describe
and discuss relevant studies that have used bilingual participants, whether exclu
sively or in comparison to monolinguals. To date, there has been relatively little
use of RSVP in bilingual research. However, this chapter provides rationale for its
use as a well-controlled experimental method that is especially well-suited for use
with bilinguals (whose reading speeds tend to vary a great deal). Suggestions for
future research are also provided

Introduction

Throughout this volume. the various methods used to study bilingual reading and
related processes are presented along with discussions on how these methods inform
theory and research in bilingualism. The focus of this chapter is on rapid serial
visual presentation (RSVP). RSVP is a method in which letters, digits, or words are
presented one at a time for a designated brief period of time. For example, Fig. 4.1, below,
shows a sample experiment that uses an RSVP stream of eight items presented
serially for 100 milliseconds (ms) with no pause in between (0 ms interstimulus
interval; ISI). The boxes in the figure indicate what the participant would be viewing
on the computer screen. proceeding chronologically from the upper left corner to
the lower right comer. Stimuli may comprise a list of items or a full phrase or sen
tence. The greatest strength of this method is flexibility and control in manipulating

J.M. Marlin, M.A. (ET-S) J. Altarriba. PhD.
Dcpartment of Psychology, University at Albany. State University of New York
Social Science Building-Room 399 1400 Washington] Avenue. Albany. NY I2222, USA
e-mail: jmaninS @albany.cdu: .lAltartiba@albany.edu

E) Springer Science+Business Media New York 2016
RR. Hercdia cl al. (eds). Methods in Bilingual Reading7 Comprehension
Research. The Bilingual Mind and Brain Book Series I
DOI [0.1007/978-1«1939-29934 4

FIGURE 1.14
Extracted text information from the documented image (text data file).

detected image, text blocks detected image, etc.), also known as the system's intermediate outputs. The main limitation was that the proposed text-extraction system could not remove undesirable text or symbols from images. It also provided poor results in extracting bent or arched text objects from images.

Furthermore, the system faced troubles in handling those images containing more photos or figures than text content. As a result, it generated useless characters or symbols in extracting such types of image content. As a result, the proposed OCR-based text-extraction system is the finest for text mining in scanned documents with more text content.

1.5 Conclusion

The majority of information is now available on paper, pictures, or videos. Images contain a lot of information. OCR allows a machine to read data from natural sceneries or other resources in any format. Several related technologies and studies have been reviewed and analyzed for developing the proposed text-extraction approach. Information extraction is made up of several components, including its kind, orientation, method, and a strategy for carrying out the entire procedure. Before introducing the OCR tool, this chapter covers the fundamentals of image processing and information extraction. The developed system successfully retrieved text data from scanned documents and displayed only its text content. It received image files or scanned textbook pages as inputs and mined only text information as outputs. The findings for the regular recorded images and scanned pages, on the other hand, were more accurate with minimal undesired characters. We believe that this method is helpful for students' scientific research and academic data storage applications and saves them necessary typing time. It is also valuable for text-based applications like picture database retrieval and library management (to convert the scanned page to the image).

In summary, the contribution of this study includes a new framework for text information extraction using the Tesseract OCR engine in the Ubuntu (Linux) environment. In addition, the C++ framework is used to construct all essential algorithms and functions, including the Qt creator tool with its integrated development environment (IDE). Although the proposed method extracted correct text from documented images, it has one major flaw: it could not delete unwanted text or symbols from images. Handling curved or arched text material and numerous figures in a picture was extremely tough. In conclusion, the presented OCR-based text-extraction method is the best for text mining in scanned documents that include more text. In the future, an intelligent information extraction mechanism will be implemented that will automatically skip any unwanted characters or symbols. This sort of equipment may be used to create analog images, among other purposes. Furthermore, this method may be improved by extracting text from photos and videos.

References

[1] C. Kaundilya, D. Chawla, and Y. Chopra, "Automated text extraction from images using OCR system," in *2019 6th International Conference on Computing for Sustainable Global Development (INDIACom)*, 2019, pp. 145–150: IEEE.

[2] C. M. Mizan, T. Chakraborty, and S. Karmakar, "Text recognition using image processing," *International Journal of Advanced Research in Computer Science*, vol. 8, no. 5, 2017.

[3] S. M. S. Ismail, S. N. H. S. Abdullah, and F. Fauzi, "Detection and recognition via adaptive binarization and fuzzy clustering," *Pertanika Journal of Science & Technology*, vol. 27, no. 4, pp. 1759–1781, 2019.

[4] J. Gllavata, R. Ewerth, and B. Freisleben, "A text detection, localization and segmentation system for OCR in images," in *IEEE Sixth International Symposium on Multimedia Software Engineering*, 2004, pp. 310–317: IEEE.

[5] M. B. Halima, H. Karray, and A. M. Alimi, "A comprehensive method for Arabic video text detection, localization, extraction and recognition," in *Pacific-Rim Conference on Multimedia*, 2010, pp. 648–659: Springer.

[6] C. Wolf, J.-M. Jolion, and F. Chassaing, "Text localization, enhancement and binarization in multimedia documents," in *Object Recognition Supported by User Interaction for Service Robots*, 2002, vol. 2, pp. 1037–1040: IEEE.

[7] S. J. Perantonis, B. Gatos, and N. Papamarkos, "Image segmentation and linear feature identification using rectangular block decomposition," in *Proceedings of Third International Conference on Electronics, Circuits, and Systems*, 1996, vol. 1, pp. 183–186: IEEE.

[8] D. Gera and N. Jain, "Comparison of text extraction techniques—A review," *International Journal of Innovative Research in Computer Communication Engineering*, vol. 3, pp. 621–626, 2015.

[9] V. Rajan and S. Raj, "Text detection and character extraction in natural scene images using fractional Poisson model," in *2017 International Conference on Computing Methodologies and Communication (ICCMC)*, 2017, pp. 1136–1141: IEEE.

[10] Q. Ye and D. Doermann, "Text detection and recognition in imagery: A survey," *IEEE Transactions on Pattern Analysis Machine Intelligence*, vol. 37, no. 7, pp. 1480–1500, 2014.

[11] T. A. Setu and M. Rahman, "Human face detection and segmentation of facial feature region," *Global Journal of Computer Science Technology Health Care*, vol. 16, no. 1, pp. 1–8, 2016.

[12] H. Yang, B. Quehl, and H. Sack, "A framework for improved video text detection and recognition," *Multimedia Tools Applications*, vol. 69, no. 1, pp. 217–245, 2014.

[13] R. Mittal and A. Garg, "Text extraction using OCR: A systematic review," in *2020 Second International Conference on Inventive Research in Computing Applications (ICIRCA)*, 2020, pp. 357–362: IEEE.

[14] G. Vamvakas, B. Gatos, N. Stamatopoulos, and S. J. Perantonis, "A complete optical character recognition methodology for historical documents," in *2008 the Eighth IAPR International Workshop on Document Analysis Systems*, 2008, pp. 525–532: IEEE.

[15] A. Gupta, R. Mishra, and A. K. Singh, "Performance optimization of text extraction technique for complex degraded images," *Journal of Xi'an Shiyou University, Natural Science Edition*, vol. 17, no. 9, pp. 627–637, 2021.

[16] A. Mate, M. Gurav, K. Babar, G. Raskar, and P. Kshirsagar, "Extraction of text from image," *International Journal of Advanced Research in Science, Communication and Technology*, vol. 6, no. 1, 2021.

[17] K. Yindumathi, S. S. Chaudhari, and R. Aparna, "Analysis of image classification for text extraction from bills and invoices," in *2020 11th International Conference on Computing, Communication and Networking Technologies (ICCCNT)*, 2020, pp. 1–6: IEEE.

[18] P. S. Giri, "Text information extraction and analysis from images using digital image processing techniques," *Special Issue of International Journal on Advanced Computer Theory and Engineering*, vol. 2, no. 1, pp. 66–71, 2013.

[19] T. Tasneem and Z. Afroze, "A new method of improving performance of Canny edge detection," in *2019 2nd International Conference on Innovation in Engineering and Technology (ICIET)*, 2019, pp. 1–5: IEEE.

[20] R. Chatterjee and A. Mondal, "Effects of different filters on text extractions from videos using Tesseract," 2021. https://github.com/cserajdeep/Impacts-of-Filters-on-Video-Text-Extraction.

[21] C.-L. Huang and D.-H. Huang, "A content-based image retrieval system," *Image Vision Computing*, vol. 16, no. 3, pp. 149–163, 1998.

[22] K. Jung, K. I. Kim, and A. K. Jain, "Text information extraction in images and video: A survey," *Pattern Recognition*, vol. 37, no. 5, pp. 977–997, 2004.

[23] M. M. Rahman, M. R. Rinty, and F. Risdin, "Extracting text information from digital images," *International Journal of Scientific & Engineering Research*, vol. 10, no. 6, pp. 1350–1356, 2019.

[24] R. Lienhart and A. Wernicke, "Localizing and segmenting text in images and videos," *IEEE Transactions on Circuits Systems for Video Technology*, vol. 12, no. 4, pp. 256–268, 2002.

[25] J. Zhang and R. Kasturi, "Extraction of text objects in video documents: Recent progress," in *2008 the Eighth IAPR International Workshop on Document Analysis Systems*, 2008, pp. 5–17: IEEE.

[26] S. W. Smoliar and H. Zhang, "Content based video indexing and retrieval," *IEEE Multimedia*, vol. 1, no. 2, pp. 62–72, 1994.

[27] B. B. Chaudhuri, *Digital Document Processing: Major Directions and Recent Advances*. Springer Science & Business Media, 2007.

[28] A. Chaudhuri, K. Mandaviya, P. Badelia, and S. K. Ghosh, "Optical character recognition systems," in *Optical Character Recognition Systems for Different Languages with Soft Computing.* Springer, 2017, pp. 9–41.

[29] G. Mukarambi, H. Gaikwadl, and B. Dhandra, "Segmentation and text extraction from document images: Survey," in *2019 Innovations in Power and Advanced Computing Technologies (i-PACT)*, 2019, vol. 1, pp. 1–5: IEEE.

[30] A. Thilagavathy, K. Aarthi, and A. Chilambuchelvan, "A hybrid approach to extract scene text from videos," in *2012 International Conference on Computing, Electronics and Electrical Technologies (ICCEET)*, 2012, pp. 1017–1022: IEEE.

[31] D. M. Nor, R. Omar, M. Z. M. Jenu, and J. M. Ogier, "Image segmentation and text extraction: Application to the extraction of textual information in scene images," in *International Seminar on Application of Science Mathematics (ISASM2011)*, 2011. https://core.ac.uk/download/pdf/12007356.pdf.

[32] J. Gllavata, R. Ewerth, and B. Freisleben, "A robust algorithm for text detection in images," in *3rd International Symposium on Image and Signal Processing and Analysis, 2003. ISPA 2003. Proceedings of the*, 2003, vol. 2, pp. 611–616: IEEE.

[33] D. K. Sarmah, A. J. Kulkarni, and A. Abraham, *Optimization Models in Steganography Using Metaheuristics.* Springer Nature, 2020.

[34] A. McAndrew, *A Computational Introduction to Digital Image Processing.* CRC Press Boca Raton, 2016.

[35] A. A. Rafiq and M. Yusuf, "Implementation of digital image processing using NI myRIO and Arduino Mega 2560 as controller on Rover bogie robot," in *2018 International Conference on Applied Science and Technology (iCAST)*, 2018, pp. 210–215: IEEE.

[36] R. Dastres and M. Soori, "Advanced image processing systems," *International Journal of Imagining Robotics*, vol. 21, no. 1, pp. 27–44, 2021.

[37] N. Al-Najdawi, M. Biltawi, and S. Tedmori, "Mammogram image visual enhancement, mass segmentation and classification," *Applied Soft Computing*, vol. 35, pp. 175–185, 2015.

[38] M. R. Banham and A. K. Katsaggelos, "Digital image restoration," *IEEE Signal Processing Magazine*, vol. 14, no. 2, pp. 24–41, 1997.

[39] F. Mentzer, L. V. Gool, and M. Tschannen, "Learning better lossless compression using lossy compression," in *Proceedings of the IEEE/CVF Conference on Computer Vision and Pattern Recognition*, 2020, pp. 6638–6647: IEEE.

[40] J. Uthayakumar, T. Vengattaraman, and P. Dhavachelvan, "A survey on data compression techniques: From the perspective of data quality, coding schemes, data type and applications," *Journal of King Saud University-Computer Information Sciences*, vol. 33, no. 2, 2018: Elsevier.

[41] G. Kumar and P. K. Bhatia, "A detailed review of feature extraction in image processing systems," in *2014 Fourth International Conference on Advanced Computing & Communication Technologies*, 2014, pp. 5–12: IEEE.

[42] S. S. Varshney, N. Rajpal, and R. Purwar, "Comparative study of image segmentation techniques and object matching using segmentation," in *2009 Proceeding of International Conference on Methods and Models in Computer Science (ICM2CS)*, 2009, pp. 1–6: IEEE.

[43] T. M. Breuel, "The OCRopus open source OCR system," in *Document Recognition and Retrieval XV*, 2008, vol. 6815, p. 68150F: International Society for Optics and Photonics.

[44] H.-K. Kim, "Efficient automatic text location method and content-based indexing and structuring of video database," *Journal of Visual Communication Image Representation*, vol. 7, no. 4, pp. 336–344, 1996.

[45] H. Zhang, K. Zhao, Y.-Z. Song, and J. Guo, "Text extraction from natural scene image: A survey," *Neurocomputing*, vol. 122, pp. 310–323, 2013.

[46] C. Sumathi, T. Santhanam, and G. G. Devi, "A survey on various approaches of text extraction in images," *International Journal of Computer Science Engineering Survey*, vol. 3, no. 4, p. 27, 2012.

[47] K. Rajeswari, S. Nakil, N. Patil, S. Pereira, and N. Ramdasi, "Text categorization optimization by a hybrid approach using multiple feature selection and feature extraction methods," *International Journal of Engineering Research Applications*, vol. 4, 2014.

[48] A. Kolcz, V. Prabakarmurthi, and J. Kalita, "Summarization as feature selection for text categorization," in *Proceedings of the Tenth International Conference on Information and Knowledge Management*, 2001, pp. 365–370: ACM.

[49] M. Arora and V. Kansal, "Character level embedding with deep convolutional neural network for text normalization of unstructured data for Twitter sentiment analysis," *Social Network Analysis Mining*, vol. 9, no. 1, pp. 1–14, 2019.

[50] M. Allahyari et al., "A brief survey of text mining: Classification, clustering and extraction techniques," *arXiv preprint arXiv:1707.02919*, 2017.

[51] C. D. Paice, "Method for evaluation of stemming algorithms based on error counting," *Journal of the American Society for Information Science*, vol. 47, no. 8, pp. 632–649, 1996.

[52] Z. Huang and J. Leng, "Text extraction in natural scenes using region-based method," *Journal of Digital Information Management*, vol. 12, no. 4, pp. 246–254, 2014.

[53] A. Sharma, A. Dharwadker, and T. Kasar, "MobLP: A CC-based approach to vehicle license plate number segmentation from images acquired with a mobile phone camera," in *2010 Annual IEEE India Conference (INDICON)*, 2010, pp. 1–4: IEEE.

[54] T. Kumuda and L. Basavaraj, "Edge based segmentation approach to extract text from scene images," in *2017 IEEE 7th International Advance Computing Conference (IACC)*, 2017, pp. 706–710: IEEE.

[55] K. I. Kim, K. Jung, and J. H. Kim, "Texture-based approach for text detection in images using support vector machines and continuously adaptive mean shift algorithm," *IEEE Transactions on Pattern Analysis Machine Intelligence*, vol. 25, no. 12, pp. 1631–1639, 2003.

[56] A. Mirza, M. Fayyaz, Z. Seher, and I. Siddiqi, "Urdu caption text detection using textural features," in *Proceedings of the 2nd Mediterranean Conference on Pattern Recognition and Artificial Intelligence*, 2018, pp. 70–75: ACM.

[57] H. J. Heijmans, "Mathematical morphology: A modern approach in image processing based on algebra and geometry," *SIAM Review*, vol. 37, no. 1, pp. 1–36, 1995.

[58] Y. M. Hasan and L. J. Karam, "Morphological text extraction from images," *IEEE Transactions on Image Processing*, vol. 9, no. 11, pp. 1978–1983, 2000.

[59] J.-C. Wu, J.-W. Hsieh, and Y.-S. Chen, "Morphology-based text line extraction," *Machine Vision Applications*, vol. 19, no. 3, pp. 195–207, 2008.

[60] Y. Hawwar and A. Reza, "Spatially adaptive multiplicative noise image denoising technique," *IEEE Transactions on Image Processing*, vol. 11, no. 12, pp. 1397–1404, 2002.

[61] L. Fan, F. Zhang, H. Fan, and C. Zhang, "Brief review of image denoising techniques," *Visual Computing for Industry, Biomedicine, Artificial Intelligence in Agriculture*, vol. 2, no. 1, pp. 1–12, 2019.

[62] M. Abo-Zahhad, R. R. Gharieb, S. M. Ahmed, and A. A. E.-B. Donkol, "Edge detection with a preprocessing approach," *Journal of Signal Information Processing*, vol. 5, no. 04, p. 123, 2014.

[63] R. Maini and H. Aggarwal, "Study and comparison of various image edge detection techniques," *International Journal of Image Processing*, vol. 3, no. 1, pp. 1–11, 2009.

[64] G. M. H. Amer and A. M. Abushaala, "Edge detection methods," in *2015 2nd World Symposium on Web Applications and Networking (WSWAN)*, 2015, pp. 1–7: IEEE.

[65] J. Canny, "A computational approach to edge detection," *IEEE Transactions on Pattern Analysis Machine Intelligence*, no. 6, pp. 679–698, 1986.

[66] P. Roy, S. Dutta, N. Dey, G. Dey, S. Chakraborty, and R. Ray, "Adaptive thresholding: A comparative study," in *2014 International Conference on Control, Instrumentation, Communication and Computational Technologies (ICCICCT)*, 2014, pp. 1182–1186: IEEE.

[67] D. Ghai, D. Gera, and N. Jain, "A new approach to extract text from images based on DWT and K-means clustering," *International Journal of Computational Intelligence Systems*, vol. 9, no. 5, pp. 900–916, 2016.

[68] J. F. Canny, "Finding edges and lines in images," Master's thesis, Massachusetts Inst of Tech Cambridge Artificial Intelligence Lab, 1983.

[69] S. Lee, "Lines detection with Hough transform," 2020. https://towardsdatascience.com/lines-detection-with-hough-transform-84020b3b1549.

[70] N. Efford, *Digital Image Processing: A Practical Introduction Using Java*. Addison-Wesley Longman Publishing Co., Inc., 2000.

[71] B. Gatos, N. Papamarkos, and S. Perantonis, "Comparing point and block representation in computer vision and image processing tasks." https://core.ac.uk/download/pdf/12007356.pdf.

[72] R. Smith, "An overview of the Tesseract OCR engine," in *Ninth International Conference on Document Analysis and Recognition (ICDAR 2007)*, 2007, vol. 2, pp. 629–633: IEEE.

[73] R. W. Smith, "The extraction and recognition of text from multimedia document images," Doctoral dissertation, University of Bristol, 1987.

2

Extracting Pixel Edges on Leaves to Detect Type Using Fuzzy Logic

Lakshmi JVN and Kamalraj R

CONTENTS

2.1 Introduction

Image processing is a huge research-oriented domain in various fields, including astronomy, medicine, national security, product quality, industrialization, etc. Modeling complex systems requires treating data that are uncertain and subjective. Among the complex systems, image recognition and classification from photos and images have become a significant area of research. Much research has been undertaken in developing methods for edge detection and image recognition, addressing conventional logic and models.

Edges are significant features, as they define structure and form in the identification of the image. In many visual applications, identifying the object and displaying the name as a tag are current features in development for future applications. The framework that can be defined as a function of the structure is the object. With the defined frame structure, objects are extracted from the homogeneous background of the images or video clips. Regardless of surface orientation and light variations, an edge determines physical building. An edge can be differentiated by the greyscale in the pixels connected between the regions. These edges are most frequently used in image segmentation and structural operations.

DOI: 10.1201/9781003218111-2

Digital image processing techniques are used to extract needed details from the enhanced images by enriching the features of images. A variety of electronic gadgets and devices in many different application areas are used to produce the images that are processed and analysed to help people make decisions. The focus of the current study is on extracting useful details from images.

Orientation and localization of a particular image can be derived using the second-order derivatives on the image function. Many methods are implemented on localization in order to extract the required features. Some of these techniques and their limitations are presented in Table 2.1.

These limitations are addressed using the image segmentation and fuzzy logic techniques. Image segmentation, boundary detection, edge recognition and contour extraction are the significant applications of fuzzy logic. Fuzzy sets combined with filters assess the similarity between the segments and detect the weak edges efficiently. Also, a combination of machine learning technique transfer learning and fuzzy logic is applied for effective edge recognition. This combination method can be applied in the medical field for seeking the optimal solution in detecting edges while dealing with crucial image segmentation. It is an important contribution, as it detects the minute edges as a pre-processing step and also classifies the type based on the sharpness and thickness of the edges.

Fuzzy logic is better than other classifier methods because it is more similar to how humans think and gain knowledge to classify objects present in the external environment. Because of this, it produces accurate results used in the problem domain to get expected results. The rules can easily be made in fuzzy systems, and they could be used to derive results by mapping the conditions according to the rules. Fuzzy logic can be modelled with three parts such as 'fuzzifier', 'controller' and 'defuzzifier'. The fuzzifier role is making of linguistic variables from the given input values or numbers. From this, the normalized fuzzy values are obtained which are feasible to apply in the working model of the problem to solve.

The controller part consists of an inference engine and a knowledge base. The knowledge base will store all fuzzy rules and functions to provide input to the inference engine for performing its assigned responsibility in the domain. Finally, the defuzzifier converts back to normal values from the obtained fuzzy results. The fuzzy logic model is completely rigid in deriving the results based on the knowledge and rules given to it. Hence, the accuracy of results and flow of steps in deriving the solution in a given problem will be more accurate compared to all other different classifier approaches.

Transfer learning is the technique of reusing the model from the already solved problem domain to solve the new problem. The performance of the existing model will be

TABLE 2.1

Edge Detection Techniques with Their Limitations

Method	Application	Drawback
Laplacian	Isolated edges	Sensitive to the impulse noise
Gaussian/Canny convolutional edge detector	Edge points closer to the real edges	Improper edge localization
Adaptive bilateral filtering/adaptive thresholding/unsharp masking	Ill-posed problem	Feeble edges are not detected
Bacterial foraging algorithm	Detect the weak edges	Discriminate false edges from the non-noise background

analysed to apply in framing the solution. If the performance of the existing model is acceptable when it produces accurate results, then it may be tuned by adding a proper set of data features to improve the performance. This also depicts human behaviour when understanding the pattern of any natural language character to identify the language of the particular character obtained as an input from the environment. Hence, transfer learning contributes to identifying the model from past experience to solve the given new one. Thus, this may improve the results' accuracy and the performance of the system in terms of time and other resource usage to obtain the solution. The proposed research in the fuzzy rule–based transfer learning approach is to identify the leaves of various fruits, including apple, orange, papaya, banana, mango, pomegranate, guava, strawberry, grape and pineapple. An aggregate membership function is used for selective edge processing in spite of noisy pixels.

The remaining paper is organized as follows: a comprehensive study on several edge detection methods using fuzzy logic with machine learning are discussed in Section 2.2. Pixel pre-classification, sparse representation, edge detection and mapping are described in Section 2.3. The methodology evaluation metrics and comparison with existing techniques are demonstrated in Section 2.4. Finally, the chapter concludes in Section 2.5 and presents future directions.

2.2 Related Study on Edge Detection Methods

Edge detection is applied on clinical images using a 3×3 mask directed as a fuzzy rule set. The mask integrated for edge detection in clinical images adjusts the contrast to darken the smoother edges. The window mask function is designed by considering the difference between the values of eight neighbouring pixels P_j and central pixel P. The window mask function is given in Equation 2.1 (Izhar, Anwar, Kamran, Muhammad, & Shaukat, 2015).

$$\Delta P_j = \left| P_j - P \right| for\ j = 1, 2 \ldots 8 \tag{2.1}$$

The sliding window technique processes the image edges slowly and is lacking for small images. The kernel fuzzy system outperforms in recasting the original image to a new greyscale image on different types of images. The fuzzy membership function discriminates the adjacent pixel points of an edge and a curve (Anas, 2016).

The spatial convolution technique is applied using low-pass, Sobel edge enhancement and high-pass filters on 3×3 digital images to optimize the edginess for each pixel. Gaussian membership and fuzzy system rules classify the pixel as either edge or non-edge based on its intensity. The Mamdani defuzzifier method is robust in classifying the captured image pixel with Prewitt and Sobel operators (Aborisade, 2010).

The contour sensing technique is tested on a color image repository. The approach to detecting blurred edges in color images is to compare greyscale intensity of images and also verify the noise in the corrupted images. Claudia et al. compare general Type 2 fuzzy logic with other edge detection algorithms, such as those based on Type 1 and Range 2 fuzzy systems. The simulation results show that edge detection based on a Type 2 fuzzy system exceeds other methods due to its ability to handle the inherent vagueness in edge detection (Claudia, Patricia, & Oscar, 2017).

The algorithm proposed by Andrea and Eyberth defines the creation of a fuzzy inference system that evaluates the prevailing connection between the pixels in the image by finding variations in the greyscale of the adjacent linked pixels. Later, it shows an implementation of the OTSU's method on a binary image that was obtained from the fuzzy process and thus produces an image containing only extracted edges, collateral methodology using humanoid League imagery. This method improves the processing time by 35% and 52% less noise susceptibility (Andrea, Eyberth, Carlos, Jorge, & Juan, 2013).

Images can be extracted from various modalities beyond the normal greyscale and color photographs, such as infrared, X-rays, as well as the new generation of hyperspectral satellite data sets. Edge pixels are mapped over a range of discrete values. The robustness of the results from the proposed method for different captured images is compared with that obtained with the linear operator Sobel. It is given a permanent effect in the softness and rectitude of the lines to the straight lines and a good roundness to the curved lines. While processing, the corresponding edges become sharper and easily recognizable (Alshennawy & Aly, 2009).

The algorithm uses a fuzzy set of rules to assess the force of the edges. This is followed by selecting a threshold; only pixels with a contour strength higher than the threshold are considered to be edge pixels. The threshold is nominated so that the total probability of error in the identification of edge pixels is minimized. The sum of the probability of misinterpretation and the probability of false alarm are minimal. This minimization is achieved by adapting the particle swarm optimization (PSO) technique for optimization. The experimental results demonstrate the efficacy of the proposed border detection method and other standard gradient-based methods (Khunteta & Ghose, 2014).

A fuzzy logic technique is based on modified rules because fuzzy logic is desirable for converting the uncertainties that exist in many aspects of picture processing. First, both gradient and standard deviation are calculated and used as input data for a fuzzy system. The traditional algorithms such as Sobel, Prewitt, and LoG are carried out. The three edge resistance values used as fuzzy system inputs were blurred using Gaussian adhesion features. Fuzzy if-then rules are applied to change membership in one of the lower, middle, or upper classes (Manpreet & Kaur, 2011).

A histogram in association with fuzzy logic for edge detection of a digital image uses BSD for color representation. Brightness, hue and saturation are psychological color variations that a human eye recognizes. Hence, RGB color images are converted into hue-saturation-intensity (HSI) images. Once HSI images are extracted, the saturation component is not of concern, but hue and intensity are of concern. If the peak in a histogram is high, then the membership value in fuzzy logic is computed to be 1; otherwise, it varies as per the greyscale intensities at the appropriate segmentation. Hence, an output image can be obtained by convoluting the horizontal and vertical directions (Khaire & Thakur, 2012).

Type 2 Fuzzy is another pixel intensity distinguisher technique in fuzzy logic to interpret the changes between intensities of each pixel in an image. The method considers a 3×3 mask that is slided over the image, pixel by pixel more focusing on fuzzy rules. The fuzzy inference system has four gradients to classify a pixel to be an edge or not an edge (Neena, 2018).

Digital image processing represents the physical quantity, radiation, digital memory and processing hardware to interpret the edges of an image. Edges characterize limits, and edge detection is one of the most stimulating tasks in image processing. By using the edges of images, areas have high-intensity contrast, and a leap of intensity from pixel to pixel creates major variations in image quality. Detection of the edges of an image will reduce the amount of data and filter out unnecessary information, while structural properties of an image are preserved (Malarvizhli, Revathi, & Nevitha, 2018).

Fuzzy logic provides a good mathematical framework to manage information uncertainty. The processing of images of the collection from all approaches will represent an understanding of their segments and their characteristics as fuzzy games. The imaging and processing depend on the chosen interference technique and the problem to be solved. This research issue relates to the fuzzy inference system (FIS), which represents greater robustness to contrast and illumination variations. Further weight adjustments associated with fuzzy inference rules are still required to further reduce the inclusion in the output image of non-border pixels (Malarvizhli, Revathi, & Nevitha, 2018).

The health of a leaf's nutrient content can be detected using veins and edges of a leaf to detect deficiencies and symptoms of fungi. These deficiencies can be observed between interveinal areas along the edges. An effective algorithm is applied using Canny edge technique to detect the leaf edges for smoothness by reducing the image noise. Edge local gradient and direction are represented in Equations 2.2 and 2.3 (Radha & Jeyalakshmi, 2014):

$$\nabla f = \sqrt{g_x^2 - g_y^2} \tag{2.2}$$

$$\text{Edge Direction} = \frac{g_x}{g_y} \tag{2.3}$$

A plant can be identified using several features of a leaf, such as smell, color, leaf shape and taste. Accuracy in detection of a leaf is achieved by extracting the features in realistic and appropriate way. Contour-based Canny edge detection to emphasis the edges for plant identification. The extracted features from the plant are used in identifying the type of plants accurately. The algorithm proposed by Dubey follows the steps as described in Figure 2.1 (Thanikkal, Dubey, & Thomas, 2018).

Plants are the major species of the earth. The identification of plants is extremely important in the fields of Ayurvedic medicine, agriculture and biology. The work helps humans in the classification of medicinal plants in the real world and is seen as an essential task in the pharmaceutical industry, for Ayurvedic practitioners and for botanists. The computerization of plant species and their management is growing in importance. The process of identifying plants is performed by gathering common characteristics of the leaves. As a result, information about leaf veins plays an important role in identifying living plants. This chapter features Canny edge, characteristic of Gabor, and color histogram descriptors that have low, efficient and simple dimensions. In this case, a support vector machine (SVM) is used as a classifier. The process of identifying the leaves takes time manually and was primarily performed by botanists. In our proposed system, the machine-assisted plant recognition system is proposed in which k-mean is used for image segmentation. Good results are achieved through the combination of color, edge and texture (edge) characteristics. As it turns out, classification accuracy is better with the SVM classifier (Sneha & Pankaja, 2016).

FIGURE 2.1
Edge detection algorithm by Dubey and Thomas.

Research is ongoing to discover unknown plants and their classification and use. The plant classifications and recognition of leaves for plant identification play an essential role in all of these initiatives. Edge detection is considered one of the key steps in pre-treatment for leaf identification and recognition. Now the present need is to have a fast and efficient edge sensor for a sheet image. This proposed technique was introduced for detecting the base edges of wavelets, which used dyadic transformation of the wavelets and a p-tile thresholding method to find the edges. The proposed methodology was compared to conventional onboard detectors such as Canny, Sobel, Prewitt, Roberts, and Log. Based on the experimental results, the proposed method was found to be beneficial and capable of detecting edges (Valliammal & Geethalakshmi, 2010).

Removing the edge in the sheet images is an important step in computer inspection of the sheets. It is important to detect the edges and preserve detailed information about the texture of the leaf, such as vein, color, etc. The image on the original sheet is taken with a digital camera. The resulting sheet is initially treated by an adhesion function. Then, a fuzzy morphological mathematical algorithm is used to detect the boundary. The efficiency of edge detection based on fuzzy mathematical morphology is proven by comparing with the results of other edge detection algorithms such as binary morphology, Sobel in different conditions.

To implement intelligent farming techniques, an Android application is present that diagnoses and identifies the symptoms and maps to the corresponding disease on plant leaves. The Android app carries out basic operations like transforming colors found from the input images, thresholding and performing edge detection. The system works on such leaves of plants that are affected by many diseases—virus, fungus, excess nutrients and insects. The illness classification on plants will be done by using image processing operations. It determines the type of condition and its symptoms. Finally, the SVM-GA classifier is used for the diagnosis of cotton leaf disease. Using the Android app, the type of illness, symptoms, corrective actions and recovery suggestions are given at a very reduced time and low cost (Deepa, Nagarajan, PalanivelRajan, & Balamurali, 2019).

Pictures provide important data and information for the biological sciences. Plant diseases can be devastating and may lead to reduced quality and quantity of farm products. Farmers suffer from problems resulting from different kinds of plant characteristics/diseases. A successful sampling technique to identify plant diseases is proposed that automatically identifies based on colour, edges and histogram mapping. The methodology of this research is divided into two main phases. Phase one is the formation of a healthy sample and a diseased sample. The second phase involves the formation of the test sample and generates an outcome based on edge detection and histogram matching (Shital, Ajita, Pranali, & Sunil, 2014).

2.3 Proposed Methodology

The methodology aims to classify the type of leaf by detecting the edge points and monitoring the impulse noise. This method identifies the defective pixels from the brightness range of an image. The process initially begins by classifying the image pixel points into edge, regular or noisy based on random valued computational specifications. A fuzzy rule scheme applied in the proposed work will define the map accenting the edge pixels. The current research study used a high-resolution camera and Core i7 processor for collecting the leaf images of various fruits. Around 1,000 images of each type of fruit leaves are captured and processed for edge detection and thereby classification. All the images have the same size of 4×6.

2.3.1 Pre-classification

Image binarization maps the image pixels with black and white for classifying the different leaf structures from the data set. Fuzzy observes the uncertainty in the pixels to minimize the classification error. Fuzzification function for composing the grayscale image to map the pixels on the background is defined in Equations 2.4 and 2.5. The grayscale representation is given in Table 2.2.

TABLE 2.2

Grayscale Representation of Various Leaves in the Data Set

$$\mu_{1j}\left(l_j\right)=\left(gray\ level\ of\ l_j\right)/255 \tag{2.4}$$

$$\mu_{2j}\left(l_j\right)=1-\mu_{1j}\left(l_j\right) \tag{2.5}$$

2.3.2 Detection of Edge Pixels Using Fuzzy Sets

In edge detection, applying the Laplace second-order difference between the current pixel and neighbouring pixel will result in noise removal. If the magnitude is large, then consider the pixel is noisy as computed using Equation 2.6. Hence, the basic classification applying this technique is representing the fruit leaves of apple, orange, papaya, banana, mango, pomegranate, guava, strawberry, grape, and pineapple using Table 2.3. From the

TABLE 2.3

Edge Detection Using Fuzzy Sets

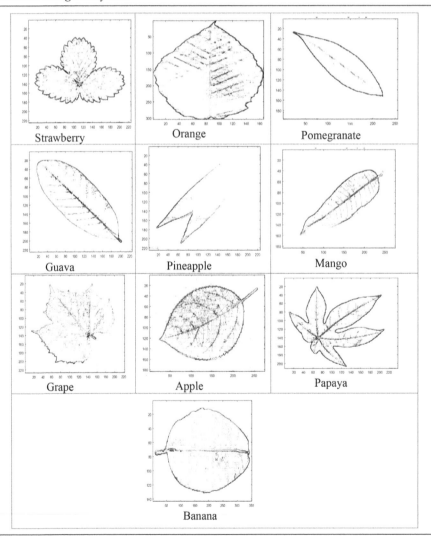

observation collected in the initial classification, the fuzzy model would provide 57% accuracy when tested on images like papaya and grape leaves. On pomegranate and mango leaves, the accuracy was 67% because of the resembling structures. Applying the fuzzy edge detection model on guava and banana leaves, the accuracy was 58%.

$$W = \left[c_{i+m,j+n} \right]; -1 \le m,n \le 1 \tag{2.6}$$

The membership function representing the pixel value for an image denoise is computed using Equation 2.7, where J represents the image pixel value, $a = 50$ and $b = 180$. The membership function for the papaya leaf image is represented in Figure 2.2.

$$\mu_m = \left(0 \; J \le a \; \frac{J-a}{b-a} \; a < J \le b1 \; b < J \le 255 \right) \tag{2.7}$$

2.3.3 Sparse Representation

The sparse matrix takes only the non-zero values from the input matrix which supplies both zero and non-zero values collected from the input domain. The sparse matrix will be suggested for use where memory is a constraint and less non-zero values are generated to process in application. For an example, the deployed sensors in a real-time system may get value 0 frequently until a particular event happens in its environment. The design of the sparse matrix may reduce the waste of memory space to store zero values, so instead of that, it takes only non-zero values to keep in memory for system processes.

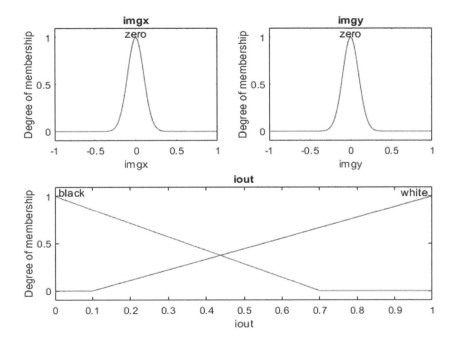

FIGURE 2.2
Degree of membership function of papaya leaf.

Image processing is a wide area that is the basis for developing very advanced or high-level applications solving real-time issues or problems. The captured input image will be converted into an intermediate representation which may be feasible to process in the programming script. The sparse representation is depicted in Table 2.4 for various leaves (pomegranate, apple, banana, strawberry, grape, guava, papaya, pineapple, mango and orange) of the data set.

The data extracted from the input image will be huge in size and can be represented using matrix form. But most of the parts of the input image may not have expected information, such as black pixels' data, to process. So, those portions may not be necessary to generate the expected results.

2.3.4 Edge Mapping with Kernel Function

In order to improve the edge detection, kernel functions are incorporated. Laplacian and Sobel filter functions are applied to improve the resolution, thereby removing the noise. A Sobel filter approximation kernel mask on horizontal and vertical axes are given in Equation 2.8:

$$H_x^S = \begin{bmatrix} -1 & 0 & 1 & -2 & 0 & 2 & -1 & 0 & 1 \end{bmatrix} \quad H_Y^S = \begin{bmatrix} -1 & -2 & -1 & 0 & 0 & 0 & 1 & 2 & 1 \end{bmatrix} \tag{2.8}$$

A Laplacian kernel mask computes the second-order derivative for accurate image intensity computation. This filter is preferred over Sobel for smoother edges, and its kernel mask is given in Equation 2.9:

$$K(LoG) = \begin{bmatrix} 1 & 1 & 11 & -8 & 11 & 1 & 1 \end{bmatrix} \tag{2.9}$$

To enhance the image quality, the Gaussian filter from Canny is applied as given in Equation 2.10. The approximated gradients strengthen the edges in both X and Y directions,

TABLE 2.4

Sparse Matrix Representation of Fruit Leaves

Sparse Matrix	Pomegranate	Apple	Banana	Strawberry	Grapes	Guava	Papaya	Pineapple	Mango	Orange
(1,1)	112	97	98	115	103	103	112	112	109	111
(1,2)	111	112	97	116	114	117	97	105	97	114
(1,3)	109	112	110	114	97	97	112	110	110	97
(1,4)	101	108	97	97	112	118	97	101	103	110
(1,5)	103	101	110	119	101	97	121	97	111	103
(1,6)	114	46	97	98	115	46	97	112	46	101
(1,7)	97	106	46	101	46	106	46	112	106	46
(1,8)	110	112	106	114	106	112	106	108	112	106
(1,9)	97	103	112	114	112	103	112	101	103	112
(1,10)	116		103	121	103		103	46		103
(1,11)	101			46				106		
(1,12)	46			106				112		
(1,13)	106			112				103		
(1,14)	112			103						
(1,15)	103									

removing the noise and perceiving the fainted edges of an image. Equation 2.11 is used to find the gradient's magnitude. The Canopy kernel mask is given in Equation 2.12.

$$|G| = \sqrt{G_X^2 + G_Y^2} \tag{2.10}$$

$$\theta = arctag\left(\frac{|G_X|}{|G_Y|}\right) \tag{2.11}$$

$$K(Canny) = \begin{bmatrix} -1 & 2 & -1 & 2 & -4 & 2 & -1 & 2 & -1 \end{bmatrix} \tag{2.12}$$

In this section papaya leaf (Table 2.5) is considered for representing the various kernel filters such as Sobel, and Laplacian mask is applied as shown in Figure 2.3. A Laplacian kernel mask filter represents the edge in a better way, as also depicted in Figure 2.3.

TABLE 2.5

Edge Detection Using Canopy Technique on Different Leaves in the Data Set

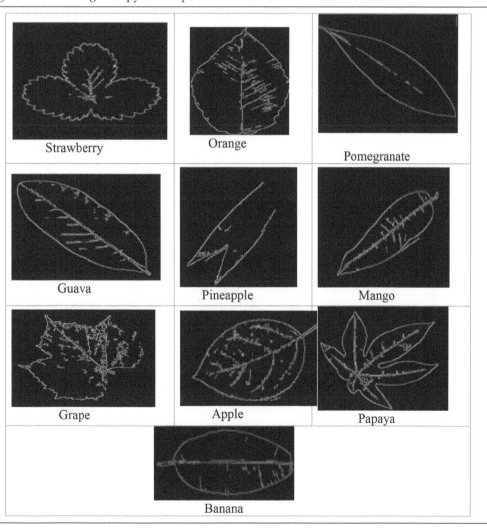

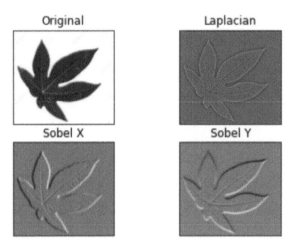

FIGURE 2.3
Filter representation of papaya leaf.

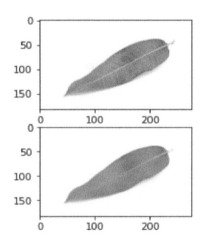

FIGURE 2.4
Denoising the image of a mango leaf using *FastNlMeans* function.

Segmentation is the basic image processing that partitions the image into regions that consist of homogeneous pixels and attributes. The noise component needs to be removed from the image preserving the pixel content intact. Gray-level intensity can be emphasised on the edge of an image by examining the neighbouring points. The *fastNlMeansDenoisingColored()* function is applied on the image for noise removal as depicted in Figure 2.4.

2.3.5 Principal Steps for Proposed Method

The following steps in Figure 2.5 summarize detection of the leaves using transfer learning from the fuzzy edge detection images.

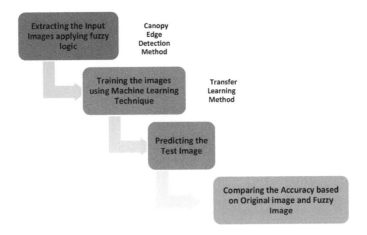

FIGURE 2.5
Proposed method for predicting the type of leaf.

1. The input images are converted to fuzzy images by applying the Canopy filtering mask for extracting edge detection features.
2. These fuzzy images are trained using the transfer learning technique using an eight-layer model as depicted in Figure 2.6. The training parameters are as follows: learning rate, 0.0001; validation frequency, 5; MaxEpochs, 10; and MiniBatchSize, 11.
3. Once the training has been finished, the test image is fed to check the accuracy by exporting the trained network. The accuracy is represented on a graph based on epoch iteration.
4. Finally, prediction accuracy is compared between the original image and fuzzy-based image.

2.4 Experimental Result Analysis

The interpretation results of the proposed methodology were verified and tested on 10,023 images of leaves. For experimenting with the method, 10 different leaves with different shapes and sizes are considered (see Appendix). Original images are displayed in Figure 2.7.

2.4.1 Parameter Selection

For each leaf in the data set, optimal true edges and noisy pixel points are discriminated. Hence, among the various filter types, canopy kernel mask is applied for appropriate feature selection. From these features, the model is able to identify the exact type of the leaf. The variations in the image horizontally and vertically with properties of fuzzy rule such as antecedent, consequent, weight and connection are represented in Table 2.6.

The effect of variation from Table 2.7 has been analysed using peak signal-to-noise ratio (P) using the following Equation 2.13:

$$P = 20 \log_{10} \left(\frac{MAX_f}{\sqrt{MSE}} \right)$$

(2.13)

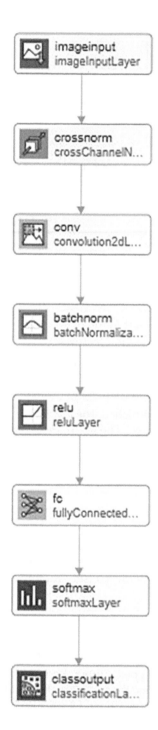

FIGURE 2.6
Eight-layer transfer learning technique.

FIGURE 2.7
Original leaf images in the data set.

TABLE 2.6

Image Representation in Horizontal and Vertical Considering Fuzzy Properties

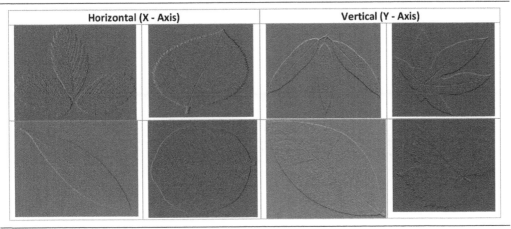

MAX_f is the maximum possible pixel for an input image, and MSE is the mean squared error with variance range on the horizontal axis as 56% and variance range for the vertical axis 65%. After these corrections, the images are restored for training on the transfer learning model. This improvement stabilizes the optimal recognition of the leaf by 50% and also degrades the unwanted noise pixels.

2.4.2 Computational Complexity

Time complexity is computed before and after the application of fuzzy image generation for the real-time prediction. Accuracy is improved for the fuzzy-based image over the original image by 56.4%. Considering the amount of training, the model also has better performance by representing the image in fuzzy logic, as shown in Table 2.7.

TABLE 2.7

Time Complexity on Fuzzy versus Original Image

Fuzzy Image	Time Complexity	Amount of Time Taken
Fuzzy and sparse representation	$O(n^2) + O(n) + O(1)$	5 sec
Transfer learning algorithm	$O(n^2) + O(n) + O(1)$	00:11:53 sec [training]
Original image	Time complexity	Amount of time taken
Colour representation	$O(n) + O(1)$	5 sec
Transfer learning algorithm	$O(n^2) + O(n) + O(1)$	00:15:56 sec [training]

TABLE 2.8

Accuracy of Training Model on Fuzzy Images

Input Data Normalization	Accuracy
Mini Batch	73.33%
Validation	57.14%

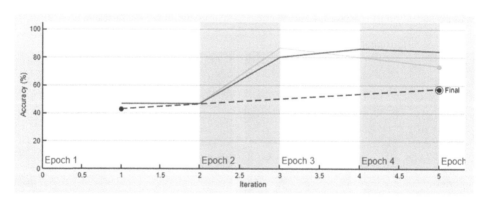

FIGURE 2.8
Original image accuracy for the training process.

2.4.3 Performance Comparison

Image classification is based on the accuracy of the prediction on the original image and that of the fuzzy representation. The performance accuracy and loss function metrics are presented in Table 2.8. At a learning rate of 0.0001 for five epochs, Mini Batch and Validation accuracy are given in Table 2.8. Accuracy gradually improved as the number of iterations increased on fuzzy-based images. Figures 2.8 and 2.9 represent the accuracy of original and canopy fuzzy images, respectively.

2.4.4 Prediction Evaluation

Once the training process is elapsed, a test image is fed to the deep network for observing the prediction accuracy. The model demonstrates the disrupted performance on the original image. But once the image is transformed into a fuzzy image by applying the canopy kernel mask, the model performance has a drastic improvement. The prediction was accurate for many test images that are fuzzy represented.

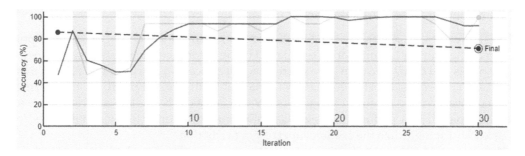

FIGURE 2.9
(Canopy) Fuzzy image accuracy for the training process.

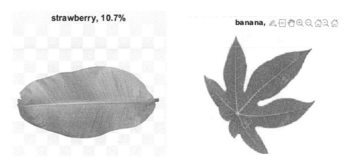

FIGURE 2.10
Prediction metrics of original images from the data set.

FIGURE 2.11
Prediction metrics of fuzzy represented images from the data set.

For the test images, banana leaves, papaya leaves and strawberry leaves are considered. The model on the original images predicted the banana leaf to be a strawberry and the papaya leaf to be a banana as presented in Figure 2.10. In the proposed study, fuzzy images usage has reduced the time consumption while training the model as presented in Table 2.7.

Testing the fuzzy kernel masked images predicted the leaf type with 89% accuracy as depicted in Figure 2.11.

2.5 Conclusion and Future Directions

The canopy kernel mask applied on blurred representations for leaf images and the application of the transfer learning approach paved the way for accurate prediction. Removing noisy pixels and defuzzification have aggregated the process in classifying the leaves more precisely. The proposed technique has been tested on both original and fuzzy transformed images. The accuracy for fuzzy images was 89%, whereas 40% was the accuracy score for original images. This performance signifies that the application of fuzzy as a pre-processing step will standardize the accuracy metrics in prediction.

The proposed work can be further extended to optimize the control parameters and also to minimize the computational complexity.

References

Aborisade, D. (2010). Fuzzy Logic Based Digital Image Edge Detection. *Global Journal of Computer Science and Technology*, Vol. 10, Issue 14 (Ver. 1.0), 78–83.

Alshennawy, A. A., & Aly, A. A. (2009). Edge Detection in Digital Images Using Fuzzy Logic Technique. *World Academy of Science, Engineering and Technology*, 178–186.

Anas, E. (2016). Edge Detection Techniques Using Fuzzy Logic. *International Conference on Signal Processing and Integrated Networks (SPIN)* (pp. 169–173). Lancashire.

Andrea, K., Eyberth, G., Carlos, S., Jorge, L., & Juan, M. (2013). Edge Detection Algorithm Based on Fuzzy Logic Theory for a Local Vision System of Robocup Humanoid League. *TecnoLógicas*, No. 30, 33–50.

Claudia, I., Patricia, M., & Oscar, C. (2017). Edge Detection Method Based on General Type-2 Fuzzy Logic Applied to Color Images. *Special Issue Fuzzy Logic for Image Processing*, 45–56.

Deepa, N., Nagarajan, N., PalanivelRajan, D., & Balamurali, R. (2019). Image Processing System for Detecting and Recovering from Cotton Leaf Disease Using the Android Application. *International Journal of Innovative Technology and Exploring Engineering*, 3367–3381.

Izhar, H., Anwar, S., Kamran, S., Muhammad, T., & Shaukat, A. (2015). Fuzzy Logic Based Edge Detection in Smooth and Noisy Clinical Images. *PLOS ONE*. Retrieved from https://journals.plos.org/plosone/article?id=10.1371/journal.pone.0138712#sec002

Khunteta, A., & Ghose, D. (2014). Edge Detection via Edge-Strength Estimation Using Fuzzy Reasoning and Optimal Threshold Selection Using Particle Swarm Optimization. *Advances in Fuzzy System—Hindawi*, 1–15.

Malarvizhli, A., Revathi, S., & Nevitha, R. (2018). Image Edge Detection Using Fuzzy Logic. *International Journal of Engineering Research & Technology*, 15–19.

Manpreet, K., & Kaur, S. (2011). A New Approach to Edge Detection Using Rule Based Fuzzy Logic. *Journal of Global Research in Computer Sciences*, 15–19.

Neena, A. (2018). A Novel Method for Edge Detection using Type 2 Fuzzy Logic. *International Journal of Engineering Research & Technology*, 1–8.

Khaire, P. A., & Thakur, N. V. (2012). Image Edge Detection Based on Soft Computing Approach. *International Journal of Computer Applications*, 12–14.

Radha, R., & Jeyalakshmi, S. (2014). An Effective Algorithm for Edges and Veins Detection in Leaf Images. *World Congress on Computing and Communication Technologies*, 128–131.

Shital, B., Ajita, D., Pranali, K., & Sunil, D. (2014). Plant Disease Detection Techniques Using Canny Edge Detection and Color Histogram in Image Processing. *International Journal of Computer Science and Information Technologies*, 1165–1168.

Sneha, & Pankaja, K. (2016). Identification of Leaf by Using Canny Edge Detection and SVM Classifier. *International Journal of Advanced Research in Electrical, Electronics and Instrumentation Engineering*, 3360–3363.

Thanikkal, J., Dubey, A., & Thomas, M. (2018). Advanced Plant Leaf Classification through Image Enhancement and Canny Edge Detection. *International Conference on Reliability, Infocom Technologies and Optimization (Trends and Future Directions) (ICRITO)*. Kerala.

Valliammal, N., & Geethalakshmi, S. (2010). Performance Analysis of Various Leaf Boundary Edge Detection Algorithms. Coimbatore, India: ACM.

Appendix

```
>> a=imread('a.jpg');
g1=rgb2gray(a);
g=imresize(g1,[200 200]);
[m,n]=size(g);
%figure, imshow(g)
%edge detection part
t=readfis('edge.fis');
z=uint8(zeros(m,n));
for i=2:m-1
  for j=2:n-1
      F = [g(i-1,j-1) g(i-1,j) g(i,j-1) g(i,j)];
      h=double(F);
      z(i,j)=evalfis(h,t);
  end
end
disp(z)
figure, imshow(z)
%noise removal part
z2=uint8(zeros(m,n));
for i=2:m-1
  for j=2:n-1
      if ((0<=z(i-1,j-1)<=50) & (0<=z(i-1,j)<=50) & (0<=z(i-1,j+1)<=50) &
(0<=z(i,j-1)<=50) & (0<=z(i,j)<=50) & (0<=z(i,j+1)<=50) & (0<=z(i+1,j-1)<=50) &
(0<=z(i+1,j)<=50) & (0<=z(i+1,j+1)<=50))
   %      if z1(i-1,j-1)==0 && z1(i-1,j)==0 && z1(i-1,j+1)==0 && z1(i,j-1)==0 &&
z1(i,j)==0 && z1(i,j+1)==0 && z1(i+1,j-1)==0 && z1(i+1,j)==0 && z1(i+1,j+1)==0
     z2(i,j)=128;
    else
      z2(i,j)=z(i,j);
    end
  end
end
>> Irgb = imread('a.jpg');
>> Igray = rgb2gray(Irgb);

figure
image(Igray,'CDataMapping','scaled')
colormap('gray')
title('Input Image in Grayscale')
>> I = im2double(Igray);
>> Gx = [-1 1];
Gy = Gx';
```

```
Ix = conv2(I,Gx,'same');
Iy = conv2(I,Gy,'same');
>> figure
image(Ix,'CDataMapping','scaled')
colormap('gray')
title('Ix')
>> figure
image(Iy,'CDataMapping','scaled')
colormap('gray')
title('Iy')
>> edgeFIS = mamfis('Name','edgeDetection');
>> edgeFIS = addInput(edgeFIS,[-1 1],'Name','Ix');
edgeFIS = addInput(edgeFIS,[-1 1],'Name','Iy');
>> sx = 0.1;
sy = 0.1;
edgeFIS = addMF(edgeFIS,'Ix','gaussmf',[sx 0],'Name','zero');
edgeFIS = addMF(edgeFIS,'Iy','gaussmf',[sy 0],'Name','zero');
>> edgeFIS = addOutput(edgeFIS,[0 1],'Name','Iout');
>> wa = 0.1;
wb = 1;
wc = 1;
ba = 0;
bb = 0;
bc = 0.7;
edgeFIS = addMF(edgeFIS,'Iout','trimf',[wa wb wc],'Name','white');
edgeFIS = addMF(edgeFIS,'Iout','trimf',[ba bb bc],'Name','black');
>> figure
subplot(2,2,1)
plotmf(edgeFIS,'input',1)
title('Ix')
subplot(2,2,2)
plotmf(edgeFIS,'input',2)
title('Iy')
subplot(2,2,[3 4])
plotmf(edgeFIS,'output',1)
title('Iout')
>> r1 = "If Ix is zero and Iy is zero then Iout is white";
r2 = "If Ix is not zero or Iy is not zero then Iout is black";
edgeFIS = addRule(edgeFIS,[r1 r2]);
edgeFIS.Rules

ans =
1x2 fisrule array with properties:

  Description
  Antecedent
  Consequent
  Weight
  Connection
Details:
        Description

  _____
  1 "Ix==zero & Iy==zero => Iout=white (1)"
  2 "Ix~=zero | Iy~=zero => Iout=black (1)"
```

```
>> Ieval = zeros(size(I));
for ii = 1:size(I,1)
    Ieval(ii,:) = evalfis(edgeFIS,[(Ix(ii,:));(Iy(ii,:))]');
end
>> figure
image(I,'CDataMapping','scaled')
colormap('gray')
title('Original Grayscale Image')
>> figure
image(Ieval,'CDataMapping','scaled')
colormap('gray')
title('Edge Detection Using Fuzzy Logic')
>> Irgb = imread('b.jpg');
>> figure
image(Igray,'CDataMapping','scaled')
colormap('gray')
title('Input Image in Grayscale')
>> Igray = rgb2gray(Irgb);

figure
image(Igray,'CDataMapping','scaled')
colormap('gray')
title('Input Image in Grayscale')
>> I = im2double(Igray);
>> Gx = [-1 1];
Gy = Gx';
Ix = conv2(I,Gx,'same');
Iy = conv2(I,Gy,'same');
>> figure
image(Ix,'CDataMapping','scaled')
colormap('gray')
title('Ix')
>> figure
image(Iy,'CDataMapping','scaled')
colormap('gray')
title('Iy')
>> edgeFIS = mamfis('Name','edgeDetection');
>> edgeFIS = addInput(edgeFIS,[-1 1],'Name','Ix');
edgeFIS = addInput(edgeFIS,[-1 1],'Name','Iy');
>> sx = 0.1;
sy = 0.1;
edgeFIS = addMF(edgeFIS,'Ix','gaussmf',[sx 0],'Name','zero');
edgeFIS = addMF(edgeFIS,'Iy','gaussmf',[sy 0],'Name','zero');
>> edgeFIS = addOutput(edgeFIS,[0 1],'Name','Iout');
>> wa = 0.1;
wb = 1;
wc = 1;
ba = 0;
bb = 0;
bc = 0.7;
edgeFIS = addMF(edgeFIS,'Iout','trimf',[wa wb wc],'Name','white');
edgeFIS = addMF(edgeFIS,'Iout','trimf',[ba bb bc],'Name','black');
>> figure
subplot(2,2,1)
```

```
plotmf(edgeFIS,'input',1)
title('Ix')
subplot(2,2,2)
plotmf(edgeFIS,'input',2)
title('Iy')
subplot(2,2,[3 4])
plotmf(edgeFIS,'output',1)
title('Iout')
>> r1 = "If Ix is zero and Iy is zero then Iout is white";
r2 = "If Ix is not zero or Iy is not zero then Iout is black";
edgeFIS = addRule(edgeFIS,[r1 r2]);
edgeFIS.Rules
ans =
  1×2 fisrule array with properties:
      Description
      Antecedent
      Consequent
      Weight
      Connection
  Details:
          Description
      _____
  1 "Ix==zero & Iy==zero => Iout=white (1)"
  2 "Ix~=zero | Iy~=zero => Iout=black (1)"
>> Ieval = zeros(size(I));
for ii = 1:size(I,1)
  Ieval(ii,:) = evalfis(edgeFIS,[(Ix(ii,:));(Iy(ii,:))]');
end
>> figure
image(I,'CDataMapping','scaled')
colormap('gray')
title('Original Grayscale Image')
>> figure
image(Ieval,'CDataMapping','scaled')
colormap('gray')
title('Edge Detection Using Fuzzy Logic')
>> fuzzy1
```

3

Water Surface Waste Object Detection and Classification

Jayanand P. Gawande, Rakesh P. Borase and Sushant N. Pawar

CONTENTS

3.1 Introduction

3.1.1 Motivation

Water pollution has become a serious problem in some parts of world. The water waste objects such as plastic cups, bottles, bags, etc., in lakes, rivers, reservoirs and oceans affect the water quality and living environment. Water contamination is a major concern in many countries around the world, including India, due to fast urbanisation, industrialisation and population growth [1]. The pollutants cause pollution, which poses a threat to the marine ecology and has significant environmental consequences [2–4]. The destruction of the aquatic ecosystem will not only have an impact on the environment but will also put small-scale economic activity associated with aquatic life in jeopardy. This leads to degradation of water bodies and increases biological oxygen demand (BOD) in water. This has adverse effects on the animals, humans and aquatic life relying on that water. Cleaning the contamination on a large scale is a tedious task. Hence, the water waste objects must be detected and cleaned automatically without human efforts. Vision-based robots are emerging as new tools for water surface waste cleaning [5–8]. However, the design of an autonomous robot which can function on the water surface remains a difficult issue due to the lack of waste object detection capability. Inspired by the workings of a garbage collection robot, this study aims to develop an intelligent robot which can detect the water surface garbage and pick it up automatically.

DOI: 10.1201/9781003218111-3

3.1.2 Significance of the Study

The detection and collection of water waste is not a new problem in real-world applications. Researchers from various fields, mechanical, civil, medical, environmental, etc., have made significant efforts in garbage collection from the sea, rivers and ponds. We employed a state-of-the-art deep learning (DL)–based object detection technique in this research study. This allows us to detect and classify water surface waste objects which will aid in waste mapping and water body cleaning. Furthermore, this aids in clean-up efforts and reduces water pollution levels, both of which are beneficial to aquatic life.

In recent years, object detection techniques have been used in many applications by the researchers. The classical image processing methods such as background subtraction, frame difference, Hough transform and image segmentation have been popularly used in object detection applications. However, to extract specific properties, these methods necessitate handcrafted models. Furthermore, the retrieved characteristics are lacking in representativeness and robustness, resulting in low generalisation ability. Object detection systems based on deep learning and video cameras have therefore arisen and been effectively implemented in self-driving cars [9], facial recognition [10] and pedestrian detection [11]. DL-based methods are more expressive than traditional methods. The most advanced DL-based object identification models can locate waste objects, assisting in the clean-up of water bodies and contributing to the environment by sustaining the aquatic ecosystem [12].

In this work, a new approach is presented to detect water surface waste objects which are captured by a digital camera on an aquatic cleaning robot. It can be used to clear up garbage on the water's surface, reduce the number of sanitation staff in the workplace, and improve the water's natural habitat. Waste object detection, waste capture and waste collection are the three key objectives for the waste object collecting robot. The waste object images are processed by means of a new deep learning framework called as YOLO (you only look once). The YOLO algorithm is modified by decreasing the detection scales from three to two to improve the performance of waste object detection. The four classes of waste objects, viz. plastic bottles, wrappers, paper cups and plastic bags, have been used in the training and testing phases of a modified YOLO algorithm. The performance of the modified YOLO algorithm is analysed in regard to precision and detection speed.

The following are the major findings of the current study:

- We developed an efficient and accurate DL-based approach to detect the water surface waste objects.
- We proposed a modified YOLO algorithm for waste object detection of four classes, viz. plastic bottles, wrappers, paper cups and plastic bags.
- We evaluated the classification performance of the proposed approach on four class customised data sets of water surface waste objects.
- We designed a prototype of a waste-collecting aquatic robot and implemented the proposed YOLOv3 algorithm in real time for intelligent detection and collection of waste objects independently.

The remaining content of the chapter is framed as follows. First, related review work is discussed in detail, and then the proposed detection method is elaborated effectively. Finally, the experimental results are reported, and this article is concluded.

3.2 Related Work

Automatic object detection systems can extract in the same way that humans can. Because of its rapid feature extraction speed and ability to convey object edge information, the Haar features extraction method [13] has been chosen. The textural information of objects can be better expressed using a local binary pattern (LBP) [14]. A histogram of oriented gradient (HOG) is widely applied to count the edges of objects [15]. Also, a multidirectional grayscale-based detection method is applied in fault detection [16]. A candidate region in an image is identified via sliding window in traditional object detection methods. The candidate regions are categorised using Adaboost and support vector machine after the Haar, HOG or LBP features are retrieved from them. Another popular object detector is deformable part module (DPM) which splits the image of the object into root model (HOG feature) and part model (template) [17]. However, it has been discovered in the literature that the manual-designed features have been used in these object detection methods [13–17]. Designing features manually is particularly troublesome, insufficient, incomplete and application specific [18]. These limitations have been overcome by a convolutional neural network (CNN) in various applications of object detection [19–21].

DL has proven considerable performance in the object detection algorithms because of improved computational power and developments in graphics processing units (GPUs). Two types of DL-based object detection systems exist: two-stage networks and one-stage networks. Regions with convolutional neural network (R-CNN) [22], Fast R-CNN [23] and Faster R-CNN [24] are included in the two-stage network. R-CNN with a region proposal network (RPN) can detect objects accurately, but the training process is very complex and requires large storage space. Also, the computational burden on RPN reduces the detection speed.

YOLOv1 (you only look once version 1) [25], YOLOv2 [26], YOLOv3 [27], and SSD (single-shot detector) [28] are examples of one-stage networks. Object detection and classification are transformed into regression using these strategies. Among other one-stage networks, the YOLOv3 object detection method performs exceptionally well in regard to speed and accuracy [29]. Objects are detected using YOLOv3 with three scales. As a feature extraction network, it employs Darknet-53. The entire convolution and residual structures are used in Darknet-53. By leveraging the deep and shallow features across the route layer, this technique enhances the recall rate and accuracy of YOLOv3 [30].

Various researchers have made efforts to detect the water waste objects using the DL techniques previously mentioned. Plastic marine debris [31] and river plastic waste [32] have been identified using CNN algorithm (VGG-16). Faster R-CNN is used in waste object detection and classification. A DL-based object detection model is proposed by Kulkarni and Raman [33] to detect the waste objects using SSD and RetinaNet architecture. The presented floating garbage data set is used to train the YOLOv3 network, which allows for accurate and real-time garbage identification [8]. Comparing with Faster R-CNN and SSD, the YOLOv3 algorithm achieves high speed and better accuracy. In this work, the YOLOv3 algorithm is modified and employed in the detection of four types of water surface waste objects including plastic bottles, wrappers, paper cups and plastic bags.

3.3 Water Surface Waste Collecting Robot

We designed a vision-based waste collecting robot for intelligent detection and collection of objects independently. The construction details of the aquatic robot are depicted in Figure 3.1. The robot was designed in the Autodesk FUSION 360 software, which is a three-dimensional computer-aided design and manufacturing and computer-aided engineering (CAE) tool. Lightweight fibreglass and PVC material are used to construct the robot body. The dimensions of the robot are 800 mm length, 440 mm width and 250 mm height. The 8-megapixel Raspberry Pi NoIR camera placed at the top of the robot captures the images of waste objects on the water's surface. The waste objects are detected by means of YOLOv3 algorithm implemented in a 64-bit quad-core Raspberry Pi processor. The robot actuated by two propellers moves towards the objects and collects the waste in a collecting box with the help of a conveyer belt. The waste collection box can carry the maximum 5 Kg capacity of water waste. The weight of collected waste can be measured by a load cell placed at the bottom of the waste collecting box. A 12 V, 10,000mAH Lithium-Ion rechargeable battery is used as the power supply. The designed aquatic robot is suitable for the collection of waste objects in lakes, rivers and ponds. It can be employed in the detection of water surface waste objects, mainly plastic bottles, wrappers, paper cups and plastic (polythene) bags.

3.4 Proposed Water Surface Waste Object Detection

The DL-based algorithms are proven to work competently in object detection. The modified YOLOv3 network for waste object detection was deduced from the YOLOv1 [25] and

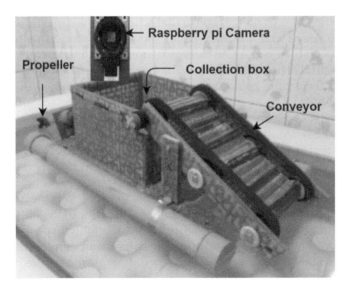

FIGURE 3.1
Prototype of the designed aquatic robot.

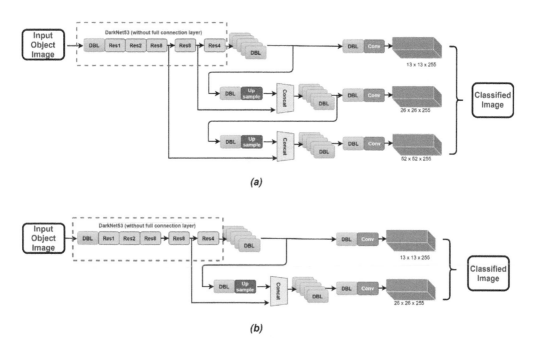

FIGURE 3.2
Framework of YOLOv3: (a) three-scale and (b) two-scale.

YOLOv2 [26] networks proposed in this chapter. YOLO framework does not require the RPN module. The bounding box coordinates and probabilities of each class are generated in YOLO directly through regression. The YOLOv3 uses Darknet-53 framework as shown in Figure 3.2. It is used to detect four different types of floating objects on the water's surface: plastic bottles, wrappers, paper cups and plastic bags.

YOLOv3 employs multiscale prediction for the detection of objects. Three bounding boxes are predicted in YOLOv3 for each multiscale grid. As illustrated in Figure 3.3, the network detects four coordinates for each bounding box: t_x, t_y, t_w, t_h. The predicted values are determined by Redmon and Farhadi [27], where the bounding box beforehand has width p_w, and height p_h.

$$b_x = \sigma(t_x) + c_x \tag{3.1}$$

$$b_y = \sigma(t_y) + c_y \tag{3.2}$$

$$b_w = p_w e^{t_w} \tag{3.3}$$

$$b_h = p_h e^{t_h} \tag{3.4}$$

where $\sigma(\cdot)$ is the sigmoid function which predicted the values in the interval [0, 1]. The input image with any size will be scaled first to 416×416 pixels. The output feature will map in three sizes of this image after transit through the YOLOv3 network, i.e. $13 \times 13 \times 3 \times (4+1+N)$, $26 \times 26 \times 3 \times (4+1+N)$ and $52 \times 52 \times 3 \times (4+1+N)$ cells, where

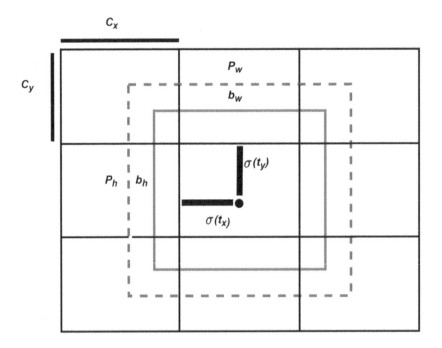

FIGURE 3.3
Prediction of bounding boxes in YOLOv3 algorithm [27].

   i. The feature map's side lengths are 13, 26 and 52.
   ii. The number 3 indicates three sizes of bounding box to predict the objects.
   iii. $(4 + 1)$ are the variables in the predicted box, i.e. $\{w, h, x, y,$ confidence$\}$. Here, (x, y) indicates the centre coordinate; (w, h) are the width and height of the box, respectively; and confidence specifies the possibility of the object. The confidence value will be nearer to one if the object is in the bounding box, else it is near zero.
   iv. N denotes the possible outcome values which is equal to the number of object categories, e.g. four classes of objects in this work.

Each scale's output is made up of $\{w, h, x, y,$ confidence$\}$ for each bounding box, as well as probability for the four classes. Therefore, the total channels of output is $3 \times (4+1+4) = 27$. The non-maximum suppression (NMS) approach is utilised to choose the best bounding box from the predicted bounding boxes. Using dimension clusters as anchor boxes, the system predicts bounding boxes.

The loss function in YOLOv3 is defined in Li et al. [18] which uses the sum of the squared error between the predicted value and ground truth value. For category prediction, YOLOv3 employs binary cross-entropy loss and logistic regression. This will make it easier to use YOLOv3 in more complicated situations and to detect objects more precisely and efficiently. Also, it can be helpful for classification of objects with multiple labels.

The k-means clustering is used to obtain the initial sizes of bounding boxes in YOLOv3. At first, k objects are selected randomly as the initial center of clusters, then the distance between each object and the center of the cluster is obtained and the object is assigned to the nearest clustering center. Euclidean distance is used as a distance measure which is defined as

$$D_{xy} = \left[\sum_{i=1}^{n} (x_i - y_i)^2 \right]^{\frac{1}{2}}$$

(3.5)

where D_{xy} is the Euclidean distance between the points (x_i, y_i) in n-dimensional space. At each iteration, the clustering center is updated until the best clustering results are obtained. In the original YOLOv3 algorithm, nine clustering results are obtained on a COCO data set which are (10 × 13), (16 × 30), (33 × 23), (30 × 60), (60 × 45), (59 × 119), (116 × 90), (156 × 198), (373 × 326), [27]. However, due to redundancy and increased computation time, combining the item anchor boxes obtained from the COCO data set may not be adequate for water surface waste object detection. Hence, the original prior anchor boxes are replaced with new object bounding boxes obtained from a water surface waste object data set. In our experimentation, six clustering results are obtained as (47 × 57), (62 × 68), (59 × 119), (142 × 104), (161 × 306), (373 × 326).

3.5 Experimental Results and Discussions

The performance of the modified YOLOv3 algorithm is analyzed on the data set created for the four classes of water surface waste objects, i.e. plastic bottles, wrappers, paper cups and plastic bags.

3.5.1 Data Set Information

Since the data set for water surface waste objects is not available, we need to make our own waste object image database. Most of the images are collected in real environments (water tank and lake) by means of a digital camera, while a few images have been downloaded from the internet. The collected images are annotated for labelling using an online open-source software. It allows the user to create and save annotations in the format required by YOLOv3. Each object in the image is labelled with a rectangular box which corresponds to the object class. The coordinates of the rectangular boxes' top-left corner and bottom-right corner are recorded as a text file in the labelled file. Table 3.1 highlights the objects for every category in the data set used during the experimentation's training and testing phases. The sample images of the data set are depicted in Figure 3.4.

TABLE 3.1

Data Set Information

Object Class	Plastic Bottles	Plastic Bags	Paper Cups	Wrappers	Multiple Objects
Number of images	42	46	40	31	15

FIGURE 3.4
Sample images in the water surface waste object data set.

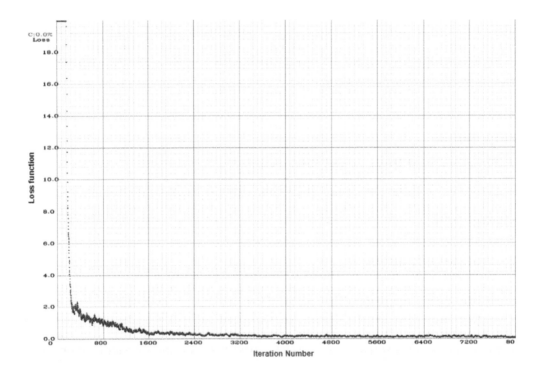

FIGURE 3.5
Plot of cross-entropy loss function versus number of iterations.

3.5.2 Object Detection Results and Discussions

During experimentation, four classes of water surface objects (bottles, wrappers, paper cups and plastic bags) have been detected by means of the proposed modified YOLOv3 algorithm. The training and testing of the YOLOv3 network is accomplished with standard rule 80% to 20% of the images in the data set. Using YOLOv3, we have trained our custom object for garbage detection. A weight is saved at every 1,000 iterations. Thus, eight weights are saved until the iteration reaches 8,000. The cross-entropy loss function computed during the training phase is plotted in Figure 3.5.

The classification performance is analysed by the performance parameter, mean average precision (MAP) which is a commonly used measure of recognition accuracy of the object detection algorithm. The average precision (AP) of the area is calculated by integrating the curve function, and the MAP is calculated by averaging the detection accuracy of all classes. The accuracy indicates the proportion of successfully identified objects to the total number of objects identified. The precision (P) and recall rate (R) are given by

$$P = \frac{TP}{TP + FP} \tag{3.6}$$

$$R = \frac{TP}{TP + FN} \tag{3.7}$$

Here, TP gives the number of objects exactly classified as positive. The number of samples wrongly categorised as positive is given by FP. FN gives the number of instances that are incorrectly classified as negative.

The experiments are performed on NVIDIA MX150 and Tesla-K80 GPU. The proposed waste object detection algorithm is implemented in Python programming. A snippet of Python code of waste object detection is presented in the Appendix. Here, we used the two-scale YOLOv3 network instead of three-scale YOLOv3 in order to improve the detection speed. The original anchor boxes in three-scale YOLOv3 are substituted with the anchor boxes retrieved from our data collection. The AP values are measured for each object class, plastic bottle, plastic bag, paper cup and wrapper, and are tabulated in Table 3.2. Since all the images are from water surface scenes, the robot can adapt to the aquatic environment and performs well in terms of recognition accuracy. Out of the four categories, the plastic bag and wrapper objects are detected more precisely as compared to the other two categories. The plastic bag and wrapper images in the data set have larger uniform object (foreground) area than plastic bottles and paper cups. The detection results of the YOLOv3 algorithm are shown in Figure 3.6 for the different object categories.

In Table 3.3, we compared the results of the proposed water surface waste object detection method with recently published work. As seen from Table 3.3, the proposed method achieved remarkable MAP value compared to the existing work in the literature [8, 12, 18, 33]. The results show that a modified two-scale YOLOv3 network outperforms faster than R-CNN [33] and SSD [12] algorithms in terms of precision. It can be noted that in existing works, few images are from surface water sights, and others are from other sights. The detection performance may be influenced by the environment. In the proposed method, the YOLOv3 algorithm is modified by decreasing the detection scales from three to two to improve the performance of waste object detection. Some of YOLOv3's original anchor boxes have been replaced with anchor boxes retrieved from our own data gathering, allowing YOLOv3 to attain high accuracy. In this way, the computational burden on the processor to detect the object area has been reduced. Moreover, the YOLOv3 algorithm is capable of detecting objects of small sizes. In our experimentation, we scaled the original frame or image to 416 × 416 pixels for further processing of the YOLOv3 network. The object bounding boxes obtained from the water surface waste object data set results in six clustering results: $(47 \times 57), (62 \times 68), (59 \times 119), (142 \times 104), (161 \times 306), (373 \times 326)$. Thus, the minimum size of the object in an image is required to be (47 × 57)pixels after rescaling. In addition, the proposed algorithm can detect multiple objects in an image with high precision.

TABLE 3.2

Average Precision Values Using YOLOv3 on the Dataset

Object Class	This Work	Li et al. [18]	Kong et al. [8]
Plastic bottle	0.9757	0.8894	0.8799
Plastic bag	0.9819	0.9378	0.9376
Paper cup	0.9642	—	—
Wrapper	0.9831	—	—

TABLE 3.3

Performance of Proposed Work Compared to Existing Methods

Ref.	Year	Number of Objects	Algorithm	MAP
Kulkarni et al. [33]	2019	6 (cardboard, glass, metal, paper, plastic, trash)	Faster R-CNN	0.8416
Panwar et al. [12]	2020	4 (glass, metal, paper, plastic)	SSD	0.8148
Li et al. [18]	2020	3 (bottle, bag, Styrofoam)	SSD	0.8596
			YOLOv3	0.9143
Kong et al. [8]	2020	3 (bottle, bag, Styrofoam)	YOLOv3	0.9119
Proposed work	2021	4 (plastic bottle, plastic bag, paper cup, wrapper)	YOLOv3	0.9756

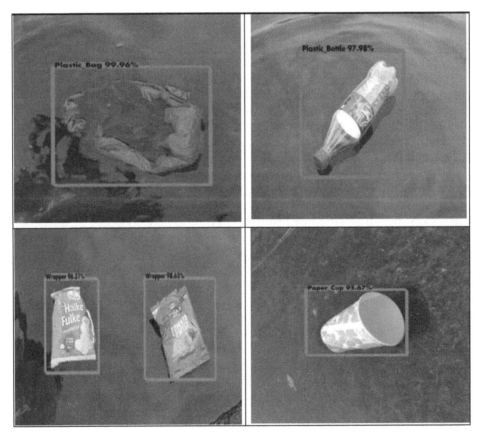

FIGURE 3.6

Object detection results: (a) with single object and (b) with multiple objects.

FIGURE 3.6
(Continued)

During the field experiment, the two-scale YOLOv3 algorithm is implemented on Raspberry Pi processor for real-time application. We conducted the field experiments using the designed aquatic robot with a camera. As the robot cruised on the water surface of a lake, it moved in the forward direction until the waste object on the water surface was detected. The detected objects were collected by the conveyer and placed in the waste collection box on the floating robot. The designed robot with the YOLOv3 algorithm detected the waste objects accurately and in real time.

3.6 Conclusion

In this work, an efficient approach based on a DL technique is presented to detect water surface waste objects. The four categories of waste objects are captured by a digital camera on an aquatic cleaning robot. Plastic bottles, plastic bags, paper cups and wrappers are among the four kinds of floating items detected using a modified YOLOv3 algorithm. The scales in the YOLOv3 network were changed from three to two for faster object detection. The experimental results prove that the proposed method performs better considering mean average precision as compared to the similar existing techniques. Also, the multiple objects in an aquatic scene can be detected accurately using the modified YOLOv3 algorithm. The proposed algorithm is deployed successfully on a designed aquatic robot for real-time application of waste object detection. In the future, the proposed intelligent algorithm can be applied to detect and classify underwater objects and solid wastes.

References

[1] Rakhecha, P. R. (2020). Water environment pollution with its impact on human diseases in India. *International Journal of Hydrogen*, 4(4), 152–158. https://doi.org/10.15406/ijh.2020.04.00240.

[2] Bilal, M., & Iqbal, H. M. (2020). Microbial bioremediation as a robust process to mitigate pollutants of environmental concern. *Case Studies in Chemical and Environmental Engineering*, 2, 100011. https://doi.org/10.1016/j.cscee.2020.100011.

[3] Coyle, R., Hardiman, G., & O'Driscoll, K. (2020). Microplastics in the marine environment: A review of their sources, distribution processes, uptake and exchange in ecosystems. *Case Studies in Chemical and Environmental Engineering*, 2, 100010. https://doi.org/10.1016/j.cscee.2020.100010.

[4] Bilal, M., Ashraf, S. S., Barcelo, D., & Iqbal, H. M. (2019). Biocatalytic degradation/redefining "removal" fate of pharmaceutically active compounds and antibiotics in the aquatic environment. *Science of the Total Environment*, 691, 1190–1211. https://doi.org/10.1016/j.scitotenv.2019.07.224.

[5] Albitar, H., Dandan, K., Ananiev, A., & Kalaykov, I. (2016). Underwater robotics: Surface cleaning technics, adhesion and locomotion systems. *International Journal of Advanced Robotic Systems*, 13(1), 7. https://doi.org/10.5772/62060.

[6] Bai, J., Lian, S., Liu, Z., Wang, K., & Liu, D. (2018). Deep learning-based robot for automatically picking up garbage on the grass. *IEEE Transactions on Consumer Electronics*, 64(3), 382–389. https://doi.org/ 10.1109/TCE.2018.2859629.

[7] Kim, J., Mishra, A. K., Limosani, R., Scafuro, M., Cauli, N., Santos-Victor, J., & Cavallo, F. (2019). Control strategies for cleaning robots in domestic applications: A comprehensive review. *International Journal of Advanced Robotic Systems*, 16(4), 1729881419857432. https://doi.org/10.1177/1729881419857432.

[8] Kong, S., Tian, M., Qiu, C., Wu, Z., & Yu, J. (2020). IWSCR: An intelligent water surface cleaner robot for collecting floating garbage. *IEEE Transactions on Systems, Man, and Cybernetics: Systems*, 51(10), 6358–6368. https://doi.org/10.1109/TSMC.2019.2961687.

[9] Campmany, V., Silva, S., Espinosa, A., Moure, J. C., Vázquez, D., & López, A. M. (2016). GPU-based pedestrian detection for autonomous driving. *Procedia Computer Science*, 80, 2377–2381. https://doi.org/10.1016/j.procs.2016.05.455.

[10] Ranjan, R., Patel, V. M., & Chellappa, R. (2017). Hyperface: A deep multi-task learning framework for face detection, landmark localization, pose estimation, and gender recognition. *IEEE Transactions on Pattern Analysis and Machine Intelligence*, 41(1), 121–135. https://doi.org/10.1109/TPAMI.2017.2781233.

[11] Li, J., Liang, X., Shen, S., Xu, T., Feng, J., & Yan, S. (2017). Scale-aware fast R-CNN for pedestrian detection. *IEEE Transactions on Multimedia*, 20(4), 985–996. https://doi.org/10.1109/10.1109/TMM.2017.2759508.

[12] Panwar, H., Gupta, P. K., Siddiqui, M. K., Morales-Menendez, R., Bhardwaj, P., Sharma, S., & Sarker, I. H. (2020). AquaVision: Automating the detection of waste in water bodies using deep transfer learning. *Case Studies in Chemical and Environmental Engineering*, 2, 100026. https://doi.org/10.1016/j.cscee.2020.100026.

[13] Whitehill, J., & Omlin, C. W. (2006, April). Haar features for FACS AU recognition. In *7th International Conference on Automatic Face and Gesture Recognition (FGR06)* (pp. 5-pp). IEEE. https://doi.org/10.1109/FGR.2006.61.

[14] Ojala, T., Pietikainen, M., & Maenpaa, T. (2002). Multiresolution gray-scale and rotation invariant texture classification with local binary patterns. *IEEE Transactions on Pattern Analysis and Machine Intelligence*, 24(7), 971–987. https://doi.org/10.1109/TPAMI.2002.1017623.

[15] Dalal, N., & Triggs, B. (2005, June). Histograms of oriented gradients for human detection. In *IEEE Computer Society Conference on Computer Vision and Pattern Recognition (CVPR'05)* (Vol. 1, pp. 886–893). IEEE. https://ieeexplore.ieee.org/document/1467360, https://doi.org/10.1109/CVPR.2005.177.

[16] Ma, Y., Li, Q., Zhou, Y., He, F., & Xi, S. (2017). A surface defects inspection method based on multidirectional gray-level fluctuation. *International Journal of Advanced Robotic Systems*, 14(3), 1729881417703114. https://doi.org/10.1177/1729881417703114.

[17] Ali, A., Olaleye, O. G., & Bayoumi, M. (2016). Fast region-based DPM object detection for autonomous vehicles. In *IEEE 59th International Midwest Symposium on Circuits and Systems (MWSCAS)* (pp. 1–4). IEEE. https://doi.org/10.1109/MWSCAS.2016.7870113.

[18] Li, X., Tian, M., Kong, S., Wu, L., & Yu, J. (2020). A modified YOLOv3 detection method for vision-based water surface garbage capture robot. *International Journal of Advanced Robotic Systems*, 17(3), 1729881420932715. https://doi.org/10.1177/1729881420932715.

[19] Szarvas, M., Yoshizawa, A., Yamamoto, M., & Ogata, J. (2005). Pedestrian detection with convolutional neural networks. *IEEE Proceedings. Intelligent Vehicles Symposium, 2005* (pp. 224–229). IEEE. https://doi.org/10.1109/IVS.2005.1505106.

[20] Chen, F. C., & Jahanshahi, M. R. (2017). NB-CNN: Deep learning-based crack detection using convolutional neural network and naïve Bayes data fusion. *IEEE Transactions on Industrial Electronics*, 65(5), 4392–4400. https://doi.org/10.1109/TIE.2017.2764844.

[21] Kagaya, H., Aizawa, K., & Ogawa, M. (2014, November). Food detection and recognition using convolutional neural network. In *Proceedings of the 22nd ACM International Conference on Multimedia* (pp. 1085–1088). https://dl.acm.org/doi/10.1145/2647868.2654970, https://doi.org/10.1145/2647868.2654970.

[22] Girshick, R., Donahue, J., Darrell, T., & Malik, J. (2014). Rich feature hierarchies for accurate object detection and semantic segmentation. *In Proceedings of the IEEE Conference on Computer Vision and Pattern Recognition* (pp. 580–587). IEEE. https://ieeexplore.ieee.org/document/6909475, https://doi.org/10.1109/CVPR.2014.81.

[23] Girshick, R. (2015). Fast R-CNN. In *Proceedings of the IEEE International Conference on Computer Vision* (pp. 1440–1448). IEEE. https://ieeexplore.ieee.org/document/7410526, https://doi.org/10.1109/ICCV.2015.169.

[24] Ren, S., He, K., Girshick, R., & Sun, J. (2016). Faster R-CNN: Towards real-time object detection with region proposal networks. *IEEE Transactions on Pattern Analysis and Machine Intelligence*, 39(6), 1137–1149. https://doi.org/10.1109/TPAMI.2016.2577031.

[25] Redmon, J., Divvala, S., Girshick, R., & Farhadi, A. (2016). You only look once: Unified, real-time object detection. In *Proceedings of the IEEE Conference on Computer Vision and Pattern Recognition* (pp. 779–788). IEEE. https://ieeexplore.ieee.org/document/7780460, https://doi.org/10.1109/CVPR.2016.91.

[26] Redmon, J., & Farhadi, A. (2017). YOLO9000: Better, faster, stronger. In *Proceedings of the IEEE Conference on Computer Vision and Pattern Recognition* (pp. 7263–7271). IEEE. https://ieeexplore.ieee.org/document/8100173, https://doi.org/10.1109/CVPR.2017.690.

[27] Redmon, J., & Farhadi, A. (2018). YOLOv3: An incremental improvement. *arXiv preprint arXiv:1804.02767*.

[28] Liu, W., Anguelov, D., Erhan, D., Szegedy, C., Reed, S., Fu, C. Y., & Berg, A. C. (2016, October). SSD: Single shot multibox detector. In *European Conference on Computer Vision* (pp. 21–37). Springer, Cham. http://doi.org/10.1007%2F978-3-319-46448-0_2.

[29] Benjdira, B., Khursheed, T., Koubaa, A., Ammar, A., & Ouni, K. (2019). Car detection using unmanned aerial vehicles: Comparison between Faster R-CNN and YOLOv3. In *2019 1st International Conference on Unmanned Vehicle Systems-Oman (UVS)* (pp. 1–6). IEEE. https://doi.org/10.1109/UVS.2019.8658300.

[30] Park, J. H., Hwang, H. W., Moon, J. H., Yu, Y., Kim, H., Her, S. B., & Lee, S. J. (2019). Automated identification of cephalometric landmarks: Part 1—Comparisons between the latest deep-learning methods YOLOv3 and SSD. *The Angle Orthodontist*, 89(6), 903–909. https://doi.org/10.2319/022019-127.1.

[31] Kylili, K., Kyriakides, I., Artusi, A., & Hadjistassou, C. (2019). Identifying floating plastic marine debris using a deep learning approach. *Environmental Science and Pollution Research*, 26(17), 17091–17099. https://doi.org/10.1007/s11356-019-05148-4.

[32] Van Lieshout, C., van Oeveren, K., van Emmerik, T., & Postma, E. (2020). Automated river plastic monitoring using deep learning and cameras. *Earth and Space Science*, 7(8). https://doi.org/10.1029/2019EA000960.

[33] Kulkarni, H. N., & Raman, N. K. S. (2019). Waste object detection and classification. *Turkish Journal of Computer and Mathematics Education (TURCOMAT)*, 12(6), 5583–5595.

Appendix

Python code snippet of proposed method

```
cd Object-Detection-API/

conda env create -f conda-gpu.yml
conda activate yolov3-gpu
python load_weights.py

python load_weights.py --weights './weights/yolov3_custom_8000.weights'
--output './weights/yolov3_custom_8000.tf' --num_classes '4'
python app.py

python detect_video.py --video 0 --output './data/video/output.avi'

python detect_video.py --video './data/video/waste.mp4' --output
'./data/video/output1.avi'

python detect.py --images "data/images/dog.jpg, data/images/office.jpg"
```

4

A Novel Approach for Weakly Supervised Object Detection Using Deep Learning Technique

Jyoti G. Wadmare and Sunita R. Patil

CONTENTS

DOI: 10.1201/9781003218111-4

4.1 Introduction

Due to rapid development in the computer vision arena and the availability of large amounts of images, object detection tasks using deep learning techniques play an important role in finding the instances of predefined object classes in an images or videos. Automatically learning the features from the raw data is possible due to the powerful techniques of deep learning. In this decade, many researchers' attention has been on solving real-time problems like disease detection, automatic road sign detection, face detection, retail management, etc. with the help of object detection using deep learning techniques such as convolutional neural network (CNN), region-based convolutional neural networks (R-CNNs), single-shot detectors (SSDs), YOLO you only look one), etc. [1].

As the world is facing the problem of huge amounts of waste generation daily, the proper classification and detection of solid waste materials into categories like glass, paper, metal, cardboard and plastic helps to increase the recycling process and scrapping of other waste materials. Manual sorting of these materials is a time-consuming, expensive process, and it may lead to health-related problems due to harmful substances. Keeping that in mind, it motivated us to solve the problem using an automated system. Computer vision technology can be an economical solution due to a weakly supervised approach where the deep learning model is trained solely on image-level annotations and is an environmentally friendly solution to detect solid wastes from garbage [2].

To achieve this goal, this chapter makes the following key contributions:

- The main contribution is to choose the best pre-trained deep learning model for features extraction from the input images so that the object detection model will perform better.
- The other sub-contribution of the present study is the development of a custom dataset consisting of small-scale waste materials so that the object detection model can detect small-sized objects effectively.

This chapter focuses on an automated way of detecting solid waste materials using a weakly supervised object detection (WSOD) approach—an effective solution to channelize the recycling process.

This chapter is organized as follows: Section 4.1 introduces computer vision, its application domains, milestones of object detection and different challenges faced during object detection. Section 4.2 summarises deep learning approaches for WSOD and different datasets used for object detection. Section 4.3 describes the methodology for WSOD in detail. Section 4.4 presents and discusses the research findings. Section 4.5 concludes with some observations and suggestions for future research.

4.1.1 Introduction to Computer Vision

Computer vision is a branch of study that aims to help computers interpret images and videos and determine what the machine "sees" and "recognizes". Humans can recognize the objects which are present in an image, human eyes act as sensors and that information is sent to the brain that then interprets that information and classifies and recognizes the objects present in an image. The same phenomenon is applied in computer vision, where the input image or video is captured via camera and sent to the computer, where different computer vision–based algorithms extract the features from images and recognize different objects present in an image.

4.1.2 Computer Vision Application Domains

Computer vision has a wide range of applications like in self-driving cars in which pedestrian and other vehicle detection is a crucial task, face recognition and objects detection. Self-driving, driverless or autonomous cars are a current emerging application of computer vision in which pedestrian and other vehicle detection is a crucial task. Companies like Google and Tesla are competing to launch the first self-driving car [3]. Following are some of the most well-known computer vision application domains.

4.1.2.1 Face Detection and Recognition

Face detection is the same as object class detection in that it seeks out the locations and sizes of all items in an image that belong to a particular category. A face detection algorithm focuses on frontal human faces; it localizes the face with a bounding box in an image.

A smile detection algorithm allows the camera to take a picture automatically when a person is smiling.

4.1.2.2 Optical Character Recognition

Computer vision–based algorithms are used to recognize numbers or digits, characters, zip codes, etc. This optical character recognition is the oldest application of computer vision, used, for example, in handwriting recognition, license plate recognition, etc.

4.1.2.3 Three-Dimensional Modelling

Images are captured with drone cameras, and computer vision techniques are used to render all the images into a three-dimensional model.

4.1.2.4 Object Detection

This is a technique for recognising and locating objects in an image or video. The state-of-the-art algorithms are designed to detect the objects by drawing a bounding box around the object and assigning a label to all detected objects present in an image.

This chapter is primarily concerned with the application of computer vision: object detection.

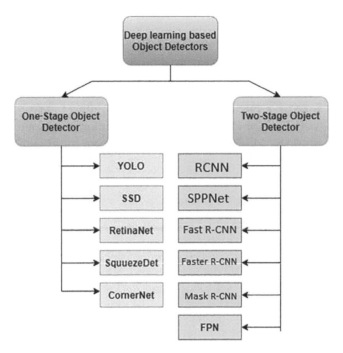

FIGURE 4.1
Milestones of object detectors.

4.1.3 Milestones of Object Detection

In traditional object detectors, manually defined feature extractors were used which have low detection accuracy and precision. Due to an exponential growth in data generation, deep learning has become a solution in many computer vision–based object detection. There has been remarkable growth in deep learning–based object detectors, and there are two types of detectors: one-stage and two-stage, as shown in Figure 4.1.

4.1.3.1 Two-Stage Detectors

Two-stage detectors are commonly employed to achieve localization and classification accuracy. The following are two-stage detector networks.

1. R-CNN (region-based convolutional neural network)

   In the first stage of R-CNN, a selective search method extracts 2,000 sections from the input image; these regions are called region proposals. We have to deal with more areas in a CNN, but we just have to work with 2,000 regions in an R-CNN. The selective search algorithm uses four measures: colour, shape, size and texture. In the second stage of R-CNN, a strong classifier support vector machine (SVM) is applied to predict the object present within each region proposal. The main limitation of R-CNN is its training time; for each image, there are 2,000 region proposals, so it requires more training time [4].

2. SPPNet (spatial pyramid pooling network)

   The spatial pyramid pooling layer replaces the previous pooling layer in SPPNet. In the spatial pyramid pooling layer, three kinds of pooling operations are performed, i.e. level 0 (256 dimensions), level 1 (4*256 dimensions) and level 2 (16*256 dimensions), and at the end we get (21*256 dimensions) feature output. It is independent of size and aspect ratio of the input image. Although it has better accuracy in classification and detection tasks than R-CNN, it requires multistage training [5].

3. Fast R-CNN (fast region-based convolutional neural network)

In Fast R-CNN, a single grid of 7*7 is used instead of having multiple grids of different sizes, unlike SPPNet. This kind of pooling is called region of interest (ROI) pooling. It uses a softmax classifier instead of SVM and a bounding box regressor per class. It has two fully connected layers, one for learning the weights of classification and one for learning the weights for bounding box regressor. It uses only one-stage training, and to fine-tune the network, classification and regression losses are back-propagated. It has higher accuracy as compared to R-CNN and is 146 times faster than R-CNN [6].

4. Faster R-CNN (faster region-based convolutional neural network)

This CNN is an extension of Fast R-CNN. Instead of using selective search, it uses RPN (region proposal network). It uses anchor boxes of different sizes, i.e. three different scales and three aspect ratios. ROI pooling takes different sizes of feature maps as input and reduces all the feature maps to the same size. Training of Faster R-CNN is completed in four phases. First, train the region proposal network using ConvNet1 second, train Fast R-CNN using ConvNet2 and RPN proposals. Third, fine-tune RPN using ConvNet2, and last, fine-tune Fast R-CNN using ConvNet2 and new RPN proposals. It has two fully connected layers: one for classification and one for the bounding box regressor. Although it is faster than Fast R-CNN, it faces computational redundancy at the last stage [7].

5. Mask R-CNN (mask region-based convolutional neural network)

This is an approach of instance segmentation which we get from combining object detection and semantic segmentation. For object detection, it uses similar architecture like Faster R-CNN, and for semantic segmentation, it uses FCN (fully convolutional network). The limitation of the ROI pooling layer is loss of data due to quantizing the stride. The ROI-align method is used to overcome the problem of ROI pooling by applying a bilinear interpolation operation. The class label, bounding box coordinates, and object mask are the three outputs of Mask R-CNN. It is widely used in computer vision applications like medical image analysis. It uses the ResNet-FPN model to extract the features from the input image or video. It has small computational overhead on the network [8].

6. FPN (feature pyramid network)

In FPN, low-level features at last layers are merged with the feature maps from early layers to improve the resolution of feature maps. It has bottom-up and top-down paths of CNNs. The output of the bottom-up path is given to input to each convolutional layer of the top-down path so that it produces high-quality features as output. FPN is a method of upsampling the features. It is not a stand-alone detector; it is used with other region-based neural networks for detecting small-scale objects in an image [9].

4.1.3.2 One-Stage Detectors

To achieve high inference speed, one-stage object detectors are used. One-stage detector models are as follows:

1. YOLO (you only look once)

   The YOLO object detection algorithm is faster and simpler to use for real-time object detection. It is entirely different from the previous object detectors; it takes an input image and divides it into grids of any size. For each grid, it predicts the bounding box and class probabilities. This algorithm may predict multiple bounding boxes for a given object; this problem is solved by calculating the IOU (intersection of union). There are many YOLO versions available, like YOLOv2 and YOLOv3 which have good accuracy. To overcome the challenge of recognising little objects in an image, the Tiny YOLO model is utilised [10].

2. SSD (single-shot detector)

   SSD produces 8732 predictions for each object in an image by using six convolution layers. It uses non-maximum suppression to remove duplicate predictions. An SSD network checks the confidence score of each box and picks the top 200 predictions of each object by calculating IOU. It is faster than the YOLO object detector. It has a large number of classification errors but minimal localization errors [11].

3. RetinaNet

   One-stage detectors surpass the two-stage detectors. Class-imbalance problems in SSD and YOLO happen due to inefficient training, as most locations are easy negatives. That contributes no useful signal and thus leads to degenerate models. RetinaNet uses focal loss during training to avoid the problem of class imbalance. It is more focused on misclassified objects [12].

4. SqueezeDet

   SqueezeDet is used in autonomous driving systems for detecting objects. It consists of stacked convolution filters for extracting low- and high-resolution feature maps of input images. The convolutional layer ConvDet is used to generate the bounding boxes and predict its class. Filtering is applied on these bounding boxes and detects objects. It consumes less energy (1.4 J per image) and is an extremely fast network. The SqueezeNet network is the backbone of SqueezeDet architecture. The size of the model is very small compared with AlexNet [13].

5. CornerNet

   This is a novel way of detecting objects. The object bounding boxes are detected by CornerNet as a pair of key points, namely, top-left and bottom-right. It eliminates the use of anchor boxes by introducing corner pooling. It uses a single convolutional network to predict heat-maps of the top-left and right-bottom corners of all the instances of the same object, later embedding vector groups in top-left and right-bottom corners [14].

4.1.4 Different Challenges Faced During Object Detection

- Despite advances in computer vision–based object detection algorithms, recognising or identifying objects of various orientations, scales or sizes remains a difficult task.
- The images or pictures are captured from different viewpoints and different cameras.
- Another challenge is lighting conditions, scaled objects and variations of a single object.

The researchers addressed all of these issues, which are as follows:

1. Variation in viewpoint

   The object looks different from different viewpoints, and it is difficult to detect the objects due to variation in viewpoint. Glasner et al. [15] proposed a joint task of detection and viewpoint estimation in six-dimensional parameter space which serves to improve the performance of the detector.

2. Deformation

   Many objects are not rigid in nature, and they can be deformed in many ways. So an object detector should detect such deformed objects and undertake the challenging task of analysing the deformed object. Felzenszwalb et al. [16] proposed that deformable part modules (DPMs) have discriminative model training by using latent information.

3. Occlusion

   Sometimes objects of interest can be occluded, but some part of the object is visible; in such conditions, detecting such occluded objects is challenging. Angtian Wang et al. [17] proposed compositional nets which classify occluded objects. They have used a part-based voting mechanism for robust bounding box estimation under severe occluded conditions.

4. Illumination conditions

   Images captured during daylight, evening and night light have different pixel intensities of the same object. The object looks different in such changing illumination. This affects the performance of the object detector. Atoum [18] proposed an iterative CNN model to produce good lighting illumination to recover from dark images.

5. Cluttered background

   Objects of interest may blend into the background, and it is difficult to identify them from the cluttered background. Varatharasan et al. [19] proposed a SEg-CK framework in which they have used DeepLab and chroma key concept to merge the extracted objects into a predefined background.

6. Intraclass variance

   One object may appear in different sizes and shapes, so it is a challenging task to detect such objects. Rafał Pilarczyk et al. [20] proposed an optimization technique through the Hadamard layer to minimize intraclass variance.

4.2 Deep Learning Approaches for Object Detection

Due to exponential growth in data generation, deep learning has become the solution in many computer vision–based object detection applications like pedestrian detection, human computer interaction, crowd detection, military applications, medical image analysis, solid waste segregation and other domains. This section of this chapter focuses on object detection applications in various domains.

4.2.1 Need for Deep Learning in Object Detection Task and Its Applications

Pedestrian detection is useful in video surveillance applications and autonomous cars, but the main challenges are to detect pedestrians in occluded, dense conditions and small pedestrian detection. A major military application is detection of objects in remote areas using remote sensing. In this application, the main challenges are to detect objects in complex backgrounds.

In medical image analysis, infectious regions or abnormalities can be detected with the help of vision-based techniques, like detection of lung cancer, breast cancer, tumours and skin disease. Researchers can use a variety of available image datasets to do research in the healthcare field.

Crowd detection is one of the most difficult tasks using object detection. In a crowded situation, there are many confused people, which leads to panicked motions by everyone. To avoid this, automatic detection of a dense crowd is very important to alert the emergency controls for the safety of people. Such applications are useful in disaster management and public gathering programs [21].

Vision-based object detection techniques can be used in other domains like agriculture for detecting plant disease, automatic fruit detection and counting, etc. It can be used to help visually impaired people as an assistive technology and to monitor elderly people at home.

The object detection technique gives an artifical intelligence–based solution for waste segregation. This technique is used to identify and locate solid waste materials like glass, plastic, paper, metal, cardboard and trash items from input images/videos. This chapter provides an approach to solve this real-time problem of waste segregation using the deep learning technique.

4.2.2 Deep Learning Approaches for Weakly Supervised Object Detection

The state-of-the-art fully supervised object detector requires bounding box annotations during training the model. Such manual annotation of the bounding box is a very time-consuming process. Due to this and the availability of a large number of images with image-level labels, researchers are more interested to work toward a WSOD approach.

For training, the WSOD model leverages image-level annotations. Classification and localization accuracy in real-time application is a challenging task in object detection. Researchers have used a variety of techniques for WSOD, as shown in Table 4.1.

According to a review of the research, existing deep learning weakly supervised algorithms for object detection have some drawbacks, such as the inability to recognise target objects in congested environments and the difficulty of locating small-scaled objects.

4.2.3 Object Detection Datasets

All deep learning–based object detection approaches need datasets for model training and verification of the output. Table 4.2 shows the most commonly used latest version datasets for object detection.

As per the application of object detection, many image datasets are available freely for researchers. But in some cases, we need custom datasets as well as per the requirement of the application. These custom datasets are generated by clicking the photographs;

TABLE 4.1

Summary of Weakly Supervised Object Detection Techniques Used for Object Detection

Serial Number	Title	Description	Limitation	Dataset
1	Weakly Supervised Group Mask Network (WSGMN) for Object Detection	Images and their proposed area proposals are sent into this network, which produces a score of images for each label. The image-level annotations are used for training the network. For predicting the target objects, convolutional filters are used [22].	Automatic estimation of the grouping of class labels is missing.	ImageNet Detection Dataset, MS-COCO Dataset
2	Weakly Supervised Region Proposal Network and Object Detection	For proposal generation in weakly supervised object detection (WSOD), they developed a two-stage region proposal network. To generate proposals, low-level information from first convolutional layers are utilized, and the second stage is a region-based CNN to fine-tune the first-stage proposals [23].	Investigate new approaches to use low-level and high-level data in CNN to generate proposals.	PASCAL VOC 2012 dataset
3	WSOD Using Complementary Learning and Instance Clustering	The proposed method's core module is the fused complementary network, which is followed by the inter-class clustering module. The main aim is to extract features; any pre-trained convolutional neural network (CNN) can be used as a backbone network. The classification branch computes class probabilities for each area proposal using the features given to FuCN. [24].	—	PASCAL VOC 2007, PASCAL VOC 2012 datasets
4	Coupled Multiple Instance Detection Network (C-MIDN) with Segmentation Guidance for WSOD	C-MIDN has two MIDNs with similar structure. The proposal with the highest score and nearby proposals will be excluded from the second MIDN's input. Due to this second detector, catching up the same object as the first detector can be prevented. So, there will be a possibility to detect an entire object [25].	MIDN essentially searches for a discriminative component of an object rather than the whole object.	PASCAL VOC 2007, PASCAL VOC 2012 datasets

(Continued)

TABLE 4.1

(Continued)

Serial Number	Title	Description	Limitation	Dataset
5	Weakly supervised easy-to-hard learning for object detection in image sequences	They have used Faster R-CNN as an object detector. First, the detector is trained on simple samples; later it is trained on complex samples. This detector easily distinguishes the objects and background regions for simple samples, while it hardly distinguishes the objects and background regions for complex samples [26].	There is room for improvement in heavy inter-occlusions	PETS09
6	A weakly supervised framework for abnormal behavior detection and localization in crowded scenes	Faster R-CNN has been used for detecting pedestrians, vehicles, etc. For behaviour description, the histogram of the Large-Scale Optical Flow descriptor is extracted. The Multiple Instance Support Vector Machine (SVM) is used to determine whether an object's behaviour is normal [27].	It is still a hybrid learning system, and end-to-end learning cannot detect anomalous behavior.	UCSD dataset
7	Dissimilarity Coefficient-Based WSOD	They have used the Fast R-CNN model. The proposed framework represents the uncertainty in the localization of objects by using a probabilistic objective based on the dissimilarity coefficient [28].	Investigate the use of active Learning.	PASCAL VOC 2012
8	A progressive learning framework based on single-instance annotation for WSOD	In this they have used single-instance annotations in weakly supervised object detection (WSOD). In addition, They have integrated image level, single-instance and multiple instance learning into end-to-end network [29].	Partially locates objects.	PASCAL VOC 2007
9	Weakly Supervised Object Localization with Multifold Multiple Instance Learning	It consists of two detectors. For training the first detector, a multifold procedure is used similar to cross-validation. For relocating images from positive images, the approach separates the positive training images into K disjoint folds. The second detector performs mining on negative training [30].	Computational cost increases due to multifold.	PASCAL VOC 2007

Serial Number	Title	Description	Limitation	Dataset
10	WSOD via Object-Specific Pixel Gradient (OPG)	To infer the correct object localization, it uses OPG map rather than score map. Resolution of OPG map is same as resolution of input image. Instead of using traditional classifiers like SVM, selective search, they have used two classifiers which perform classification and localization [31].	More iterations are required for fine-tuning of both the classifiers	PASCAL VOC 2007
11	Weakly supervised detection with decoupled attention-based deep representation	It uses a set of convolutional layers to extract the features from input images and then it is given to the object representation block. This block finds attention maps with the help of full convolution layers. The object localization task is done by the attention pooling layer [32].	High computation time due to selective search.	PASCAL VOC 2007
12	Continuation Multiple Instance Learning (C-MIL) for WSOD	By smoothing the loss function, this approach solves a difficult optimization problem. It treats image areas generated by an object proposal technique as instances and considers images as bags [33].	—	PASCAL VOC 2012

TABLE 4.2

Most Commonly Used Datasets for Object Detection

Serial Number	Name of the Dataset	Number of Classes/ Categories	Number of Total Images	Training Images	Testing Images
1	CIFAR10	10	60,000	50,000	10,000
2	CIFAR100	100	60,000	500 Images/class	100 Images/class
3	OpenImage	600	9 Million	9,011,219	125,436
4	ImageNet	1,000	14,197,122	1,281,167	100,000
5	MS-COCO 2017	80	328,000	118,000	41,000
6	PASCAL- VOC2012	20	11,540	5,717	5,823

the real-world images are collected with the help of programmed cameras in the environment.

Data augmentation is also a powerful technique to increase the size of training images in the case of a small size dataset. In some applications, real data may not available, so a generative adversarial network (GAN) is used for synthetic data generation.

4.3 Methodology for Weakly Supervised Object Detection

This section provides the steps to perform the WSOD to solve the real-world problem of solid waste material detection.

4.3.1 Need of Object Detection Task to Solve Real-World Problem

Globally, 2.01 billion tonnes of solid waste are produced annually, and by 2050, it will grow to 3.40 billion tonnes. In India, everyday, 1 lakh metric tonnes waste is generated which needs to be managed in a streamlined and effective manner. Garbage segregation is usually done by the rag pickers which affects their health if it is not done correctly. Solid waste management is very important for the protection of common public health and quality of the environment. So, a technological approach would be a better solution for solid waste treatment by automatically identifying the solid waste materials which are used for the recycling process [34].

4.3.2 Methodology for Detecting Recyclable Items Using Weakly Supervised Object Detection Approach on Solid Waste Material Dataset

The proposed concept focuses primarily on the detection of solid waste materials that are used for recycling. These materials are glass, metal, plastic, cardboard, trash and paper. This proposed system can detect garbage without the need for human involvement based on the waste item's material, regardless of its shape, colour or size. WSOD, which employs a deep learning approach, will be used to detect garbage automatically. It provides a cost-effective solution because image-level annotations will be used during model training.

Solid waste material detection using the WSOD approach mainly covers six significant stages as shown in Figure 4.2. The first step is collection of the data (images), the second step is data pre-processing, the third step consists of a solid waste material detection model which comprises a feature extractor using transfer learning and an object localization model, the fourth step consists of training the model, the fifth step is related testing of the model and the last stage consists of results validation.

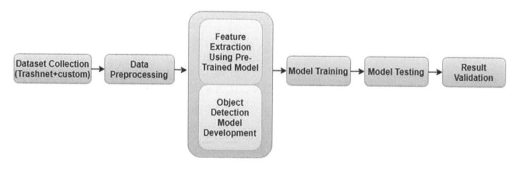

FIGURE 4.2
Flow diagram of solid waste material detection using WSOD approach.

4.3.2.1 Data Collection

The TrashNet dataset [35] along with a custom dataset are used for this work. This dataset contains paper, glass, plastic, metal, trash and cardboard subclasses. The custom dataset is made mainly for small-scaled objects so that the proposed approach becomes a robust detector of all kinds of objects irrespective of size. Figure 4.3 shows some of the dataset's sample images.

4.3.2.2 Data Pre-processing

It is necessary to have a correct input data format to build an effective neural network model. Image pre-processing may increase the model inference speed and decrease the model training time by applying pre-processing steps like image resizing, scaling, data

FIGURE 4.3
Custom dataset sample images.

augmentation [36], etc. The pre-trained modes will be used for feature extraction; such a model needs input images in a particular size, e.g. InVGG requires a fixed 224*224 RGB image. The image resizing output is as shown in Figure 4.4.

To reduce the overfitting problem, data augmentation techniques are used. It artificially increases the size of the training dataset by data warping or oversampling. It transforms existing images such that their label is preserved as shown in Figure 4.5. It consists of geometric and color transformations, neural style transfer and adversarial training.

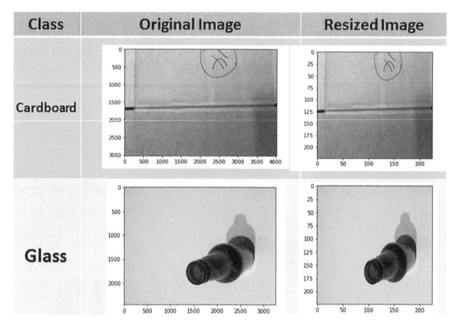

FIGURE 4.4
Image resizing output.

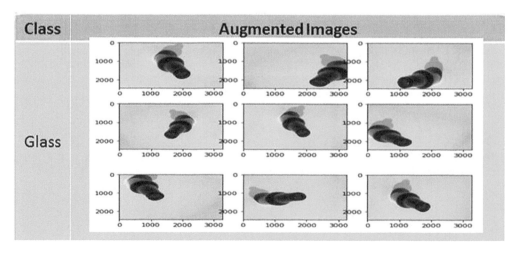

FIGURE 4.5
Data augmentation output.

4.3.2.3 Feature Extraction Using Pre-trained Model

Transfer learning is a machine learning technique in which a model is trained and built for one task and then used for a related activity. When a new dataset is smaller than the original dataset, transfer learning is generally used to train the pre-trained model. There are many pre-trained models like VGG16, VGG19, ResNet50, DenseNet, AlexNet, etc. are used as starting points for any computer vision task like feature extraction.

1. VGG16 (Visual Geometry Group) pre-trained model

As per extensive literature review and obtained results, this pre-trained model is one of the best. The architecture of VGG16 [37] is as shown in Figure 4.6.

It consists of a total of 16 layers and requires input image size 224*224*3. The first two convolutional layers use 64 filters of size 3*3 with stride of 1, which results in a volume of 224*224*64, a pooling layer with 2*2 size and stride equal to 2, which results in a volume of 112*112*64 and such a stack of convolution layers with different filter sizes, like 128, 266 applied along with a pooling layer of stride equal to 2. The last layer is a fully connected layer having softmax activation function.

2. VGG19 (Visual Geometry Group) pre-trained model

The architecture of VGG-19 consists of a total of 19 layers as shown in Figure 4.7.

It also requires input image size 224*224*3. It consists of a stack of convolution layers of a varying number of filters like 64, 128, 256 and 512 of size 3*3. It consists of a pooling layer with stride equal to 2 of size 2*2. It has three fully connected (dense) layers to predict the specified classes [38].

4.3.2.4 Object Localization and Detection Module

For object localization and detection, a Faster R-CNN architecture is composed of a pre-trained network for extracting features which acts as a predecessor. After that, it has two sub-networks: region proposal network (RPN) which is used for generating the proposals

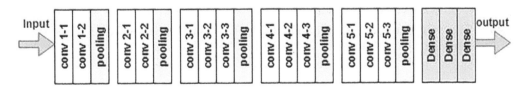

FIGURE 4.6
Layered architecture of VGG16.

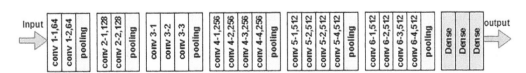

FIGURE 4.7
Layered architecture of VGG-19.

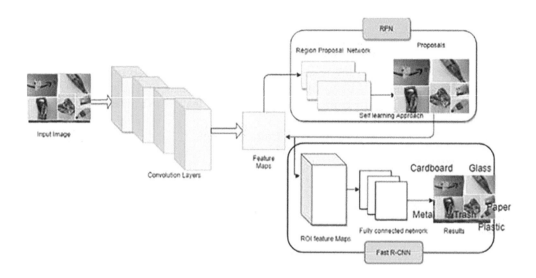

FIGURE 4.8
Proposed weakly supervised object detection architecture diagram.

instead of using selective search and Fast R-CNN to predict the class of the object. The ROI polling layer takes region proposals from the first sub-network and after that the class of the object along with bounding boxes around the detected object task done by the fully connected layers. Both sub-networks are trainable. The proposed WSOD diagram architecture [39] is as shown in Figure 4.8.

The following points are summarised steps to perform the object detection task:

- Use a pre-trained VGG16 CNN that has been trained (i.e., ImageNet)
- Extract feature maps from the last convolution layer
- Train an RPN using a self-learning technique to determine whether there is an object in the image and to indicate a box placement
- Give proposals to ROI pooling layer
- Send to a fully connected layer after all proposals have been resized to a fixed size to continue the categorization and bounding box regression

4.3.2.5 Object Detection Model Training

The waste material dataset for training should be divided into three parts: training, validation and testing:

Training: Training uses up to 75% of the total dataset. The training set is used to provide the weights and biases.

Validation: About 15% to 20% of the data are utilised to evaluate initial accuracy, assess how the model learns and fine-tune hyper-parameters while the model is being trained. Validation data are seen by the model but not used to learn weights and biases.

Test: The final evaluation uses between 5% and 10% of the data. The model is bias-free because it has never seen this dataset before.

The network's accuracy is entirely dependent on the Faster R-CNN's RPN. We present a computationally powerful self-paced learning technique for training an RPN for WSOD. It will contribute to improving the model's performance. A self-paced learning algorithm uses the concepts of curriculum learning. It takes input samples in meaningful manner means in each iteration it chooses easy samples first and accordingly updates the parameters and then takes hard samples for training the model.

4.3.2.6 Hyper-Parameter Tuning

Hyper-parameters are the parameters which define the deep learning models' architecture. These hyper-parameters are not changed with model training and not learnt from the model training. Every deep learning model has its own hyper-parameters. Deep CNNs consist of convolution layers, pooling layers and fully connected layers:

- Convolution layer hyper-parameters are kernel size, number of kernels, stride, padding and activation function.
- Pooling layer hyper-parameters are filter size, stride and padding.
- Fully connected hyper-parameters are number of weights and activation function.
- Other hyper-parameters include optimizer, model architecture, loss function, learning rate and number of epochs.

The tuning of hyper-parameter helps to find the optimum solution in order to achieve the balance between overfitting and underfitting. The model performance is based on selection of all these hyper-parameters. Finding the solution that does not overfit is the most important.

Speed of convergence during training should be high and optimal, so tuning of the optimizer hyper-parameter is required. For a good hyper-parameters grid search, random search techniques are used [40].

4.3.2.7 Model Testing

In this stage, the implemented model will be tested on the test dataset. The trained model processes the test dataset. Python script will be written to test the newly trained waste material detection model which will accurately classify the recyclable items.

Training and testing sets are not sufficient to test the performance of a model, so the validation set plays a very important role in evaluation of the model. A cross-validation approach will also be a solution in case of a small dataset.

4.3.2.8 Result Validation

To evaluate the performance of any deep learning model, different evaluation metrics are used like accuracy, loss, confusion matrix and precision recall. According to a survey of the literature, the performance of object detection deep learning models is analyzed using the average precision (AP) and mean AP (mAP) evaluation metrics. The localization accuracy is also measured using the correct localization (CorLoc) parameter.

Image-level mean average precision (mAP)

It is a popular metric used by many researchers to assess object detector accuracy.

Average precision value is calculated by averaging precision value for recall value over 0 to 1.

Correct localization (CorLoc)

The neural networks will give a bounding box for a target object, and CorLoc evaluates only positive images which contain the target class, and counts the percentage of images for IOU > 0.5:

CorLoc = (the boxes that IOU > 0.5)/(all boxes belong to the target class)

4.4 Results and Discussion

The extraction of features from the input image is a primary step of object detection. As there are many pre-trained networks used for this operation like VGG16, VGG19, ResNet50 and AlexNet, but as per an extensive literature survey, the VGG16 pre-trained model is more accurate. In this section, VGG16 and VGG19 performance is analysed for different epoch size, and it is observed that VGG16 is more accurate than VGG19.

VGG16 has 3*3 of fixed size of convolution filters in all layers which shows significant improvement on the previous architectures. It can be achieved by increasing the depth of 16 layers. This fixed size kernel and smaller stride value of the first convolution layer help to increase the accuracy of classification and recognition. Training and testing of VGG16 network densely over the whole image strives to increase the accuracy. Resizing of the input image to 224*224 is essential to reduce the training time of the model, and computational cost as well. The TrashNet dataset along with a custom dataset are used for VGG-16 and VGG19 training.

4.4.1 VGG16 Filters

The VGG16 and VGG19 pre-trained models training was performed with epoch size 20 and batch size 32. Both the models use filters of size 3*3. The first convolution layer of VGG16 has 64 filters of size 3*3. The remaining convolution layers of VGG16 have 128, 256, 512 filters of size 3*3.

4.4.2 Feature Extraction Using VGG16

As VGG16 requires 224*224 input image size, the input images are supplied, and it extracts the features from the input image which is the first essential step in the object detection task. After applying the first layer of convolution, features are extracted as shown in Figure 4.9.

4.4.3 VGG16 and VGG19 Model Training for Epoch20

The number of epochs is an important hyper-parameter during training of a neural network model. It helps to decide whether the model is underfit, optimal or overfit. To check the validation loss, this number of epoch hyper-parameter is used. The result after Epoch10

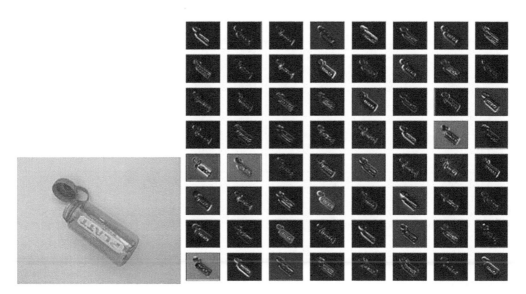

FIGURE 4.9
Feature extraction of input image of plastic by VGG16.

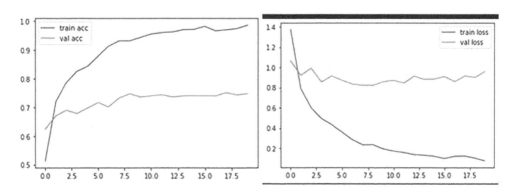

FIGURE 4.10
VGG16 accuracy and loss plot for Epoch20.

and Epoch20 is analyzed; it shows that after Epoch10 the validation loss and training loss start decreasing, and after Epoch20, it starts increasing so training is stopped at Epoch20 to prevent the model from overfit.

The TrashNet dataset of solid waste material along with a custom dataset are used for VGG16 and VGG19 model training. The TrashNet dataset is composed of images of six classes of solid waste materials, i.e. plastic, glass, cardboard, paper, trash and metal. The Custom dataset is made by collecting images of small-sized objects of each category, like images of nails, small plastic material, plastic bottle caps, small glass bottles, etc. so that the model can detect the objects irrespective of their size. In the VGG16 model, training and validation accuracy is 98% and 76%, respectively, for Epoch20 and its corresponding losses are as shown in Figure 4.10. In the VGG19 model, training and validation accuracy is 96% and 70%, respectively, for Epoch20 and its corresponding losses as shown in Figure 4.11.

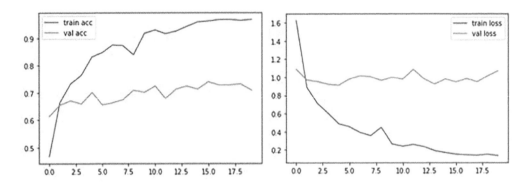

FIGURE 4.11
VGG19 accuracy and loss plot for Epoch20.

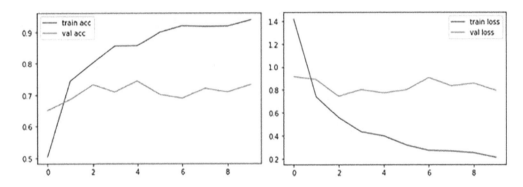

FIGURE 4.12
VGG16 accuracy and loss plot for Epoch10.

In VGG16, validation loss is in decreasing order, and validation accuracy is in increasing order which means the model has been working fine.

But in VGG19, validation loss is in increasing order during the last epoch as shown in Figure 4.11.

4.4.4 VGG16 and VGG19 Model Training for Epoch10

The TrashNet dataset of solid waste material along with a custom dataset are used for VGG16 and VGG19 model training. In the VGG16 model, training and validation accuracy are 93% and 73%, respectively, for Epoch10, as shown in Figure 4.12. In the VGG19 model, training and validation accuracy are 91% and 72%, respectively, for Epoch10 as shown in Figure 4.13.

4.4.5 Comparison of Different Pre-trained Models

Table 4.3 shows the training and validation accuracy of different pre-trained models for Epoch20.

From Table 4.3, it is observed that the VGG16 model is more accurate and can be used as a feature extractor.

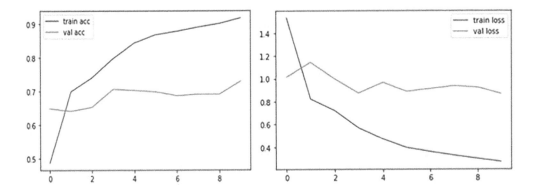

FIGURE 4.13
VGG19 accuracy and loss plot for Epoch10.E

TABLE 4.3

Comparison of Different Pre-trained Models

Pre-trained Model	Training Accuracy (%)	Validation Accuracy (%)
VGG16	98	76
VGG19	96	70
ResNet50	48	39
AlexNet	62	24

The AlexNet model consists of eight layers only; hence, it is not a deep neural network model compared with VGG16, VGG19 and ResNet50. So the feature extraction is difficult from the input images. It also takes more time to achieve good accuracy.

The complex architecture and variable filter size in each convolution layer affect the accuracy of the ResNet50 model on a given solid waste material dataset. As per phenomenon, the depth of the network increases, and the training error also increases. VGG16 has obtained good experimental results on a given dataset.

4.5 Conclusion and Future Directions

Computer vision–based object detection using deep learning provides a cost-effective solution for solid waste material detection. A novel weakly supervised approach uses only image-level annotations so that the tedious task of manually annotating bounding boxes is eliminated. A VGG16 pre-trained model has been used as a feature extractor because its training and validation accuracy are 98% and 76%, respectively. It is a more accurate model than other pre-trained models like VGG19, AlexNet and ResNet50. These extracted features are given to the detection model. A self-paced learning algorithm will be used for training the proposed object detection model. It helps to automate the process of solid waste material detection and give a better solution to solve the environmental pollution problem effectively.

Such object detectors can be used to solve many problems in various domains like medical image analysis, video surveillance, retail management and crowd detection to avoid panic situations. The object detection model should be robust in spite of occlusions, cluttered background and different sizes of objects.

References

[1] Ajeet Ram Pathak, Manjusha Pandey, and Siddharth Rautaray, "Application of Deep Learning for Object Detection," *Procedia Computer Science*, vol. 132, 2018, p. 17061717. https://doi.org/10.1016/j.procs.2018.05.144.

[2] M. Anjum and M. S. Umar, "Garbage Localization Based on Weakly Supervised Learning in Deep Convolutional Neural Network," in *2018 International Conference on Advances in Computing, Communication Control and Networking (ICACCCN)*, 2018, pp. 1108–1113. https://ieeexplore.ieee.org/stamp/stamp.jsp?tp=&arnumber=8748568, https://doi.org/10.1109/ICACCCN.2018.8748568.

[3] Asharul Khan, "Machine Learning in Computer Vision," *Procedia Computer Science*, vol. 167, 2020. https://doi.org/10.1016/j.procs.2020.03.355.

[4] Ross B. Girshick, Jeff Donahue, Trevor Darrell, and Jitendra Malik, "Rich Feature Hierarchies for Accurate Object Detection and Semantic Segmentation," *CoRR, abs/1311.2524*, 2013. http://arxiv.org/abs/1311.2524.

[5] K. He, Xiangyu Zhang, Shaoqing Ren, and Jian Sun, "Spatial Pyramid Pooling in Deep Convolutional Networks for Visual Recognition," *IEEE Transactions on Pattern Analysis and Machine Intelligence*, vol. 37, 2015, 1904–1916.

[6] R. Girshick, "Fast R-CNN," in *Proceedings of the International Conference on Computer Vision*, Santiago, Chile, 13–16 December 2015, pp. 1440–1448.

[7] S. Ren, K. He, R. Girshick, and J. Sun, "Faster R-CNN: Towards Real-time Object Detection with Region Proposal Networks," in *Advances in Neural Information Processing Systems*, Curran Associates, Inc., San Diego, CA, 2015, pp. 91–99.

[8] K. He, G. Gkioxari, P. Dollár, and R. Girshick, "Mask R-CNN," in *Proceedings of the IEEE International Conference on Computer Vision*, Venice, Italy, 22–29 October 2017, pp. 2961–2969.

[9] T.Y. Lin, P. Dollár, R. Girshick, K. He, B. Hariharan, and S. Belongie, "Feature Pyramid Networks for Object Detection," in *Proceedings of the Conference on Computer Vision and Pattern Recognition*, Honolulu, HI, 21–26 July 2017, pp. 2117–2125.

[10] Joseph Redmon, "You Only Look Once: Unified, Real-Time Object Detection," *arXiv:1506.02640v5* [cs.CV], 9 May 2016.

[11] Wei Liu, "SSD: Single Shot MultiBox Detector," *arXiv:1512.02325v5* [cs.CV], 29 December 2016.

[12] Tsung-Yi Lin, "Focal Loss for Dense Object Detection," *arXiv:1708.02002v2* [cs.CV], 7 February 2018.

[13] Bichen Wu, and SqueezeDet, "Unified, Small, Low Power Fully Convolutional Neural Networks for Real-Time Object Detection for Autonomous Driving," *arXiv:1612.01051v4* [cs.CV], 11 June 2019.

[14] Hei Law, "CornerNet: Detecting Objects as Paired Keypoints," *arXiv:1808.01244v2* [cs.CV], 18 March 2019.

[15] Daniel Glasner, "Viewpoint-Aware Object Detection and Continuous Pose Estimation," Image and Vision Computing," *Image and Vision Computing*, vol. 30, no. 12, 2012, pp. 923–933. http://doi.org/10.1016/j.imavis.2012.09.006.

[16] Pedro F. Felzenszwalb, "Object Detection with Discriminatively Trained Part Based Models," *IEEE Transactions on Pattern Analysis and Machine Intelligence*, vol. 32, no. 9, September 2010.

[17] Angtian Wang, "Compositional Convolutional Neural Networks: A Robust and Interpretable Model for Object Recognition Under Occlusion," *International Journal of Computer Vision*, no. 3, 2021.

[18] Yousef Atoum, *Detecting Objects Under Challenging Illumination Conditions*, ProQuest Dissertations Publishing, 2018, p. 10746014.

[19] Vinorth Varatharasan, "Improving Learning Effectiveness for Object Detection and Classification in Cluttered Backgrounds," *arXiv:2002.12467v1* [cs.CV], 27 February 2020.

[20] Rafał Pilarczyk, "On Intra-Class Variance for Deep Learning of Classifiers," *Arxiv:1901.11186v2* [Cs.CV], 22 April 2019.

[21] Chinthakindi Balaram Murthy, "Investigations of Object Detection in Images/Videos Using Various Deep Learning Techniques and Embedded Platforms—A Comprehensive Review," *Applied Sciences*, vol. 10, 2020, p. 3280. http://doi.org/10.3390/app10093280.

[22] Lingyun Song, "Weakly Supervised Group Mask Network (WSGMN) for Object Detection," *International Journal of Computer Vision*, 30 October 2020.

[23] Peng Tang, *Weakly Supervised Region Proposal Network and Object Detection*, Springer Nature Switzerland AG, 2018.

[24] Mehwish Awan, "Weakly Supervised Object Detection Using Complementary Learning and Instance Clustering," *IEEE Access*, vol. 8, 2020.

[25] Yan Gao, Boxiao Liu, Nan Guo, Xiaochun Ye, Fang Wan, Haihang You, and Dongrui Fan, "C-MIDN: Coupled Multiple Instance Detection Network with Segmentation Guidance for Weakly Supervised Object Detection," *IEEE/CVF International Conference on Computer Vision (ICCV)*, 2019.

[26] Hongkai Yu, "Weakly Supervised Easy-to-Hard Learning for Object Detection in Image Sequences," *Neurocomputing*, vol. 398, 2020, pp. 71–82. https://doi.org/10.1016/j.neucom.2020.02.075.

[27] Xing Hu, "A Weakly Supervised Framework for Abnormal Behavior Detection and Localization in Crowded Scenes," *Neurocomputing*, vol. 383, 2020, pp. 270–281. https://doi.org/10.1016/j.neucom.2019.11.087.

[28] Aditya Arun, C. V. Jawahar, and M. Kumar, *Dissimilarity Coefficient Based Weakly Supervised Object Detection*, 2019, pp. 9424–9433. https://arxiv.org/abs/1811.10016, https://doi.org/10.1109/CVPR.2019.00966.

[29] Ming Zhang, and Bing Zeng, "A Progressive Learning Framework Based on Single-Instance Annotation for Weakly Supervised Object Detection," *Computer Vision and Image Understanding*, vol. 193, 2020, p. 102903. https://doi.org/10.1016/j.cviu.2020.102903.

[30] R. G. Cinbis, J. Verbeek, and C. Schmid, "Weakly Supervised Object Localization with Multi-Fold Multiple Instance Learning," *IEEE Transactions on Pattern Analysis and Machine Intelligence*, vol. 39, no. 1, 1 January 2017, pp. 189–203. https://doi.org/10.1109/TPAMI.2016.2535231.

[31] Y. Shen, R. Ji, C. Wang, X. Li, and X. Li, "Weakly Supervised Object Detection via Object-Specific Pixel Gradient," *IEEE Transactions on Neural Networks and Learning Systems*, vol. 29, no. 12, December 2018, pp. 5960–5970. https://doi.org/10.1109/TNNLS.2018.2816021.

[32] W. Jiang, Z. Zhao, and F. Su, "Weakly Supervised Detection with Decoupled Attention-Based Deep Representation," *Multimedia Tools and Applications*, vol. 77, 2018, pp. 3261–3277. https://doi.org/10.1007/s11042-017-5087-x.

[33] Fang Wan, Chang Liu, Wei Ke, Xiangyang Ji, Jianbin Jiao, and Qixiang Ye, *C-MIL: Continuation Multiple Instance Learning for Weakly Supervised Object Detection*, 2019, pp. 2194–2203. https://arxiv.org/abs/1904.05647, https://doi.org/10.1109/CVPR.2019.00230.

[34] Daniel Octavian Melinte, Ana-Maria Travediu, and Dan N. Dumitriu, "Deep Convolutional Neural Networks Object Detector for Real-Time Waste Identification, MDPI," *Applied Sciences*, vol. 10, 2020, p. 7301.

[35] G. Thung, *TrashNet. GitHub Repository*. Available online: https://github.com/garythung/trashnet.

[36] Barret Zoph, "Learning Data Augmentation Strategies for Object Detection," *arXiv:1906.11172v1* [cs.CV], 26 June 2019.

[37] Karen Simonyan, and Andrew Zisserman, "Very Deep Convolutional Networks for Large-Scale Image Recognition," 2015. http://arxiv.org/abs/1409.1556.

[38] Jian Xiao, "Journal of Physics: Conference Series, Volume 1518," *2020 4th International Conference on Machine Vision and Information Technology (CMVIT 2020)*, 20–22 February 2020, Sanya, China.

[39] Jyoti Wadmare, and Sunita Patil, "Improvising Weakly Supervised Object Detection (WSOD) Using Deep Learning Technique," *International Journal of Engineering and Advanced Technology (IJEAT)*, vol. 9, no. 3, February 2020.

[40] Mohd Aszemi, "Hyperparameter Optimization in Convolutional Neural Network Using Genetic Algorithms," *International Journal of Advanced Computer Science and Applications*, vol. 10, 2019, pp. 269–278. http://doi.org/10.14569/IJACSA.2019.0100638.

Appendix

Code snippet to get filters of first convolution layer of VGG16

```
Figure=plt.figure(figsize=(8, 12))
columns = 8
rows = 8
Total _ filters = columns * rows
for i in range(1, Total _ filters +1):
    T = filters[:, :, :, i-1]
    Figure =plt.subplot(rows, columns, i)
    Figure.set _ xticks([])
    Figure.set _ yticks([])
    plt.imshow(T[:, :, 0], cmap='gray')
plt.show()
```

Code snippet of extracting features of input image by VGG16

```
from keras.preprocessing.image import load _ img, img _ to _ array
image = load _ img('/content/drive/MyDrive/PhD Implementation/waste image
dataset/Copy of dataset-original.zip (Unzipped Files)/dataset-original/
glass/glass502.jpg', target _ size=(224, 224))
image = img _ to _ array(image)
image = np.expand _ dims(image, axis=0)
feature _ Extraction = model _ short.predict(image)
columns = 8
rows = 8
for ftr in feature _ Extraction:
    figure =plt.figure(figsize=(12, 12))
    for i in range(1, columns*rows +1):
        figure =plt.subplot(rows, columns, i)
        figure .set _ xticks([])
        figure .set _ yticks([])
        plt.imshow(ftr[0, :, :, i-1], cmap='gray')
    plt.show()
```

Code snippet to analyze the performance of the model

```
from tensorflow.keras.preprocessing.image import ImageDataGenerator

train _ data = ImageDataGenerator(rescale = 1./255,
            shear _ range = 0.2,
            zoom _ range = 0.2,
            horizontal _ flip = True)

test _ data = ImageDataGenerator(rescale = 1./255)
train _ set = train _ data.flow _ from _ directory('/content/drive/MyDrive/PhD
Implementation/waste image dataset/custom splitted dataset/train',
```

```
                                        target _ size = (224,  224),
                                        batch _ size = 32,
                                        class _ mode = 'categorical')
test _ set= test _ data.flow _ from _ directory('/content/drive/MyDrive/PhD
Implementation/waste image dataset/custom splitted dataset/test',
                                        target _ size = (224,  224),
                                        batch _ size = 32,
                                        class _ mode = 'categorical')
new = model.fit _ generator(
       train _ set,
       validation _ data=test _ set,
       epochs=20,
       steps _ per _ epoch=len(train _ set),
       validation _ steps=len(test _ set)
)
```

5

Image Inpainting Using Deep Learning

Yogesh H. Dandawate, Tushar R. Jadhav and Paritosh J. Marathe

CONTENTS

5.1 Introduction

Since time immemorial, humans have created art as a mark of their culture which survives through time as a symbol of that period.

Images have been an integral part of human culture, providing a visual representation of data, events, person or stature, right along to the thoughts of the creator itself. It provides an indispensable medium of communication not only in terms of data conveyance but also in terms of impression.

Beginning with cave paintings showing traces of battles fought long ago, right along the works of masters like Michelangelo, Leonardo Da Vinci, Botticelli and many others who froze on a canvas the depictions of events and notable persons of that period, right along to the visual imagery that presented itself to the author of that art. Thus, these images provide us a window to that past as an illustration of that era.

However, even these cannot escape the ravages of time and hence require maintenance and repair to maintain the depictions as the creator intended them. This requires skilled people to fill in the missing parts of the canvas in a way which looks similar to the original part itself such that a common observer should not be able to distinguish the additions from the original.

DOI: 10.1201/9781003218111-5

FIGURE 5.1
Piero Della Francesca—scene after and before inpainting.

This process is referred to as image inpainting (Figure 5.1).

The field of inpainting has been active over many years with the first scientific approach established (by Pierto Edwards) way back in 1744 for the restoration of old art pieces.

This was initially achieved via physical means. It involved the compensation of paint losses by the ravages of time to remake the missing parts of the image in an attempt to improve its overall perception.

The advent of computers has allowed image inpainting to take a more computational approach for the reconstruction of damaged digital images and videos.

Images could now be digitised which resulted in the expansion of inpainting to include the restoration of digital images having scratches, lines or textual overlays; image degradation due to loss of packets during transmission; and the removal of an object in the context of image editing.

This chapter aims to introduce the concept of image inpainting and its technique both in the traditional context and using deep learning. The traditional methods encompass diffusion and exemplar-based methods (both pixel and patch based). For deep learning, we aim to introduce the use of convolutional neural networks (CNNs) and generative adversarial networks (GANs) to the problem domain.

5.2 Traditional Methods

Traditional inpainting involves the use of both human artists using software such as Adobe Photoshop as well as automatic image-inpainting methods. This chapter discusses the use of automatic image-inpainting methods.

Traditional methods make use of two primary methods for digital inpainting, namely, diffusion-based and exemplar-based approaches.

5.2.1 Diffusion-Based Methods

The term *diffusion* refers to the movement of anything from higher concentration to lower concentration based on the gradient of that concentration (physical analogy could be heat propagation).

Hence, diffusion-based methods work by filling the missing part of the image by evenly spreading image content (diffusing it) from the boundary towards the center of the missing patch.

They try to find a good continuation of the surrounding lines. Hence, they are also referred to as geometry-driven algorithms.

The concept of automatic digital inpainting was introduced in Bertalmio et al. [1]. It makes use of partial differential equations (PDEs) for isophote propagation. Isophotes are lines connecting pixels or points where the intensity of light is the same (Figure 5.2).

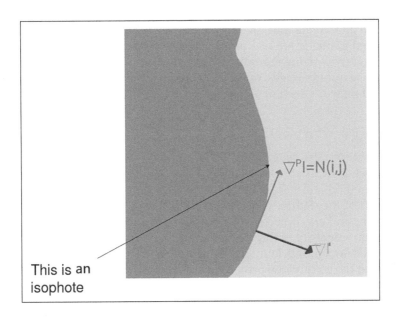

FIGURE 5.2
Isophote.

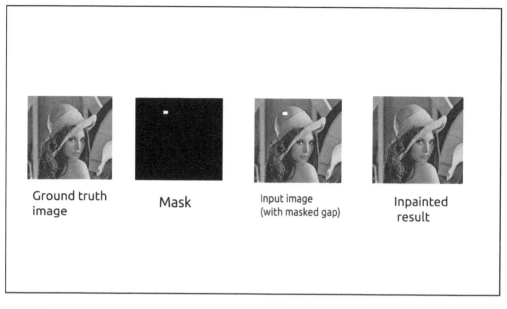

FIGURE 5.3
Diffusion-based inpainting.

The principle is that there is an innate tendency of a line to be seen as continuing its established direction.

Using this, the goal is then to continue the isophotes into the gap to fill the colour and texture (here texture refers to a visual pattern that can be seen on an image) preserving the 'angle of arrival'.

Therefore, the pixel information (pixel values) for the isophotes approaching the boundary is allowed to fill into the hole, thereby effectively filling it.

Diffusion-based methods are useful for smooth images or for images containing well-defined structures (well-defined gradients) and filling up small patches. However, they are not adaptable to textured images, especially those having larger patches to fill. The result is then a blurred image as seen in Figure 5.3.

5.2.2 Exemplar-Based Methods

The exemplar method (also referred to as patch-based method) is another type of inpainting method which is focused towards a more texture-preserving approach.

Patch-based methods work by filling the missing regions with patches that may match (candidate patches) the damaged areas. The patches are selected from the undamaged parts of the image and are copied to their corresponding areas. The patches are chosen on the basis of visual similarity of the source sample.

Exemplar-based inpainting is inspired mostly by local region-based methods which work on growing the texture one pixel or one set of pixels (patch) at a time (Figure 5.4).

Many of the pixel-based techniques work using Markov random fields for learning to calculate the missing pixel for the area to be filled.

Using that, a candidate patch is chosen (sampled) from a set of candidate patches taken from the source region Φ to fill the target region Ω. The sum of squared differences (SSD)

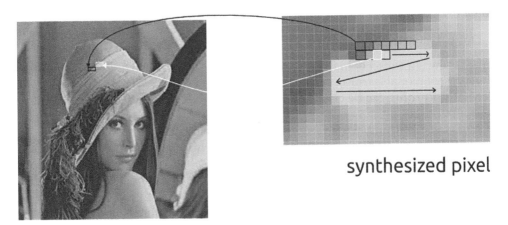

synthesized pixel

FIGURE 5.4
Pixel-based exemplar method.

FIGURE 5.5
Exemplar inpainting. (One of the popular applications of inpainting is object removal.)

is used to calculate scores for identifying the best matching patch to be filled into the gap. (The goal is for the chosen patch texture to be similar to the target region texture.)

The chosen patch is then copied into the designated place ψ_p achieving a partial filling of the target region. This process is carried on iteratively until the target region has been completely filled (Figure 5.5).

However, the random patch selection method of exemplar inpainting may lead to a skewed alignment with the texture. This may lead to a disruption in the texture, or the expected smoothness may not be achieved.

5.3 Deep Learning

Deep learning is a subset of machine learning methods based on artificial neural networks with representational learning.

Generally, learning can be classified into three categories: supervised, semi-supervised and unsupervised.

In supervised learning, we present the model with a dataset D such that $D = \{x, y\}_n$, for n number of input features x and their label pairs y. This y can take other forms, based on the task to be learnt. For example, in a classification setting y is generally a scalar representation of the class labels, whereas for regression tasks it can be a vector of continuous variables.

When one tries to design a model for the purpose of segmentation, y can even be a multidimensional label for an image input x.

It finally boils down to finding model parameters that best predict the data based on the loss defined by the loss function $L(Y, \hat{Y})$. In this context, $\hat{y}$ symbolizes the output of the model obtained by entering a data row x_i for $i : \{0, n-1\}$ (n = number of inputs) to the function $f(x)$ representing the model.

Unsupervised learning algorithms use data without any labels, trying to discover some patterns, such as latent subspaces. Some examples of unsupervised learning algorithms are principal component analysis (PCA) and clustering methods like K-means.

Deep learning provides a unique angle to the problem of inpainting. It provides an essential representation of the sample domain in a compressed format. Since deep learning comes under representational learning, it allows the machine to learn from multiple instances to achieve a particular task more efficiently as demonstrated by Köhler et al. [3] by their use of multilayer perceptron (MLP).

This allows for a better inpainting result based on the input of multiple data samples as compared to the more traditional methods.

Architectures such as GAN also provide an approach for generative inpainting where the missing patches are generated instead of being selected and patched from the image itself.

5.4 Convolutional Neural Networks

Convolutional neural networks (also referred to as CNNs or ConvNets) is a kind of deep neural net commonly applied towards visual imagorial data. They are also known as shift invariant or space invariant artificial neural networks (SIANN), based on their shared-weights architecture and translation invariance (i.e. the filter slides over the data without rotation). They are called convolutional as they perform the mathematical operation of convolution on the images. Convolution is a specialized kind of linear operation. This way the model is not required to learn separate detectors for the same object occurring at different locations in an image, making it equally symmetrical with respect to translations of the input. It also greatly reduces the number of parameters (i.e. since there is an aggregation of features, there is no need for representation of every pixel in input sample space) that need to be learned.

For one-dimensional convolution, the input image undergoes a convolution operation with a set of kernels K generating weights $W = \{W_1, W_2, \ldots, W_K\}$ and biases $B = \{b_1, \ldots, b_K\}$, for a feature map for input X_k. These features are provided to an activation function with the same being repeated for every convolutional layer l:

$$X_k^l = \sigma\left(W_k^{l-1} * X^{l-1} + b_k^{l-1}\right)$$

The latter part of the convolution operation involves the use of pooling layers in CNNs where the values of neighborhood pixels are aggregated using the max or mean operation. Usually, a convolutional network ends with fully connected (FC) layers (Figure 5.6).

A distribution over the output classes is then obtained by feeding the output from the final layer through a softmax activation function. The network is trained using the maximum likelihood approach (Figure 5.6).

The convolution operation acts over the entire input image, effectively splitting the image into smaller patches. These patches can effectively be considered as a sub-image over some part of the main image.

For example, we can consider Cai et al. [4] blind inpainting convolutional neural network (BICNN) (Figures 5.7 and 5.8).

It can utilize a fully convolutional network (there is no fully connected layer) consisting of three cascading layers: patch extraction and representation, nonlinear mapping and output of a reconstructed image for the task of inpainting.

The first part involves the extraction of the subpatches from the corrupted image and is represented as a multidimensional array.

The second part maps a high-dimensional vector to another high-dimensional vector. It is the conceptual mapping of the corrupted subpatches to the completed counterpart.

The latter part aggregates the corrected subpatches into a final completed image. The end goal is to learn an end-to-end mapping between the input-corrupted patches and the ground truth patches.

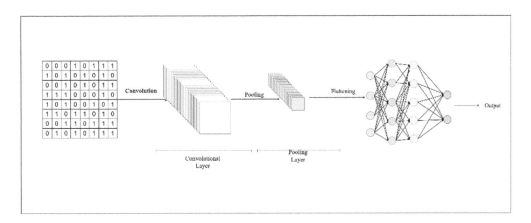

FIGURE 5.6
A typical convolutional neural network.

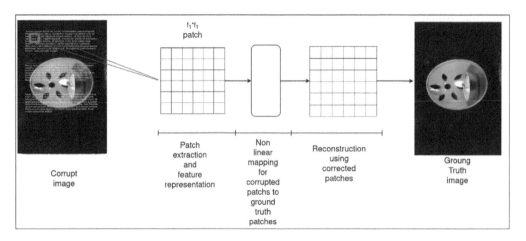

FIGURE 5.7
Convolutional neural network based approach (based on) [2]

FIGURE 5.8
Convolutional neural network based inpainting method output.

Given **X** as a corrupted image and Y as a clean image that is as close as possible to the ground truth image, we may define the network as

$$h^l = \sigma \left(W^l * h^{l-1} + b^l \right)$$

$$Y = W^l * h^{l-1} + b^l$$

where l is the number of layers, W is the weight and * is the convolution operation with σ serving as the nonlinear mapping (RELU).

Furthermore, CNN may be used in an encoder–decoder network (in some cases as a convolutional denoising autoencoder [DAE]).

Input   Output

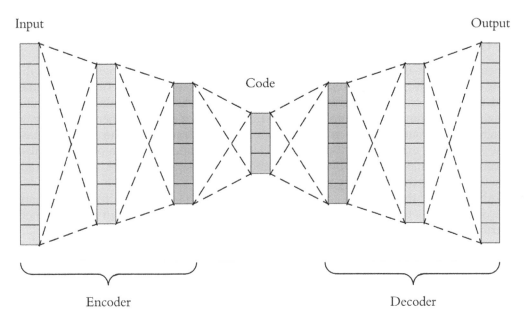

Code

Encoder   Decoder

FIGURE 5.9
General autoencoder architecture.

The encoder extracts the feature representation of an input image with the decoder then reconstructs the final image from the compressed feature map (Figure 5.9).

CNNs hold a distinctive advantage over the traditional methods with their ability to capture the contents of the entire image. This led to many works utilizing CNN for the task of inpainting.

For example, Yan et al. [5] introduced a special shift-connection layer referred to as 'Shift Net' into a U-net architecture. It shifts the known encoded features as an approximation of the missing parts with the decoder 'guiding' the shift from the known region during reconstruction.

Weerasekera et al. [6] utilizes CNN for real-time inpainting on sparse depth maps from a monocular simultaneous localization and mapping (SLAM), providing dense depth maps for certain visual guided task (e.g., autonomous cars).

Hardeberg et al. [7] proposed a fully convolutional encoder–decoder model for the combined purpose of denoising, inpainting and super-resolution of hyper-spectral images. They designed an approach to an algorithm that attempts to optimize the networks weights on corrupted images only. This approach was chosen for the inherent lack of datasets for that approach.

Zeng et al. [8] built a pyramidal-context encoder architecture with a multi-scale decoder network called PEN-NET for high-resolution image inpainting. An attention network was added to learn the relationship between the damaged area and visible part and then convert that visible area characteristics into a feature map to fill the missing parts.

Liu et al. [9] proposed a coherent semantic attention layer to the encoder under a U-Net architecture. This was done in an attempt to preserve the context of the structure in question and to provide better prediction for the missing parts.

5.5 Generative Adversarial Network

Generative adversarial networks (GANs) are an approach towards generative modelling using deep learning (Figure 5.10). Deep generative models used deep networks with many hidden layers to create an approximation of a high-dimensional probability distribution utilizing a large number of samples. Successfully trained models can then be used to create new approximations that could have been plausibly drawn from the original dataset. However, due to many difficult problems related to the approximation of a probabilistic outcome in the maximum likelihood estimation or its related strategies, deep generative networks did not create a heavy impact.

GAN proposed the use of an adversarial network which is pitted against the generative network. It learns to discriminate a sample as to whether it was drawn from the model distribution or the data distribution.

$$\min_G \max_D V(D, G) = E_{x \sim pdata(x)}[\log D(x)] + E_{z \sim pz(z)}[\log(1-D(G(z)))].$$

In other words, the discriminator and the generator play the this two-player min/max game with value function $V(G, D)$. An analogy may be made with the generative model being a counterfeit maker and discriminator being the police. The counterfeit maker must make good counterfeits, and the police must identify those to stop them. Thus, the generative network must keep generating images to the point where the discriminator cannot identify the original from the generated image.

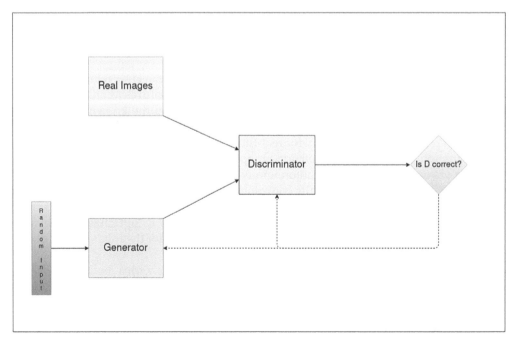

FIGURE 5.10
Typical model architecture of a generative adversarial network.

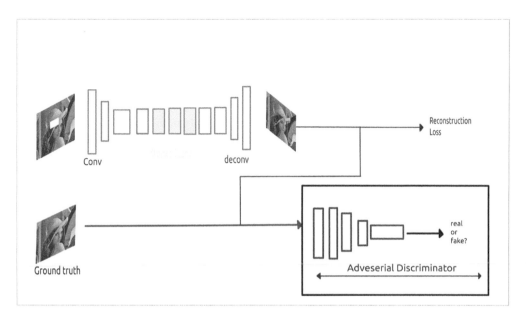

FIGURE 5.11
Example of the general architecture of a generative adversarial network based inpainting method.

Typically, GAN reconstructs the image with the appropriate patch plugged in. The discriminator compares it to the ground truth image in an attempt to discern whether the generated patch looks real. The training is done when the discriminator can discern a generated image from the training data sample.

GAN-based approaches give good performance and are proven to be helpful for inpainting (Figure 5.11). For example, Hsu et al. [11] proposed the use of GAN in combination with s CNN-based texture encoder and a super-resolution network to provide a high-resolution repaired image output. Pathak et al. [10 and 12] and Jianwu Li [13] proposed a context-driven approach based on GAN.

For the task of handwritten Chinese character recognition, Li et al. [14] proposed a method using deep convolutional generative adversarial networks (DCGANs) to reconstruct corrupted handwritten character images. An improved GoogleLeNet with traditional feature extraction methods is then used to recognize those characters.

Shin et al. [14] proposed a GAN-based method called a parallel extended decoder path for semantic inpainting (PEPSI) having a single-stage encoder–decoder network for inpainting. It utilizes the parallel decoding network with a coarse and fine network to reduce the number of required convolutional operations reducing the operation time while giving performance [15].

Wang et al. [16] made use of an encoder-decoder network with a multiscale GAN for image inpainting. A similar combination was utilized in Dhamo et al. [17] for inpainting and image transformation purposes.

The process used in Dhamo et al. [17] works for layer depth images. It aims to retrieve a scene geometry from a RGB image for three-dimensional content. A CNN added with a GAN model has been used to create the background of a scene by eliminating the object in the foreground image. It is then utilized to create an RGB-D image. Vitoria et al. [18] proposed an improved version of the Wasserstein GAN with the introduction of a residual learning framework for both the generator and discriminator parts for improved performance. Similarly, Dong et al. [19] and S. Lou et al. [20] proposed the use of a DCGAN for filling the missing parts of the sea surface temperature images. N. M. Salem [21] used self learning encoder-decoders with GAN adversarial loss. H. Liu [22] extensively used GAN for image inpainting.

Structural consistency and textural clarity are required for a good image restoration. Han et al. [23] proposed a DCGAN architecture restoration of facial images. FiNet [24] is another approach for the popular task of fashion image inpainting that consists of inpainting (generating) different styles of clothes of a person's representation.

5.6 Evaluation

The task of training a model is achieved by corrupting a ground truth image and then reconstructing a new image using that corrupted image. The goal of training the model can be said to be achieved when the reconstructed image is as close as possible to the original ground truth image. However, that requires a comparison to be made between the reconstructed and ground truth image for us to tune the model. This is done by the use of metrics.

Metrics are a quantitative measure which provide us with a good idea about the progress of the model. It allows for a comparison for performance between multiple architectures and solutions.

Some of the more commonly used metrics are as follows.

5.6.1 Mean Squared Error

Mean squared error (MSE) measures the average squared difference between the estimated values and the actual value. It is represented as

$$MSE = \frac{1}{n}\sum_{i=1}^{n}(Y_i - \widehat{Y}_i)^2$$

It is one of the most common metrics used for calculation of error. However, it cannot capture the structural differences between the images.

5.6.2 Peak Signal-to-Noise Ratio

Peak signal-to-noise ratio (PSNR) is the ratio between the maximum possible power of a signal and the power of corrupting noise which affects the accuracy of its representations. It can be easily explained via the MSE as

$$PSNR = 10\frac{L^2}{MSE}$$

where L is maximum pixel value.

5.6.3 Structural Similarity Index Measure

The structural similarity index measure (SSIM) is used for measuring the similarity between two images. With the original image as a reference, SSIM looks at three key points for comparison, namely, luminance, contrast and structure:

- Luminance (μ): $\mu_x = \dfrac{1}{N}\sum_{i=1}^{x} x_i$

  For two images (x, y), the luminance comparison is given as $l(x,y) = \dfrac{2\mu_x\mu_y + C_1}{\mu_x^2 + \mu_y^2 + C_1}$

- Contrast (σ): $\sigma_x = \left(\dfrac{1}{N-1}\sum_{i=1}^{N}(x_i - \mu_x)^2\right)^{\frac{1}{2}}$

  For two images (x, y), the contrast comparison is given as $c(x,y) = \dfrac{2\sigma_x\sigma_y + C_2}{\sigma_x^2 + \sigma_y^2 + C_2}$

- Structure comparison function (s): $s(x,y) = \dfrac{\sigma_{xy} + C_3}{\sigma_x\sigma_y + C_3}$

  where $\sigma_{(x,y)}$

$$\sigma_{xy} = \dfrac{1}{N-1}\sum_{i=1}^{N}(x_i - \mu_x)(y_i - \mu_y)$$

- Finally, SSIM is given as $SSIM(x,y) = [l(x,y)]^{\alpha} \cdot [c(x,y)]^{\beta} \cdot [s(x,y)]^{\gamma}$

5.6.4 Datasets

Datasets are a requirement for the training of a model for any particular task. The problem domain of image inpainting has many large and public datasets for the evaluation and comparison of proposed methods. Some of the commonly used datasets are as follows:

- *Paris street view* [24]: It is a dataset based on Google Street view dataset which comprises multiple images collected from many cities worldwide. It contains about 15,000 images having 936*537 resolution.
- *Berkeley segmentation dataset* [25]: It is a dataset containing 12,000 images having hand-labeled segmentations. The dataset contains both RGB and grayscale images.
- *ImageNet* [26]: It is a large-scale dataset with as many as 14,197,122 images with 1,034,908 annotated with bounding boxes. There are about 21,841 sysnet with each having thousands of images.
- **Celebface** [27]: It is a large dataset with more than 200K celebrity images, each having 40 attribute annotations.

5.7 Conclusion

Image inpainting is one of the important problems in the computer vision domain. There is an ever-growing number of tools available for image editing leading to a large amount of modified data. Inpainting finds its application in many ways including image restoration, correction of transmitted images and image quality enhancement, among many others.

This chapter gives a brief overview of inpainting along with its traditional and non-traditional (deep learning–based) methods. The various methods of inpainting approached in this chapter have been used to tackle various kinds of distorted images including inscribed text, object removal, scratched image along with some more specialized datasets like RGB-D and hyper-spectral images.

The traditional methods include diffusion and exemplar-based methods, whereas the deep learning methods contain CNN and GAN for their functioning.

Traditional methods do not require any dataset (they work on data available from image itself), whereas deep learning–based approaches require large amounts of data to achieve a particular accuracy in a task.

We may conclude that no particular method may be able to solve all the inpainting problems.

Every learning technique has its own niche of performance in certain tasks. However, we may expect promising new techniques which offer good performance in most of the available cases.

References

[1] Marcelo Bertalmio, Guillermo Sapiro, Vincent Caselles, Coloma Ballester. Image inpainting. In *Proceedings of the 27th Annual Conference on Computer Graphics and Interactive Techniques (SIGGRAPH '00)*. ACM Press/Addison-Wesley Publishing Co., 2000, pp. 417–424.

[2] A. Criminisi, P. Perez, K. Toyama. Object removal by exemplar-based inpainting. In *2003 IEEE Computer Society Conference on Computer Vision and Pattern Recognition, 2003. Proceedings (Vol. 2, pp. II–II)*. IEEE, 2003 June.

[3] R. Köhler, C. Schuler, B. Schölkopf, S. Harmeling. Mask-specific inpainting with deep neural networks. In *German Conference on Pattern Recognition* (pp. 523–534). Springer, Cham, 2014 September.

[4] N. Cai, Z. Su, Z. Lin, H. Wang, Z. Yang, B. W.-K. Ling. Blind inpainting using the fully convolutional neural network. *The Visual Computer* 33.2 (2017): 249–261.

[5] Z. Yan, X. Li, M. Li, W. Zuo, S. Shan. Shift-net: Image inpainting via deep feature rearrangement. In *Proceedings of the European Conference on Computer Vision (ECCV)*. Springer, 2018, pp. 1–17.

[6] C. S. Weerasekera, T. Dharmasiri, R. Garg, T. Drummond, I. Reid. Just-in-time reconstruction: Inpainting sparse maps using single view depth predictors as priors. In *2018 IEEE International Conference on Robotics and Automation (ICRA)*. IEEE, 2018, pp. 1–9.

[7] O. Sidorov, J. Y. Hardeberg. Deep hyperspectral prior: Denoising, inpainting, super-resolution, 2019. *arXiv preprint arXiv:1902. 00301*.

[8] Y. Zeng, J. Fu, H. Chao, B. Guo. Learning pyramid-context encoder network for high-quality image inpainting. In *Proceedings of the IEEE Conference on Computer Vision and Pattern Recognition*. IEEE, 2019, pp. 1486–1494.

[9] H. Liu, B. Jiang, Y. Xiao, C. Yang. Coherent semantic attention for image inpainting, 2019. *arXiv preprint arXiv:1905.12384*.

[10] D. Pathak, P. Krahenbuhl, J. Donahue, T. Darrell, A. A. Efros. Context encoders: Feature learning by inpainting. In *Proceedings of the IEEE Conference on Computer Vision and Pattern Recognition*. IEEE, 2016, pp. 2536–2544.

[11] Chihwei Hsu, Feng Chen, Guijin Wang. High-resolution image inpainting through multiple deep networks. In *2017 International Conference on Vision, Image and Signal Processing (ICVISP)*. IEEE, 2017.

[12] Deepak Pathak, et al. Context encoders: Feature learning by inpainting. In *Proceedings of the IEEE Conference on Computer Vision and Pattern Recognition*. IEEE, 2016.

[13] Jianwu Li, Ge Song, Minhua Zhang. Occluded offline handwritten Chinese character recognition using deep convolutional generative adversarial network and improved GoogLeNet. *Neural Computing and Applications* 32.9 (2020): 4805–4819.

[14] Yong-Goo Shin, et al. PEPSI++: Fast and lightweight network for image inpainting. *IEEE Transactions on Neural Networks and Learning Systems* 32.1 (2020): 252–265.

[15] H. Wang, L. Jiao, H. Wu, R. Bie. New inpainting algorithm based on simplified context encoders and multi-scale adversarial network. *Procedia Computer Science* 147 (2019): 254–263.

[16] C. Wang, C. Xu, C. Wang, D. Tao. Perceptual adversarial networks for image-to-image transformation. *IEEE Transactions on Image Processing* 27.8 (2018): 4066–4079.

[17] Helisa Dhamo, et al. Peeking behind objects: Layered depth prediction from a single image. *Pattern Recognition Letters* 125 (2019): 333–340.

[18] P. Vitoria, J. Sintes, C. Ballester. Semantic image inpainting through improved Wasserstein generative adversarial networks, 2018. *arXiv preprint arXiv:1812.01071.*

[19] J. Dong, R. Yin, X. Sun, Q. Li, Y. Yang, X. Qin. Inpainting of remote sensing SST images with deep convolutional generative adversarial network. *IEEE Geoscience and Remote Sensing Letters* 16.2 (2018): 173–177.

[20] S. Lou, Q. Fan, F. Chen, C. Wang, J. Li. Preliminary investigation on single remote sensing image inpainting through a modified GAN. In *2018 10th IAPR Workshop on Pattern Recognition in Remote Sensing (PRRS)*. IEEE, 2018, pp. 1–6.

[21] N. M. Salem, H. M. Mahdi, H. Abbas. Semantic image inpainting using self-learning encoder-decoder and adversarial loss. In *2018 13th International Conference on Computer Engineering and Systems (ICCES)*. IEEE, 2018, pp. 103–108.

[22] H. Liu, G. Lu, X. Bi, J. Yan, W. Wang. Image inpainting based on generative adversarial networks. In *2018 14th International Conference on Natural Computation, Fuzzy Systems and Knowledge Discovery (ICNC-FSKD)*. IEEE, 2018, pp. 373–378.

[23] X. Han, Z. Wu, W. Huang, M. R. Scott, L. S. Davis. Compatible and diverse fashion image inpainting. *arXiv preprint arXiv:1902.01096.*

[24] C. Doersch, S. Singh, A. Gupta, J. Sivic, A. A. Efros. What makes Paris look like Paris? *Communications of the ACM* 58.12 (2015): 103–110.

[25] D. Martin, C. Fowlkes, D. Tal, J. Malik, et al. A database of human segmented natural images and its application to evaluating segmentation algorithms and measuring ecological statistics. *ICCV Vancouver* (2001).

[26] O. Russakovsky, J. Deng, H. Su, J. Krause, S. Satheesh, S. Ma, Z. Huang, A. Karpathy, A. Khosla, M. Bernstein, et al. ImageNet large scale visual recognition challenge. *International Journal of Computer Vision* 115.3 (2015): 211–252.

[27] Z. Liu, P. Luo, X. Wang, X. Tang. Large-scale celeb faces attributes (celeba) dataset (2018). Retrieved August 15, 2018.

6

Watermarking in Frequency Domain Using Magic Transform

Narendrakumar R. Dasre and Pritam Gujarathi

CONTENTS

6.1 Introduction

Digital image processing has acquired a lot of importance in the era of information and data. In the last two decades, the authentication of digital information (text, audio and video) has become a challenging question [8]. In this regard, digital watermarking plays an important role in the security of digital content. Researchers are working constantly to minimise this security issue using different techniques [10]. Watermarking techniques have emerged as a viable option to authenticate the digital content and protect the copyright of the original owner [4, 6, 9]. The watermarking techniques are used in spatial and frequency domains. Researchers have put forth many algorithms for authentication of a watermark. A few of these techniques for watermarking are discussed in the literature [8–11]. In this chapter, frequency domain wavelet transform is used, incorporating three levels of decomposition. Here, Magic transform (Dasre-Gujarathi transform [DGT]) [7] is used for encrypting and decrypting the watermark. This Magic transform scrambles the watermark which makes the algorithm more secure. Multiresolution analysis is done using wavelets and three-level decomposition is obtained using Daubechies filter. After scrambling the watermark, it is added in the frequency domain. This combination of wavelet transform and Magic transform make the technique more reliable. The level of decomposition, the filter used, scaling factor and the choice of frequency channel are also the additional security keys. The statistical analysis is performed considering different parameters like mean squared error (MSE), peak signal-to-noise ratio (PSNR), structural similarity index measure (SSIM), normalized correlation and image fidelity.

Watermarking is a process of embedding information or code into image, audio or video objects which may be visible or invisible. Classification of watermarking in all possible ways is given in Figure 6.1.

Watermarking techniques mainly fall into two categories: spatial domain method and spectral domain method [6].

> *Spatial domain method*: In this, the watermark is embedded directly by modifying the pixel location of the images. These methods are less complex as no transform is used but are not robust against attacks. For example, a simple image cropping operation may eliminate the watermark. They also have relatively low bit embedding capacity and are not resistant enough to lossy image compression. The simplest example based on these methods is to embed the watermark in the least significant bit (LSB) of image pixels.
>
> *Spectral domain method*: In this method, the image is transformed into a set of a frequency domain coefficients using discrete cosine transform (DCT), discrete Fourier transform (DFT) or the discrete wavelet transform (DWT). Watermark is inserted into an image by modifying selected frequency coefficients of image pixels. These methods can embed more bits of watermark and are more robust to attacks. But both of the techniques discussed have the same defect, that is they modify the working pixels of the original image.

Some desirable properties of the watermarking technique [1–3] include the following:

- The inserted watermark should not introduce visible artifacts.
- The watermark should not be easily removable.
- The watermark should be resilient to lossy data compression such as jpeg.

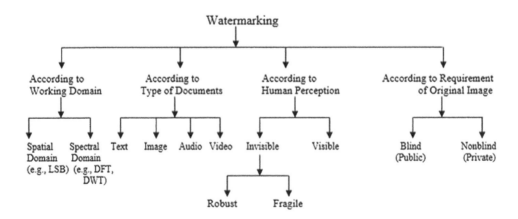

FIGURE 6.1
Classification of watermarking.

- The watermark should be resilient to an image processing technique such as median filtering and image cropping.
- The original image is not required in watermark extraction.
- The watermark can only be extracted by privileged individuals given the security key.

6.2 Proposed Algorithm Using Magic Transform

In this section, the algorithms for embedding and extracting a watermark using Magic transform are discussed. In the embedding algorithm, the watermark is scrambled using Magic transform. The host image is decomposed into three levels using wavelet transform, and then the scrambled watermark is embedded into it. For extraction of the watermark, inverse wavelet transform is used. The original watermark can be obtained using inverse Magic transform.

6.2.1 Watermark Embedding Algorithm

We consider the host image (Lena) I_0 and the watermark (logo/image) W_0. The embedding algorithm is as follows:

Step 1: Read the host image I_0 and the watermark W_0.

Step 2: Decompose the host image into different frequency regions using wavelet transform up to required levels.

Step 3: Apply Magic transform (DGT) to the watermark W_0 to obtain the scrambled watermark W_0'.

Step 4: Choose the scaling factor $k \epsilon (0,1)$ and appropriate frequency channel (C) to insert the scrambled watermark W_0'. The following formula [5] is used to insert the watermark in channel C as

$$C(m,n) = \{C(m,n) \ if \ 0 \le m,n \le \frac{N}{8} - M \ k.W_0'\left(m - \frac{N}{8} + M, \ n - \frac{N}{8} + M\right) otherwise \quad (6.1)$$

where the size of the host image is $N \times N$ and the size of the watermark is $M \times M$. As per the capacity of the channel, the restriction on the size of the logo (watermark) is $0 \le m,n \le \frac{N}{8}$ for three-level decomposition.

Step 5: Reconstruct the watermarked image I_1 using inverse wavelet transform.

6.2.2 Watermark Extraction Algorithm

In this section, the algorithm for extraction of the watermark is discussed. The algorithm for extraction of watermark is as follows:

Step 1: Consider watermarked image I_1.

Step 2: Apply wavelet transform to decompose watermarked image I_1 into different frequency regions up to required level.

Step 3: Choose the required frequency channel and extract the watermark block W_1' which is a scrambled watermark. The watermark W_1' can be extracted using the following formula:

$$W_1' = k^{-1}C\left(m + \frac{N}{8} - M, n + \frac{N}{8} - M\right)$$ (6.2)

Step 4: Apply inverse Magic transform to W_1', and the extracted watermark W_0 is obtained.

6.3 Experimental Results

For the experimental results, we have considered following test images as host image with size 256 × 256 and the watermark logo of DGT of size 16 × 16. Some standard images like Lena, cameraman, baboon, Barbara, plane, street and pepper are considered for the experiment. These images are as shown in Figure 6.2 through Figure 6.9.

Test Images

FIGURE 6.2
Lena image.

FIGURE 6.3
Cameraman image.

FIGURE 6.4
Baboon image.

FIGURE 6.5
Barbara image.

FIGURE 6.6
Plane image.

FIGURE 6.7
Street image.

FIGURE 6.8
Pepper image.

FIGURE 6.9
DGT logo/watermark.

Using these images as host image and the DGT logo as the watermark, the experiments were carried out, and the statistical parameters are noted in the form of tables. For each attack, the experimental output images and the statistical parameters corresponding to Lena image are provided as the sample. The same experiments are carried out for all the test images, and the statistical results are provided in the form of tables.

6.3.1 Insertion and Extraction of the Logo

Using the insertion algorithm 6.2.1, we considered three-level two-dimensional decomposition using wavelet transform as shown in Figure 6.10.

The mid-frequency region LH3 or HL3 is chosen for insertion of a watermark. The mid-frequency region was selected because it is robust to the attacks. Since the LL region contains the energy of the signal and the HH region is the least significant bit, these two regions are avoided. Magic transform and inverse Magic transform are the additional keys to secure the information (watermark/logo). Before insertion of a watermark, it is scrambled using Magic transform (DGT). Then the watermark (logo/information) is inserted into the target frequency channel with the scaling factor. The scaling factor controls the visibility of effects in the watermarked image. The watermarked image is reconstructed using inverse wavelet transform. This watermarked image is transmitted through the channel.

At the receiver's end, the extraction algorithm 6.2.2 is followed. The wavelet transform has been used to decompose the watermarked image into different frequency channels, and the scrambled watermark is extracted from the target channel. The original watermark (logo) is obtained using inverse Magic transform (Figure 6.11 through Figure 6.15).

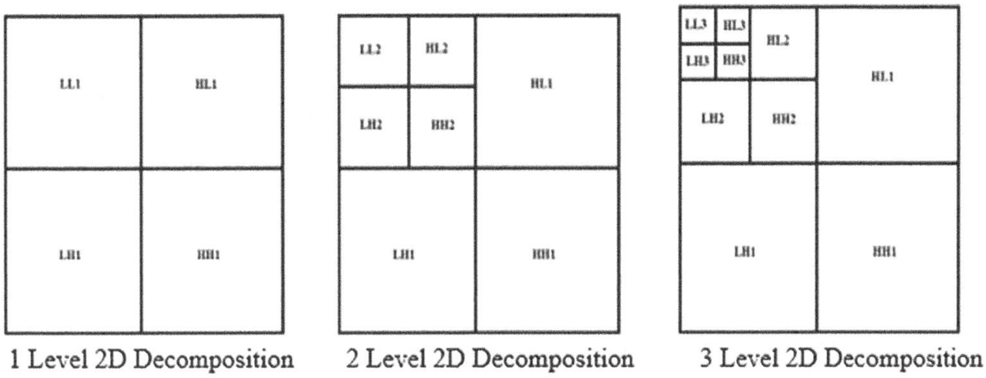

LL1	HL1
LH1	HH1

1 Level 2D Decomposition

LL2	HL2	HL1
LH2	HH2	
LH1		HH1

2 Level 2D Decomposition

LL3	HL3	HL2	HL1
LH3	HH3		
LH2		HH2	
LH1			HH1

3 Level 2D Decomposition

FIGURE 6.10
Two-dimensional decomposition.

Original Image

FIGURE 6.11
Original image.

FIGURE 6.12
Original logo.

FIGURE 6.13
Scrambled logo.

Reconstructed Watermarked Image

FIGURE 6.14
Watermarked image.

FIGURE 6.15
Logo recovered.

6.3.2 JPEG Compression Attack

The 8 × 8 mask is used for the JPEG compression attack. After the JPEG compression attack, the logo is extracted with normalised correlation coefficient (NC) 1.0. The watermarked image and the recovered logo after the JPEG compression attack are as shown in Figure 6.16 and Figure 6.17.

6.3.3 Bit Compression Attack

For the bit compression attack, two bits are reduced from the representation of every pixel in the mid-frequency region and one bit from the representation of every pixel in the high-frequency region. After bit compression attack, the logo is extracted with NC 1.0. The watermarked image and the recovered logo after bit compression attack are as in Figure 6.18 and Figure 6.19.

6.3.4 Median Filter Attack

For median filter attack, 3 × 3 mask is used. The image becomes smoother due to median filter attack. After median filter attack, the logo is extracted with NC 0.9568. The watermarked image and the recovered logo after median filter attack are as in Figure 6.20 and Figure 6.21.

FIGURE 6.16
Image after JPEG compression.

FIGURE 6.17
Recovered logo after JPEG compression.

FIGURE 6.18
Image after bit compression.

FIGURE 6.19
Recovered logo after bit compression.

FIGURE 6.20
Image after median filter.

FIGURE 6.21
Recovered logo after median filter.

6.3.5 Salt and Pepper Attack

For salt and pepper attack, 5% noise is added to the watermarked image. After salt and pepper attack, the logo is extracted with NC as 0.97. The watermarked image and the recovered logo after salt and pepper attack are as in Figure 6.22 and Figure 6.23.

6.3.6 Statistical Analysis

The statistical analysis is carried out for different attacks. The statistical measures MSE, PSNR, NC, SSIM and image fidelity are calculated between the original image and the image after each attack. Also, the statistical measures NC, SSIM are calculated for all recovered watermarks. The statistical measures and values for image and watermark are mentioned in the tables.

MSE (mean squared error) is calculated between the original image and the watermarked image by using the following formula:

$$MSE = \frac{\sum_{i=1}^{N}\sum_{j=1}^{N}(I_0 - I_1)^2}{N \times N} \tag{6.3}$$

where $N \times N$ is the size of the image; $I_0(i,j) = I_0$ is the original host image; and $I_1(i,j) = I_1$ is the watermarked image.

The disturbance into the host image is calculated with PSNR. The PSNR of an image of size $N \times N$ is calculated as

Image after Salt and Pepper

FIGURE 6.22
Image after salt and pepper.

FIGURE 6.23
Recovered logo after salt and pepper.

$$PSNR = 10log_{10}\left[\frac{N \times N \times max\left(I_1\right)^2}{\sum_{i=1}^{N}\sum_{j=1}^{N}\left(I_0 - I_1\right)^2}\right] \tag{6.4}$$

where $I_0\left(i,j\right) = I_0$ is the original host image, and $I_1\left(i,j\right) = I_1$ is the watermarked image.

The NC is calculated to measure the similarity of the original watermark and the extracted watermark. NC is calculated for the watermark of the size $M \times M$ as

$$NC = \frac{\sum_{i=1}^{M}\sum_{j=1}^{M}W_0 \times W_1}{\sum_{i=1}^{M}\sum_{j=1}^{M}W_0 \times W_0} \tag{6.5}$$

where $W_0\left(i,j\right) = W_0$ is the original watermark, and $W_1\left(i,j\right) = W_1$ is the extracted watermark.

SSIM is a measure of similarity in two signals (images). SSIM is an effective tool to compare the original signal (image) and perturbed signal. Here the original and the watermarked images are compared after attack. SSIM is also a good quantifier to understand the degradation in the original signal (image). The SSIM uses three important features of the signal (image): luminance, contrast and structure.

We calculate SSIM [12] by using the following formula:

$$SSIM(A,B) = \frac{(2\mu_A\mu_B + C_1)(2\sigma_{AB} + C_2)}{(\mu_A^2 + \mu_B^2 + C_1)(\sigma_A^2 + \sigma_B^2 + C_2)} \tag{6.6}$$

where A and B are the images for SSIM, μ denotes the mean, and σ denotes the standard deviation.

Image fidelity [9] is also one of the measures to calculate the transparency or imperceptibly of image with watermark. Image fidelity (IF) can be calculated as

$$IF = 1 - \frac{\sum_{i,j}(A(i,j) - B(i,j))^2}{\sum_{i,j}(A(i,j))^2} \tag{6.7}$$

where $A(i, j)$ is the original image and $B(i, j)$ is the image after watermarking.

The values of statistical parameters MSE, PSNR, NC, SSIM and IF after each attack are calculated for the host image. The parameters SSIM, NC are calculated for watermark. All values are given in Table 6.1 through Table 6.7.

TABLE 6.1

Statistical Parameters: Lena

Statistical parameters for host image: Lena

Attacks	MSE	PSNR	SSIM	NC	IF
Median filter	172.3397	25.7669	0.8863	0.9655	0.9893
Salt and pepper	172.3397	25.7669	0.8863	0.9655	0.0107
Bit compression	1246.8	17.1729	0.3872	0.8184	0.0669
JPEG compression	53.1824	30.8731	0.9652	0.9891	0.0032

Statistical parameters for watermark with Lena as host image

Attacks	SSIM	NC
Median filter	1.57×10^{-18}	0.9568
Salt and pepper	0.9867	0.9885
Bit compression	4.0001×10^{-6}	1.0
JPEG compression	1.0	1.0

FIGURE 6.24
Lena image.

TABLE 6.2

Statistical Parameters: Cameraman

Statistical parameters for host image: Cameraman

Attacks	MSE	PSNR	SSIM	NC	IF
Median filter	180.0859	25.5760	0.8791	0.9769	0.9890
Salt and pepper	180.0859	25.5760	0.8791	0.9769	0.0110
Bit compression	2259.9	14.5899	0.1960	0.7963	0.1170
JPEG compression	46.9394	31.4154	0.9758	0.9939	0.0029

Statistical parameters for watermark with cameraman as host image

Attacks	SSIM	NC
Median filter	1.5043×10^{-18}	0.9526
Salt and pepper	0.9823	0.9857
Bit compression	4.0001×10^{-6}	1
JPEG compression	1	1

FIGURE 6.25
Cameraman image.

TABLE 6.3

Statistical Parameters: Baboon

Statistical parameters for host image: Baboon

Attacks	MSE	PSNR	SSIM	NC	IF
Median filter	143.2512	26.5698	0.9184	0.9627	0.9925
Salt and pepper	143.2512	26.5698	0.9184	0.9627	0.0075
Bit compression	1316.2	16.9377	0.5089	0.7929	0.0688
JPEG compression	13.2512	36.9083	0.9890	0.9964	7.2319×10^{-4}

Statistical parameters for watermark with baboon as host image

Attacks	SSIM	NC
Median filter	2.1121×10^{-18}	0.9355
Salt and pepper	0.9867	0.9886
Bit compression	4.0001×10^{-6}	1
JPEG compression	1	1

FIGURE 6.26
Baboon image.

TABLE 6.4

Statistical Parameters: Barbara

Statistical parameters for host image: Barbara

Attacks	MSE	PSNR	SSIM	NC	IF
Median filter	171.3697	25.7915	0.8821	0.9627	0.9906
Salt and pepper	171.3697	25.7915	0.8821	0.9627	0.0094
Bit compression	1677.0	15.8856	0.3490	0.7769	0.1079
JPEG compression	41.6383	31.9359	0.9597	0.9907	0.0023

Statistical parameters for watermark with Barbara as host image

Attacks	SSIM	NC
Median filter	1.6130×10^{-18}	0.9188
Salt and pepper	0.9866	0.9892
Bit compression	4.0001×10^{-6}	1
JPEG compression	1	1

FIGURE 6.27
Barbara image.

TABLE 6.5

Statistical Parameters: Plane

Statistical parameters for host image: Plane

Attacks	MSE	PSNR	SSIM	NC	IF
Median filter	188.8599	25.3694	0.8816	0.9563	0.9943
Salt and pepper	188.8599	25.3694	0.8816	0.9563	0.0057
Bit compression	1966.7	15.1933	0.2642	0.7299	0.0572
JPEG compression	47.0592	31.4044	0.9701	0.9888	0.0014

Statistical parameters for watermark with plane as host image

Attacks	SSIM	NC
Median filter	1.5729×10^{-18}	0.9381
Salt and pepper	0.9816	0.9849
Bit compression	4.0001×10^{-6}	1
JPEG compression	1	1

FIGURE 6.28
Plane image.

TABLE 6.6

Statistical Parameters: Street

Statistical parameters for host image: Street

Attacks	MSE	PSNR	SSIM	NC	IF
Median filter	142.8493	26.5820	0.9149	0.9839	0.9868
Salt and pepper	142.8493	26.5820	0.9149	0.9839	0.0132
Bit compression	1396.0	16.6820	0.5021	0.8656	0.1303
JPEG compression	2.3078×10^{-23}	274.4989	0.9847	0.9966	0.0034

Statistical parameters for watermark with street as host image

Attacks	SSIM	NC
Median filter	1.7548×10^{-18}	0.9100
Salt and pepper	0.9576	0.9735
Bit compression	4.0001×10^{-6}	1
JPEG compression	1	1

FIGURE 6.29
Street Image

TABLE 6.7

Statistical Parameters: Pepper

Statistical parameters for host image: Pepper

Attacks	MSE	PSNR	SSIM	NC	IF
Median filter	163.1706	26.0044	0.8531	0.9728	0.9908
Salt and pepper	163.1706	26.0044	0.8531	0.9728	0.0092
Bit compression	1396.0	16.6820	0.5021	0.8656	0.1303
JPEG compression	28.9323	33.5170	0.9547	0.9951	0.0016

Statistical parameters for watermark with pepper as host image

Attacks	SSIM	NC
Median filter	1.3445×10^{-18}	0.9803
Salt and pepper	0.9823	0.9853
Bit compression	4.0001×10^{-6}	1
JPEG compression	1	1

FIGURE 6.30
Pepper image.

TABLE 6.8

Comparison of Attacks

Host Images	Median Filter	Salt and Pepper	Bit Compression	JPEG Compression
Lena	0.9655	0.9655	0.8184	0.9891
Cameraman	0.9769	0.9769	0.7963	0.9939
Baboon	0.9627	0.9627	0.7929	0.9964
Barbara	0.9627	0.9627	0.7769	0.9907
Plane	0.9563	0.9563	0.7299	0.9888
Street	0.9839	0.9839	0.8656	0.9966
Pepper	0.9728	0.9728	0.8656	0.9951

TABLE 6.9

Comparison of Original Watermark and Extracted Watermark after Attacks

Host Images	Median Filter	Salt and Pepper	Bit Compression	JPEG Compression
Lena	0.9568	0.9885	1.0	1.0
Cameraman	0.9526	0.9857	1.0	1.0
Baboon	0.9355	0.9886	1.0	1.0
Plane	0.9381	0.9849	1.0	1.0
Street	0.9100	0.9735	1.0	1.0
Pepper	0.9803	0.9853	1.0	1.0

All seven test images with the attacks of median filter, salt and pepper, bit compression and JPEG compression are compared, and the NC is recorded in Table 6.8.

From Table 6.8, the observed range of NC for test images after attacks is (0.7299, 0.9966). Similarly, extracted watermark after median filter, salt and pepper, bit compression and JPEG compression attacks is compared with the original watermark for all seven test images. The NC for watermark is recorded in the Table 6.9.

From Table 6.9, the observed range of NC for test watermark after attacks is (0.9100, 1.0).

6.4 Conclusion

In this chapter, a new method of watermarking using Magic transform (DGT) has been proposed and implemented. The algorithm is tested under different attacks like median filter, bit compression, JPEG compression and salt and pepper. This method provides security to the logo due to Magic transform. NCs of recovered logo and original logo are more than 0.95 for this method. Though the watermarked image is very much disturbed, still the watermark is safe and exists in the image and can be extracted properly. This has proved that the proposed method is secure and robust to all mentioned attacks.

6.5 Acknowledgement

We are thankful to Dr. Mukesh D. Patil, Principal, R. A. I. T., Nerul for his continuous support and guidance throughout the work. We are thankful to our reviewers and editors for their valuable suggestions for the improvement of this chapter.

References

1. Tay P. and Havlicek J. P., Image watermarking using wavelet, *Circuits and Systems*, 2002, MWSCAS-2002, 45th Midwest Symposium, pp-III-258–III-261(2002).
2. Dasre N. R. and Patil H. R., On watermarking in frequency domain, 2nd ICDIP, *Proceedings of SPIE*, 7546(2010), 754622-1–5.
3. Dasre N. R. and Patil H. R., A technique of watermarking using wavelet, *Proceedings of IC-RAMSA* (2011), 420–427.
4. Dasre N. R., On watermarking using Arnold and wavelet transform, *IJMCR*, 4(5) (2016), 1325–1332.
5. Dahake V. R., Dasre N. R. and Gaikwad V. B., Digital image watermarking in frequency domain using CAT mapping, *JSTM*, 4 (2011), 11–16.
6. Dasre N. R., A dual watermarking using DWT, DCT, SVED and image fusion, *International Journal of Mathematical Sciences and Engineering Applications (IJMSEA)*, 10(3) (2016), 77–89.
7. Dasre N. R. and Gujarathi P. R., Magic transformation: An introduction, *International Journal of Mathematical Sciences and Engineering Applications (IJMSEA)*, 13(1) (2019), 7–13.
8. Mohanarathinam A., Kamalraj S., Prasanna Venkatesan G.K.D., et al., Digital watermarking techniques for image security: A review, *Journal of Ambient Intelligence and Humanized Computing*, 11 (2020), 3221–3229. https://doi.org/10.1007/s12652-019-01500-1
9. Dixit A. and Dixit R., A review on digital image watermarking techniques, *International Journal of Image, Graphics and Signal Processing (IJIGSP)*, 9(4) (2017), 56–66. https://doi.org/10.5815/ijigsp.2017.04.07
10. Bellaaj M. and Ouni K., Watermarking technique for multimedia documents in the frequency domain, *Digital Image and Video Watermarking and Steganography*, Sudhakar Ramakrishnan, Intech Open (2019), 09–29. http://doi.org/10.5772/intechopen.79370
11. Fofanah A. J. and Gao T., Dual watermarking for protection of medical images based on watermarking of frequency domain and genetic programming, *The 4th International Conference on Innovation in Artificial Intelligence*, Xiamen, China, May 8–11, 2020, ACM (2020), 106–115. https://doi.org/10.1145/3390557.3394308
12. Wang Z., Bovik A. C., Sheikh H. R. and Simoncelli E. P., Image quality assessment: From error visibility to structural similarity, *IEEE Transactions on Image Processing*, 13(4) (April 2004), 600–612.

Appendix

i) Code for applying Dasre-Gujarathi Transform (Magic Transform)

```
for k=p:-1:1
    el=zeros(k);
for j=1:k
    for i=1:k
        el(i,j)=b(mod(i,k)+1,mod(j,k)+1);
    end
```

```
end
for  y=1:z
          f(x1,y1)=e1(x,y);
          f(y1,x1)=e1(y,x);
          y1=y1+1;
  end
f;
b=e1(2:k,2:k);
z=z-1;
x1=x1+1;
z1=z1+1;
y1=z1;
```

ii) Code for applying inverse Dasre-Gujarathi Transform (Magic Transform)

```
 k=2;
 b=b_ex;
 k1=p-2;
for  z=p-1:-1:1
e=b(z:p,z:p);
e1=zeros(k);
     for i=1:k
     for j=1:k
          m=mod(i-1,k);
          n=mod(j-1,k);
          if  n==0
              n=k;
          end
          if  m==0
              m=k;
          end
     e1(i,j)=e(m,n);
     end
     end
     if k==p
          b=e1;
     else
for  i=1:k
     for j=1:k
     b(k1+i,k1+j)=e1(i,j);
     end
end
     end
k=k+1;
k1=k1-1;
end
```

7

An Efficient Lightweight LSB Steganography with Deep Learning Steganalysis

Dipnarayan Das, Asha Durafe and Vinod Patidar

CONTENTS

7.1 Introduction

As we discuss the science of secret messaging, one question always comes first, what is the difference between cryptography and steganography? In cryptography [1,2], a method converts secret plain data into cipher data [3] and sends to another person who then decrypts the cipher data into plain data (secret). But in case of steganography, the secret data are unaltered and scrambled inside media for hiding. Like in image steganography, the transmission media a.k.a. cover data, is an image, and the secret data a.k. A.stego data is hidden inside the cover. The main target of steganography is not to protect from decryption but to make the transmission unsuspicious. From the definition, we got our motivation, which is human curiosity. The effect of human curiosity drives us to explore more. From a defender perspective, if we can remove the curiosity of a hacker, then we will win the war before it starts. As an example, if a hacker tried to login to an admin page and gets the response "incorrect password", then due to curiosity they will again try with a new password. But if we give a fake access without stopping, the hacker's focus will not be isolated to only that fake environment. To implement the concept in our steganography algorithm, we proposed obfuscation.

Steganography is to conceal the secret data within multimedia contents such as file, message, image, or video. [4–5] whereas is to detect secret data hidden using steganography, identify suspected packages and ascertain whether the secret data is embedded or not [6–8]. An added advantage of steganography over cryptography is that, in case of cryptography, the algorithms and keys have finite range for encryption, but in steganography, the number of media is infinite and two computations are needed (reading the cover data and analyzing the secret pattern), increasing the complexity of the process.

Though steganography has effective security, today's high-speed computations with the help of artificial intelligence (AI)automation break most of the state-of-the-art algorithms [9,10]. Under AI, machine learning is combined with deep learning networks for pattern analysis. The concepts of machine learning [11–12] and AI are becoming almost synonymous with information security as industries turn to automation [13,14]. However, where there is light, there is also dark [15]. According to ESET, in their latest finding, AI can be a major threat to organizations, leading a significant number of IT decision makers (75%) from the United States to believe that the frequency of these attacks they have to detect will increase gradually.

A LSB (least significant bit) based scheme was proposed by Mielikainen [16] which embeds two bits into a pixel pair of cover image. The exploiting modification direction (EMD) data-hiding scheme by Zhang and Wang [17] overcomes the vulnerability in [16]. It can achieve a large embedding capacity with comparatively less distortion. The authors provided an embedding technique which provides $(2n + 1)$ different ways of alteration to cover pixels, which further corresponds to $(2n + 1)$ possible values of a secret digit. In Kim et al. [18], the quality of original EMD was improved. In 2008, Chang et al. [19] proposed a Sudoku-based solution which was inspired from Zhang and Wang's method. In 2012, Hong and Chen [20] proposed an adaptive pixel pair matching (PPM) method, where the scrambled plain text can be extracted without using key or additional information. Chen [21] proposed, in 2014, a data-hiding method based on PPM. Liu and Nguyen [22] proposed a novel data-hiding scheme on the basis of turtle a shell which provides quite enough image quality and high embedding rate. It offers a flexible embedding version in [23], and in 2018 the faster search version was proposed [24]. The methodology encrypts the private data [25] in order to decrease the chances of dataleakage if the embedding algorithm goes public. Although many data-hiding schemes exist on the basis of a chaotic map [26], a better scheme through chaotic systems for security was proposed by Yadav and Ojha [27] to offer greater embedding capacity and increased perceptual quality. Rasool et al. [28] mainly focused on the steganalysis of RGB images where a dataset named "CALTECH-BMP" is utilized, and in the images, different steganography algorithms are applied to hide the secret message. From cross-validation and testing results, we can see the exactness of SVM is in between 99% and 100%. The paper proposed that their trained model has given high precision of over 99% for the consolidated RGB channels features with dual-channel combinations as well as single channels. The number of different features is not in any dependency. Inserting in one channel in particular (the blue channel), there was no decrease in the recognition accuracy. Joshi et al. [29] proposed a new method of image steganography where the seventh bit of a pixel is working as an indicator and a successive temporary pixel in the grayscale image. Rasras et al. [30] have shown a quite good PSNR value. Qin et al. [31] proposed a coverless image steganography technique where a region detection system works to find a suitable place to embed secret data into an image to make it undetectable. Durafe and Patidar [32] presented a blind color image steganography with fractal cover and compared the performance metrics with integer wavelet transform (IWT)–singular value decomposition (SVD) and discrete wavelet transform (DWT)–SVD embedding in a frequency domain. Qian et al. [33] proposed a steganography algorithm that can break a convolutional neural network based steganalysis tool, thus enhancing security of the hidden data.

Reviewing subsequent and more recent literature, it was apparent that most of the steganography approach's firewall is broken against machine learning steganalysis [34]. In a few scenarios, the mathematical computation can be reversed without complexity. This doesn't mean that the state-of-the-art methods are not good in embedding, but according to the extensive analysis done, it can be predicted that the embedding is done at specific places of the images which coordinately generate a pattern and can be exploited by feature engineering. Inspired by state-of-the-art algorithms, to protect embedding from getting an interest, the proposed work utilizes two layers of security: the obfuscation layer which makes the embedding nearly undetectable and graphical embedding which can't be breakable using visual recognition. As a significance of this study, we leveraged priority to provide enough security with less resource constraints for industrial applicability.

In the following, background materials required to understand the proposed work are explored.

7.1.1 Material and Methods

In this section some background knowledge of steganography and steganalysis will be explored as a prerequisite of the proposed work.

7.1.1.1 Steganography

In the proposed work, the image is used as a steganography medium which can be classified as lossy and lossless. Lossy compression (e.g. JPEG design) accomplishes a significant

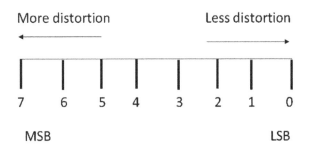

FIGURE 7.1
Embedding in eight-bit image.

level of compression and hence saves more space [35]. However, doing so, the pieces might be adjusted generally, and the inventiveness of the image might be affected, whereas lossless compression reproduces the message precisely. We have implemented our algorithm with lossless compression image formats where the results have shown satisfactory levels of robustness. In our proposed scheme, we have used spatial domain. In case of spatial, the focus is based on values of image pixels.

7.1.1.2 Steganalysis and Performance Measures

Steganalysis is the craftsmanship and science to recognize whether a given picture contains shrouded information. The steganalysis assumes a part in the determination of highlights or properties of the picture to test for concealed information and furthermore in planning of methods to distinguish or extricate the shrouded information. A steganalysis technique is considered effective if it can identify and extract the concealed information implanted [36]. The proposed work mainly focuses on targeted and blind steganalysis.

7.2 Proposed Work

Our proposed architecture is divided into two phases: embedding and extraction. In the proposed architecture, three main components are cover image, secret text to be embedded and direct key or questionnaire. For the questionnaire, the answer is inserted through the input at the beginning of the implemented program, or a direct key can be used for encryption which is also overlaid on the stego-image. Here for the implementation, the secret text and key are kept under ASCII format. For encryption, there are different cryptographic techniques already available. Among them, a very easily applicable Caesar cipher or shift cipher is used in this chapter. After inserting the cover image in the program, it checks for compression type. The algorithm is implemented to run in non-compression formatted images. After inserting the image, the program separates the channels R, G and B from the image as the system is implemented for RGB images. For each channel, the pixel value ranges from 0 to 255 [37,38]. Now according to the algorithm, the last digit will be replaced, so the value of the last digit can be from 0 to 9 which also signifies the change will be maximum up to four bits [39,40]. With only the last digit from each pixel, each channel is further serialized and visualized which is like the following waveform for better understanding.

In parallel, the secret text is also loaded and encoded into an ASCII value list, e.g., abcd -> 97-98-99-100. Now the answer or direct key, which was inserted, is used for encryption of the secret text. The serialized value string can be again visualized into waveform like Figure 7.2. At this point, there are four serialized value strings (three for RGB cover image and one for encrypted text). Now each serialized string from the cover image is fed to the differentiator with encrypted secret text's serialized value string, where least standard deviation is calculated, and that channel is selected for embedding to maximally obfuscate the secret text.

The embedding of the message is done (first layer security completed), and the rest is cryptographic key embedding which is the second layer. Most of the existing techniques embed the keys like a message so it can be extracted using the relatively same analyzing algorithm [41]. Here we propose a special type of embedding where data is not embedded

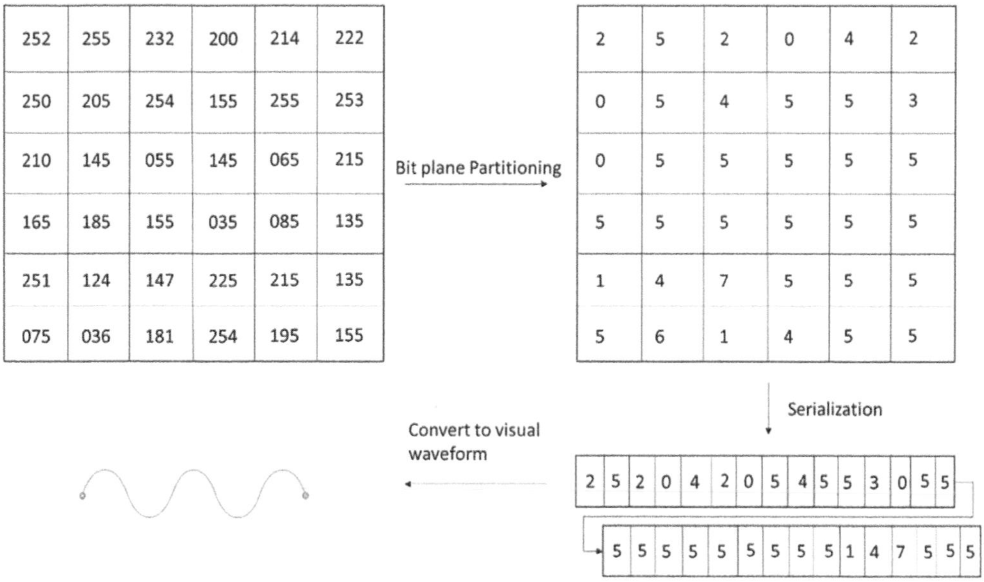

252	255	232	200	214	222
250	205	254	155	255	253
210	145	055	145	065	215
165	185	155	035	085	135
251	124	147	225	215	135
075	036	181	254	195	155

Bit plane Partitioning →

2	5	2	0	4	2
0	5	4	5	5	3
0	5	5	5	5	5
5	5	5	5	5	5
1	4	7	5	5	5
5	6	1	4	5	5

Serialization ↓

2	5	2	0	4	2	0	5	4	5	5	3	0	5	5

5	5	5	5	5	5	5	5	5	1	4	7	5	5	5

Convert to visual waveform ←

FIGURE 7.2
Image to waveform (single channel).

using its ASCII value; instead of that, we have proposed a graphical character database for specific font size. Font size should be kept as small as possible to be non-visual under normal zoom level. The character database is formed using pixel coordinates, and for overlaying first we choose the noisiest region of the image. The noisy region is chosen depending upon the number of different colors under a small block. After choosing the top, left position, using coordinates, targeted pixels are given an offset of a specific constant value (e.g. we have given 10 for implementation). The overlaying should be done on a channel where secret text is not embedded or else secret text can be destroyed.

7.2.1 Embedding Phase Proposed Architecture

Embedding Algorithm

1. Input cover image, secret text
2. Compression method is checked for cover image
3. If compression = lossless
4. Extract channels from image and serialize
5. Load secret text
6. Load character database
7. Input questionnaire
8. Encrypt secret text using Caesar cipher and serialize
9. Check least standard deviation and select channel
10. If length == 1: /* length of RGB pixel value in form of string */
11. New pixel value = new digit extracted from text digit
12. Make it three-digit value (e.g. $3 \geq 003$)
13. Else if length == 2: /* length of RGB pixel value in form of string */
14. Make it three-digit value (e.g. $37 \geq 037$)

15. Value divided by 10 = Value without last digit
16. New pixel value = Value without last digit*10 + new digit extracted from text digit
17. Else if length == 3: /* length of RGB pixel value in form of string */
18. Value divided by 10 = Value without last digit
19. New pixel value = Value without last digit*10 + new digit extracted from text digit
20. Text overlayed in done any channel except previously selected channel
21. Else /* compression = lossy */
22. Not implemented

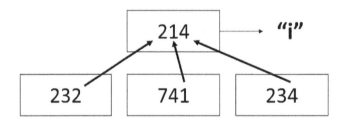

FIGURE 7.3
Secret text's character formation.

After embedding at sender's end, the extraction phase comes at the receiver end. After feeding the stego-image, it is serialized. From each subsequent three groups of pixels, the last digit is extracted and appended to form each letter of secret text as shown in Figure 7.3.

But the characters were encrypted using Caesar encryption, so further the text is decrypted using the key manually entered in run-time.

7.2.2 Extraction Phase

Extraction Algorithm

1. Take three subsequent image pixel values
2. Take an empty string
3. Loop through each pixel value
4. Value modulo 10 = last digit extracted
5. Append the digit to empty string
6. Convert the string to integer which is in ASCII for the character
7. Enter the answer/key for Caesar decryption
8. Subtract the offset value (ASCII value of key) from each character to get the secret text

7.2.3 Proposed Architecture

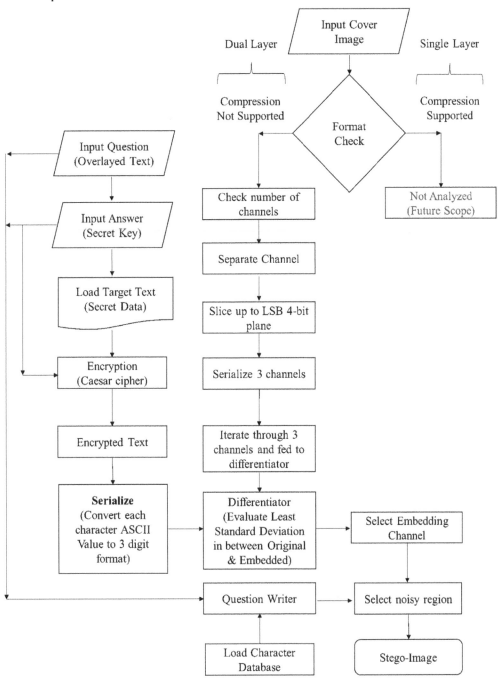

FIGURE 7.4(A)
Embedding phase.

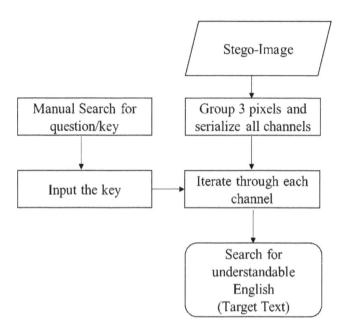

FIGURE 7.4(B)
Extraction phase.

7.3 Implementation and Analysis

In order to appraise the performance of our proposed scheme, we use difference performance and quality metrics like peak signal-to-noise ratio(PSNR), structural similarity index (SSIM); standard images like Lena, fruits, splash, etc.; and standard datasets like CALTECH-BMP, USC-SIPI are considered. We presented all system parameters under the implemented scheme.

7.3.1 Tools and Computing System Parameters

Programming languages: Python is used to build the software based on our proposed scheme, and Java is used to run StegExpose [42] and Weka [43]. The tests were performed using Intel Corei3–3210 with 3.20 GHz processor and 4.0 GB DDR3 RAM.

To execute from training to testing phase, the following steps are executed.

Step 1. Steganography was done on all images from both datasets.

Description:

If the cover image name is cover0.bmp, then the processed or stego-image can be saved as cover0-stego.bmp to discriminate both.

Step 2. Now first for doing the statistical steganalysis, we have used StegExpose tool [42].

Description:

The tool can be downloaded from GitHub. After downloading there will be one folder:"testFolder". We need to settle all the stego-images in that folder. Now to execute the StegExpose, first we need to open the command line at the same directory where StegExpose.jar is present. After that, we need to enter the following command.

Command: "java -jar StegExpose.jar test folder"

Step 3. We have used Weka [43] for machine learning performance analysis.

Description:

After embedding, we have listed all cover and stego-images in a CSV file containing two columns: Image name & Type. Image name is cover0.bmp, cover0-stego.bmp etc. and type is 0/1(Cover/Stego), respectively. After creating the list, we initiated the pre-trained deep learning network Xception for feature extraction. For each image, 2,047 features are extracted. After feature extraction, the generated CSV file was fed to Weka predefined classifiers under 10-fold cross-validation in the ratio of 67:33 (train:test).

In time of feeding a large amount of data, Weka might be stopped as it will not be able to allocate the required amount of memory to process the data [44,45]. So we have used the following command to start Weka from terminal, and explicitly we have declared to allocate 1,024 Megabytes of memory to Java virtual machine for further processing.

Command: java -Xmx1024m -jar weka.jar

7.3.2 Dataset Usage

In our implementation, we use two datasets for performance analysis: CALTECH-BMP [46] and USC-SIPI Aerials, Miscellaneous Images [47]. The USC-SIPI dataset was mainly used for quality analysis of steganography, and CALTECH-BMP was used to check performance analysis of our proposed scheme against statistical analysis and machine learning classification through deep learning feature extraction.

7.3.3 Image Size and Embedded Data Relation

In our implementation, there were mainly two resolutions of three-channel RGB images. For each resolution, we embedded a specific amount of data in one channel. In another channel, the graphical obfuscation was done, and the rest channel was kept untouched. In Table 7.1, image size and embedded data size are mentioned.

TABLE 7.1

Size Factors of Image and Embedded Data

Image Resolution (Width*Height*Channel)	Image Size (pixels)	Embedded Data Size (bits)	Embedding Capacity (bits)
256*256*3	196,608	152,000	1,048,576
512*512*3	786,432	648,000	4,194,304

7.3.4 Proposed Scheme Exceptional Case

The proposed algorithm obfuscates very well and in some cases the image is destroyed. This can be taken as a limitation of the proposed approach, though the system can measure quality of service (QoS) for better performance in hiding.

FIGURE 7.5(A)
Original cover.

FIGURE 7.5(B)
Stego-image (destroyed).

TABLE 7.2

First Four Records from Total 1,500 Records (1,500 images of CALTECH-BMP dataset)

Stego-Image	Cover-Image	Similarity Index
0_fmatted.bmp	C0001.bmp	0.9965529646735172
1_fmatted.bmp	**C0002.bmp**	**0.5974087739707975**
2_fmatted.bmp	C0003.bmp	0.9379443552261453
3_fmatted.bmp	C0004.bmp	0.9816576154939605

From Table 7.2 it is proved that the second image is destroyed after embedding which was shown in Figure 7.5(b).

7.4 Results and Discussion

In this section, our proposed scheme performance factors are evaluated to check the effectiveness. Among the two datasets, USC-SIPI was mainly used to check effectiveness against statistical steganalysis and quality factor analysis, and the other CALTECH-BMP datasets are used to check effectiveness against machine learning and statistical steganalysis.

7.4.1 Statistical Analysis with USC-SIPI Dataset

In Table 7.3, we can notice one image from Aerial was detected under statistical steganalysis.

In Figure 7.6, we represented PSNR of 37 images from Aerial USC-SIPI dataset after steganalysis.

Next, we have chosen some images from miscellaneous under the USC-SIPI dataset. Those images were used to check other statistical properties like mean, median, etc.

7.4.2 Statistical and Machine Learning Analysis with CALTECH-BMPDataset

With CALTECH-BMP dataset, there are different test scenarios which are derived in the Table 7.5.

7.4.2.1 Worst Condition (Destroyed Images Not Filtered)

In Table 7.6, we can observe that the J48 classifier gave a maximum accuracy of 74.3% under the worst condition. Figure 7.7(a) shows the ROC curves for each classifier for better representation.

7.4.2.2 Good Condition (Destroyed Images Filtered)

From Table 7.7, it is noticeable that in good condition, maximum accuracy was only 49.93% using the Decision table. Figure 7.7(b) depicts the ROC curves of different classifier's prediction results at good condition.

TABLE 7.3

Aerial Tests under USC-SIPI Dataset by StegExpose

File Name	Crossed Threshold? (T-TRUE/F-FALSE)	Data Size	Primary Sets	Chi-Square	Sample Pairs	RS Analysis	Fusion (mean)
2.1.01._fmatted.bmp	F	38891	0.04776	0.00262	0.2667	0.1756	0.1483
2.1.02._fmatted.bmp	F	42712	0.04776	0.004061	0.2880	0.1966	0.1629
2.1.03._fmatted.bmp	F	46978	0.04776	0.001359	0.3333	0.2028	0.1791
2.1.04._fmatted.bmp	**T**	**53860**	**0.04776**	**0.002382**	**0.3686**	**0.2452**	**0.2054**
2.1.05._fmatted.bmp	F	40202	0.04776	0.002492	0.2911	0.1663	0.1533
2.1.06._fmatted.bmp	F	31014	0.299953	0.004946	0.0127	0.1555	0.1183
2.1.07._fmatted.bmp	F	31257	0.0726	0.002183	0.2674	0.1346	0.1192
2.1.08._fmatted.bmp	F	39633	0.04776	0.004279	0.2872	0.1620	0.1511
2.1.09._fmatted.bmp	F	35431	0.04776	0.002176	0.2639	0.1392	0.1351
2.1.10._fmatted.bmp	F	30121	0.054389	0.002698	0.2612	0.1412	0.1148
2.1.11._fmatted.bmp	F	34402	0.04776	0.003985	0.2418	0.1478	0.1312
2.1.12._fmatted.bmp	F	40477	0.04776	0.002674	0.2899	0.1705	0.1543
2.2.01._fmatted.bmp	F	63903	0.015743	2.88E-04	0.1452	0.0824	0.0609
2.2.02._fmatted.bmp	F	44798	0.04776	7.61E-04	0.0905	0.0368	0.0427
2.2.03._fmatted.bmp	F	54288	0.04776	6.24E-04	0.1119	0.0427	0.0517
2.2.04._fmatted.bmp	F	45089	0.04776	6.51E-04	0.0836	0.0447	0.043
2.2.05._fmatted.bmp	F	48442	0.04776	9.12E-04	0.0955	0.0421	0.0461
2.2.06._fmatted.bmp	F	61995	0.014208	4.87E-04	0.1424	0.0792	0.0591
2.2.07._fmatted.bmp	F	62665	0.04776	7.78E-04	0.1207	0.0577	0.0597
2.2.08._fmatted.bmp	F	69578	0.04776	6.97E-04	0.1278	0.0705	0.0663
2.2.09._fmatted.bmp	F	41708	0.04776	3.97E-04	0.0842	0.0347	0.0397
2.2.10._fmatted.bmp	F	50626	0.04776	3.31E-04	0.0986	0.0458	0.0482
2.2.11._fmatted.bmp	F	47142	0.056992	5.83E-04	0.0909	0.0312	0.0449
2.2.12._fmatted.bmp	F	21177	0.021426	3.95E-04	0.0407	0.0182	0.0201
2.2.13._fmatted.bmp	F	52953	0.059059	5.15E-04	0.0999	0.0425	0.0504
2.2.14._fmatted.bmp	F	46047	0.047791	6.08E-04	0.0823	0.0448	0.0439
2.2.15._fmatted.bmp	F	53399	0.04776	6.69E-04	0.1066	0.0454	0.0509
2.2.16._fmatted.bmp	F	47790	0.033314	5.55E-04	0.0925	0.0559	0.0455
2.2.17._fmatted.bmp	F	43805	0.004362	0.001142	0.0979	0.0636	0.0417
2.2.18._fmatted.bmp	F	41475	0.02284	4.99E-04	0.0940	0.0407	0.0395
2.2.19._fmatted.bmp	F	52503	0.04776	7.51E-04	0.1043	0.0451	0.0500
2.2.20._fmatted.bmp	F	31143	0.00218	6.45E-04	0.0733	0.0426	0.0297
2.2.21._fmatted.bmp	F	55318	0.04776	7.23E-04	0.1013	0.0561	0.0527
2.2.22._fmatted.bmp	F	43966	0.03248	5.95E-04	0.0902	0.0443	0.0419
2.2.23._fmatted.bmp	F	37512	0.04776	6.00E-04	0.0743	0.0323	0.0357
2.2.24._fmatted.bmp	F	53343	0.03603	5.01E-04	0.1255	0.0414	0.0508
wash-ir._fmatted.bmp	F	209249	0.04776	1.50E-04	0.0680	0.0558	0.0413

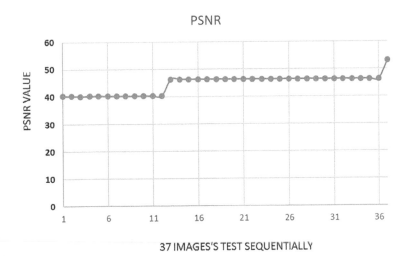

FIGURE 7.6
Thirty-seven image's PSNR under USC-SIPI dataset.

TABLE 7.4

MISC Images Test on Statistical Properties

Serial Number	Statistical Properties of Cover and Stego Images					
1	**4.1.04 Female image properties**					
	Attributes	**Values**	Cover TIFF)		Stego (BMP)	
	Stego text	19KB				
	Above stego threshold?	FALSE				
	Secret message size in bytes	8726				
	Primary Sets	0.080990432				
	Chi-square	Null				
	Sample pairs	0.153042101				
	RS analysis	0.165308962				
	Fusion (mean)	0.133113832				
	Capacity	256*256*3 bytes				
	FOBP	0				
			Attributes	**Values**	**Attributes**	**Values**
			Mean	0.567	**Mean**	0.461
			Median	0.545	**Median**	0.455
			Standard Deviation	0.208	**Standard Deviation**	0.213
			Pixels	65536	**Pixels**	196608

(Continued)

TABLE 7.4

(Continued)

Serial Number	Statistical Properties of Cover and Stego Images			

2   4.1.02 Female image properties

Attributes	Values
Stego text	19KB
Above stego threshold?	FALSE
Secret message size in bytes	11645
Primary sets	0.080990432
Chi-square	Null
Sample pairs	0.224937686
RS analysis	0.130343281
Fusion (mean)	0.177640483
Capacity	256*256*3 bytes
FOBP	0

Cover (TIFF)   Stego (BMP)

Attributes	Values	Attributes	Values
Mean	0.173	Mean	0.129
Median	0.137	Median	0.086
Standard Deviation	0.140	Standard Deviation	0.129
Pixels	65536	Pixels	196608

3   Lena image properties

Attributes	Values
Stego text	81KB
Above stego threshold?	FALSE
Secret message size in bytes	25885
Primary sets	0.018807427
Chi-square	0.001913449
Sample pairs	0.239993506
RS analysis	0.134234913
Fusion (mean)	0.098737324
Capacity	512*512*3bytes
FOBP	0

Cover (TIFF)   Stego (BMP)

Attributes	Values	Attributes	Values
Mean	0.503	Mean	0.501
Median	0.467	Median	0.467
Standard Deviation	0.231	Standard Deviation	0.230
Pixels	786432	Pixels	196608

Serial Number	Statistical Properties of Cover and Stego Images					
4	Fruits image properties					
	Attributes	**Values**	Cover (TIFF)		Stego (BMP)	
	Stego text	81KB				
	Above stego threshold?	FALSE				
	Secret message size in bytes	44471				
	Primary sets	NaN				
	Chi-square	0. 00144562				
	Sample pairs	0. 136823965				
	RS analysis	0. 136062193				
	Fusion (mean)	0. 091443926				
	Capacity	512*512*3				
	FOBP	0				
			Attributes	**Values**	**Attributes**	**Values**
			Mean	0. 434	Mean	0. 432
			Median	0. 424	Median	0. 424
			Standard Deviation	0. 260	Standard Deviation	0. 259
			Pixels	786432	Pixels	786432
5	Splash image properties					
	Attributes	**Values**	Cover (TIFF)		Stego (BMP)	
	Stego text	81KB				
	Above stego threshold?	FALSE				
	Secret message size in bytes	23973				
	Primary sets	NaN				
	Chi-square	0.00144562				
	Sample pairs	0. 136823965				
	RS analysis	0. 136062193				
	Fusion (mean)	0. 091443926				
	Capacity	512*512*3				
	FOBP	0				
			Attributes	**Values**	**Attributes**	**Values**
			Mean	0. 427	Mean	0. 425
			Median	0. 271	Median	0. 271
			Standard Deviation	0. 289	Standard Deviation	0. 289
			Pixels	786432	Pixels	786432

TABLE 7.5

Implementation Scenarios

As we already discussed regarding the exceptional negative impact in Section 7.3.4, we tested our algorithm in two cases or conditions. At one condition, after embedding image is exported even if SSIM is less than 90%, and in the other case, images are exported only when SSIM is greater than or equal to 90%. After embedding, there were datasets containing all 1,000 and remaining 832 images to be tested under worst and good conditions, respectively.

$$f(x) = \{Worst\ Case(1000\ images), SSIM < 90\% Good\ Case(832\ images), SSIM \geq 90\%$$

Worst Case	
Case	**Implemented Summary**
Statistical analysis	Total images for testing: 1,000, 5.4% of images were correctly classified
Machine learning analysis with deep learning	Total images for testing: cover (1,000) + stego (1,000) = 2,000 Total features extracted: 2,000*2,047 = approx. 40 Lakhs 94 thousand Classification result is presented in Section 7.4.2.1
Good Case	
Case	**Implemented Parameters**
Statistical analysis	Total images for testing: 832, 2.55% images were correctly classified
Machine learning analysis with deep learning	Total images for testing: cover (832) + stego (832) = 1,664 Total features extracted: 1,664*2,047 = approx. 34 Lakhs 6 thousand Classification result is presented in Section 7.4.2.2

TABLE 7.6

Different Machine Learning Classifier Results on Multiple Parameters in a Worst Condition

Technique	TP Rate	FP Rate	Accuracy (Percentage)	Precision (Percentage)	ROC-Area (Percentage)
Naive Bayes	0.65	0.34	65.2	66.5	71
Random Forest	0.71	0.28	71.1	71.1	78.1
SMO	0.735	0.265	73.5	73.5	73.5
AdaBoostM1	0.66	0.33	66.3	66.3	73.1
Bayes Net	0.64	0.35	64.8	65.1	71.2
Decision Table	0.63	0.36	63.4	63.4	68
J48	**0.74**	**0.25**	**74.3**	**74.3**	**81.2**
Logit-Boost	0.66	0.34	66	66	74.1

Note: TP, true positive; FP, false positive; ROC, receiver operating characteristics.

7.4.3 Effectiveness in Implementation

We demonstrated our scheme using different explanations and evaluated with more than one performance metric. And in this last section of the results and discussion, we discuss the effectiveness of our proposed scheme.

- Two layers of security: Obfuscation helps to meet the steganography objective and the encryption layer makes the hidden data secure from an adversary.
- Here the secret text was taken from lorem-ipsum website [48]. The 81 KB of data was made by repeatedly copying the same portion of data from lorem-ipsum website.

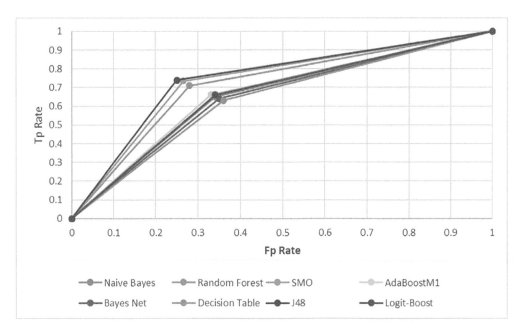

FIGURE 7.7(A)
ROC curve of different machine learning classifier's prediction results at worst condition.

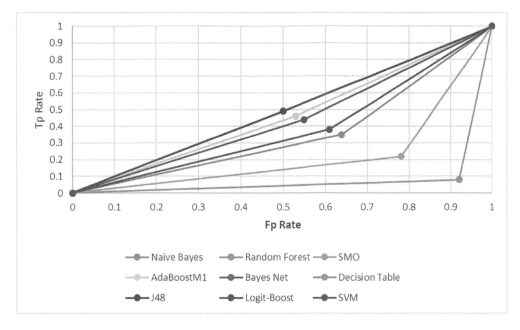

FIGURE 7.7(B)
ROC curve of different machine learning classifier's prediction result at good condition.

TABLE 7.7

Different Machine Learning Classifier's Prediction Results on Multiple Parameters at Good Condition

Technique	TP Rate	FP Rate	Accuracy (Percentage)	Precision (Percentage)	ROC-Area (Percentage)
Naïve Bayes	0.35	0.64	35.75	31.6	29.8
Random Forest	0.08	0.92	7.99	8	1.7
SMO	0.219	0.781	21.87	21.9	21.9
AdaBoostM1	0.46	0.53	46.39	46.3	44.2
Bayes Net	0.49	0.5	49.87	49.8	49.8
Decision Table	**0.49**	**0.5**	**49.93**	**49.9**	**50**
J48	0.49	0.5	49.87	49.8	49.8
Logit-Boost	0.38	0.61	38.64	38.6	34.5
SVM	0.44	0.55	44.29	44.2	44.3

Note: TP, true positive; FP, false positive; ROC, receiver operating characteristics.

FIGURE 7.8
Visual embedding of answer or key.

So, if the data is serialized, then we will see a symmetrical waveform which also signifies that the secret text contains a pattern. This could be a very exploitation against hidden though the proposed scheme successfully could obfuscate it from get detected.

- From Figure 7.8, we can see the overlaid key is nearly visible after zooming and which cannot be extracted without human intervention. Standard OCRs might not be able to do key extraction as the fontsize and visibility are less. So, if the obfuscation layer is suspected, then also with automation it is nearly infeasible to break the encryption layer.

7.5 Conclusion

We observe that deep learning in steganalysis is currently rising day by day. Taking this into consideration, this paper put forward a data-hiding scheme to address the specified challenges. The analysis was done on different standard steganography datasets with standard machine learning classifiers, deep learning feature extractor and statistical measures. Explicitly, the proposed work demonstrates quality analysis. From results, it can be inferred that the proposed steganography algorithm gives a significant performance and is capable of withstanding against statistical and machine learning steganalysis attacks. The proposed scheme is very lightweight so it can be used in different industrial security applications, e.g. Internet of Things communication under Industry 4.0 revolution. One more beneficial side of this research is that one layer of embedding was done in graphical space without ASCII value injection which is subjected to anti-automation attacks. As a future direction of the present work, instead of BMP images, GIF images as a dataset can be used to improve the capacity and security of the algorithm.

7.6 Availability of Data, Material and Code

All materials required to reproduce the results are available at the following Google drive link: https://drive.google.com/file/d/1MlRqMe01vxoAITG_3HUZTqlUWp6SMNVu/view?usp=sharing

7.7 Acknowledgements

We are grateful to the editor and other anonymous reviewers for their valuable response.

References

[1] Zhang M, Zhang Y, Jiang Y, Shen J. Obfuscating eves algorithm and its application in fair electronic transactions in public cloud systems. *IEEE System Journal*. 2019;13(2):1478–1486. [Google Scholar]

[2] Cheng K, Wang L, Shen Y, Wang H, Wang Y, Jiang X, et al. Secure K-NN query on encrypted cloud data with multiple keys. *IEEE Transactions on Big Data*. 2017;7(4):689–702. [Google Scholar]

[3] Wang H, Zhang Z, Taleb T. Special issue on security and privacy of IoT. *World Wide Web*. 2018;21(1):1–6. [Google Scholar]

[4] Ozcan S, Mustacoglu AF. Transfer learning effects on image steganalysis with pre-trained deep residual neural network model. *2018 IEEE International Conference on Big Data (Big Data)*. IEEE, 2018. http://doi.org/10.1109/bigdata.2018.8622437

[5] Khan A, Siddiqa A, Munib S, Malik SA. A recent survey of reversible watermarking techniques. *Information Sciences*. 2014;279:251–272.

[6] Subhedar MS, Mankar VH. Current status and key issues in image steganography: A survey. *Computer Science Review*. 2014;13:95–113.

[7] Nissar A, Mir AH. Classification of steganalysis techniques: A study. *Digital Signal Processing*. 2010;20:1758–1770.

[8] Cho S, Cha BH, Gawecki M, Kuo CC. Block-based image steganalysis: Algorithm and performance evaluation. *Journal of Visual Communication and Image Representation*. 2013;24:846–856.

[9] Schmidhuber J. Deep learning in neural networks: An overview. *Neural Networks*. 2015;61:85–117.

[10] Zhang M, Zhang Y, Su Y, Huang Q, Mu Y. Attribute-based hash proof system under learning-with-errors assumption in obfuscator-free and leakage-resilient environments. *IEEE Systems Journal*. 2015;11(2):1018–1026.

[11] Karampidis K, Kavallieratour E, Papadourakis G. A review of image steganalysis techniques for digital forensics. *Journal of Information Security and Applications*. 2018;40:217–235.

[12] Musumeci F, et al. 2018. An overview on application of machine learning techniques in optical networks. *Computer Science, Cornell University Library*. October 2018:1–27. https://arxiv.org/abs/1803.07976

[13] Pretrained Deep Neural Networks. https://in.mathworks.com/help/deeplearning/ug/pre-trained-convolutional-neural-networks.html

[14] Chollet F. Xception: Deep learning with depth wise separable convolutions. In: *Proceedings of the IEEE Conference on Computer Vision and Pattern Recognition*. 2017, pp. 1251–1258.

[15] Millman R. The dark side of automation. December 19, 2018. www.infosecurity-magazine.com/magazine-features/the-dark-side-of-automation/

[16] Mielikainen J. LSB matching revisited. *IEEE Signal Processing Letters*. 2006;13(5):285–287. [Google Scholar]

[17] Zhang X, Wang S. Efficient steganographic embedding by exploiting modification direction. *IEEE Communications Letters*. 2006;10(11):781–783. http://doi.org/10.1109/LCOMM.2006.060863

[18] Kim HJ, Kim C, Choi Y, Wang S, Zhang X. Improved modification direction methods. *Computers and Mathematics with Applications*. 2010;60(2):319–325. http://doi.org/10.1016/j.camwa.2010.01.006

[19] Chang C, Chou Y, Kieu T. An information hiding scheme using Sudoku. In: *2008 3rd International Conference on Innovative Computing Information and Control*. IEEE, 2008, pp. 17–17.

[20] Hong W, Chen T. A novel data embedding method using adaptive pixel pair matching. *IEEE Transactions on Information Forensics and Security*. 2012;7(1):176–184. http://doi.org/10.1109/TIFS.2011.2155062

[21] Chen J. A PVD-based data hiding method with histogram preserving using pixel pair matching. *Signal Processing: Image Communication*. 2014;29(3):375–384. http://doi.org/10.1016/j.image.2014.01.003

[22] Chang C-C, Liu Y, Nguyen T-S. A novel turtle shell based scheme for data hiding. In: *2014 Tenth International Conference on Intelligent Information Hiding and Multimedia Signal Processing*. IEEE, 2014, pp. 89–93.

[23] Liu L, Chang C, Wang A. Data hiding based on extended turtle shell matrix construction method. *Multimedia Tools and Applications*. 2017;76(10):12233–12250.

[24] Chang C-C, Liu Y. Fast turtle shell-based data embedding mechanisms with good visual quality. *Journal of Real-Time Image Processing*. 2019;16(3):589–599. [Google Scholar]

[25] Liu Y, Zhong Q, Chang L, Xia Z, He D, Cheng C. A secure data backup scheme using multi-factor authentication. *IET Information Security*. 2016;11(5):250–255.

[26] Martínez-González RF, Díaz-Méndez JA, Palacios-Luengas L, López-Hernández J, Vázquez-Medina R. A steganographic method using Bernoulli's chaotic maps. *Computers and Electrical Engineering*. 2016;54:435–449. http://doi.org/10.1016/j.compeleceng.2015.12.005

[27] Yadav GS, Ojha A. Chaotic system-based secure data hiding scheme with high embedding capacity. *Computers and Electrical Engineering*. 2018;69:447–460. http://doi.org/10.1016/j.compeleceng.2018.02.022

[28] Rasool ZI, Al-Jarrah M. The detection of data hiding in RGB images using statistical steganalysis. Thesis, CS, Middle East University.

[29]   Joshi K, Gill S, Yadav R. A new method of image steganography using 7th bit of a pixel as indicator by introducing the successive temporary pixel in the grayscale image. *Journal of Computer Networks and Communications*. 2018;2018:Article ID 9475142:10 pages. https://doi.org/10.1155/2018/9475142

[30]   Rasras R, Alqadi Z, Rasmi M, Mutaz AS. A methodology based on steganography and cryptography to protect highly secure messages. *Engineering, Technology & Applied Science Research*. 2019;9:3681–3684.

[31]   Qin J, Luo Y, Xiang X, Tan Y, Huang H. Coverless image steganography: A survey. *IEEE Access*. 2019;7:171372–171394. https://doi.org/10.1109/ACCESS.2019.2955452

[32]   Durafe A, Patidar V. Development and analysis of IWT-SVD and DWT-SVD steganography using fractal cover. *Journal of King Saud University—Computer and Information Sciences*. 2020. http://doi.org/10.1016/j.jksuci.2020.10.008

[33]   Qian Z, Huang C, Wang Z, Zhang X. Breaking CNN-based steganalysis. In: Pan JS, Lin JW, Sui B, Tseng SP (eds) *Genetic and Evolutionary Computing*. ICGEC 2018. Advances in Intelligent Systems and Computing, vol. 834. Springer, Singapore, 2019. https://doi.org/10.1007/978-981-13-5841-8_50

[34]   Lee JH, Shin J, Realff MJ. Machine Learning: Overview of the recent progresses and implications for the process systems engineering field. *Computer and Chemical Engineering*. 2018;114:111–121.

[35]   Rashid A, Rahim M. Critical analysis of steganography an art of hidden writing. *International Journal of Security and Its Applications*. 2016;10:259–282. http://doi.org/10.14257/ijsia.2016.10.3.24

[36]   Canziani A, Paszke A, Culurciello E. An analysis of deep neural network models for practical applications. *arXiv preprint arXiv:1605.07678* (2016).

[37]   Shelke SG, Jagtap SK. Analysis of spatial domain image steganography techniques. In: *2015 International Conference on Computing Communication Control and Automation*, Pune, India, 2015, pp. 665–667. http://doi.org/10.1109/ICCUBEA.2015.136.

[38]   Hussain M, Abdul Wahab AW, Idna Bin Idris YI, Ho ATS, Jung K-H. Image steganography in spatial domain: A survey. *Signal Processing: Image Communication*. 2018;65:46–66, ISSN 0923–5965. https://doi.org/10.1016/j.image.2018.03.012.

[39]   Febryan A, Purboyo TW, Saputra RE. Analysis of steganography on TIFF image using spread spectrum and adaptive method. *Journal of Engineering and Applied Sciences*. 2020;15(2):373–379, ISSN 1816–949X. http://doi.org/10.14257/ijsia.2016.10.3.24.

[40]   Sharma N, Batra U. A review on spatial domain technique based on image steganography. In: *2017 International Conference on Computing and Communication Technologies for Smart Nation (IC3TSN)*, Gurgaon, IEEE, 2017, pp. 24–27. http://doi.org/10.1109/IC3TSN.2017.8284444.

[41]   Lee C, Chang C, Wang K. An improvement of EMD embedding method for large payloads by pixel segmentation strategy. *Image and Vision Computing*. 2008;26(12):1670–1676. http://doi.org/10.1016/j.imavis.2008.05.005.

[42]   StegExpose. https://github.com/b3dk7/StegExpose

[43]   Weka, The Workbench for Machine Learning. www.cs.waikato.ac.nz/ml/weka/

[44]   Ozcan S, Mustacoglu AF. Transfer learning effects on image steganalysis with pre-trained deep residual neural network model. In: *2018 IEEE International Conference on Big Data (Big Data)*. IEEE, 2018. http://doi.org/10.1109/bigdata.2018.8622437

[45]   Jung K-H. A study on Machine Learning for steganalysis. In: *Proceedings of the 3rd International Conference on Machine Learning and Soft Computing—ICMLSC 2019*. 2019, pp. 12–15. http://doi.org/10.1145/3310986.3311000

[46]   Al-Jarrah M. RGB-BMP steganalysis dataset. *Mendeley Data*. 2018;V1. http://doi.org/10.17632/sp4g8h7v8k.1

[47]   The USC-SIPI Image Database. http://sipi.usc.edu/database/

[48]   lipsum.com

Appendix

1. Caesar encryption key, input from user

```
ques=input('Enter security key (one character) (a-zA-Z): ')
ques _ val=ord(ques)
```

2. Convert characters of string (target hidden data) to list of decimal values

```
rdata=''
with open("target.txt") as f:
    rdata=f.read()

rdata _ l=list(bytes(rdata.encode()))
rdata _ len=len(rdata _ l)
```

3. RGB channels serialization

```
for i in range(rows):
 for j in range(cols):
 blue.append(image[i,j][0])
 green.append(image[i,j][1])
 red.append(image[i,j][2])
```

4. Data embedding in each channel

```
if len(text)<=len(blue):
    temp _ ind=0
    for word in range(len(text)):
        if len(str(blue[word]))>=2:
            temp _ blue.append((10*int(blue[word]/10))+text[word])
            temp _ ind=word
        else:
            temp _ blue.append(text[word])
            temp _ ind=word
    if temp _ ind!=len(blue)-1:
        for a in range((temp _ ind+1),len(blue)):
            temp _ blue.append(blue[a])

    temp _ ind=0
    for word in range(len(text)):
        if len(str(green[word]))>=2:
            temp _ green.append((10*int(green[word]/10))+text[word])
            temp _ ind=word
        else:
            temp _ green.append(text[word])
            temp _ ind=word
    if temp _ ind!=len(green)-1:
        for a in range((temp _ ind+1),len(green)):
            temp _ green.append(green[a])

    temp _ ind=0
    for word in range(len(text)):
        if len(str(red[word]))>=2:
            temp _ red.append((10*int(red[word]/10))+text[word])
            temp _ ind=word
        else:
```

```
        temp _ red.append(text[word])
        temp _ ind=word
    if temp _ ind!=len(red)-1:
        for a in range((temp _ ind+1),len(red)):
            temp _ red.append(red[a])
```

5. After data embedding standard deviation is checked for each channel

```
result1 = np.subtract(blue,temp _ blue)
result2 = np.subtract(green,temp _ green)
result3 = np.subtract(red,temp _ red)
```

6. Graphical character embedding and stego-image export

```
diff=0
for a in ques:
        val=ord(a)
        if val>=97 and val<=122:
            val=26+(val-97)
        elif val>=65 and val<=90:
            val=val-65

        minv=min([i[0] for i in characters[val]])
        maxv=max([i[0] for i in characters[val]])
        diff+=(maxv-minv)
        for b in characters[val]:
            if choose==1:
                image[b[1],b[0]-minv+diff+40][1]+=30
                image[b[1],b[0]-minv+diff+40][2]+=30
            elif choose==2:
                image[b[1],b[0]-minv+diff+40][0]+=30
                image[b[1],b[0]-minv+diff+40][2]+=30
            else:
                image[b[1],b[0]-minv+diff+40][1]+=30
                image[b[1],b[0]-minv+diff+40][0]+=30

    cv2.imwrite('output/'+str(counter)+' _ fmatted'+'.bmp',image)
    print('Exported in output directory')
```

7. Hidden data extraction from stego-image

```
def extract(filename):
    image = cv2.imread(filename)
    rows,cols,ch = image.shape
    data=''
    blue1=[]
    green1=[]
    red1=[]
    ques1=input('Enter security key:  ')
    ques _ val1=ord(ques1)
    print('key',ques _ val1)

    for i in range(rows):
      for j in range(cols):
        blue1.append(image[i,j][0])
        green1.append(image[i,j][1])
        red1.append(image[i,j][2])
```

```
j=1
for i in zip(*[iter(red1)]*3):
    try:
        # print(int(str((i[0]%10))+str((i[1]%10))+str((i[2]%10))))
        data+=chr((int(str((i[0]%10))+str((i[1]%10))+str
        ((i[2]%10)))-ques_val1))
    except:
        pass
print(data)
```

8. PSNR calculation

```
def psnr(path1,path2):
        original = cv2.imread(path1)
        contrast = cv2.imread(path2)
        d = cv2.PSNR(original, contrast)
        return d
```

9. SSIM calculation

```
def ssim_val(path1,path2):
    imageA = cv2.imread(path1)
    imageB = cv2.imread(path2)
    # convert the images to grayscale
    grayA = cv2.cvtColor(imageA, cv2.COLOR_BGR2GRAY)
    grayB = cv2.cvtColor(imageB, cv2.COLOR_BGR2GRAY)
    (score, diff) = compare_ssim(grayA, grayB, full=True)
    diff = (diff * 255).astype("uint8")
    return score
```

8

Rectal Cancer Magnetic Resonance Image Segmentation

Srivaramangai R.

CONTENTS

8.1 Introduction

Medical image segmentation plays a very important role in the diagnosis using computer-aided systems. The radiological images such as magnetic resonance imaging (MRI), computed tomography (CT), positron emission tomography (PET), colonoscopy, etc., are obtained from the respective scanners with high-density resolutions. The images are acquired using the scanners of big companies like GE, Siemens, etc., where the proprietary software makes it possible to save and display the captured images on computers from the machines. These images are then analysed by radiologists and oncologists for further diagnosis/prognosis. Though the latest machines give a very clear image of the organ under study, when computer-aided systems are to be built for diagnosis, image processing techniques need to be used. It is essential to have an automated system for extracting the region of interest (ROI) so as to support the radiologist with granular level information about the properties of the images. In order to mine the ROI, segmentation techniques are crucial.

The American Joint Committee for Cancer (AJCC) [27] and the National Comprehensive Cancer Network (NCNN) [28] have emphasized TNM staging (Tumour-Node-Metastasis) in which for the T staging the focus is more on the affected organ under consideration. The standards of TNM staging have been prescribed in AJCC which are globally followed by

DOI: 10.1201/9781003218111-8

radiologists and oncologists. While following these standards in the automated process of medical diagnosis, one of the components of image processing of MRI images is segmentation, where so far 100% automation is yet a challenge. Though we need to work on the ROI, it has its own limitations of human intervention. There are several semi-automatic segmentation methods and also some fully automatic segmentation methods where the accuracy needs to be improved. This is because in medical diagnosis, unless all the performance measures reach 100%, the implementation in actual practice will be difficult as it will again need a human intervention or lead to wrong outputs.

Cancer found in the rectal area of the human body is known as rectal cancer. Sometimes the cancer is also referred to as colorectal cancer since the chances of spread of cancer from the colon to the rectum or the rectum to the colon are high. According to the American Cancer Society, it is the third most common cancer in men and the second most common cancer in women. The American Cancer Society predicted an increase in colorectal cancer cases with 44% being rectal cancer. Colorectal tumour areas are usually manually delineated from volumetric MRI data by an oncologist or radiologist [2]. This manual delineation or segmentation takes time and effort, and there are high chances of variability in each expert's observation. As the slices are taken in large, the shape and size also may vary. Depending on the current and voltage levels and also on Tesla, the intensity is also not consistent. So, it is essential to have automated segmentation of the ROI from large volumetric data where sometimes the nearby nodes and organs are also captured during examination. Several research works have been done on applying the segmentation techniques for rectal MRI. Yet there is a lot of room for improvement of the result since a lot of inconsistencies exist as mentioned earlier. Apart from the regular segmentation techniques, the latest research shows the application of methods like deep learning, atlas methods, super voxel clustering methods, two-dimensional convolutional neural network (CNN) and three-dimensional (3D) CNN. According to TNM staging of AJCC standards, the primary tumour detection is locus to the area under observation where T is the primary stage. If the primary stage is detected and treated, there is a high chance of recovery possible as per AJCC. The T staging diagnosis required the extraction of the rectal area alone from the entire MRI image. Though the MRI might have been taken for the abdominal pelvic area, there are chances of having nearby lymph nodes and organs captured in the image. So, it is essential to segment the region of interest, i.e. the rectal area, to diagnose the existence of malignancy and if found to further investigate the primary stages, i.e. T1, T2, T3 and T4. Thus, segmentation becomes a very important factor in the diagnosis of rectal cancer from radiological images.

This work is an attempt to have a fully automated segmentation method for the axial T2 weighted MRI images of rectal cancer. It is always better to try to work with existing techniques if they have been proven in other problem spaces. If those techniques are able to give better results, that will reduce the time of innovating new techniques. Still, when the existing technique is used, it needs a lot of preprocessing, and selection of features and masking methods will differ according to the problem space. Innovation occurs in selecting the right input, preprocessing and setting parameters for segmentation [1]. This chapter deals with comparing the existing techniques against the proposed technique known as M-R-CNN. M-R-CNN is a method used for segmentation of other types of images like road traffic images, floral images, etc. The data has been collected from various cancer hospitals, MRI scanning centres across India like MIOT Hospital, Chennai, India; Amrita Hospital, Cochin; and Lakeshore Hospital, Cochin. The author had periodic discussion with the domain experts like oncologists and radiologists belonging to Tata Memorial Hospital and Nanavati Hospital, both in Mumbai; MIOT hospital and Adyar Hospital, both in Chennai;

and Amrita Hospital and Lakeshore Hospital, both in Cochin. The method currently used by the experts are biopsy and individual scanning as per the location of the organ. Since these domain experts have suggested that MRI is widely used for rectal cancer especially and the scanners used in India are mostly from General Electric and Siemens, the MRI images data thus obtained are from these two original equipment manufacturer based MRI scanners from the previously mentioned sources. Whenever we do any research, the performance and outcome need to be tested with a large data set. The data obtained for rectal cancer from these sources were very few, and since there are ethical issues in obtaining more data, some of the radiologists suggested obtaining more data from an open data repository such as Radiopedia, Radiology Assistant, or the Cancer Genome Atlas, and these data were shown to the experts in order to clarify the understanding of the data properties. The significance of this research is to use the proven method of M-R-CNN, which is a combination of CNN, ResNet, fuzzy based convolutional neural network (F-CNN) and region proposal network (RPN) with masking. M-R-CNN has been extensively used in segmentation of remote sensed images, automobile images, etc., other than the segmentation of rectal MRI. This will contribute a lot to the radiologists as a support system in creating one more level of confirmation before diagnosing and prescribing the right treatment.

8.2 Anatomical Structure of Rectum

The rectum is the last portion of the large intestine. Figure 8.1 illustrates the position of the rectum in the human body. Here we can observe that the colon in the large intestine connects with the rectum in the posterior abdominal area. Fecal matter is collected in the rectum from the colon before being evacuated through the anus. From inside the organ, the

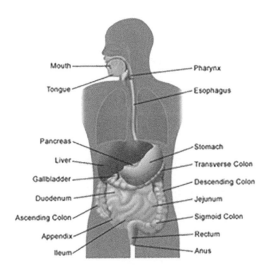

FIGURE 8.1
Anatomy of large intestine and rectum in human body (JohnHopkinsmedicine.org).

innermost layer is known as mucosa. The mucosa is protected by the next layer known as submucosa. The submucosa protects the mucosa by providing nutrients and oxygen through the blood vessels and nerves. The submucosa is covered by a muscular layer known as muscularis propia which expands and contracts, thus allowing the mucosa to expel the feces. The last and outermost layer is known as serosa which protects the entire rectum from any damage. The understanding of these layers is very important since the spread of the cancer and its staging are determined by what layer the cancer is present and has crossed.

8.3 Magnetic Resonance Imaging as Modality for Rectal Cancer

According to Horvat et al. [29], extracting the rectal region using MRI for primary staging of rectal cancer is very important and essential. MRI rectal segmentation is thus significant for the assessment of the location of the tumour and morphology which describes the shape and structure. Thus, the segmentation will help in knowing the details of primary staging, otherwise known as the 'T' category, spread of the cancer from the rectum to the anal sphincter, the status of the circumferential resection margin, the cancer spread to the pelvic sidewall, extramural vascular invasion of the cancer, and also spread to nearby nodes, called the 'N' category [4]. As per the expert's opinion, MRI is a much preferred method compared to other methods for rectal cancer detection. This is due to the clarity of the image and the granular information that can be obtained in MRI [2,26]. As per the 2018 American Cancer Society Cancer Facts and Figures, MRI helps the domain experts to plan the treatment in primary staging of rectal cancer. Figure 8.2 is an example of rectal MRI.

MRI, as the name indicates, is purely based on the magnetic properties of the atom. A magnetic field is applied uniformly to align the protons in the water nuclei of the tissues of the organ. During the process of rest by the nuclei, the radio frequency (RF) is emitted. By varying the RF pulses, the MRI is able to produce different images [25]. The following terminologies are very important in understanding the MRI image properties:

- Slice: One image at a time is a slice. There can be many slices produced during one examination. The standard is 1,000 images per exam.
- TR: Repetition Time: The time taken between one RF pulse and another for the same slice.
- TE: Time to Echo: The difference in time between the RF pulse and echo signal.

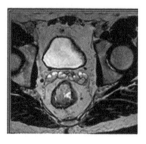

FIGURE 8.2
MRI of rectal cancer (the Cancer Genome Atlas).

MRI scans in three major orientations, namely, axial, coronal and sagittal [3]. In all these orientations, the weightage model is applied where T1 weighted and T2 weighted are contrasted in nature. The T1 and T2 weights are the relaxation time applied to the image in order to characterize the tissues. Thus, T1 is the longitudinal RT, and T2 is transverse RT. T1 is obtained by having short TE and TR times, whereas T2 is obtained by having longer TE and TR times. The MRI images are in gray colour due to which the colour of the image cannot be taken as a property. The white and black colour tissues within organ can interchange as per T1 or T2 weighted image [5]. So the features of the rectum in MRI are mainly based on the intensity levels otherwise known as textural parameters. But the irregular shapes can be considered with its variants as different shapes and can allow us to segment the images.

8.4 Literature Survey of Existing Segmentation Techniques

The research and development of computer-aided systems for diagnosis of various diseases has been taking place for more than two decades. Computer scientists along with the domain experts have been trying to bring a support system for the medical professionals, and the evolution of systems are enormous. Yet there are certain areas where there is a need for a full-fledged system. In rural areas, the lack of medical professionals and the availability of expensive medical equipment means that it takes a longer time to get the examination done. In such cases, the computer-aided systems can bring faster solutions for critical diseases like cancer. This section deals with the existing research which has already been done in the segmentation of MRI images, rectal images in particular and medical images on the whole.

Meng et al. [6] proposed a novel multi-task learning network which has a combined effort of classification, detection and segmentation. The proposed system is named as MSBC-net, and they have found that the proposed method outperforms the other methods they have compared in their literature. Hongwei et al. [7] have used the deep learning method which used a multiple view approach to segment the claustrum I brain T1-weighted MRI scans. Claustrum is the layer of gray matter in rectal tissues which gives the variation in intensity due to cell damage. So, claustrum was their focus, and they have found that the deep learning–based segmentation of claustrum was successful when a large data set is applied for training. Further, the delineation of gray matter was well done in other orientations compared to sagittal images. Zhu et al. [8] have used the U-Net model for automated segmentation of diffusion-weighted images of rectal MRI. For comparison of the result of the deep learning U-Net model, the semi-automatic segmentation with threshold value was considered. The deep learning was successfully able to identify the rectal area and surrounding area. Zhao et al. discusses segmentation of lymph nodes from the MRI images [9]. The method framed as auto-LNDS used deep learning and very efficiently segmented the lymph nodes. This system focuses on N stage diagnosis rather than T stage. The research on automated segmentation of colorectal MRI images using 3D T2 weighted images [10] deals with 3D MSDenseNet in order to segment the colorectal tumour, and they have compared the proposed method with their own earlier research methods like 3D U-Net and 3D DenseVoxNet and also with the conventional neural networks and other machine learning algorithms. The proposed method works well the 3D T2 weighted images. The work on Neutrosophic medical image analysis [11] is a compilation of various research performed on different medical images, and the main focus was given for ultrasonic images. As the behavioural properties of ultrasound images and MRI images of rectum vary, the methods used are not suitable for rectal cancer diagnosis. An automated deep learning model (DLM) was used by Laukamp et al. [12] for brain MRI segmentation and further diagnosis. Guo et al. [13] in their work on multimodality image processing have used deep learning as the technique for segmenting the images from various modalities which proved to be a successful method with convolutional neural networks. Voronstov et al. [14] illustrated how the segmentation of tumours found in the liver can be automated by using deep learning if that tumour is the result of a metastatic state from colorectal cancer. The images used are CT images, and the performance was found better with CNN with minor corrections done manually. The fully automatic method did not happen to the expected level of accuracy. Wang et al. [15] used deep learning for rectal MRI images and showed that the method used for segmentation performs to the nearest approximation of human intervention when T2 weighted images are used. Feng et al. [16] have proposed a semi-supervised deep learning model for the minimal amount of data that can be obtained and to segment the pelvic regions. Initially the system is trained with fully convolutional network (FCN) and upon that when test data are applied, the untrained data are getting segmented to obtain the focus area. The FCN trains the system with the limited labels and thus the deep learning is able to extract the unlabelled elements. Liu et al. [17], in their study on survey of applications of deep learning to MRI images, have found that in most of the medical image processing, deep learning has been found successful, though there are still some challenges with the segmentation of irregular-shaped organs or tissues. Nie et al. [18], have proposed a semi-supervised deep learning method which they named ASDNet. The training to do segmentation has been carried out by using the FCN which creates a confidence map. Using this map, they have used a semi-supervised method based on region identification which is then able to identify the unlabelled segments and extract them. The research proposed this method with better accuracy for segmentation. Kalyani and Swami [19] have used K-means clustering for segmenting the rectal region from the pelvic MRI images. They used MATLAB coding for carrying out the task and found the accuracy to be higher than other earlier methods in segmentation. The earlier research work to all these have shown that deep learning is very heavily used, though some have proposed methods of support vector machines, decision trees, etc. Most of the earlier work on segmentation deals with semi-automated segmentation where a manual intervention is required [22]. The latest works discuss fully automated segmentation, and deep learning with some modifications or combinations have been heavily used for this purpose [20,21].

8.5 Comparison of Existing Techniques

The methods which were proposed in some of the earlier research with a comparatively higher accuracy were taken for comparison. As per the expert opinion, axial images play a more important role than other orientations [24]. So, for this research purpose, the axial T2 weighted images were taken, and the images were obtained from some collections from leading hospitals. The Cancer Genome Atlas data repository, Radiopedia and PubMed also provided a lot of data with the description of each image and its properties and the diagnosis reports from the domain experts. Following are the existing techniques most widely used which are taken for comparison to apply on the collected data set:

1. 3D MSDenseNet
2. FCN
3. DLM

8.5.1 Three-Dimensional MSDenseNet

Three-dimensional MSDenseNet [10], which is nothing but a 3D multiscale densely connected CNN is an automated segmentation method proposed in the referred research paper for 3D volumetric segmentation of colorectal cancer MRI. The method used coarser scales for 2D depth 3D densely interconnected convolutional layers. The scale is used to generate individually low- and high-level features. In order to improve the segmentation results and to have efficient results, they have used a propagation layout of diagonal in nature where the first layer has coarse features, followed by depth features with local and global information describing the contextual part the network. The method is based on volume-to-volume learning and interference, that eradicates computation redundancy. This method has been tested and evaluated on colorectal tumor segmentation in 3D MRI, and it has attained outperformed segmentation results in comparison with previous baseline methods compared by the authors in their research work.

Figure 8.3 illustrates the working of MSDenseNet in which the first layer is a unique layer where the division of the feature map present in the first convolution layer is in terms of scale s2 via pooling of step raised to 2. Here the feature maps and the horizontal paths are densely connected with each other. The resolution of the feature maps X^1l is very high along the next layers l > 1. The output feature maps are brought out in the next layers in

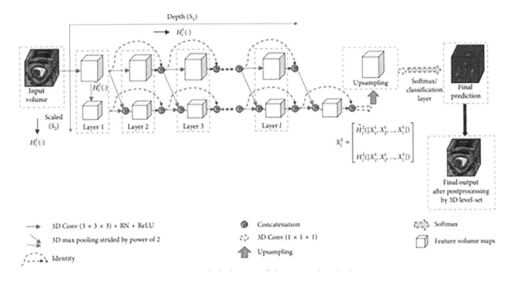

FIGURE 8.3
Working of 3D MSDenseNet [10].

a vertical path by means of concatenating the transformed feature maps of the previous layers in s1 and s2 using coarse scaling technique. This method is incorporated in the current research to test whether it can be the powerful method of obtaining the rectal region, overcoming the drawbacks of the earlier methods. The experimental results are discussed with other methods of comparison in this section.

8.5.2 Fully Convolutional Network

An FCN is another machine learning artificial neural network in which 1×1 convolutions are used to perform the task equivalent to the dense layers found in other network algorithms. In FCN, the first step is to extract image features (for image segmentation) using CNN. The obtained numbers of channels are then transformed into that many numbers of classes using $1 \times 11 \times 1$ convolutional layer. The final step is to transform or map the height and width of the feature maps with that of the input image using transposed convolution instead of $1 \times 11 \times 1$ convolution layer. Since a mapping is done with that of the input image, the model output also has the same height and width. Thus, the obtained output channel has the predicted classes for the input pixel from the input image locating at the same spatial position.

8.5.3 Deep Learning Model

The DLM is a subset of machine learning algorithms and works on the principle of a dense training scheme for training sets which indeed is an efficient and effective method. When training takes place, one pathway is created for the adjacent images into this single pathway through the network established [8,9]. At the same time, the method also learns to automatically study the existing classes, both balance and imbalanced, in the data. This model is similar to DLMs employed in other research works since it uses a dual pathway architecture for local and larger information with its contextual details. For this, it used multiple scales at a time in all input images. As the performance can be increased and improved on the number of true positives, it is necessary to remove the false positives. This is done using 3D fully connected conditional random field in the soft segmentation

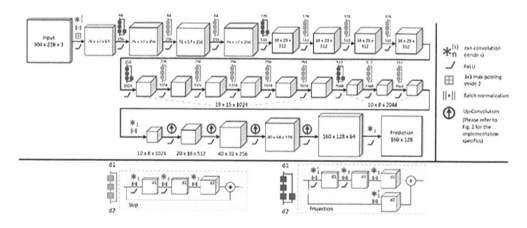

FIGURE 8.4
Fully convolutional network [30].

methods. This was used in brain MRI data [7,12] which has been currently used in this study for comparison of the performance with other methods and to find the effective method of segmenting the rectal area from the rectal MRI image.

Nearly 200 images were collected, and 10× validation was done having 150 images as training and 50 images for testing. All these input images were applied to the previously discussed three methods, and the experimental results were compared. The initial data set obtained is given below. Sample of six images are shown in Figure 8.6.

The results of these images after segmentation using the methods discussed earlier are shown in Figure 8.7.

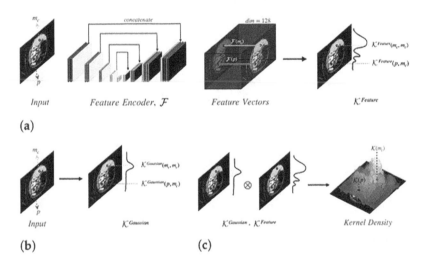

FIGURE 8.5
Deep learning method model for brain tumour magnetic resonance imaging segmentation [12].

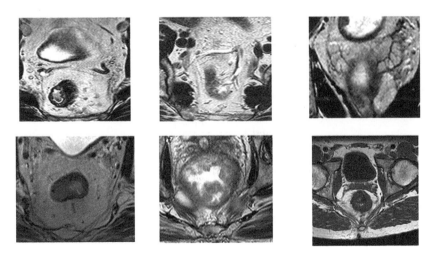

FIGURE 8.6
Six sample images of unsegmented rectum MRI images.

3D
MSDenseN
et

FCN

DLM

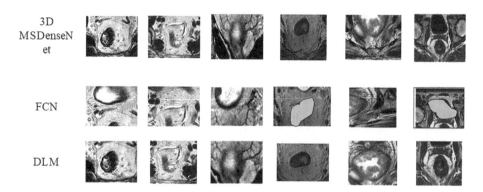

FIGURE 8.7
Output from three segmentation techniques for a sample of six rectal MRI.

Throughout the research for all methods (existing and proposed methods), a confusion matrix with 10 cross-validation is used along with the performance parameters such as accuracy and precision.

Recall and FScore are calculated from the confusion matrix using the following standard formula. Confusion matrix (CM) is a tabular or pictorial representation of the performance values obtained during the validation of the segmentation results. To achieve this, the segmented image section is pixel-wise compared against the pixels of the manually segmented images (ground truth image) with the support of domain experts and are then recorded to evaluate the performance of the process.

Here, true positive (TP) is the number of true cases predicted, which means number of images segmented properly as the ground truth segmented images. False positive (FP) is the number of true cases predicted as false, which means the number of images segmented properly but in evaluation found to be false. True negative (TN) is the number of false cases, which means the number of images that were segmented wrongly and evaluated as wrong segmentation. False negative (FN) is the number of false cases, which means the number of segmented images which are segmented incorrectly but evaluated as correct segmentation. From these values, the performance of classification techniques is measured by calculating the following parameters for each classifier.

Accuracy: It is the proportion of the total number of correct predictions, which means the correct segmentations of true cases and false cases. It is calculated as the ratio between the number of cases correctly classified to the total number of cases:

$$\text{Accuracy} = \frac{TP + TN}{TP + TN + FP + FN}$$

Precision: It is the proportion of the correct true segmentations to that of cases predicted as true:

$$\text{Precision} = \frac{TP}{TP + FP}$$

Recall: It is the proportion of the correct true segmentations to that of predicted true cases:

$$\text{Recall} = \frac{TP}{TP + FN}$$

FScore: It is the harmonic mean of two measures precision and recall and is given by

$$FScore = \frac{2*Precision*Recall}{Precision + Recall}$$

Figure 8.8 depicts the graphical representation of the performance evaluation of 10× validation using a confusion matrix for each of the methods.

The 3D MSDenseNet performance is low in all the performance parameters. This is proved in each cross-validation. DLM has consistently outperformed in all cross-validations. FCN is the second highest performer. On taking the average of the cross-validated measures, the results of these performance parameters such as accuracy, recall, FScore and precision for each method are shown in Table 8.2. From Table 8.2, it is evident that the DLM outperforms the other two segmentation techniques as far as rectal MRI is concerned.

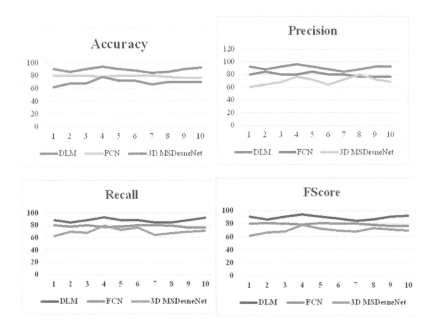

FIGURE 8.8
Performance parameters of 10× validation for the three segmentation methods.

TABLE 8.1

Confusion Matrix

	Predicted Classes	
	True Class **Automated Correct** **Segmentation**	**False Class** **Automated Incorrect** **Segmentation**
True class Ground truth image	TP	FP
False class Ground truth image with some errors	FN	TN

TABLE 8.2

Performance Parameters Obtained through Confusion Matrix

Method	Accuracy	Precision	Recall	FScore
3D MSDenseNet	69.60	69.60	69.84	69.72
FCN	78.80	79.60	78.36	78.98
DLM	**89.00**	**90.40**	**87.94**	**89.15**

8.6 Proposed Method of Segmentation

Medical diagnosis is a crucial and sensitive area where the life of humans is involved. Therefore, utmost care has to be taken when developing computer-aided systems for diagnosis. The accuracy of the system thus becomes more challenging and critical and cannot be compromised. This research is an attempt to further improve on the accuracy and other performance measures with some enhanced technique so that the progress of the system should reach 100% correct output. The literature survey depicts that deep learning is widely used and has given good results [23]. Considering that, the proposed method for segmentation is deep learning using M-R-CNN. Many articles and research have discussed the use of M-R-CNN for object detection for other images. In rectal MRI image segmentation also, there is a need for the correct ROI detection. The proposed method therefore used masked M-R-CNN to detect the rectal area and extract the region for further process of classification.

The working of the proposed M-R-CNN as shown in Figure 8.9 is as follows:

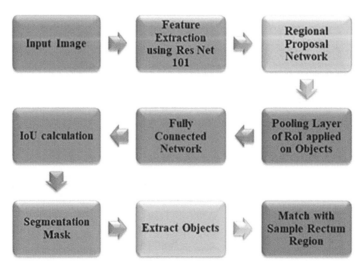

FIGURE 8.9
Working of M-R-CNN.

The deep learning CNN based on region is known as R-CNN. In order to use mask R-CNN, it should first use the F-CNN method. The F-CNN method basically detects the object. The object detection involves first extraction of feature maps from the image using the convolution network. These extracted feature maps are then given as input to the region proposal network, the function of which is to give candidate bounding boxes. The sample ROI of the rectum is then applied on these boxes to bring uniformity to the sizes of these boxes. In M-R-CNN instead of using ConvNet, the ResNet 101 architecture is used for extracting the feature maps.

Details of the concepts of ResNet, F-CNN, R-CNN and M-R-CNN follow.

ResNet:

Region Proposal Network: An RPN is another method of machine learning in which the object detection is done as follows:

1. To detect objects, it creates the object under consideration in bounding box representation.
2. For this, it takes images as input (no standardization of image required). So, the image can be of any size.
3. The output of this is a set of rectangular boxes, each box having a score for the true object-ness.

ROI Pooling: Though the previous step does not require uniformity in size for subsequent network processes, it is required. Thus, the main objective of ROI (region of interest)

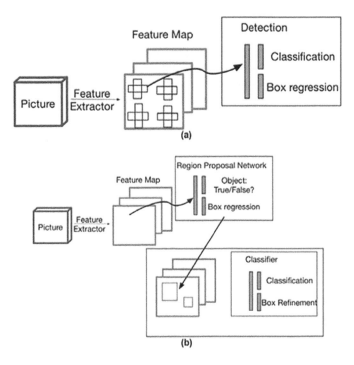

FIGURE 8.10
Working of region proposal network [14].

pooling is to adjust the output of the input images step into a standardized size, a uniform size. In ROI, the proposal that is the result of the first step is mapped, aligned to the original feature map and then divided into regions of the same size where the pooling operation is performed in each of these regions. The pooling operation involves taking either maximum fit or average fit in these regions. Thus, the ROI pooling with mapping is taken care of by introducing CNN input images.

The next step is to use a classifier or regressor to identify the object's presence from the rectangular boxes created using RPN. Anchor boxes generated are then classified as said, whether the area in the anchor box belongs to the foreground or background. The next step is to study the structure, especially the shape of the offset, to fit the objects of right shape and size into these anchor boxes.

8.6.1 M-R-CNN

Masked R-CNN is a newly developed technique which is a revised version of R-CNN where masking is done after the ROI selection. So, in this technique the first layer is a single convolutional layer. This CNN is used to take out the single building block information as a base from the 400×4 input matrix. Here, each base is a 1×4 independent code, since the size of the convolution kernel can only be 1×4. Due to this uniform sizing of the base, there is a definite entry of this information into the network while generating the 16 feature maps. Considering the input matrix sn, x, y, the design of this first layer is given by the following formula:

$$L_{n,1} = \sum_{x=1}^{400} \sum_{y=1}^{4} 8_{n,x,y}\, \omega_{x,y}^{f,1} + b^{f,1}$$

Here, $\omega_{x,y}^{f,1}$ is the weight, and $b_{f,1}$ is the respective base of the parameter or weight of the layer where f represents the convolutional filter. With this formula, the output is calculated for the first layer. This was used for DNA sequencing with 20×20 tensor and 16 channels.

When observing the second and third layers, they are the traditional convolution and pooling layers. So in these layers, the size of the convolution kernel is 3×3, the pooling method is maximum pooling and no choice for average pooling with step sizes as 1×1 and 3×3. Thus, it helps in high-level feature extraction. Following are the computations of second and third layers with a Relu function and parameter passed to this Relu function:

$$L_{n,2} = \text{Relu}\left(\sum_{x=1}^{20} \sum_{y=1}^{20} L_{n,1}\omega_{x,y}^{f,2} + b^{f,2}\right)$$

$$L_{n,3} = max_{3i\leq x, 3i\leq y}\left(L_{i,n,2}\right)$$

The MOTIF which is represented by $\omega_{x,y}^{f,2}$ will be displayed at the right position when the Relu activation function assigns all the negative values to zero. Here $L_{n,2}$ links to the proof that the MOTIG has created. There is a need of reducing the dimensions of the input tensor for which a nonoverlapping pooling is implemented. The subsequent two layers are formed as both single-convolution layers with same size and step size which is the second layer's convolution kernel. There is no activation function or any pooling linkages, as the first layer and these subsequent layers is a linear convolution operation and no convolution exists. The key objective is to improve the outcome of the convolution and nonlinear activation function, that is the outcome of the input getting into the saturated zone, where the related weights cannot be updated. At the end, the tensor obtained by the final layer is scaled through the fully connected layer. To handle the overfitting during training, a dropout function is implemented following which a methylation level could be obtained from the output layer. Mean squared error (MSE) is computed to find the loss function during the training process since MSE is the standard method of finding the solution in any problem of regression. Thus, the computation of MSE is

$$MSE\left(Y,\ Y^0\right) = \frac{\sum_{i=1}^{n}\left(Y-Y^0\right)^2}{n}$$

In this equation, Y is the predicted value of methylation, and Y^0 is the true methylation level. In this case, the predicted values are continuous and so the value may be either greater than 1 or less than 0. For a uniform model, the values are set as 1 where the prediction value is more than 1 and set as 0 where the prediction values are less than 0.

The working of the masked layer is such that it selected the positive regions from the classifier. The positive regions are selected by the ROI classifier so that the masked layer can create masks for them which are of low resolution with 28×28 pixels. Though the resolution is low, the representation is in float type so that more details are being captured rather than binary-type masks. Such soft masks usually are smaller in size to be a lightweight component. In the training phase, there is a scaledown of the ground truth masks in order to compensate and calculate the loss in the scaling down. But during testing or the inferencing phase, the predicted masks are scaled up to the original ROI boundary which is considered as the complete and final mask for each object.

Sample snippets of the Python code are as follows:

```
import os
import sys
import random
import math
import numpy as np
import skimage.io
import matplotlib
import matplotlib.pyplot as plty
R _ DIR = os.path.abspath("../")
sys.path.append(R _ DIR)
from mrcnn import utils
import mrcnn.model as modellib
from mrcnn import visualize
# Import Dataset
sys.path.append(os.path.join(R _ DIR, "RectumProject/MRI _ Images/"))
%matplotlib inline
# trained set are stored in M-DIR
M _ DIR = os.path.join(R _ DIR, "logs")
# Local path to trained weights file
DATA _ MODEL _ PATH = os.path.join(R _ DIR, "mask _ rcnn _ rproj.h10")
# The weights are downloaded from the dataset
if not os.path.exists(DATA _ MODEL _ PATH):
utils.download _ trained _ weights(DATA _ MODEL _ PATH)
# the original image directory to find the object detection with data
model
I _ DIR = os.path.join(R _ DIR, "images")
```

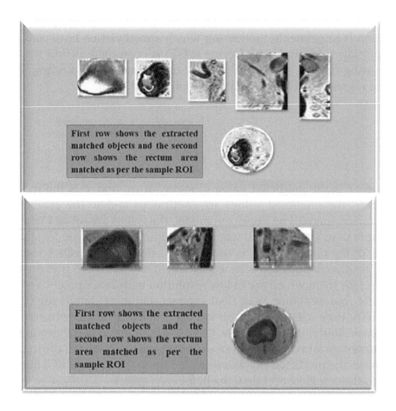

FIGURE 8.11
Output of the M-R-CNN applied on two of the rectal MRI images.

The M-R-CNN method was applied in all the 200 images, and the system was trained with 10× validation with 150 images for training and the remaining 50 images for testing. The output images thus obtained through M-R-CNN for two of the six images given for comparison of earlier segmentation methods are given in Figure 8.11.

The matched region in the image is the final object for processing further for diagnosis of malignancy. This image will be given as input to classifiers for further predictions as per the standard methods of diagnosis.

8.7 Experimental Results and Conclusion

The performance parameters of the M-R-CNN weres calculated using the same method of confusion matrix, and the measures such as accuracy, precision, recall and FScore were compared with the DLM which is the best performer of the earlier comparison. The experimental results are shown in Figure 8.12.

The average of all cross-validations for M-R-CNN is consistent for all measures at 96, and that is higher than DLM. In this chapter, a novel mask R-CNN rectal MRI image

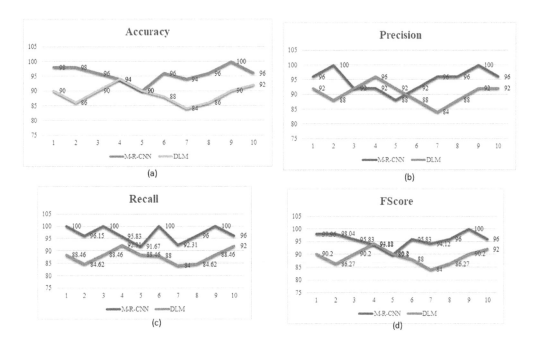

FIGURE 8.12A,B,C,D
Performance measures for the two methods DLM and M-R-CNN.

segmentation is proposed, which combines CNN, ResNet, F-CNN, RPN along with masking, and effectively improves the segmentation performance by training the 10-fold cross-validation data. Initially the predominant methods like 3D MSDesneNet, FCN and DLM are implemented for the collected data and compared, and it was found that DLM performs with better accuracy and precision level than the other two methods. Then the proposed M-R-CNN method is applied to the same data set and the results are compared with DLM, and it is found that M-R-CNN segmentation is well suited for rectal MRI images.

8.8 Limitations and Future Enhancements

When keenly observing the results, in each method only images of one orientation are taken as the complexity increases when dealing with all orientations. The same method also will not be applicable in all orientations. This gives a lot of room in which to perform new research areas in the direction of segmentation itself, focusing on each orientation with various Tesla values. There is also a need of generalizing the technique for all radiology centres and all types of instruments from various original equipment manufacturers. Moreover, the volume of the data set needs to be increased in order to prove the efficiency as 100% of performance. Since medical diagnosis needs to be foolproof to apply in real-world applications, due to human life being at stake, if wrong predictions are done, the system with more retrospective data needs to be tested several times and the results need to be keenly observed.

References

1. Gonzalez, Rafael C., and Richard E. Woods. "Digital image processing." (2018), Pearson Education.
2. Santiago, Inês, Nuno Figueiredo, Oriol Parés, and Celso Matos. "MRI of rectal cancer—Relevant anatomy and staging key points." *Insights into Imaging* 11, no. 1 (2020): 1–21.
3. Horvat, Natally, Camila Carlos Tavares Rocha, Brunna Clemente Oliveira, Iva Petkovska, and Marc J. Gollub. "MRI of rectal cancer: Tumor staging, imaging techniques, and management." *Radiographics* 39, no. 2 (2019): 367–387.
4. van Loenhout, Rhiannon, Frank Zijta, Max Lahaye, Regina Beets-Tan, and Robin Smithuis. "Rectal cancer MR imaging." *Radiology Assistant.* https://radiologyassistant.nl/abdomen/rectum/rectal-cancer-mr-staging-1.
5. Gowdra Halappa, Vivek, et al. "Rectal imaging: Part 1, High-resolution MRI of carcinoma of the rectum at 3 T." *AJR American Journal of Roentgenology* 199, no. 1 (2012): W35–W42.
6. Meng, Ping, Chao Sun, Yi Li, Long Zhou, Xinyu Zhao, Zichao Wang, Wei Lu, Min Hou, Jinguo Li, and Jihong Sun. "MSBC-Net: Automatic Rectal Cancer Segmentation from MR Scans." *TechRxiv. Preprint.* https://doi.org/10.36227/techrxiv.16577417.v1.
7. Li, Hongwei, Aurore Menegaux, Benita Schmitz-Koep, Antonia Neubauer, Felix J.B. Bäuerlein, Suprosanna Shit, Christian Sorg, Bjoern Menze, and Dennis Hedderich. "Automated claustrum segmentation in human brain MRI using deep learning." *Human Brain Mapping* 42, (2021): 5862–5872.
8. Zhu, Hai-Tao, Xiao-Yan Zhang, Yan-Jie Shi, Xiao-Ting Li, and Ying-Shi Sun. "Automatic segmentation of rectal tumor on diffusion-weighted images by deep learning with U-Net." *Journal of Applied Clinical Medical Physics* 22, (2021): 324–331.
9. Zhao, Xingyu, Peiyi Xie, Mengmeng Wang, Wenru Li, Perry J. Pickhardt, Wei Xia, Fei Xiong et al. "Deep learning–based fully automated detection and segmentation of lymph nodes on multiparametric-MRI for rectal cancer: A multicentre study." *EBioMedicine* 56 (2020): 102780.
10. Soomro, Mumtaz Hussain, Matteo Coppotelli, Silvia Conforto, Maurizio Schmid, Gaetano Giunta, Lorenzo Del Secco, Emanuele Neri, Damiano Caruso, Marco Rengo, and Andrea Laghi. "Automated segmentation of colorectal tumor in 3D MRI using 3D multiscale densely connected convolutional neural network." *Journal of Healthcare Engineering* 2019 (2019).
11. Sengur, Abdulkadir, Umit Budak, Yaman Akbulut, Murat Karabatak, and Erkan Tanyildizi. "7 - A survey on neutrosophic medical image segmentation." In Yanhui Guo, Amira S. Ashour, (eds.), *Neutrosophic Set in Medical Image Analysis*, pp. 145–165. Academic Press, 2019, ISBN 9780128181485, https://doi.org/10.1016/B978-0-12-818148-5.00007-2.
12. Laukamp, Kai Roman, Frank Thiele, Georgy Shakirin, David Zopfs, Andrea Faymonville, Marco Timmer, David Maintz, Michael Perkuhn, and Jan Borggrefe. "Fully automated detection and segmentation of meningiomas using deep learning on routine multiparametric MRI." *European Radiology* 29, no. 1 (2019): 124–132.
13. Guo, Zhe, Xiang Li, Heng Huang, Ning Guo, and Quanzheng Li. "Deep learning-based image segmentation on multimodal medical imaging." *IEEE Transactions on Radiation and Plasma Medical Sciences* 3, no. 2 (2019): 162–169.
14. Vorontsov, Eugene, Milena Cerny, Philippe Régnier, Lisa Di Jorio, Christopher J. Pal, Réal Lapointe, Franck Vandenbroucke-Menu, Simon Turcotte, Samuel Kadoury, and An Tang. "Deep learning for automated segmentation of liver lesions at CT in patients with colorectal cancer liver metastases." *Radiology: Artificial Intelligence* 1, no. 2 (2019): 180014.
15. Wang, Jiazhou, Jiayu Lu, Gan Qin, Lijun Shen, Yiqun Sun, Hongmei Ying, Zhen Zhang, and Weigang Hu. "A deep learning-based auto segmentation of rectal tumors in MR images." *Medical Physics* 45, no. 6 (2018): 2560–2564.
16. Feng, Zishun, Dong Nie, Li Wang, and Dinggang Shen. "Semi-supervised learning for pelvic MR image segmentation based on multi-task residual fully convolutional networks." In *2018 IEEE 15th International Symposium on Biomedical Imaging (ISBI 2018)*, pp. 885–888. IEEE, 2018.
17. Liu, Jin, Yi Pan, Min Li, Ziyue Chen, Lu Tang, Chengqian Lu, and Jianxin Wang. "Applications of deep learning to MRI images: A survey." *Big Data Mining and Analytics* 1, no. 1 (2018): 1–18.

18. Nie, Dong, Yaozong Gao, Li Wang, and Dinggang Shen. "Asdnet: Attention based semi-supervised deep networks for medical image segmentation." In *International Conference on Medical Image Computing and Computer-assisted Intervention*, pp. 370–378. Springer, Cham, 2018.

19. Srivaramangai, R., Prakash Hiremath, and Ajay S. Patil. "Preprocessing MRI images of colorectal cancer." *International Journal of Computer Science Issues (IJCSI)* 14, no. 1 (2017): 48.

20. Kalyani, C.S., and Mallikarjuna Swamy. "Segmentation of rectum from CT images using K-means clustering for the EBRT of prostate cancer." In *2016 International Conference on Electrical, Electronics, Communication, Computer and Optimization Techniques (ICEECCOT)*, pp. 34–39. IEEE, 2016.

21. van Heeswijk, Miriam M., Doenja M.J. Lambregts, Joost J.M. van Griethuysen, Stanley Oei, Sheng-Xiang Rao, Carla A.M. de Graaff, Roy F.A. Vliegen, Geerard L. Beets, Nikos Papanikolaou, and Regina G.H. Beets-Tan. "Automated and semiautomated segmentation of rectal tumor volumes on diffusion-weighted MRI: Can it replace manual volumetry?" *International Journal of Radiation Oncology* Biology* Physics* 94, no. 4 (2016): 824–831.

22. Srivaramangai, R., and Ajay S. Patil. "Survey of segmentation techniques of cancer images emphasizing on MRI images." *International Journal of Computer Science Trends & Technology* 3, no. 3 (2015): 304–311.

23. Namías, Rafael, J.P. D'Amato, Mariana del Fresno, and M. Vénere. "Automatic rectum limit detection by anatomical markers correlation." *Computerized Medical Imaging and Graphics* 38, no. 4 (2014): 245–250.

24. Nelikanti, Arjun, Narasimha L.V. Prasad, and Naresh M. Goud. "Colorectal cancer MRI image segmentation using image processing techniques." *International Journal on Computer Science and Engineering* 6, no. 7 (2014): 280.

25. Joshi, Niranjan, Sarah Bond, and Michael Brady. "The segmentation of colorectal MRI images." *Medical Image Analysis* 14, no. 4 (2010): 494–509.

26. Gaillard, F., and M. Niknejad. "Rectal cancer." Reference article, *Radiopaedia.org* (2009). https://radiopaedia.org/articles/7172.

27. Jessup, J. Milburn, Richard M. Goldberg, Elliot A. Asare, Al B. Benson III, James D. Brierley, George J. Chang, Vivien Chen, Carolyn C. Compton, Paola De Nardi, Karyn A. Goodman, Donna Gress, Justin Guinney, Leonard L. Gunderson, Stanley R. Hamilton, Nader N. Hanna, Sanjay Kakar, Lauren A. Kosinski, Serban Negoita, Shuji Ogino, Michael J. Overman, Philip Quirke, Eric Rohren, Daniel J. Sargent, Lynne T. Schumacher-Penberthy, David Shibata, Frank A. Sinicrope, Scott R. Steele, Alexander Stojadinovic, Sabine Tejpar, Martin R. Weiser, Mark Lane Welton, Mary Kay Washington. "Colon and rectum." *AJCC Cancer Staging Manual, 8th Edition American Joint Committee on Cancer*, 2016, Version 1, pp. 1–8.

28. Benson, Al B., Tanios Bekaii-Saab, Emily Chan, Yi-Jen Chen, Michael A. Choti, Harry S. Cooper, Paul F. Engstrom et al. "Rectal cancer." *Journal of the National Comprehensive Cancer Network* 10, no. 12 (2012): 1528–1564.

29. Horvat, Natally, Camila Carlos Tavares Rocha, Brunna Clemente Oliveira, Iva Petkovska, and Marc J. Gollub. "MRI of rectal cancer: Tumor staging, imaging techniques, and management." *Radiographics* 39, no. 2 (2019): 367–387.

30. Laina, Iro, C. Rupprecht, Vasileios Belagiannis, Federico Tombari, and Nassir Navab. "Deeper depth prediction with fully convolutional residual networks." *2016 Fourth International Conference on 3D Vision (3DV)* (2016): 239–248.

9

Detection of Tuberculosis in Microscopy Images Using Mask Region Convolutional Neural Network

Nasir Khan, Hazrat Ali, Muhammad Shakaib Iqbal,
Muhammad Arfat Yameen and Christer Grönlund

CONTENTS

9.1 Introduction

Tuberculosis (TB) is caused by *Mycobacterium tuberculosis*. TB is an infectious, re-emerging, and fatal disease (Díaz-Huerta et al. 2019). The World Health Organization (WHO) has termed TB as a contagious disease. TB may affect a specific organ or multiple organs causing extrapulmonary TB, though pulmonary TB is the most common type (85% cases) (Díaz-Huerta et al. 2019; Guler et al. 2015). According to a WHO report (World Health Organization 2019) in 2019, 1.5 million people lost their lives due to TB. TB affects all age groups and genders. Typically, males are affected more than females (57% males and 32% females with TB cases in 2018). According to WHO, the Southeast Asian region has the highest proportion of TB cases (44%), followed by the African region (24%), and the Western Pacific (18%). In Pakistan, approximately 44,000 people died of TB in 2019 (World Health Organization 2019).

Timely detection and cure of TB are vital because it is a communicable disease. If it is not cured at an early stage, it may transfer to other persons in the community. There are different approaches for TB analysis such as GeneXpert, chest X-ray, Mantoux tuberculin test, and microscopy (Ryu 2015). In developing economies, the manual Ziehl-Neelsen stained sputum smear test is a popular choice for pulmonary TB identification (Van Rie et al. 2008) as it is a simple and inexpensive method. However, manual microscopy screening technique is time-consuming and susceptible to error given the heavy workload and lack of appropriately skilled technicians. This often leads to low sensitivity. According to WHO, for precise diagnosis of pulmonary TB disease, 300 fields of view of smear have to be examined within a day of collection of specimens (Leung 2011). Usually, the diagnosis process may involve 40

DOI: 10.1201/9781003218111-9

minutes to 3 hours of examination of around 40 to 100 view fields images from one slide to identify the bacilli under a microscopy analysis (Díaz-Huerta et al. 2019). So, the test performance varies and depends heavily on the expertise of a laboratory technician.

Computer-aided detection of TB bacilli from smear microscopy not only helps in automating the detection process but also results in saving time and improving the diagnosis process. A programmed and automated technique for detection of the TB bacilli would lessen the workload of the lab technician and the pathologist, reduce error, and increase the precision of the testing process. It would also reduce the requirement of human resources such as lab technicians and facilitate rapid detection of TB in remote regions where expert microbiologists are not available (Van Deun et al. 2002).

Machine learning methods have the potential to provide aid in the diagnosis process either by refining the visual appearance of the TB bacilli (Salleh et al. 2007; Osman et al. 2009) or by detecting the bacilli within a given sputum smear microscopy image (Costa et al. 2008). Costa et al. (2008) presented a method based on red minus green (R-G) images to detect TB bacilli. A histogram of the R-G image was computed that was used to compute a threshold value for bacilli segmentation. In addition, they applied filtering to remove artifacts. Ayma et al. (2015) used adaptive signal processing techniques (Eigen decomposition) for bacilli segmentation. Adaptive filters were used for features extraction. Ayas and Ekinci (2014) trained supervised Random Forest model followed by support vector machine for segmentation and classification of bacilli. Riries et al. (Rulaningtyas et al. 2012) used a naïve Bayesian method to detect bacilli based on color segmentation. CostaFilho et al. (2012) separated the images on the basis of background density (low versus high) and then performed segmentation of the bacilli using color features. Nayak, Shenoy, and Galigekere (2010) used a proximity text algorithm for segmentation and proposed a color-based classification to separate the bacteria and the image background. Zhai et al. (2010) performed segmentation on both the HSV and the CIE-Lab color spaces that was developed as an auto-focus algorithm for the sputum image. Kant and Srivastava (2018) used a neural network for detection of bacilli in Ziehl-Neelsen sputum microscopy images. They divided a microscopy image into smaller patches such that a TB bacilli occurred in each patch.

A careful review of the aforementioned methods reveals that there is greater room for improving performance of the bacilli identification. Besides, although deep learning has shown tremendous potential for medical images, we only found two previous papers for this task (El-Melegy et al. 2019; Kant and Srivastava 2018). These works have addressed localization and classification of the bacilli. On the contrary, our work addresses the instance segmentation task on top of the localization.

In this chapter, a deep learning method for automated TB bacilli detection and segmentation is presented. The approach uses the recently developed instance segmentation framework, i.e., mask region convolution neural network (mask R-CNN) (He et al. 2017). It is a promising technique to segment single as well as overlapping TB bacilli in Ziehl-Neelsen sputum microscopy images. This is the first attempt to explore the mask R-CNN model for the detection of TB bacilli, as most previous methods are limited to the use of conventional machine learning models and shallow networks. Since the dataset is available without ground truth labels, we developed our own ground truth labels under the supervision of domain experts. We experienced that assigning the labels to the examples in this dataset is a time-consuming effort. Further, it could be deduced that the performance of the model was only limited by the noisy image acquisition processes. Our primary comparison is with the performance of the U-Net model; however, we also make comparison with a convolutional neural network (CNN) model (Kant and Srivastava 2018).

9.2 Dataset

For this work, we use ZNSM-iDB dataset (Shah et al. 2017) of Ziehl-Neelsen sputum smear microscopy images, which is publicly available. The dataset consists of various categories of images, i.e., images with overlapping bacilli, images with over-stained views of bacilli and artifacts, images with single or very few bacilli, and images without bacilli. The dataset consists of two groups of images acquired using two different microscopes. Figure 9.1 shows different categories of ZNSM-iDB dataset images.

The ground truth of these images is not present. So we manually annotate the images to compile the ground truth set. This is done under the supervision of domain experts. The ground truth is obtained by locating the TB bacilli and drawing polygons around them as shown in Figure 9.2. For annotation purposes, we used the VGG Image Annotator (VIA) tool and annotated about 520 images.[1] The VIA tool stores the file in the *json* format, which keeps the positions of all polygons along with their labels.

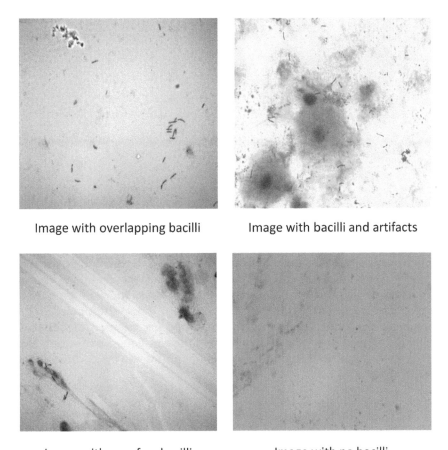

Image with overlapping bacilli   Image with bacilli and artifacts

Image with very few bacilli   Image with no bacilli

FIGURE 9.1
Ziehl-Neelsen sputum microscopy images of various categories, showing the possible variations in sputum microscopy images.

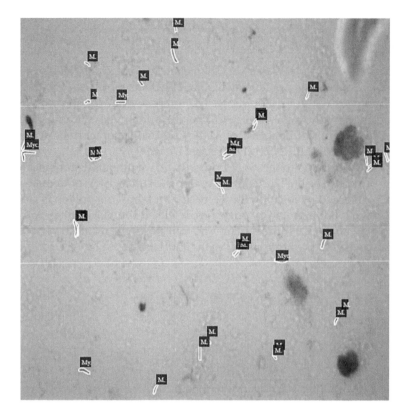

FIGURE 9.2
An annotated image by VGG image annotator.

The annotation is indeed a laborious and time-consuming task and requires a lot of patience since every image may contain approximately 5 to 30 bacilli. Some of the challenges in the annotation process as we experienced are mentioned here. The Ziehl-Neelsen sputum microscopy images contained TB bacilli as well as artifacts. It was a challenge to differentiate between TB bacilli and artifacts. The inconsistency of image brightness was another problem we faced during the annotation. These slides were prepared through a manual process. Hence, after completion of staining, the sputum most probably gave uneven texture to the slides. During the image acquisition, the user might have recorded images from different angles. This ultimately had the consequence of variation in brightness of images when captured from different angles and with various brightness settings of the microscope.

9.3 Proposed Pipeline

The annotated images are fed to the proposed model for training purposes. After training of the model, we evaluate the detection and segmentation performance on an independent test set. Also see Figure 9.3.

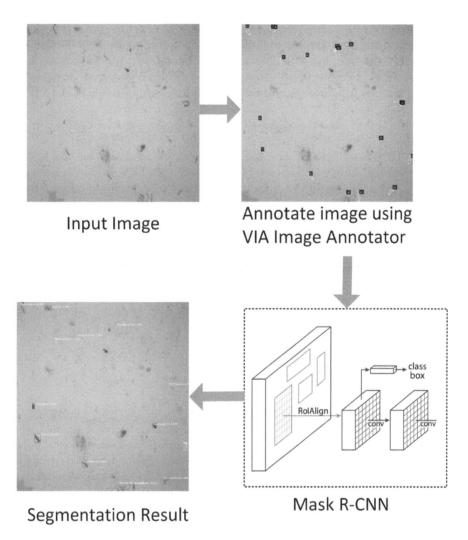

FIGURE 9.3
Workflow of the proposed approach.

The proposed pipeline uses the mask R-CNN model—a technique that has proved useful for segmentation (He et al. 2017). It is a variant of the fast R-CNN (Girshick 2015; Ren et al. 2015) developed for pixel-level segmentation. The mask R-CNN model has an open-source implementation available at the link.[2] We also encourage readers to explore the architecture of the mask R-CNN as explained in He et al. (2017). Mask R-CNN is an example of a pixel-level segmentation approach that depends on a region proposal algorithm.

The mask R-CNN model has two base phases. The first phase scans the input image and outputs region(s) of interest (ROI) on the image, showing the regions where the objects (the bacilli) might occur. The second phase performs classification and identifies the bacilli by generating the bounding box and masks. At a higher level, the mask R-CNN consists of a feature pyramid network (FPN) plus a backbone, followed by a region proposal network (RPN), which generates positive regions/ROIs (objects) and bounding box refinement.

The proposed regions have different sizes and shapes. In order to convert these proposed regions to a standard size suitable for input to a classifier, mask R-CNN uses the ROI-align technique. After that, mask R-CNN adds a network head for mask generation. This CNN-based network digs out the positive regions and then generates a mask for them. Consequently, the loss function encompasses multiple losses (as in He et al. [2017]):

$$L = L_{classification} + L_{localization} + L_{segmentation}$$

The use of an FPN-based model as a backbone network for the mask R-CNN helps to improve the overall accuracy and speed (He et al. 2017). An FPN derives relevant features at many scales that carry significance for object detection and segmentation (also refer to He et al. [2017]).

For comparison, we also use the U-Net model on the same dataset. U-Net is an encoder-decoder framework for medical image segmentation and does not depend on the region proposal algorithm (Ronneberger, Fischer, and Brox 2015). U-Net architecture comprises two phases. The first phase is the construction phase (encoder) that captures the context in the image. The second phase is the expanding path (decoder). It is used for exact localization using transposed convolutions.

9.4 Experimental Setup

First, all the images are resized to 1,000 × 1,000 pixels. We use 520 images selected from the two groups of images as described in Section 9.2. To further increase the available data, we use different data augmentation methods. In the overall dataset, 85% of the dataset is used for training and validation subsets, and 15% is used for testing. We use Res-Net101 pyramid network as a backbone for features extraction. We use the weights from pre-training on the Microsoft COCO dataset (Lin et al. 2014). To achieve good accuracy and fast training speed at the same time, we keep the minimum region proposal confidence to 0.9. This means that only regions with more than 90% confidence of potentially containing TB bacilli are considered, and regions with less than 90% confidence are discarded. A summary of the training parameters and the computing hardware is shown in Figure 9.4.

9.5 Results and Discussion

For evaluating the model performance, the recall, precision, F1-score, and classification accuracy are calculated. Recall shows how good the model is at detecting positive cases, while precision shows how many of the positively classified were relevant.

A comparison of results for different models is shown in Table 9.1, comparing the performance of the proposed pipeline with U-Net and a CNN (Kant and Srivastava 2018) for the same dataset. It appears that mask R-CNN can achieve a higher classification accuracy, recall (hence lower false negatives), and F1-score compared to other methods. Table 9.2 shows comparisons of trainable parameters for the two models.

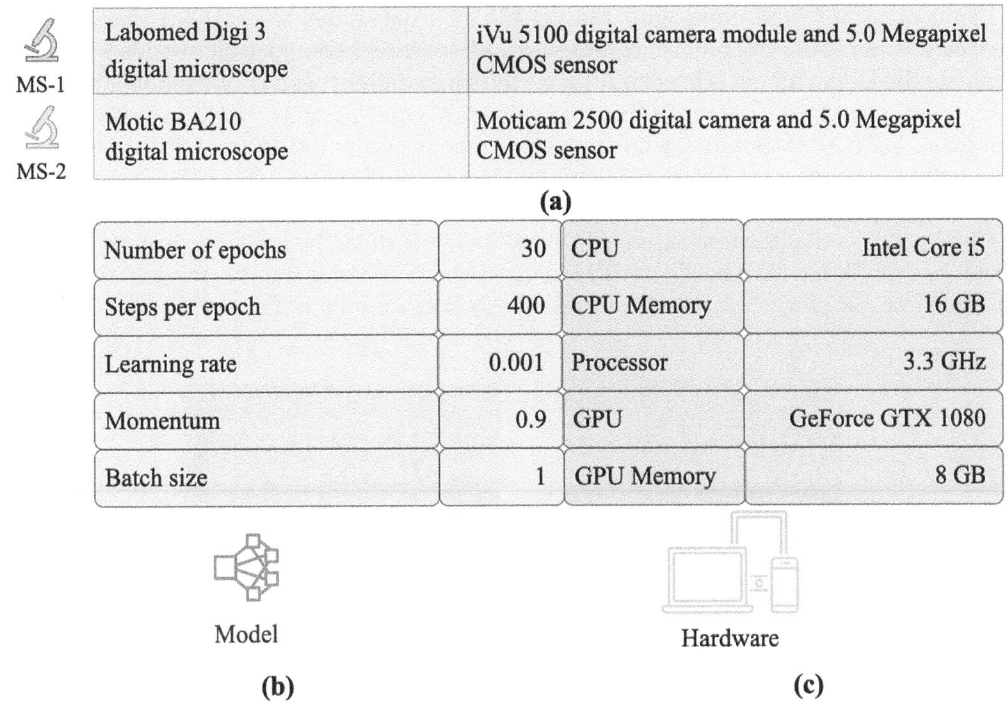

MS-1	Labomed Digi 3 digital microscope	iVu 5100 digital camera module and 5.0 Megapixel CMOS sensor
MS-2	Motic BA210 digital microscope	Moticam 2500 digital camera and 5.0 Megapixel CMOS sensor

(a)

Number of epochs	30	CPU	Intel Core i5
Steps per epoch	400	CPU Memory	16 GB
Learning rate	0.001	Processor	3.3 GHz
Momentum	0.9	GPU	GeForce GTX 1080
Batch size	1	GPU Memory	8 GB

Model   Hardware

(b)   **(c)**

FIGURE 9.4

Summary: (a) microscopes for dataset collection, (b) summary of parameters of the model, and (c) hardware resources.

TABLE 9.1

Results Comparison (only available metrics are reported)

Model	Classification Accuracy	Recall	Precision	F1 score
Mask R-CNN	98%	98%	86%	91.6%
U-Net	93%	93%	90%	91.4%
CNN [17]	-	83.8%	67.5%	74.8%

TABLE 9.2

Trainable Parameters for the Two Models

	Mask R-CNN	U-Net Model
Total parameters	63,749,552	31,056,397
Trainable parameters	63,638,064	31,044,617
Non-trainable parameters	111,488	11,780

Note: Since we use the pretrained models, not all these parameters are trained from scratch, and fine-tuning is done only in the final layers.

Using mask R-CNN along with ResNet-101 as a backbone, we get 98% classification accuracy, 98% recall, 86% precision, and 91.6% F1-score. For comparison purposes, we also evaluate the U-Net model (He et al. 2016) on the same dataset. The U-Net model gives classification accuracy of 93%, recall 93%, precision 90%, and F1-score 91.4%. We observe that the mask R-CNN gives a more false-positive rate as compared to the U-Net model and hence the precision score of the U-Net model is greater than mask R-CNN, demonstrated with the help of Figure 9.5. The image shown in Figure 9.5 has no TB bacilli, but mask R-CNN predicts that the image has a TB bacillus while the U-Net model correctly predicts that it has no TB bacilli. The TB bacilli identification results for the two models are shown in Figure 9.6. Similarly, the results of mask R-CNN are shown in Figure 9.7.

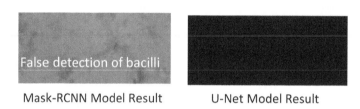

Mask-RCNN Model Result   U-Net Model Result

FIGURE 9.5
False positive detected by mask R-CNN. For the same image, U-Net does not give false positive.

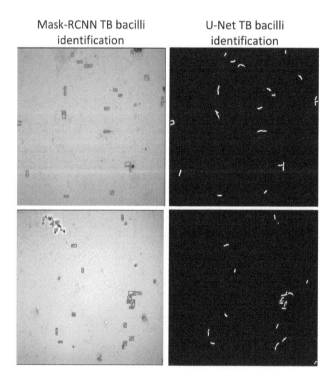

FIGURE 9.6
Samples of TB bacilli identification results of mask R-CNN model (left) and U-Net model (right). Both the models have the same test image as input and the dark background for the output of U-Net does not imply the use of different input images.

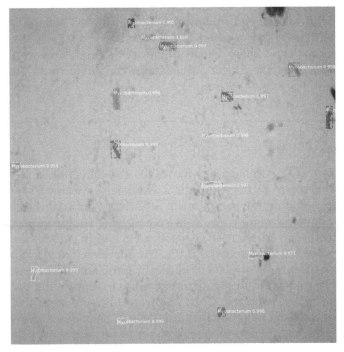

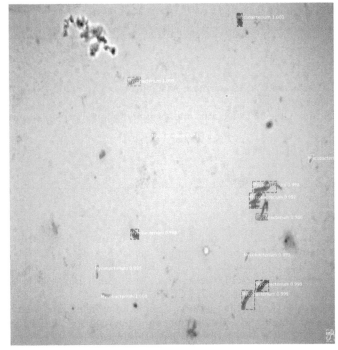

FIGURE 9.7

Examples of results of mask R-CNN. TB bacilli are successfully segmented even though quality and background of the input images have variations. Best seen in color.

From experimental results, we can conclude that the proposed pipeline can identify TB bacilli in the given Ziehl-Neelsen sputum microscopy images for a variety of images having single/few bacilli, overlapped, and over-stained TB bacilli. The results obtained in the experiments show that the performance of the proposed model is better for images with better visibility of bacilli and lower density of the background. However, the performance drops when the bacilli are out of focus or the images contain too many artifacts.

9.6 Conclusion

We have proposed an automated technique for the detection and segmentation of *Mycobacterium tuberculosis* occurring in the Ziehl-Neelsen stained sputum microscopy images. The proposed pipeline uses a mask R-CNN model with ResNet-101 backbone architecture. We have compared results with a U-Net. The proposed model has successfully performed segmentation of TB bacilli with a high confidence factor giving an overall accuracy of 98% and F1-score of 91.6%. The automated detection and localization of TB bacilli can reduce the workload of clinical technicians and speed up the diagnosis processes, and provide aid to the microbiologists by improving the performance of the sputum smear microscopy test. Thus, an overall help to control TB spread can be achieved. The instance segmentation by mask R-CNN provides added value in terms of explainability for the technicians who may prefer to verify the detection by the model.

Notes

1 A. Dutta, A. Gupta, and A. Zisserman, VGG Image Annotator (VIA). www.robots.ox.ac.uk/~vgg/software/via
2 Mask R-CNN for Object Detection and Segmentation. https://github.com/matterport/Mask_RCNN

References

Ayas, Selen, and Murat Ekinci. 2014. "Random Forest-Based Tuberculosis Bacteria Classification in Images of ZN-Stained Sputum Smear Samples." *Signal, Image and Video Processing* 8 (1): 49–61.
Ayma, V, R De Lamare, and B Castañeda. 2015. "An Adaptive Filtering Approach for Segmentation of Tuberculosis Bacteria in Ziehl-Neelsen Sputum Stained Images." In *2015 Latin America Congress on Computational Intelligence (LA-CCI)*, 1–5. IEEE.
Costa, Marly GF, Cicero FF Costa Filho, Juliana F Sena, Julia Salem, and Mari O de Lima. 2008. "Automatic Identification of Mycobacterium Tuberculosis with Conventional Light Microscopy." In *2008 30th Annual International Conference of the IEEE Engineering in Medicine and Biology Society*, 382–385. IEEE.
CostaFilho, Cicero FF, Pamela C Levy, Clahildek M Xavier, Marly GF Costa, Luciana BM Fujimoto, and Julia Salem. 2012. "Mycobacterium Tuberculosis Recognition with Conventional Microscopy." In *2012 Annual International Conference of the IEEE Engineering in Medicine and Biology Society*, 6263–6268. IEEE.

Díaz-Huerta, Jorge Luis, Adriana del Carmen Téllez-Anguiano, Miguelangel Fraga-Aguilar, Jose Antonio Gutierrez-Gnecchi, and Sergio Arellano-Calderón. 2019. "Image Processing for AFB Segmentation in Bacilloscopies of Pulmonary Tuberculosis Diagnosis." *PLoS ONE* 14 (7): e0218861.

El-Melegy, Moumen, Doaa Mohamed, Tarek ElMelegy, and Mostafa Abdelrahman. 2019. "Identification of Tuberculosis Bacilli in ZN-Stained Sputum Smear Images: A Deep Learning Approach." In *Proceedings of the IEEE/CVF Conference on Computer Vision and Pattern Recognition Workshops*. IEEE. https://ieeexplore.ieee.org/document/9025589.

Girshick, Ross. 2015. "Fast R-Cnn." In *Proceedings of the IEEE International Conference on Computer Vision*, 1440–1448. IEEE. https://ieeexplore.ieee.org/document/7410526.

Guler, Selma Ates, Fulsen Bozkus, Mehmet Fatih Inci, Omer Faruk Kokoglu, Hasan Ucmak, Sevinc Ozden, and Murvet Yuksel. 2015. "Evaluation of Pulmonary and Extrapulmonary Tuberculosis in Immunocompetent Adults: A Retrospective Case Series Analysis." *Medical Principles and Practice* 24 (1): 75–79.

He, Kaiming, Georgia Gkioxari, Piotr Dollár, and Ross Girshick. 2017. "Mask R-CNN." In *Proceedings of the IEEE International Conference on Computer Vision*, 2961–2969. IEEE. https://ieeexplore.ieee.org/document/8237584.

He, Kaiming, Xiangyu Zhang, Shaoqing Ren, and Jian Sun. 2016. "Deep Residual Learning for Image Recognition." In *Proceedings of the IEEE Conference on Computer Vision and Pattern Recognition*, 770–778. IEEE. https://ieeexplore.ieee.org/document/7780459.

Kant, Sonaal, and Muktabh Mayank Srivastava. 2018. "Towards Automated Tuberculosis Detection Using Deep Learning." In *2018 IEEE Symposium Series on Computational Intelligence (SSCI)*, 1250–1253. IEEE.

Leung, Chi Chiu. 2011. "Reexamining the Role of Radiography in Tuberculosis Case Finding." *The International Journal of Tuberculosis and Lung Disease* 15 (10): 1279–1279.

Lin, Tsung-Yi, Michael Maire, Serge Belongie, James Hays, Pietro Perona, Deva Ramanan, Piotr Dollár, and C Lawrence Zitnick. 2014. "Microsoft Coco: Common Objects in Context." In *European Conference on Computer Vision*, 740–55. Springer.

Nayak, Rohit, Vishnu Prasad Shenoy, and Ramesh R Galigekere. 2010. "A New Algorithm for Automatic Assessment of the Degree of TB-Infection Using Images of ZN-Stained Sputum Smear." In *2010 International Conference on Systems in Medicine and Biology*, 294–299. IEEE.

Osman, MK, MY Mashor, Z Saad, and H Jaafar. 2009. "Contrast Enhancement for Ziehl-Neelsen Tissue Slide Images Using Linear Stretching and Histogram Equalization Technique." In *2009 IEEE Symposium on Industrial Electronics & Applications*, 1:431–435. IEEE.

Ren, Shaoqing, Kaiming He, Ross Girshick, and Jian Sun. 2015. "Faster R-Cnn: Towards Real-Time Object Detection with Region Proposal Networks." *Advances in Neural Information Processing Systems* 28.

Ronneberger, Olaf, Philipp Fischer, and Thomas Brox. 2015. "U-Net: Convolutional Networks for Biomedical Image Segmentation." In *International Conference on Medical Image Computing and Computer-Assisted Intervention*, 234–241. Springer.

Rulaningtyas, Riries, Andriyan B Suksmono, Tati LR Mengko, and Putri Saptawati. 2012. "Color Segmentation Using Bayesian Method of Tuberculosis Bacteria Images in Ziehl-Neelsen Sputum Smear." *Proceedings of WiSE Health*. Institut Teknologi Bandung.

Ryu, Yon Ju. 2015. "Diagnosis of Pulmonary Tuberculosis: Recent Advances and Diagnostic Algorithms." *Tuberculosis and Respiratory Diseases* 78 (2): 64–71.

Salleh, Zaleha, MY Mashor, NR Mat Noor, Shazmin Aniza, N Abdul Rahim, ASW Wahab, SS Md Noor, F Mohamad Idris, and Habsah Hasan. 2007. "Colour Contrast Enhancement Based on Bright and Dark Stretching for Ziehl-Neelsen Slide Images." In *Third International Conference on Intelligent Information Hiding and Multimedia Signal Processing (IIH-MSP 2007)*, 2:205–208. IEEE.

Shah, Mohammad Imran, Smriti Mishra, Vinod Kumar Yadav, Arun Chauhan, Malay Sarkar, Sudarshan K Sharma, and Chittaranjan Rout. 2017. "Ziehl-Neelsen Sputum Smear Microscopy Image Database: A Resource to Facilitate Automated Bacilli Detection for Tuberculosis Diagnosis." *Journal of Medical Imaging* 4 (2): 027503.

Van Deun, A, A Hamid Salim, E Cooreman, Md Anwar Hossain, A Rema, N Chambugonj, Md Hye, A Kawria, and E Declercq. 2002. "Optimal Tuberculosis Case Detection by Direct Sputum

Smear Microscopy: How Much Better Is More?" *The International Journal of Tuberculosis and Lung Disease* 6 (3): 222–230.

Van Rie, A, D Fitzgerald, G Kabuya, A Van Deun, M Tabala, N Jarret, F Behets, and E Bahati. 2008. "Sputum Smear Microscopy: Evaluation of Impact of Training, Microscope Distribution, and Use of External Quality Assessment Guidelines for Resource-Poor Settings." *Journal of Clinical Microbiology* 46 (3): 897–901.

World Health Organization, WHO. 2019. "Global Tuberculosis Report 2019." www.who.int/tb/publications/global_report/en/.

Zhai, Yongping, Yunhui Liu, Dongxiang Zhou, and Shun Liu. 2010. "Automatic Identification of Mycobacterium Tuberculosis from ZN-Stained Sputum Smear: Algorithm and System Design." In *2010 IEEE International Conference on Robotics and Biomimetics*, 41–46. IEEE.

Appendix: Code Snippets

A1 Code Snippets for Mask R-CNN

```
"""
@author: Nasir Khan, Hazrat Ali
"""
# example of testing the model for bacteria detection after importing
weights from pre-trained model
from keras.preprocessing.image import load _ img
from model _ mrcnn.model import MaskRCNN as MRN
# The class names contains the names of the two classes (the labels)
class _ names = ['BG', 'Mycobacterium']
# configure the test class
class TestConfig(Config):
     NAME = "test"
     IMAGES _ PER _ GPU = 1
     NUM _ CLASSES = 1 + 1
# the deep learning mask RCNN model is initiated
model _ rcnn = MRN(mode='inference', model _ dir='E:/khan _ nasir/MASK-RCNN/
mrcnn', config=TestConfig())
# load the weights of the pre-trained model
model _ rcnn.load _ weights('TB _ bacilli _ 21.h5', by _ name=True)
# load test image to test the model.
test _ img = load _ img('17.jpg')
test _ img = img _ to _ array(test _ img)
# for the test image in test _ img, use the model to make detection
detect _ results = rcnn.detect([test _ img])
# get the output
result _ on _ image = detect _ results[0]
# display the test images and identify the detection with bounding box
and score
display _ instances(test _ img, result _ on _ image['rois'], result _
on _ image['masks'], result _ on _ image['class _ ids'], class _ names,
result _ on _ image['scores'])
Note: The official implementation is available from "https://github.com/
matterport/Mask _ RCNN". The implementation is in Python 3 using Tensorflow
and Keras libraries.
```

A2 Code Snippets for U-Net model

```
"""
@author: Nasir Khan
"""
from model import *
from data import *
model=unet()

testGene=testGenerator("E:/khan _ nasir/unet/unet-master/data/tb/train/
test")
model = unet()
model.load _ weights("unet _ tb.hdf5")
results = model.predict _ generator(testGene,1,verbose=1)
saveResult("E:/khan _ nasir/unet/unet-master/data/tb/test",results)
Note: The Tensorflow implementation of the U-Net segmentation model is
available from  https://github.com/jakeret/unet
```

10

Comparison of Deep Learning Methods for COVID-19 Detection Using Chest X-ray

Archana Chaudhari, Nikita Kotwal, Gauri Unnithan and Anaya Pawar

CONTENTS

10.1 Introduction

In the last decade, many forms of viruses (such as SARS, MERS, flu, etc.) have come into the picture, but they have only been around for a few days or a couple of weeks. At the end of 2019, humans witnessed an outbreak of severe acute respiratory syndrome coronavirus 2 (SARS-CoV-2). Although the outbreak of COVID-19 started in Wuhan, China, due to the global widespread of the epidemic in January 2020, the World Health Organization (WHO) (International Committee on Taxonomy of Viruses, 2020) declared a globally relevant public health emergency.

The early detection of COVID-19–positive cases now became critical for saving lives and also avoiding the virus's spread.

The common method for identifying COVID-19 is known as reverse transcriptase-polymerase chain reaction (RT-PCR). This test determines COVID-19 through the collection of respiratory specimens of nasopharyngeal or oropharyngeal swabs. However, the RT-PCR test is timeconsuming and demonstrates poor sensitivity [1, 2] during the initial days of exposure to the virus [3].

Patients who receive false-negative tests may come in contact with healthy individuals and infect them. It therefore becomes necessary to find alternative ways to detect COVID-19. Table 10.1 summarizes the most widely used tests for COVID-19.

After RT-PCR, computed tomography (CT) images are widely used for COVID-19 detection as summarized in Table 10.1. Based on imaging parameters, numerous retrospective examinations have found CT scans had a better sensitivity (86%–98%) and lower false-negative rates than RT-PCR. The drawback of using CT images for detection of COVID-19 is that the specificity (25%) is poor due to imaging findings that overlap with those of other viral pneumonias.

Pneumonia-like symptoms or clinical features can be detected in chest X-rays. Hence, chest X-ray can play an important role in detection of COVID-19. Although a normal chest radiograph does not exclude COVID-19 pneumonia [13], no fixed definition of COVID-19 pneumonia exists.

Like other pneumonias, COVID-19 pneumonia causes the density of the lungs to increase. This may be seen as whiteness in the lungs on radiography which, depending on

TABLE 10.1

Review of Generally Used Tests for COVID-19

Testing Type	Diagnosis	Research Work
Nucleic acid testing	COVID-19 is diagnosed primarily by nucleic acid testing. SARS-CoV-2 has been genetically detected using a number of reverse transcription polymerase chain reaction (RT-PCR) assays. The reverse transcription of SARS-CoV-2 RNA into complementary DNA (cDNA) strands is followed by amplification of particular sections of the cDNA in the RT-PCR method. There are two primary phases in the design process: 1. Sequence alignment and primer creation and 2. Assay tuning and testing.	[4–6]
Computed tomography	Bilateral and peripheral ground-glass opacities (areas of hazy opacity) and lung consolidations are the most prevalent hallmark signs of COVID-19 (fluid or solid material in compressible lung tissue). Ground-glass opacities are typically noticeable 0–4 days following symptom start, according to research. Crazy-paving patterns (i.e., irregular-shaped paved stone pattern) occur when a COVID-19 infection proceeds, in addition to ground-glass opacities, followed by increased lung consolidation.	[7–8]
Emerging diagnostic tests for COVID-19	Unlike nucleic acid testing, these assays allow for detection after recovery. This allows doctors to keep track of both ill and recovered patients, giving them a clearer idea of the total number of SARS-CoV-2 infections.	[9]
Protein testing	COVID-19 can be diagnosed using viral protein antigens and antibodies produced in response to a SARS-CoV-2 infection.	[10]
Point-of-care testing	Individuals are diagnosed without sending samples to centralised facilities via point-of-care diagnostics, allowing areas without laboratory capacity to discover infected patients.	[11]
Chest X-ray (CXR)	CXR equipment is widely available in hospitals, and CXR images are cheap and fast to acquire. They can be inspected by radiologists and show visual indicators of the virus	[12]

the severity of the pneumonia, obscures the lung markings that are normally seen; however, this may be delayed in appearing or absent [13].

When lung markings are partially obscured by the increased whiteness, a ground-glass pattern occurs. This can be subtle and might need confirmation with a radiologist. COVID-19 pneumonia can be classed as an atypical pneumonia because of the radiographic appearances of multifocal ground-glass opacity, linear opacities and consolidation. These changes are also seen in other atypical pneumonias, including other coronavirus infections (severe acute respiratory system [SARS] and Middle East respiratory syndrome [MERS]). Figure 10.1 represents the chest X-ray images of normal, COVID-19 positive and COVID-19 negative individuals [14].

This typical ground-glass pattern of pneumonia along with other clinical features observed in the clinical chest X-rays of patients with coronavirus when compared to clinical chest X-rays of people not diagnosed with coronavirus but having pneumonia can be used to detect COVID-19.

These clinical image features in chest X-rays can be extracted and exploited by using convolutional neural networks (CNNs) for COVID-19 detection. Thus, chest X-ray provides a less expensive and faster solution for COVID-19 detection than CT and RT-PCR. Detecting potential infections with COVID-19 on chest X-ray will benefit patients with highrisk by quarantining them while waiting for test results. In most healthcare systems, X-ray machines are already available. There is no transport time needed for the samples either, and most existing X-ray devices have also been digitized. The use of chest X-ray in research work is advised in order to give preference to patients' alternatives for more RT-PCR studies. This may be helpful in an inpatient setting where current services are unable to decide whether to keep a patient in the ward with other patients or to isolate them in places of COVID-19.

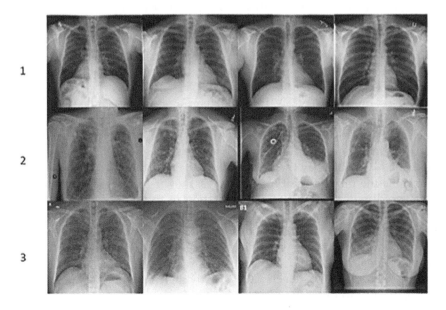

FIGURE 10.1
Chest X-rays. Class 1 are normal images, Class 2 are non-COVID-19 (pneumonia) images and Class 3 are COVID-19 images. All images belong to the training set of the COVIDx dataset [15].

The motivation behind the research work is to develop an automated and fast technique for early detection of COVID-19 using chest X-rays.

The main contributions to the research work are as follows: Various approaches to detect COVID-19 from chest X-rays using machine learning and deep learning architectures are compared and reviewed from the point of view of database used, accuracy, features of the architectures and purpose. In addition, a new approach using CNN and GoogLeNet is proposed for COVID-19 detection.

The research paper is summarized as follows: Section 10.1 provides an introduction and discusses the rationale for COVID-19 detection using chest X-rays. Section 10.2 presents a comprehensive literature survey of various deep learning techniques used for COVID-19 detection using chest X-rays in recent years along with database description and experimental analysis. Section 10.3 proposes a new method for COVID-19 detection. Section 10.4 presents the experimental results of the proposed method. Conclusions and future directions are discussed in Section 10.5.

10.2 Literature Review

In recent years, CNNs have been very popular for image classification. In case of medical imaging, these advances in image classification algorithms are also explored for the detection and classification of pathology.

Detection of COVID-19 using chest X-rays is widely used to surpass the limitations of RT-PCR test kits [2]. This section presents a comprehensive review of the existing deep learning algorithms for COVID-19 detection using chest X-rays.

In Afshar et al. [16], using X-ray images, the authors proposed a structural model focused on CAPSULE NETWORK to diagnose COVID-19. Using X-ray images, the authors suggested a Capsule Networks structure model to diagnose COVID-19 disease (i.e., COVIDCAAPS). In this proposed work, several convolution layers and capsules are used to solve the class-imbalance problem. They demonstrate the satisfactory performance of COVIDCAPS in experimental testing on a smaller number of trainable parameters.

In Ozkaya et al. [17], the authors extracted two subsets (16*16 and 32*32) of patches and called 3,000 X-ray images for COVID-19. Furthermore, fusion and ranking approaches were used to improve the efficacy of the proposed technique. The authors used support vector machine (SVM) to classify the processed data, and the CNN model was used to pass learning. As a result, they showed that set2 had good accuracy compared to set1.

In Chan et al. [18], to classify the pneumothorax, the authors used the SVM technique. In order to mine the properties of lung pictures, they used a local binary pattern (LBP). The authors used multiscale texture segmentation in the proposed detection model by removing impurities from chest images to segment the regions of irregular lungs; this transformation was used to find several overlapping blocks for a change of texture. Finally, to find an entire area of disease with the abnormal part, the authors used rib boundary (with Sobel edge detection).

A model that automatically detects COVID-19 using chest X-ray images was suggested by Ozturk et al. [19]. To identify the real-time object detection process, the authors proposed the DarkNet model.

In the preceding paragraph, a brief summary of a few deep learning methods has been presented. There still exist several deep learning models for detection of COVID-19. Table 10.2 presents a comparison of various deep learning architectures along with the

TABLE 10.2

Summary of Deep Learning Architecture for COVID-19

Serial Number	Authors	Convolutional neural Network (CNN) Architecture Used for COVID-19 Detection Using Chest X-Ray (CXR)	Dataset Details	Performance metrics (accuracy)	Features of the Proposed Method	Purpose
1.	Abbas et al. (2020) [20]	Decompose, transfer and compose (DeTraC)	Combination of two small datasets, totaling 196 images	95.1%	Data augmentation step is performed to remove limitation of few images. Frontal images of the CXRs are used for processing	Detection and diagnosis of COVID-19
2.	Alazab et al. (2020) [21]	Long short term memory (LSTM)	1,000 X-ray images of real patients	94.8%	Three forecasting methods—the prophet algorithm (PA), autoregressive integrated moving average (ARIMA) model, and long- and short-term memory neural network (LSTM)—used to forecast the numbers of COVID-19 confirmations, recoveries and deaths over the next 7 days using real-world datasets	COVID-19 detection
3.	Alawad et al. (2021) [22]	VGG-16 and VGG16+SVM VGG-16+RF VGG-16+XGBoost classifier	Combination of five datasets, totaling 7329 images	VGG-16 VGG16+SVM 99.82%	Comparative study of hybrid CNN models is presented	COVID-19 classification
4.	Alqudah et al. (2020) [23]	CNN-Softmax	71 CXR images (48 cases for COVID-19 and 23 for Non-COVID-19)	95.2%	The classification, to COVID-19 or Non-COVID-19, is achieved using different machine learning algorithms such as CNN, support vector machine (SVM), and random forest (RF) to obtain the best recognition performance.	COVID-19 classification
5.	Apostolopoulos and Mpesiana (2020) [24]	VGGNet Transfer learning using CNNs	Two datasets	96.78%	Transfer learning is explored over small datasets	Detection and diagnosis of COVID-19

(Continued)

TABLE 10.2
(Continued)

Serial Number	Authors	Convolutional neural Network (CNN) Architecture Used for COVID-19 Detection Using Chest X-Ray (CXR)	Dataset Details	Performance metrics (accuracy)	Features of the Proposed Method	Purpose
6.	Basu et al. (2020) [25]	AlexNet VGGNet ResNet DETL	Normal 350, pneumonia 322, other disease 300, COVID-19 305	90.13%		Screening of COVID-19
7.	Chhikara et al. (2021) [26]	InceptionV3 based model	Three different datasets with 11,244; 8,246; and 14,486 images	97.7%		COVID-19 classification
8.	Chowdhury et al. (2020) [27]	CNN	19 positive; 1,341 normal; 1,345 viral pneumonia CXR images	96.5%		Detection and diagnosis of COVID-19
9.	Cohen et al. (2020) [28]	DenseNet model	94 images COVID-19 positive	Not mentioned		Prediction COVID-19
10.	Dominik (2021) [29]	BaseNet, ensemble composed of BaseNet, VGG16, VGG19, ResNet50, DenseNet121, and Xception optimal classification thresholding using ensemble	COVIDx8B	95.50% 97.75% 99.25%	Lightweight architecture	COVID-19 classification
11.	Hall et al. (2020) [30]	CNN	135 COVID-19 cases	89.2%		Detection and diagnostic of COVID-19
12.	Haghanifar et al. (2020) [31]	CheXNet COVID-CXNet	3,628 images: 3,200 normal CXRs; 428 COVID-19 CXRs	87.21%		Detection and diagnosis of COVID-19
13.	Hassantabar et al. (2020) [32]	CNN	315 images total: 271 COVID-19, 44 non-COVID-19	93.2%		Detection and diagnosis of COVID-19

No.	Author	Method	Dataset	Accuracy	Notes	Purpose
14.	Hemdan et al. (2020) [33]	COVIDX-Net	Various datasets	90.0%		Detection and diagnosis of COVID-19
15.	Heidari et al. (2020) [34]	VGG16	8,474 CXR images	94.5%	Primary focus on preprocessing algorithms for performance improvement of VGG16	COVID-19 classification
16.	Hira et al. (2021) [35]	AlexNet, GoogleNet, ResNet-50, Se-ResNet-50, DenseNet121, Inception V4, Inception ResNet V2, ResNeXt-50, and Se-ResNeXt-50 architectures	Combination of four datasets, totaling 8,830 CXR images.	Se-Res NeXt-50 –99.32%		COVID-19 classification
17.	Islam et al. (2020) [36]	CNN-LSTM	915 overall cases: 305 COVID-19, 305 normal, 305 pneumonia	99.4%		Detection and diagnosis of COVID-19
18.	Ismael and Sengur (2021) [37]	ResNet18, ResNet50, ResNet101, VGG16 and VGG19 for deep feature extraction and support vector machines (SVMs)	Small dataset with 380 images	ResNet50 94.7%		COVID-19 classification
19.	Karthik et al. (2021) [38]	CNN architecture which they called channel-shuffled dual-branched (CSDB)	Combination of seven datasets, totaling 15; 265 images	99.80%		COVID-19 detection
20.	Khan et al. (2020) [39]	CNN CoroNet	310 normal images, 330 bacterial pneumonia and 327 viral pneumonia along with 284 COVID-19 images	89.6%		Detection and diagnosis of COVID-19
21.	Kumar et al. (2020) [40]	ResNet152 SMOTE algorithm	5,840 images; 5,216 images for training; 624 testing	97.7%		Prediction COVID-19

(Continued)

TABLE 10.2
(Continued)

Serial Number	Authors	Convolutional neural Network (CNN) Architecture Used for COVID-19 Detection Using Chest X-Ray (CXR)	Dataset Details	Performance metrics (accuracy)	Features of the Proposed Method	Purpose
22.	Li et al. (2020) [41]	COVID-MobileXpert	Various datasets	93.5%	DenseNet-121 architecture is adopted to pre-train and fine-tune the network; for on-device COVID-19 screening purposes, lightweight MobileNetv2, SqueezeNet and ShuffleNetV2 used	Detection and diagnosis of COVID-19
23.	Minaee et al. (2020) [42]	ResNet18, ResNet50, SqueezeNet, DenseNet-121	200 COVID-19 Images; 5,000 non-COVID images	Not mentioned		Detection and diagnosis of COVID-19
24.	Monshi et al. (2021) [43]	CovidXrayNet	COVIDx dataset with 15,496 images	95.82%	Focused on data augmentation and CNN hyperparameter optimization	COVID-19 classification
25.	Mostafiz et al. (2020) [2]	ResNet50	Combined different datasets and total of 4,809 images	98.5%	CNN (ResNet50) along with discrete wavelet transform (DWT) features is used; for classification random forest-based bagging approach adapted and data augmentation techniques were used to increase dataset size	COVID-19 classification
26.	Mohammad Shorfuzzaman (2020) [44]	Ensemble of four models: best models using majority voting (VGG16, ResNet50V2, Xception, MobileNet and DenseNet121)	678 images from various sources were used for database creation	ResNet50V2, 98.15%; Ensemble model, 99.26%	Used transfer learning	COVID-19 classification
27.	Mukherjee et al. (2020) [45]	MobileNet VGG16; shallow CNN (proposed)	130 COVID-19 Positive, 51 non-COVID-19	96.92%		Screening of COVID-19
28.	Narin et al. (2020) [46]	Deep CNN and ResNet50	GitHub repository	98%	50 images of each class have been used; therefore, the different variations of the virus spread may have not been exploited	Detection and diagnosis of COVID-19

No.	Author	Method	Dataset	Accuracy	Notes	Task
29.	Narin et al. (2021) [47]	ResNet50, ResNet101, ResNet152, InceptionV3 and Inception-ResNetV2. ResNet50	Three different datasets, totalling 7,406 images	ResNet50 99.7%		COVID-19 classification
30.	Nigam et al. (2021) [48]	VGG16, DenseNet121, Xception, NASNet and EfficientNet	Various private hospitals from Maharashtra and Indore regions from India; dataset not publicly available	79.01%, 89.96%, 88.03%, 85.03%, 93.48%	Popular deep learning architectures are used to develop coronavirus diagnostic systems	Detection and diagnosis of COVID-19
31.	Nour et al. (2020) [49]	CNN	Normal 1,341; viral pneumonia 1,345; total 2,905	97.01%		Detection and diagnosis of COVID-19
32.	Oh et al. (2020) [50]	Patch-based CNN	Various datasets	93.3%	A solution for handling limited dataset for neural network training is proposed	Detection and diagnosis of COVID-19
33.	Ozturk et al. (2020) [19]	DarkCovidNet	Various datasets	98.08%		Detection and diagnosis of COVID-19
34.	Ouchicha et al. (2020) [51]	CVDNet	219 COVID-19; 1,341 normal; 1,345 viral pneumonia; COVID-19 219	96.69%		Detection and diagnosis of COVID-19
35.	Pavlova et al. (2021) [52]	CNN specially tailored for COVID-19	COVIDx8B	95.5%		COVID-19 detection
36.	Sethy and Behera (2020) [53]	ResNet50 + SVM	GitHub repository and Kaggle X-ray dataset for pneumonia	95.38%		Detection and diagnosis of COVID-19
37.	Shibly et al. (2020) [54]	CNN	Non-COVID pneumonia 950; COVID-19 20; total 970	97.36%		Detection and diagnosis of COVID-19
38.	Talaat et al. (2020) [55]	Deep features and fractional-order marine predators algorithm	Various datasets	98.7%		Detection and diagnosis of COVID-19
39.	Varela-Santos and Melin (2021) [56]	CNN		83.2%		Classification of COVID-19

(Continued)

TABLE 10.2

(Continued)

Serial Number	Authors	Convolutional neural Network (CNN) Architecture Used for COVID-19 Detection Using Chest X-Ray (CXR)	Dataset Details	Performance metrics (accuracy)	Features of the Proposed Method	Purpose
40.	Wang and Wong (2020) [57]	COVID-Net	Various datasets	93.3%	Light architecture with less parameters and less computational complexity of the network	Detection and diagnosis of COVID-19
41.	Xu et al. (2020) [58]	ResNet and location-based attention	Private dataset and influenza A pneumonia dataset	99.6%		Detection and diagnosis of COVID-19
42.	Zhao et al. (2021) [59]	ResNet50V2	COVIDx8B	965.%		COVID-19 classification
43.	Zhang et al. (2020) [60]	18-layer residual CNN	Various datasets	96.6%		Detection and diagnosis of COVID-19

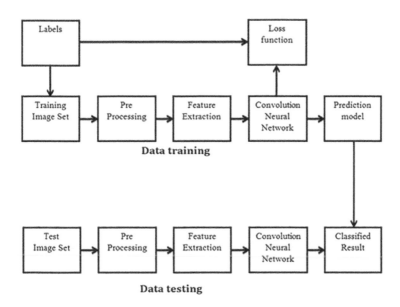

FIGURE 10.2
Proposed system architecture for COVID-19 detection.

database used and their performance accuracy and feature for detection, diagnosis, classification and prediction of COVID-19.

The following papers published in 2021 present an elaborate review of the previously mentioned methods for the detection, diagnosis and classification of deep learning methods for COVID-19 detection using chest X-ray images [61, 62]. From Table 10.2, it can be observed that the accuracy of the methods proposed depends on the CNN architectures as well as the purpose such as diagnosis, detection, classification or prediction of COVID-19.

10.3 Proposed System Architecture

The proposed method focuses on the prediction of COVID-19 positive cases. the proposed method, the input to the neural network is the chest X-ray of the patient and normal chest X-rays to train the model. And the output will be a prediction of COVID-19-positive cases.

The CNN forms the basis of the proposed method. A CNN is a network specialized in the gathering of information with a grid-like topology, such as an image (also known as CNN or ConvNet). CNNs are commonly employed in recent systems for picture classification and segmentation since they are parameter-friendly and straightforward to train.

Transfer learning, a technique that repurposes previously taught CNNs, allows for a reduction in training time and improves the performance of the trained CNNs. CNNs do not need to be trained from scratch as a result of this. The pretrained CNNs may be taught on comparable datasets as well as completely distinct datasets.

Chest X-rays of patients assumed to be infected with COVID-19 are used to feed the system. To categorise pictures into healthy and diseased groups, CNN is employed as a baseline. In order to improve the performance of the proposed CNN model, GoogLeNet was implemented.

Thus, the research work proposes a comparison of two architectures: one using a simple CNN model and another using GoogLeNet for classification.

Transfer learning was utilized to transfer the classification job instead of training CNN from scratch in the proposed system. To accomplish the classification objective in the initial step, the top layers of GoogLeNet are deleted and replaced with new fully linked layers. To avoid the problem of overfitting, the dropout approach was utilized. Figure 10.2 represents a proposed system architecture for COVID-19 detection.

10.4 Algorithmic Review

10.4.1 Proposed Convolutional Neural Network Model

Usually, a CNN has three layers: a convolution layer, a pooling layer and a fully linked layer.

Convolutional Layer: The fundamental building block of CNN is the convolutional layer. It plays a major role of carrying the network's computational load. CNN layer performs a dot product between two matrices. One matrix is the set of learnable parameters also known as the kernel, and the other matrix is the restricted part of the receptive field. The kernel in space is smaller than an image but is more in-depth. This means that if the image consists of three (RGB) channels, the height and width of the kernel will be small in space, but the depth will be expanded to all three channels. During the forward movement, the kernel slides across the height and width of the image and produces the image representation of that receptive area. This creates a two-dimensional image representation known as an activation map, which gives the response of the kernel at each spatial position of the image. Slipping the scale of the kernel is called a stride.

The number of convolutional layers plays a significant role in training the model. The more convolutional layers, the better, as each convolutional layer reduces the number of input features to the fully connected layer. However, it has been observed that after about two or three layers, the accuracy gain becomes rather small. Hence, we used three convolutional layers to train our model.

If calculating one feature at a spatial point (x1, y1) is helpful, it should also be helpful, such as (x2, y2) at some other spatial point (x2, y2). It implies that neurons are restricted to a single two-dimensional slice using the same set of weights, i.e., to construct one activation map. Each weight matrix function is used once and then never revisited in a traditional neural network, whereas the convolutional network has mutual parameters, i.e., weights assigned to one input are the same as the weight applied to the output.

If we have an input of the size $w \times w \times D$ and D_o is the number of kernels with a spatial size of F with phase s and the sum of padding P formula, the size of the output volume can be determined by Equation 10.1:

$$w_o = \frac{w - F + 2P}{s} + 1 \qquad (10.1)$$

Pooling Layer: The pooling layer derives a summary of statistical neighborhoods and replaces the output of the network at certain locations. This step thus assists to reduce the spatial size of the image, reducing the amount of measurement and weight required. On each slice of the representation, the pooling procedure is independently processed.

There are several functions for pooling, such as the average rectangular neighborhood, the regular rectangular neighborhood L2, and a weighted average centered on the central pixel distance. However, the most popular approach is max pooling, which reports the maximum output of the neighborhood.

If we have a map of activation size $w{\times}w{\times}D$, a kernel of pooling spatial size F, and phase S, the output volume size can be determined using Equation 10.2:

$$w_o = \frac{w-F}{s} + 1 \tag{10.2}$$

The fully connected layer neurons in this layer have full communication with all neurons in the preceding and following layers, as seen in regular F-CNN. This is why it is possible to calculate multiplication of the matrix followed by a bias effect as usual. The FC layer helps to map the display between the output and the input.

Nonlinearity Layers: As convolution is a linear operation and images are far from linear, layers of nonlinearity are often positioned to add the activation map to nonlinearity immediately after the convolution layer. Nonlinear actions are of many forms, as follows:

1. Sigmoid: The mathematical form of sigmoid nonlinearity is $\sigma(r) = 1/(1+\bar{e})$. A real-value number is taken and "squashed" A size of between 0 and 1.

2. Tanh: A real-value number is squashed to a range of [–1, 1] by Tanh. Like the sigmoid, the stimulus saturates, but its output is zero-centred, unlike the sigmoid neurons.

3. ReLU: In the last few years, the RECTIFIED LINEAR UNIT (ReLU) has become very common. It calculates the $x(x)=\max(0, x)$ function. That is, in most other words, the activation is merely a 0-threshold.

ReLU is more reliable and, compared to sigmoid and tanh, accelerates the convergence by six times. Figure 10.3 represents CNN models.

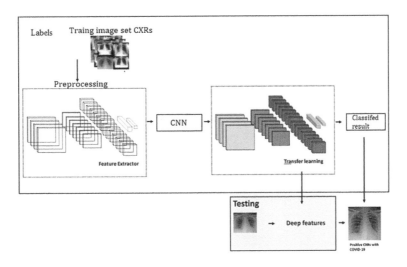

FIGURE 10.3
Convolutional neural network model

10.4.2 Proposed GoogLeNet Model

This section provides a brief introduction to GoogLeNet. GoogLeNet is a 22-layer-deep CNN built by Google researchers as a version of the Inception Network, a deep CNN. GoogLeNet is now utilized for a variety of computer vision applications, including face detection and identification, adversarial training and so on. Two pairs of convolutional layers and max-pooling layers are utilized for feature extraction and feature reduction at the bottom of GoogLeNet. The inception block in the center of GoogLeNet, which uses parallel convolution to expand the breadth as well as the depth of networks, earned GoogLeNet first prize in the ILSVRC 2014 competition. In GoogLeNet, there are a total of nine inception blocks, each of which has four parallel pathways. Figure 10.4 represents the inception block in GoogLeNet.

Four routes seek to extract rich spatial information in each inception block. To minimize feature size and computational expense, 1*1 convolutions are applied. Because features are concatenated after each inception block, computation costs would skyrocket with the growth in feature dimensions in just a few steps if no restrictions were implemented. The dimensions of the intermediate features are decreased by using 1*1 convolutions. Following convolution units in each path have various filter widths to ensure that distinct local spatial information may be retrieved and merged. It is worth noting that the last path employs max-pooling, which not only adds no new parameters but also allows for the extraction of additional features. GoogLeNet outperformed ImageNet on the classification task after incorporating all of the meticulously built architecture.

The proposed work modifies and transfers GoogLeNet in the detection system since it is very shallow compared to state-of-the-art CNNs while maintaining fantastic performance. GoogLeNet was created with a 1,000-category categorization in mind. The proposed GoogLeNet detection algorithm, on the other hand, solely considers binary categorization. As a result, the completely connected layer and output layer were deleted, and four new top layers were added: dropout layer, fully connected layer with 128 neurons, fully connected layer with 2 neurons, and output layer. To avoid overfitting, the dropout layer is used. We utilized a completely connected layer with 128 neurons as a transitional layer before final fully connected levels with 2 neurons to prevent information loss. The transferred GoogLeNet is named as GoogLeNet-COD.

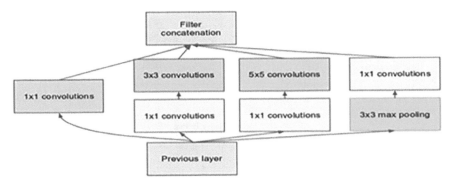

FIGURE 10.4
Inception block in GoogLeNet.

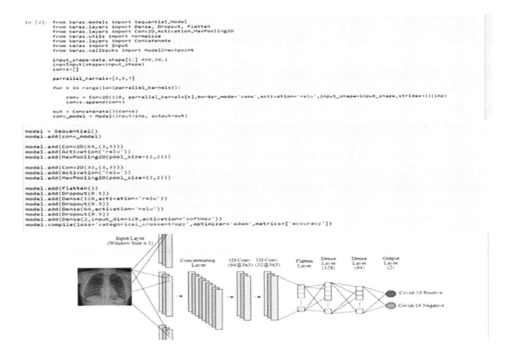

FIGURE 10.5
GoogLeNet-COD model.

10.4.3 Implementation Steps of GoogLeNet-COD

The proposed architecture is implemented using the following steps:

Step1: Load GoogLeNet trained on ImageNet

Step2: Remove the last two top layers

Step3: Add Dropout layer;

Step4: Add FC128 and FC2 fully connected layer

Step5: Add output layer

Step6: Training GoogLeNet-COD with the training set of COVID-19

(FC128 and FC2 denote completely connected layers containing 128 and 2 neurons, respectively.) Figure 10.5 illustrates the GoogLeNet-COD.

10.5 Results and Discussion

This section presents the experimental results and discussion along with the validation metrics and database used.

10.5.1 Dataset Used for COVID-19 Detection

The datasets are downloaded from the following publicly available datasets:

[1] IEEE 8023, *covid chestxray dataset.* Accessed on November 9, 2020. [Online]. Available: https://github.com/ieee8023/covid-chestxray-dataset

[2] Praveen Govi, *coronahack chest xray dataset.* Accessed on November 9, 2020. [Online]. Available: www.kaggle.com/praveengovi/coronahack-chest-xraydataset

For experimental analysis in the proposed method, 907 training images are used and 101 testing images. Figure 10.6 demonstrates the training loss and validation loss for the proposed CNN model. Figure 10.7 represents training accuracy and validation accuracy for the proposed CNN model. Figure 10.8 represents the training accuracy and validation accuracy for the proposed CNN model with GoogLeNet. Figure 10.9 demonstrates the training loss and validation loss for the proposed CNN model with GoogLeNet. The code snippet for GoogLeNet-COD is added in the appendix as Figure 10.10.

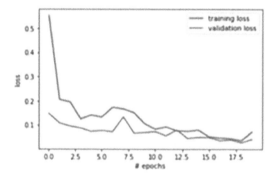

FIGURE 10.6
Training loss and validation loss for proposed CNN model.

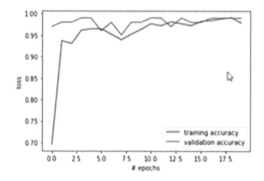

FIGURE 10.7
Training accuracy and validation accuracy for proposed convolutional neural network model.

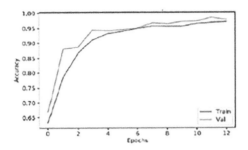

FIGURE 10.8
Training accuracy and validation accuracy for proposed convolutional neural network model with GoogLeNet.

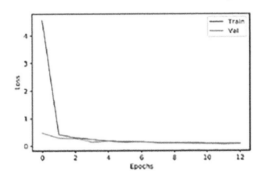

FIGURE 10.9
Training loss and validation loss for proposed convolutional neural network model with GoogLeNet.

10.5.2 Results and Discussion

Validation of the proposed method is computed using accuracy. Accuracy is the ratio between the number of predictions that are accurate and the total number of input samples. For detection, we trained models on 907 samples and tested on 101 samples for both models.

Table 10.3 demonstrates the accuracy, validation loss and validation accuracy using simple CNN. Table 10.4 demonstrates the accuracy, validation loss and validation accuracy using GoogLeNet-COD.

The performance metrics from Table 10.2 and Table 10.3 demonstrate that GoogLeNet-COD performs better in terms of accuracy for COVID-19 detection. This is because the proposed GoogLeNet-COD solely considers binary categorization as a result, the completely connected layer and output layer are deleted and four new top layers were added. Also, the dropout layer is used to avoid overfitting. In order to prevent information loss, a completely connected layer with 128 neurons is utilized as a transitional layer before final fully connected levels with 2 neurons. Also, the use of pretrained weights helps to improve the accuracy of the GoogLeNet-COD.

TABLE 10.3

Evaluation Metrics Using Proposed Convolutional Neural Network Method

Epochs (20)	Accuracy (%)	Validation Loss (%)	Validation Accuracy (%)
1	69.57	14.81	90
2	93.72	10.82	90
3	93.05	9.57	90
4	96.14	8.77	90
5	96.47	7.37	90
6	96.47	7.73	90
7	95.26	7.26	90
8	93.94	13.36	90
9	95.26	6.67	90
10	96.36	6.90	90
11	97.68	7.29	90
12	97.24	5.58	90
13	98.13	7.95	90
14	97.68	4.44	90
15	97.24	4.94	90
16	98.24	4.85	90
17	98.46	3.56	90
18	98.79	3.91	90
19	99.12	2.75	90
20	97.91	4.09	90

TABLE 10.4

Evaluation Metrics Using Convolutional Neural Network with GoogLeNet

Epochs (20)	Accuracy (%)	Validation Loss (%)	Validation Accuracy (%)
1	83.57	10.81	95
2	87.72	9.82	95
3	93.17	9.57	95
4	95.14	9.77	95
5	96.33	8.37	95
6	96.47	8.73	95
7	96.26	8.26	95
8	96.94	10.36	95
9	97.23	7.67	95
10	97.43	7.90	95
11	97.68	6.29	95
12	97.44	5.58	95
13	98.13	5.95	95
14	98.68	4.44	95
15	97.24	3.94	95
16	98.23	3.85	95
17	98.46	2.56	95
18	97.79	2.91	95
19	99.12	2.75	95
20	98.91	2.09	95

10.6 Conclusions and Future Directions

This research initially presents a comprehensive overview of deep learning methods for the detection, diagnosis, classification and prediction of COVID-19 using chest X-rays. In addition, the work proposes the detection of COVID-19 using chest X-ray.

In the proposed research work, two methods are proposed for detection of COVID-19. In the first method, simple CNN is proposed, while in the second method, using transfer learning for GoogLeNet and the CNN model, GoogLeNet-COD is proposed. The proposed GoogLeNet-COD is also modified for overfitting and information loss. Further, both methods are compared for their performance using accuracy as the comparison metrics.

From the experimental results, it can be concluded that the proposed GoogLeNet-COD method outperforms the earlier CNN method. The proposed CNN method demonstrates an accuracy of 90% for 20 epochs, while the proposed GoogLeNet-COD demonstrates 95%.

The increased accuracy using GoogLeNet-COD is because GoogLeNet-COD is a solely binary classification model, as the completely connected layer and output layer are deleted and four new top layers were added. It also utilizes a completely connected layer with 128 neurons as a transitional layer before final fully connected levels with 2 neurons. The use of pretrained weights helps to improve the accuracy of the GoogLeNet-COD.

The key drawback of the research work is the lack of adequate data to train the prediction model. In order to improve its accuracy, further different methods for data augmentation to increase dataset can be explored. Methods like CNN, LSTM and ensemble methods can be explored for improving the prediction accuracy.

References

1. Monshi, M., Poon, J., Chung, V., & Monshi, F.M. (2021). CovidXrayNet: Optimizing data augmentation and CNN hyperparameters for improved COVID-19 detection from CXR. *Computers in Biology and Medicine*, 133, 104375.
2. Mostafiz, R., Uddin, M.S., Reza, M.M., Rahman, M.M., et al. (2020). COVID-19 detection in chest x-ray through random forest classier using a hybridization of deep CNN and DWT optimized features. *Journal of King Saud University-Computer and Information Sciences*, 34(6), 3226–3235.
3. Long, D.R., Gombar, S., Hogan, C.A., Greninger, A.L., O'Reilly-Shah, V., Bryson-Cahn, C., Stevens, B., Rustagi, A., Jerome, K.R., Kong, C.S., Zehnder, J., Shah, N.H., Weiss, N.S., Pinsky, B.A., & Sunshine, J.E. (2020). Occurrence and timing of subsequent severe acute respiratory syndrome coronavirus 2 reverse-transcription polymerase chain reaction positivity among initially negative patients. *Clinical Infectious Diseases*, 72, 323–326.
4. Freeman, W.M., Walker, S.J., & Vrana, K.E. (1999). Quantitative RT-PCR: Pitfalls and potential. *BioTechniques*, 26(1), 112–125.
5. Kageyama, T., Kojima, S., Shinohara, M., Uchida, K., Fukushi, S., Hoshino, F.B., Takeda, N., & Katayama, K. (2003). Broadly reactive and highly sensitive assay for Norwalk-like viruses based on real-time quantitative reverse transcription-PCR. *Journal of Clinical Microbiology*, 41(4), 1548–1557.
6. Corman, V.M., Landt, O., Kaiser, M., Molenkamp, R., Meijer, A., Chu, D.K., Bleicker, T., Brünink, S., Schneider, J., Schmidt, M.L., Mulders, D. G., Haagmans, B. L., van der Veer, B., van den Brink, S., Wijsman, L., Goderski, G., Romette, J. L., Ellis, J., Zambon, M., Peiris, M., . . .& Drosten, C. (2020). Detection of 2019 novel coronavirus (2019-nCoV) by real-time RT-PCR. *Euro Surveillance: Bulletin Europeen sur les maladies transmissibles = European communicable disease bulletin*, 25(3), 2000045.

7. Bernheim, A., et al. (2020). Coronavirus disease-19 (COVID-19) chest CT findings in coronavirus disease-19 (COVID-19): Relationship to duration of infection. *Radiology*, 295(3), 685–691.

8. Pan, F., Ye et al. (2020). Time course of lung changes on chest CT during recovery from 2019 novel coronavirus (COVID-19). *Radiology*, 295(3), 715–721.

9. Mahmoudi, T., et al., (2020). A review of current progress and future trends in lateral flow assays for point-of-care cancer detection. *Trends in Analytical Chemistry*, 125, 115842.

10. To, K., et al. (2020). Temporal viral load in posterior oropharyngeal saliva samples and serum antibody responses during SARS-CoV-2 infection: An observational cohort study. *The Lancet Infectious Diseases*, 20(5), 565–574.

11. Huang, P., et al. (2018). MERS-CoV detection by a rapid and specific assay. *Frontiers in Microbiology*, 9.

12. Feng, H., Liu, Y., Lv, M., & Zhong, J. (2020). A case report of COVID-19 with false negative RT-PCR test: Necessity of chest CT. *Japanese Journal of Radiology*, 38, 409–410.

13. Cleverley, J., Piper, J., & Jones, M. M. (2020). The role of chest radiography in confirming COVID-19 pneumonia. *BMJ*, 370.

14. Hosseiny, M., Kooraki, S., Gholamrezanezhad, A., Reddy, S., & Myers, L. (2020). Radiology perspective of coronavirus disease 2019 (COVID-19): Lessons from severe acute respiratory syndrome and Middle East respiratory syndrome. *American Journal of Roentgenology*, 214(5), 1078–1082.

15. Wang, L., Lin, Z.Q., & Wong, A. (2020) COVID-Net: A tailored deep convolutional neural network design for detection of COVID-19 cases from chest X-ray images. *Scientific Reports*, 10, 19549.

16. Afshar, P., Afshar, P., Heidarian, S., Naderkhani, F., Oikonomou, A., Plataniotis, K. N., & Mohammadi, A. (2020). COVID-CAPS: A capsule network-based framework for identification of COVID-19 cases from X-ray images. *Pattern Recognition Letters*, 138, 638–643.

17. Ozkaya, U., Ozturk, S., & Barstugan, M. (2020). Coronavirus (COVID19) classification using deep features fusion and ranking technique. *arXiv preprint arXiv:2004.03698*.

18. Chan, Y., Zeng, Y., Wu, H., Wu, M., & Sun, H. (2018). Effective pneumothorax detection for chest X-ray images using local binary pattern and support vector machine. *Journal of Healthcare Engineering*, 1–11.

19. Ozturk, T., Talo, M., Yildirim, E. A., Baloglu, U. B., Yildirim, O., & Rajendra Acharya, U. (2020). Automated detection of COVID-19 cases using deep neural networks with X-ray images. *Computers in Biology and Medicine*, 121, 103792.

20. Abbas, A., Abdelsamea, M.M., & Gaber, M.M. (2021). Classification of COVID-19 in chest x-ray images using detrac deep convolutional neural network. *Applied Intelligence*, 51, 854–864.

21. Alazab, M., Awajan, A., Mesleh, A., Abraham, A., Jatana, V., & Alhyari, S. (2020). COVID-19 prediction and detection using deep learning. *International Journal of Computer Information Systems and Industrial Management Applications*, 168–181.

22. Alawad, W., Alburaidi, B., Alzahrani, A., & Alaj, F. (2021). A comparative study of stand-alone and hybrid CNN models for COVID-19 detection. *International Journal of Advanced Computer Science and Applications*, 12.

23. Alqudah, A., Qazan, S., Alquran, H., Qasmieh, I., & Alqudah, A. (2020). COVID-19 789 detection from X-ray images using different artificial intelligence hybrid models. *Jordan Journal of Electrical Engineering*, 6(2), 168.

24. Apostolopoulos, I.D., & Mpesiana, T.A. (2020). COVID-19: Automatic detection from X-ray images utilizing transfer learning with convolutional neural networks. *Physical and Engineering Sciences in Medicine*, 43, 635–640.

25. Basu, S., Mitra, S., & Saha, N. (2020). Deep learning for screening COVID-19 using chest X-ray images. *ArXiv*, Ml.

26. Chhikara, P., Gupta, P., Singh, P., & Bhatia, T. (2021). A deep transfer learning based model for automatic detection of COVID-19 from chest X-rays. *Turkish Journal of Electrical Engineering & Computer Sciences*, 29, 2663–2679.

27. Chowdhury, N. K., Rahman, M. M., & Kabir, M. A. (2020). PDCOVIDNeT: A parallel- dilated convolutional neural network architecture for detecting COVID-19 from chest X-ray images. *ArXiv*.

28. Cohen, J. P., Dao, L., Morrison, P., Roth, K., Bengio, Y., Shen, B., Abbasi, A., Hoshmand- Kochi, M., Ghassemi, M., Li, H., & Duong, T. Q. (2020). Predicting COVID-19 pneumonia severity on chest x-ray with deep learning. *ArXiv.*

29. Dominik, C. (2021). *Detection of COVID-19 in X-ray Images Using Neural Networks.* Bachelor's thesis. Czech Technical University in Prague, Faculty of Information Technology.

30. Hall, L. O., Paul, R., Goldgof, D. B., & Goldgof, G. M. (2020). Finding COVID-19 from chest X-rays using deep learning on a small dataset. *ArXiv*, 1–8.

31. Haghanifar, A., Majdabadi, M. M., & Ko, S. (2020). Covid-cxnet: Detecting COVID-19 in frontal chest x-ray images using deep learning. *Multimedia Tools and Applications*, 81(21), 30615–30645.

32. Hassantabar, S., Ahmadi, M., & Sharifi, A. (2020). Diagnosis and detection of infected tissue of COVID-19 patients based on lung x-ray image using convolutional neural network approaches. *Chaos, Solitons and Fractals*, 140, 110170.

33. Hemdan, E. E. D., Shouman, M. A., & Karar, M.E. (2020). COVIDX-net: A framework of deep learning classifiers to diagnose COVID-19 in X-ray images. *arXiv preprint* arXiv:2003.11055.

34. Heidari, M., Mirniaharikandehei, S., Khuzani, A. Z., Danala, G., Qiu, Y., & Zheng, B. (2020). Improving the performance of CNN to predict the likelihood of COVID-19 using chest X-ray images with preprocessing algorithms. *International Journal of Medical Informatics*, 144, 104284.

35. Hira, S., Bai, A., & Hira, S. (2021). An automatic approach based on CNN architecture to detect COVID-19 disease from chest X-ray images. *Applied Intelligence*, 51, 2864–2889.

36. Islam, M. Z., Islam, M. M., & Asraf, A. (2020). A combined deep CNN-LSTM network for the detection of novel coronavirus (COVID-19) using X-ray images. *Informatics in Medicine Unlocked*, 20, 100412.

37. Ismael, A. M., & Şengur, A. (2021). Deep learning approaches for COVID-19 detection 961 based on chest X-ray images. *Expert Systems with Applications*, 164.

38. Karthik, R., Menaka, R., & Hariharan, M. (2020). Learning distinctive filters for COVID-19 detection from chest X-ray using shuffled residual CNN. *Applied Soft Computing Journal*, 106744.

39. Khan, M., Mehran, M.T., Haq, Z.U., Ullah, Z., Naqvi, S.R., Ihsan, M., & Abbass, H. (2021). Applications of artificial intelligence in COVID-19 pandemic: A comprehensive review. *Expert Systems with Applications*, 185,115695.

40. Kumar, R., Arora, R., Bansal, V., Sahayasheela, V., Buckchash, H., Imran, J., Narayanan, N., Pandian, G., & Raman, B. (2020). Accurate prediction of COVID-19 using chest X-ray images through deep feature learning model with SMOTE and machine learning classifiers. *medRxiv preprint* medRxiv:2020.04.13.20063461.

41. Li, M. (2020). Chest CT features and their role in COVID-19. *Radiology of Infectious Diseases*, 7(2), 51–54.

42. Minaee, S., Kafieh, R., Sonka, M., Yazdani, S., & Soufi, G. J. (2020). Deep-COVID: Predicting COVID-19 from chest X-ray images using deep transfer learning. *ArXiv*, 1–9.

43. Monshi, M. M. A., Poon, J., & Chung, V. (2020). Deep learning in generating radiology reports: A survey. *Artificial Intelligence in Medicine*, 106, 101878.

44. Mohammad Shorfuzzaman, M.M. (2020). On the detection of COVID-19 from chest X-ray images using CNN-based transfer learning. *Computers, Materials & Continua*, 64, 1359–1381.

45. Mukherjee, H., Ghosh, S., Dhar, A., Obaidullah, S. M., Santosh, K. C., & Roy, K. (2020). Shallow convolutional neural network for COVID-19 outbreak screening using chest X-rays. *ArXiv*, 1–10.

46. Narin, A., Kaya, C., & Pamuk, Z. (2020). Automatic detection of coronavirus disease (COVID-19) using X-ray images and deep convolutional neural networks. *arXiv preprint* arXiv:2003.10849.

47. Narin, A., Kaya, C., & Pamuk, Z. (2021). Automatic detection of coronavirus disease (COVID-19) using x-ray images and deep convolutional neural networks. *Pattern Analysis and Applications*, 1–14.

48. Nigam, B., Nigam, A., Jain, R., Dodia, S., Arora, N., & Annappa, B. (2021). COVID-19: Automatic detection from X-ray images by utilizing deep learning methods. *Expert Systems with Applications*, 176, 114883.

49. Nour, M., Cömert, Z., & Polat, K. (2020). A novel medical diagnosis model for COVID-19 infection detection based on deep features and Bayesian optimization. *Applied Soft Computing Journal*, 106580.

50. Oh, Y., Park, S., & Ye, J. C. (2020). Deep learning COVID-19 features on CXR using limited training data sets. *IEEE Transactions on Medical Imaging*, 1.

51. Ouchicha, C., Ammor, O., & Meknassi, M. (2020). CVDNet: A novel deep learning architecture for detection of coronavirus (COVID-19) from chest x-ray images. *Chaos, Solitons and Fractals*, 140.

52. Pavlov, Y. L. (2019). Random forests. *Random Forests*, 1–122.

53. Sethy, P. K., Behera, S. K., Ratha, P. K., & Biswas, P. (2020). Detection of coronavirus disease (COVID-19) based on deep features and support vector machine. *International Journal of Mathematical, Engineering and Management Sciences*, 5(4), 643–651.

54. Shibly, K. H., Dey, S. K., Islam, M. T. U., & Rahman, M. M. (2020). COVID faster R—CNN: A novel framework to Diagnose Novel Coronavirus Disease (COVID-19) in X-ray images. *Informatics in Medicine Unlocked*, 20, 100405.

55. Talaat, A., Yousri, D., Ewees, A., Al-qaness, M. A. A., Damasevicius, R., & Elsayed Abd Elaziz, M. (2020). COVID-19 image classification using deep features and fractional order marine predators algorithm. *Scientific Reports*, 10,15364.

56. Varela-Santos, S., & Melin, P. (2021). A new approach for classifying coronavirus COVID-19 based on its manifestation on chest X-rays using texture features and neural networks. *Information Sciences*, 545, 403–414.

57. Wang, L., Lin, Z.Q., & Wong, A. (2020) COVID-Net: A tailored deep convolutional neural network design for detection of COVID-19 cases from chest X-ray images. *Scientific Reports*, 10, 19549.

58. Xu, X., Jiang, X., Ma, C., Du, P., Li, X., Lv, S., Yu, L., Chen, Y., Su, J., & Lang, G. (2020). Deep learning system to screen coronavirus disease 2019 pneumonia. *arXiv preprint* arXiv: 2002.09334.

59. Zhao, W., Jiang, W., & Qiu, X. (2021). Fine-tuning convolutional neural networks for COVID-19 detection from chest X-ray images. *Diagnostics*, 11, 1887.

60. Zhang, J., Xie, Y., Li, Y., Shen, C., & Xia, Y. (2020). COVID-19 screening on chest X-ray images using deep learning based anomaly detection. *arXiv:2003.12338*.

61. Khan, M., Mehran, M.T., Haq, Z.U., Ullah, Z., Naqvi, S.R., Ihsan, M., & Abbass, H. (2021). Applications of artificial intelligence in COVID-19 pandemic: A comprehensive review. *Expert Systems with Applications*, 185, 115695.

62. Breve, F. (2021). COVID-19 detection on chest X-ray images: A comparison of CNN architectures and ensembles. *arXiv preprint* arXiv:2111.09972.

Appendix

Code snippet for GoogLeNet-COD is presented as Figure 10.10.

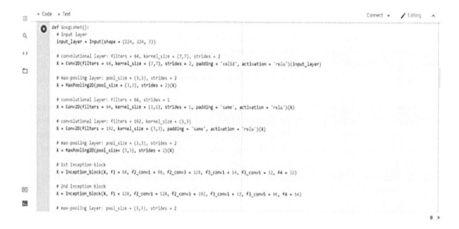

FIGURE 10.10
Code snippets for GoogLeNet model.

11

Video Segmentation and Compression

Nithya K, Mythili S, Krishnamoorthi M and Kalamani M

CONTENTS

11.1 Introduction

There is a possibility of having the extension on signal processing and image processing techniques. This leads to concentrating on video processing. In general, the motion of pictures is called as video. Advancements in the computer society and its technology make the process of video segmentation and compression more advanced.

11.1.1 Motivation

The appearance and the detailed information about the target always attract humans visually. To fetch even a minute detail from the video, the segmentation process is more supportive.

11.1.2 Significance of the Study

Basically, the video segmentation is a process of dividing a video into different sets based on its characteristic homogeneity. The appeared model of the video and its annotations are

DOI: 10.1201/9781003218111-11

highly concentrated to extract the absolute information on the basis of temporal and spatial domains. The great concern on computer vision, on the basis of supervised interaction between the objects involved in a video, is devised with various artificial learning algorithms. The video segmentation process helps to track things even in fast motion video that contains heterogeneous objects throughout the video duration. The reliability and the contextual content between the frames are extracted by this.

11.1.3 Contributions

There are a wide variety of segmentation techniques available to improve video quality and extract information in a much better way. The semantic segmentation and instance segmentation help to distinguish the different objects and identify the correlation between the same objects to treat the instances in a useful way. Pixel information is even more valuable for the autonomous car driving system. It is executed and projected in the proposed work.

Further, the substantial increase in the storage and transmission cost makes use of the video compression process. It is actually used to compress the video content without modifying the actual information. The correspondence of quality is purely based on the types of lossy and lossless compression. In general, the compression can be done by minimizing the resolution or adjusting it based on the desired application. And in another way, the frames per second can be adjusted. These dramatic changes lead to utilizing the minimal data required to view the video content. The only thing is that the quality level is compromised by this. So, the machine learning algorithms are used for better codec fidelity. There are a wide variety of benefits achieved by using machine learning. The learning-based compression with the convolutional neural network (CNN) and recurrent neural network (RNN) are involved in the developmental platform of video compression. Thus, in this way, the available bandwidth is efficiently used.

The straightforward technique of the proposed model is organized as follows: the first section of this chapter explains the necessity of video segmentation and compression. The second section covers the relevant deep learning algorithms for achieving perfect signal quality. This is followed by the proposed method which holds the architecture and experimental results.

11.2 Necessity of Video Segmentation and Compression

The most common and unified process of improving video processing is achieved with the help of segmentation and compression. An entire video is partitioned into several segments, i.e. it is segmented into several frames per second. These frames are useful to classify the different objects. And then each object is classified according to various classes like background objects, colours, etc. Finally, there will be a group of segmented images which will be the output of this. The segmentation can be of current segmentation which segments the objects which are having coherency. If importance is given to the foreground and as well as to the background, then the ground segmentation is applicable which segments the objects from the background. For activity and movement recognition, this segmentation is used. The grouping of similar neighbors called superpixels of the object leads to feasible information extraction. It is very useful to sort out the problems occurring in our day-to-day life, like to control the crowd of people occupied in a busy place, to maintain the traffic in a structured way, to maintain social distancing, etc. The concerned region is grouped based on the different inputs which are segregated on the space-time regions and appearance.

The video may consist of the same or different backgrounds, images of any size, music of any length and redundant sounds which may be present at times. Actually, video modeling is a part that is done with segmentation, whereas it has to be compact by minimizing the redundancy in the video content by applying different methods to achieve a high compression rate and video quality in a superior manner. This is used to quantify the accuracy of video. The computational complexity of segmentation and compression is quite simple. The subsequent frames are fully compressed using the number of codec algorithms. This helps to minimize the amount of bandwidth used for the luminance and chrominance of a video.

According to a survey, there will be around 2 billion users who are internet video users. So, trillions of trillions of minutes are used to watch the videos. This directly conveys that the timeline of every video is taken into consideration; if it is not taken care of, then it leads to huge internet traffic. Handling the timeline and its effectiveness for a real-time video is quite tedious. Potential technologies and its measures help to encounter the problems facing in real-time video compression. There are various standard formats like h.264, h.265 which are followed to transport the video from one point to another point. The video resolution is purely based on the product of the pixel width and pixel height. The video quality is ensured by the number of pixels realistically held in the frame with the appropriate aspect ratio. There are wide varieties of video quality available like high definition (HD) where the pixels are of 1080*720, standard definition (SD) where the pixels are of 640*480 and full high definition where the pixels are of 1920*1080. The dominant process of compression affects the video quality and influences viewing the video. So, the enhanced visual effects are achieved with the optimized compression process for better video quality at the user end.

11.3 Existing Video Segmentation and Video Compression Techniques

To extract common information from a set of video frames, a proposal-driven segmentation method is suggested [1]. CNN simultaneously segments similar object information from two different video frames and patches the combined information into one video. Similar pairs of frames are identified using ResNet architecture, and to segment the region of interest from those frames, PSPNet architecture is used which uses the datasets such as VOT 2016, DAVIS 2017 and SegTrack v2. The proposal-driven segmentation method provides improved accuracy over single-frame segmentation methods.

Multimodel temporal video segmentation methods extract the thumbnail from video frames [2]. The model includes the relevant ad in the video segment based on the context. It identifies the instance which is more relevant for inserting the context-relevant advertisement clip. In this, a deep CNN approach is applied for performing various operations such as shot boundary detection, scene/story segmentation and thumbnail extraction. Videos from French National Television and US TV series are considered for segmentation. A temporal video segmentation technique provides the superior F-score result compared with other techniques.

The video object segmentation method [3] uses the bilateral grid for reducing the computational cost. In a bilateral grid, foreground objects and the background scene are segregated using dynamic color modeling and reliability measurement algorithms. Each cell in the bilateral grid stores the spatial and temporal information. Efficient video object segmentation is achieved by reducing the size of the graph. Experiments are conducted over DAVIS 2016, YouTube-Objects and SegTrack v2 datasets. It gives the average object detection accuracy of 78% and does not process multiple objects in a frame.

The conditional random field (CRF) based optimized labelling approach automatically analyzes the computerized video and segments the objects in the videos [4]. To perform optimized labelling, the CRF approach considers various features such as higher-order CRF labeling, feature fusion, unary potential of higher-order CRF labelling and making the algorithm affordable. It considers the spatial and temporal information to perform region-based segmentation. Over the YouTube Action Dataset, video object segmentation [5] is performed which gives the average precision and recall values of 0.97 and 0.87, respectively.

The semantic object–based segmentation technique is used for segmenting the objects from the video [6, 7] which are collected using a vision-based robot. In each batch of the video, objects are segmented, and all the segmented objects are grouped together by using the notebook-based bidirectional connection technique. A standard publicly available Safari_1.0 Dataset [8] with nine different videos is considered for analysis. Performance of the model is evaluated using two metrics, IoU and NDI; both metrics give the highest average result compared with other traditional methods.

Video compression is done by a pixel motion-predictive CNN algorithm. The supervised learning model [9, 10] describes the process of video compression by iterative analysis, its synthesis and binarization. The block prediction is done to represent the data in fewer bits by decreasing the energy in calculating the residual. The preprocessing followed is motion extension which uses the reference frame to reconstruct the current block. The non-predictive mode is compared with a pixel-predicted CNN, and the results are tested with different motion categories such as local motion and global motion. In this way, the improved form of compression is achieved by using the standard H.264 codec format and proved by comparing it with traditional video codecs.

The low-resolution video is compressed with a focus on temporal sequences. The autoencoder is utilized for end-to-end autoencoders. The deep learning generative algorithm is trained on generic video and its content. The stochastic recurrent variational autoencoder is used to convert the obtained local variables and global state information into a frame sequence. The Bayesian posterior model is used as the optimal analytical encoder used for the distribution prediction. The quantitative model of local state bidirectional LSTM is considered [11]. The evaluation metric of distortion rate by bits per second and signal-to-noise ratio in the video content are estimated, and the results are extracted with the neural codec section and inferred that better video compression is achieved from the distribution for lossless compression with prior models.

Machine learning–based video compression is introduced in which the segmented frames are assigned with variable bit rates. This improves the computational efficiency and is applicable for the minimal latency mode of video. The encoding and decoding are tuned with the LSTM architecture for the appropriate prediction with the mean and variance distribution estimation [12]. The temporal variation is detected by its feature connections and modeled with the ReLu modules.

11.4 Proposed Model with Its Results

In video segmentation, object detection is the basic process of extracting the desired feature. In this, the exact position of the object is extracted based on the given frames. We tested the segmentation and object detection methods on a VIRAT video dataset [13]. It contains the high-definition videos as well as sample videos which are collected by different camara points. Most of the videos cover natural scenes and daily activities.

11.4.1 Video Segmentation Process

Video segmentation breaks the entire video into shot-based frame chunks and extracts the region of interest from every frame [14]. It also splits the foreground region from the background by using object segmentation [5]. It is used for various purposes such as face segmentation, moving object segmentation, etc. Shots in videos are differentiated by the threshold value of the number of pixels changed from previous frame to current frame.

In this work, the end-to-end video segmentation is done. Basically, semantic segmentation is used which incorporates the conditional random field for operating on the pixels of the objects in the frame. The potential evidence from the objects is extracted with proper label assignments. If the objects are identified with the same category of input, then the semantic segmentation process will not distinguish it properly. In that case, the instance segmentation is being used and fetches the information from the classes which are segmented. In this way, the refined results can be obtained as shown in Figure 11.1. So, the social distance [15, 16] can be maintained throughout the tracking region. In order to ensure the social distancing in public places, humans are considered as the desired phenomena, and this feature is being extracted. These details help to track the people and ensure the social distance at public places in a wide variety. In this, the distance between people is calculated based on the pixel and its assigned range. There are various techniques that are available to calculate the correlation among the pixels and its distance.

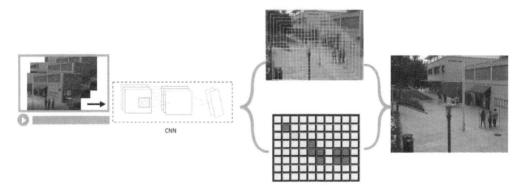

FIGURE 11.1
Convolutional neural network based video segmentation via object detection.

They are Euclidean distance, Minkowski distance, Manhattan distance, Hamming distance and Cosine distance.

- **Euclidean distance**

  If we take the Euclidean distance, the distance between the pairs of the centroids are taken as reference. The reference is the threshold point which is set as 100 for ensuring the social distance among people in a crowded area. Its inherent properties of non-negativity, symmetry and triangle inequality satisfy the need for distance space calculation between two points. With this, the similarities are identified using this Euclidean distance.

- **Manhattan distance**

  In Manhattan distance, the calculation will take the sum of absolute distances between the data points in N-dimensional space.

- **Minkowski distance**

  The generalized form of Euclidean and Manhattan distance is the Minkowski distance. If the normalized value is of order 1, then it is considered to follow the Manhattan distance. If the value is of order 2, then the distance metric has to be adapted to Euclidean distance.

- **Hamming distance**

  The categorical variables similarity index is calculated with Hamming distance. If the lengths of the two strings are equal, then it is applied for the similarity distance estimation.

- **Cosine distance**

  It is a measure of similarity between two vector spaces. If the similarity of the vectors increases, then its distance decreases. If the distance increases, then the similarity decreases. So the important estimation is its angle.

11.4.1.1 Results of Video Segmentation Process

Social distancing is tracked by the process of object detection. Among the listed distances, the Euclidean distance metrics are considered as the best suitable for this scenario. If the Euclidean distance between the adjacent humans is below the threshold level 50, then it is highlighted with red color to alert them. If they are maintaining the distance of greater than the threshold level 50, then it is highlighted with green color which shows that the social distancing is followed.

Figure 11.2 shows the YOLO (you only look once) model which acts as an object detector in video segmentation. In this object detection model, the video is split into several frames. The probabilities of different classes are tuned by the CNN algorithm followed in the YOLO model. The real-time objects are predicted even in distributed variants involved in the frame sequences. Initially the frames are divided into grids of equal dimension. All grids are purely responsible for the objects located in its cell and detect them. The outline shown for the detected object is highlighted with a solid color line which is known as a boundary level of the box where the height and width of the object is determined and marked. The objects appearing in the grid cells are purely based on the probabilistic phenomenon. It is an intersection over the union concept. Based on this, the object is detected among the different classes. All these predictions are done by the CNN.

FIGURE 11.2
Transformed social distancing breaches using object detection in video.

FIGURE 11.3
Resultant categorical view of the people in a place using semantic segmentation.

The Coco dataset is used for the experimentation which comprises 80 classes. The minimum Euclidean distance set here is 50, which is considered as a safe distance among the people. It is considered as a variable factor on the basis of application. The Coco dataset is trained with effective YOLO object detection. This kind of dataset with the semantic labels is supportive for categorization and better boundary prediction.

In Figure 11.3, it is observed that the informative objects are segmented which helps to determine the interlinking relation among the objects using semantic segmentation. In

FIGURE 11.4
Detailed views of consistent masks on every instance using instance segmentation.

this, the inherent properties of semantic segmentation and single label assigned for the scenario transform the region-based prediction to a pixel-based prediction, shown with bright contrast.

The information in the frames is easily extracted with the semantics. In Figure 11.4, it is clear that multiple objects of the same class are considered as separate entities and segmented further for better clarity. The task per pixel-based mask displayed here is distinguishing the objects with different colours.

11.4.2 Video Compression Process

The process will include the techniques to obtain lossless and quality compression, which includes high-level encoding and decoding. The network model designed comprises encoding and decoding modules in its multilayer architecture. The temporal resolution and spatial resolution are the considering factors.

The video content should be maintained and delivered to reach the utmost information in it. In the traditional approaches, in order to reduce the redundancy, the well-standardized discrete cosine transforms are used for end-to-end optimization. And then the neural network–based autoencoder helps to open the problem involved in the standard codec formats. The motion estimation, residual effects, frame rate distortion and bit rate are jointly influenced in the video viewing quality. So, the approach of mapping one-to-one components makes a clear structure for compression. The predictive coding techniques followed in the traditional compressions are H.264 and H.265. The DNN and RNN model has some trade-offs in compressing the video with optimal quality. The lag of the system arises due to the misinterpreted motion estimation and compression. In that case, the CNN is employed to avoid misinterpretation while encoding and decoding. The effectiveness is demonstrated with the CNN approach for compressing the video by reducing the bit rate and loss between the frames.

The general categories of compression are as follows:

- Lossy compression leads to eliminating the redundant data permanently so the file compression ratio is too high, which further reduces the quality at decoding side. Thus, the obtained file is of very small size.
- The lossless compression helps to delete only the redundant data, but the quality is not affected by it. Through this approach, the file size will not be reduced much. Usually, it can be an intra-frame compression or inter-frame compression. Based on the format, the compression factor is achieved. The successive frames which are segmented are compressed by eliminating the redundant data using inter-frame compression, whereas the redundant data in the frames like the repetitive backgrounds and objects are eliminated in the intra-frame compression.

The compatible and popular compression standards such as MPEG and MJPEG are having quality degradation due to the processing between the frames. But if video streaming is considered, then it attains better perception in terms of viewing ability. The traditional approach requires time to compress the video separately, whereas using the deep learning algorithms, the compressions are automated based on necessity. With little human intervention, the adaptive algorithm is deployed for compressing the video and lessening the uploading time of it. Instead of utilizing the central processing unit for the compression process, the graphical processing unit is used at which the deep learning algorithms are implemented. The simple parallel computation makes the process simpler and utilizes less computing power. Using the neural network algorithm, the input is learned and reproduced with less supervision. The cognitive tasks through deep learning algorithms and its better ways outperform the traditional compression procedures.

The advancements consider that the less sensible nature of the human eye for the colors leads to a way of compressing the video by converting it from high contrasts of RGB to YUV components. In the first phase, these components are reduced to half of the pixel in the horizontal or vertical direction. This kind of sub-sampling tends to reduce data utilization.

Then in the second phase, the motion estimation is done for the frames which are sampled. Of the two successive frames, there will be a difference between them. There are three different frames that are actually considered for encoding purposes. They are as follows:

I frames stands for intra-frames. It will not consider any frame as the reference; since it is absent, the compression factor of it is not too high. It requires more space to store the data.

P frames stands for predicted frames. In this, the current frame is compared with the reference frame, and its difference will be stored in a disk space. So, the occupied frame size is minimal.

B frames stands for bidirectional frames. It refers to the frame that is generated by using the previous and future frames as reference frames. If the B frames are preferred, then the visual data is not accompanied for all types of streams. It is compatible with H.264. But for Apple Inc., it is not supportive and produces unexpected anomalies.

So, the compression process requires the adaptive P frames for its efficient working. This P frame is also called delta frame. The P slice is considered in P frames that encode the data which is spatially distinct from other regions separately. The predictions on the segmented blocks are considered with switching P frames in order to improve the quality by facilitating the exchange of coded streams in a wide variety. This ensures the error correction in a better way while decoding it. The P frame contains the information about the picture and its motion vector displacement. The standard H.264 format helps for the optimal decoding phase by comparing multiple previously decided frames. Fewer bits are required for this encoding and decoding purpose.

11.4.2.1 Working of Computational Neural Network Model in Video Compression Process

CNN is the deep learning algorithm that supports this kind of prediction with its convoluted layers. The considered video in Figure 11.5 circumstances is performing the video compression process by having the CNN algorithm for the motion estimation. The video sequences are segmented into a number of frames which are indicated as consecutive frames 1, 2, 3 . . . n ordered on a time basis. And its distribution is formulated as the probability of $| f1, f2, f3, fn |$. The spatial-temporal correlation between the frames improves the capability of extracting the motion displacement and tends to smooth the prediction progress in a sustained manner.

The architecture components are shown in Figure 11.5. It explains the video compression model using convoluted layers. The feeder input is first segmented into a number of frames and then the compression process is started. In the initial stage of compression, the sampling process is carried out which samples the given input into a number

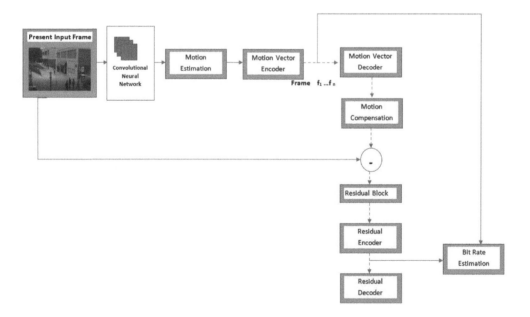

FIGURE 11.5
Developed sequential process involved in video compression.

of samples. The sampled data is considered as blocks or slices. After the sampling, the encoding phase is started which encodes the data based on the spatial and temporal correlation. The encoding is performed by having the reference frame. The motion information is compared, and the position is fixed while decoding. The predictive coding takes the side information which is known as residual information. It is created by subtracting the current frame with the predicted frame. Each stage of it gives a compact representation. The efficiency is estimated from the comparison of the target frame and the reconstructed frame. And the bit rate estimation also supports it. Various contributions are towards the machine learning formulation, motion estimation and its compensation.

11.4.2.2 Computational Neural Network Adoption Parameters and Validation of Obtained Results

The parameters determined for the video segmentation process are as follows:

- Person and the camera distance
- Object detection accuracy
- Person recognition accuracy
- Surrounding size

If the surrounding size is less than 200 persons, then its accuracy will be 82%, whereas if the surrounding size is greater than 200 persons, then its accuracy is quite appreciable which is 87%. This incremental factor is purely based on the observed pedestrians through the proposed CNN model. The factors that are considered with utmost priority are region uniformity measure, texture and mean values. With this, the obtained measures are as shown in Table 11.1.

TABLE 11.1

Proposed computational neural network model validation statistics.

Measures	Level
Precision	80%
Recall	79%
Accuracy	82%

Thus, the proposed video segmentation and compression model eradicates the traffic in all aspects and leads to smooth maintenance of social distancing.

11.5 Conclusion

The end-to-end video segmentation and compression necessity is detailed, and the work is purely based on a learning-based model and its prediction efficiency. The predictive algorithm CNN supports automating the compression with its layers for compact storage and processing of a video. The extended view focused on social distancing in a crowded area and tracking of it. This optimal solution leads to support for better detection, segmentation and compression for enhanced computational efficiency, even though the videos are of different classes. Its enhancements are proved with the inter-frame and intra-frame prediction, refinement of post-processing and the rate control.

References

1. J. Li, S. He, H. Wong and S. Lo, "Proposal-Driven Segmentation for Videos," in *IEEE Signal Processing Letters*, vol. 26, no. 8, pp. 1098–1102, Aug. 2019, doi:10.1109/LSP.2019.2921654.
2. R. Tapu, B. Mocanu and T. Zaharia, "DEEP-AD: A Multimodal Temporal Video Segmentation Framework for Online Video Advertising," in *IEEE Access*, vol. 8, pp. 99582–99597, 2020, doi:10.1109/ACCESS.2020.2997949.
3. Y. Gui, Y. Tian, D.-J. Zeng, Z.-F. Xie and Y.-Y. Cai, "Reliable and Dynamic Appearance Modeling and Label Consistency Enforcing for Fast and Coherent Video Object Segmentation with the Bilateral Grid," in *IEEE Transactions on Circuits and Systems for Video Technology*, vol. 30, no. 12, pp. 4781–4795, December 2020, doi:10.1109/TCSVT.2019.2961267.
4. J. Jiang and X. Song, "An Optimized Higher Order CRF for Automated Labeling and Segmentation of Video Objects," in *IEEE Transactions on Circuits and Systems for Video Technology*, vol. 26, no. 3, pp. 506–516, March 2016, doi:10.1109/TCSVT.2015.2416557.
5. C. Cigla and A. A. Alatan, "Depth Assisted Object Segmentation in Multi-View Video," in *2008 3DTV Conference: The True Vision—Capture, Transmission and Display of 3D Video*, IEEE, 2008, pp. 185–188, doi:10.1109/3DTV.2008.4547839.
6. K. Li, W. Tao and L. Liu, "Online Semantic Object Segmentation for Vision Robot Collected Video," in *IEEE Access*, vol. 7, pp. 107602–107615, 2019, doi:10.1109/ACCESS.2019.2933479.
7. "Semantic Segmentation of Videos with PixelLib Using Pascalvoc Model" [Code]. https://pixellib.readthedocs.io/en/latest/video_pascal.html
8. "A Large-scale Benchmark Dataset for Event Recognition in Surveillance Video" by Sangmin Oh, Anthony Hoogs, Amitha Perera, Naresh Cuntoor, Chia-Chih Chen, Jong Taek Lee, Saurajit Mukherjee, J.K. Aggarwal, Hyungtae Lee, Larry Davis, Eran Swears, Xiaoyang Wang, Qiang Ji, Kishore Reddy, Mubarak Shah, Carl Vondrick, Hamed Pirsiavash, Deva Ramanan, Jenny Yuen, Antonio Torralba, Bi Song, Anesco Fong, Amit Roy-Chowdhury and Mita Desai, in *Proceedings of IEEE Computer Vision and Pattern Recognition (CVPR)*, IEEE, 2011, https://ieeexplore.ieee.org/document/5995586.
9. S. Zhu, C. Liu and Z. Xu, "High-Definition Video Compression System Based on Perception Guidance of Salient Information of a Convolutional Neural Network and HEVC Compression Domain," in *IEEE Transactions on Circuits and Systems for Video Technology*, vol. 30, no. 7, pp. 1946–1959, IEEE, July 2020, doi:10.1109/TCSVT.2019.2911396.
10. Z. Chen, T. He, X. Jin and F. Wu, "Learning for Video Compression," in *IEEE Transactions on Circuits and Systems for Video Technology*, vol. 30, no. 2, pp. 566–576, February 2020, doi:10.1109/TCSVT.2019.2892608.
11. Jun Han, Salvator Lombardo, Christopher Schroers and Stephan Mandt, "Deep Generative Video Compression," in *Advances in Neural Information Processing Systems 32 (NeurIPS 2019)*, Vancouver, Canada.
12. Siwei Ma, Chuanmin Jia, Zhenghui Zhao, Shiqi Wang and Shanshe Wang, "Image and Video Compression with Neural Networks: A Review," in *IEEE Transactions on Circuits and Systems for Video Technology*, IEEE, 2019.
13. https://viratdata.org/
14. L. Sigal, S. Sclaroff and V. Athitsos, "Skin Color-based Video Segmentation Under Time-Varying Illumination," in *IEEE Transactions on Pattern Analysis and Machine Intelligence*, vol. 26, no. 7, pp. 862–877, IEEE, July 2004, doi:10.1109/TPAMI.2004.35.
15. "Social Distancing Detection in Real Time" [Code]. https://github.com/saimj7/Social-Distancing-Detection-in-Real-Time/blob/main/Run.py

16. A. Rosebrock, "OpenCV Social Distancing Detector" [Code], June 1, 2020. https://pyimages-earch.com/2020/06/01/opencv-social-distancing-detector/

Code Snippet

Semantic Segmentation

Step 1: Pixel library is deployed
```
import pixellib
```
Step 2: Semantic segmentation process is initiated by importing its library files
```
from pixellib.semantic import semantic _ segmentation
```
Step 3: Subsequent segmentation is processed for a video
```
segment _ video = semantic _ segmentation()
segment _ video.load _ pascalvoc _ model("/content/deeplabv3 _
xception _ tf _ dim _ ordering _ tf _ kernels.h5")
segment _ video.process _ video _ pascalvoc("/content/Sample.mp4",
overlay = True, frames _ per _ second= 15, output _ video _ name="/
content/drive/MyDrive/Yolo/output _ video.mp4")
```

Boundary Conditions for the Precise Detection of Human

Step 1: Include essential packages and set initial confidence, threshold and distance values
```
MIN _ CONFIDENCE = 0.3
NMS _ THRESH = 0.3
MIN _ DISTANCE = 50
import numpy as np
import cv2
```
Step 2: Detect object
```
def detect _ people(frame, net, ln, personIdx=0):
```
Step 3: Set appropriate dimensions for the frame results
```
(H, W) = frame.shape[:2]
results = []
```
Step 4: Detect boundary boxes using YOLO model
```
blb = cv2.dnn.blobFromImage(frame, 1 / 255.0, (416, 416),
swapRB=True, crop=False)
net.setInput(blb)
l _ out = net.forward(ln)
```
Step 5: Initialize values
```
centroids = []
boxes = []
confidences = []
```
Step 6: Perform iteration on each layer
```
for sample _ out in l _ out :
    for boundary _ detection in sample _ out:
        scr = boundary _ detection[5:]
        classID = np.argmax(scr)
        confidence = scr[classID]
```

Step 7: Identify humans by object detection and verifying the confidence level

```
if classID == personIdx and confidence > MIN _ CONFIDENCE :
    box = detection[0:4] * np.array([W, H, W, H])
    (centerX, centerY, width, height) = box.astype("int")
    x = int(centerX—(width / 2))
    y = int(centerY—(height / 2))
```

Step 8: Update initialized boundary values and return the results

```
        boxes.append([x, y, int(width), int(height)])
        centroids.append((centerX, centerY))
        confidences.append(float(confidence))
idxs = cv2.dnn.NMSBoxes(boxes, confidences, MIN _ CONFIDENCE , NMS _ THRESH)
if len(idxs) > 0:
    for i in idxs.flatten():
        (x, y) = (boxes[i][0], boxes[i][1])
        (w, h) = (boxes[i][2], boxes[i][3])
        r = (confidences[i], (x, y, x + w, y + h), centroids[i])
        results.append(r)
    return results
```

Frame Separation and Social Distance Prediction

Step 1: Import essential library files

```
from google.colab.patches import cv2 _ imshow
from scipy.spatial import distance as dist
import numpy as np
import argparse
import imutils
import cv2
import os
```

Step 2: Perform parsing in various arguments

```
ap = argparse.ArgumentParser()
ap.add _ argument("-i", "--input", type=str, default="",
help="path to (optional) input video file")
ap.add _ argument("-o", "--output", type=str, default="", help="path to
(optional) output video")
ap.add _ argument("-d", "--display", type=int, default=1,
help="whether or not output frame should be displayed")
args = vars(ap.parse _ args(["--input","/content/drive/MyDrive/Yolo/
Sample.mp4","--output","my _ output.avi","--display","1"]))
```

Step 3: Train and load Yolo object detecter

```
labelsPath = os.path.sep.join(["/content/drive/MyDrive/Yolo/coco.names"])
LABELS = open(labelsPath).read().strip().split("\n")
weightsPath = os.path.sep.join(["/content/drive/MyDrive/Yolo/yolov3.weights"])
configPath = os.path.sep.join(["/content/drive/MyDrive/Yolo/yolov3.cfg"])
print("[INFO] loading YOLO from disk . . . ")
net = cv2.dnn.readNetFromDarknet(configPath, weightsPath)
ln = net.getLayerNames()
ln = [ln[i[0] — 1] for i in net.getUnconnectedOutLayers()]
print("[INFO] accessing video stream . . . ")
vs = cv2.VideoCapture(args["input"] if args["input"] else 0)
writer = None
```

Step 4: Iterate subsequent frames of video

```
while True:
    (grabbed, frame) = vs.read()
```

```
                    if not grabbed:
                    break
        frame = imutils.resize(frame, width=700)
        results = detect _ people(frame, net, ln,
        personIdx=LABELS.index("person"))
```
Step 5: Identify social distance violation
```
        violate = set()
        if len(results) >= 2:
        centroids = np.array([r[2] for r in results])
        D = dist.cdist(centroids, centroids, metric="euclidean")
        for i in range(0, D.shape[0]):
                for j in range(i + 1, D.shape[1]):
                if D[i, j] < MIN _ DISTANCE:
                violate.add(i)
                 violate.add(j)
                for (i, (prob, bbox, centroid)) in enumerate(results):
                (startX, startY, endX, endY) = bbox
                (cX, cY) = centroid
                color = (0, 255, 0)
        if i in violate:
        color = (0, 0, 255)
        cv2.rectangle(frame, (startX, startY), (endX, endY), color, 2)
        cv2.circle(frame, (cX, cY), 5, color, 1)
        text = "Social Distancing Breaches: {}".format(len(violate))
        cv2.putText(frame, text, (10, frame.shape[0] − 25),
        cv2.FONT _ HERSHEY _ SIMPLEX, 0.85, (0, 255, 255), 3)
        if args["display"] > 0:
        cv2 _ imshow(frame)
        key = cv2.waitKey(1) & 0xFF
        if key == ord("q"):
        break
```
Step 6: Write the output file
```
        if args["output"] != "" and writer is None:
        fourcc = cv2.VideoWriter _ fourcc(*"MJPG")
        writer = cv2.VideoWriter(args["output"], fourcc, 25,
        (frame.shape[1], frame.shape[0]), True)
        if writer is not None:
        writer.write(frame)
```

12

A Novel DST-SBPMRM-Based Compressed Video Steganography Using Transform Coefficients of Motion Region

Rachna Patel and Mukesh Patel

CONTENTS

12.1 Introduction

This advancing virtual digital world is characterized by the digitalization of the vast majority of information through the use of electronic broadcasting mediums for well-structured mass storage, transformation, dispersion, and quick access. In comparison to tangible forms of information, the convention of digitalized information is more appropriate for doing any work quickly and accurately.

It also provides a benefit to the user when performing multiple tasks at the same time. Digital transmission allows the sender to communicate a large amount of data to a receiver located at a different location. Moreover, a distant receiver can receive a large amount of information in a short period of time, resulting in a significant reduction in delay and loss [1, 2]. Any problem's digitalized data may be collected, researched, and evaluated in an easy manner, allowing for rapid policy decision-making on its resolution.

There are various domains in which information secrecy is critical to prevent unauthorized access to information, such as military or intelligence communications, medical records, private or personal information systems, and so on [3]. For example, film related to enemy position tracing, rescue operations, military operations, electronic signature footage of war, and surgical strikes are extremely evidentiary in the military and must be safeguarded at all

DOI: 10.1201/9781003218111-12

costs. Furthermore, the information gathered by intelligence is quite reliable, and it must be protected from being misused by an illegitimate power or a terrorist organization while being transferred to the control room through the communication network. It is necessary to maintain the privacy of video footage acquired during an investigation and analysis of a criminal case by the investigator, which is evidence that will be subjected to forensic examination [4].

In the medical industry, personal identity enables approved access to be granted through the use of a biometric technology. Biometrics of the human being consisting of psychological, behavioral, and physiological aspects of the individual. The emotions felt by a human being are among the psychological biometric information collected by the Norco Test, which is heavily medically evaluated during the procedure. In addition, behavioral characteristics include the many postures generated by a person's physique, as well as the various patterns of sitting, standing, and walking, among other things. Some of the biometric information such as the information related to eye scanning, fingerprints, face features, voice frequency, magnetic resonance imaging, DNA and electrocardiogram data of a patient has to be protected while storing and transferring from one medical center to another. There must be a safeguard in place to prevent all of this compassionate medical information from becoming public knowledge [5–7].

Social media has been exceedingly active as compared to electronic print media. This social media is an open platform where every individual can connect directly to the public domain. It is essential to maintain the confidentiality of the personal video of an individual during end-to-end communication.

As a result, video steganography in a compressed domain can be used to maintain the secure connection between sender and receiver. Among the different features of steganography that contribute to its effectiveness are invisibility, embedding capacity, and robustness [1, 2]. Invisibility is one of the characteristics that contribute to its effectiveness. In recent years, video steganography techniques, in which the cover is assumed to be a video, have dominated the market. Video steganography is a technique for concealing huge amounts of confidential data without affecting the overall quality of a video. Depending on the video compression used for the construction of a video, there are two different domains in which video steganography can be classified: uncompressed and compressed [2, 3]. Furthermore, it is considered in two different domains, such as spatial and frequency domain [2]. A significant amount of research has been done in the uncompressed domain, which is less resilient against additional noise, compression, and decryption but has a higher payload capacity [2] and is hence more often used. Because of this, compressed domain–based video steganography is widely employed by academics and researchers. The general process for video steganography is as illustrated in Figure 12.1 [22].

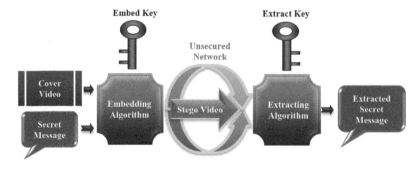

FIGURE 12.1
Video steganography procedure [22].

TABLE 12.1

Compressed-Domain Video Steganography Methods and Respective Characteristics

Video Steganography Method	Characteristics of Video Steganography Method
• Intra-frame prediction	It has a moderate level of complexity in computation.
• Inter-frame prediction	It has less complexity in computation and low-level effect on video quality.
• Motion vector estimation	Computational level of complexity is moderate, and the payload capacity for embedding the secret information is also moderate.
• Transform coefficients	With the less computational level of complexity, a high amount of hiding capacity can be accomplished.
• Entropy coding (CAVLC/CABAC)	It has less complexity in computation and a higher amount of hiding capacity.

In the compressed domain, different video steganography methods are popular: intra-frame and inter-frame prediction, estimations of motion vectors, different transform coefficients that convert an image from spatial to frequency domain, and entropy coding are examples of video steganography techniques [2, 3, 8]. The properties of these approaches for the compression of a video are expressed in Table 12.1 [2].

In addition to the superior performance of the video, the data processing techniques outlined have become more robust and secure when used in the compressed domain. Furthermore, data compression enhances hiding capacity during secure data transfer across a communication network, which is advantageous. Video compression can be accomplished using a variety of coding standards, including the Motion Picture Experts Group (MPEG) with its various versions (MPEG-1, MPEG-2, and MPEG-4), Advanced Video Coding (AVC), which is recognized as H.264, and the most recent one, High-Efficiency Video Coding, known as the H.265 video codec [9]. As video steganography has a vital role in the field of security across the various sectors as described earlier, development of an efficient video steganography method in compressed domain is essential. Therefore, the motivation toward this research is to enhance the efficiency of the video steganography method in the compressed domain in the following aspects:

- Improve the robustness using specific features (region of interest) i.e., motion region of secret cover video frame in place of entire frame
- Enhance the level of security of secret data using random least significant bit (LSB) of discrete sine transform (DST) based transform coefficient as a carrier object
- Achieve the optimum level of imperceptibility as a higher peak signal-to-noise ratio (PSNR) value and obtained as Inf (infinity) in some cases
- Enhance the embedding capacity by using more cover video frames as a carrier for hiding multiple partitions of secret message, maintaining similarity and bit error rate

In the AVC video codec, the encoder transforms the input video into the compressed format, while the decoder transforms the compressed stego video into the originally uncompressed video. Prediction, transformation, and encoding are the procedures carried out by the H.264 encoder during the encoding process. During decoding, the inverse of this process is followed by decoder, inverse transformation, and reestablishment to accomplish the video frame sequence in the decoded format [8]. In the AVC video codec, the data processed unit is macroblocks (MB) having dimension of 16×16 pixels. Different type of frames, intra-coded frames (I), predicted frames (P), and bidirectional frames (B), make up the group of pictures (GOP) in a compressed video [8].

Furthermore, the suggested discrete sine transform–secret bit positions of motion region for message (DST-SBPMRM) technique for video steganography incorporates DST transformation for digital data as part of the DST transformation process. The DST transformation raises the level of security of concealed secret information that is transferred via an unprotected network communication channel. In this experiment, both cover video and secret image are presumed to contain secret information considered in RGB format. Three criteria are used to evaluate the quality of video steganography: (i) imperceptibility, calculated by mean squared error (MSE) leads the PSNR between original and stego frame; (ii) robustness, measured by the similarity (Sim) and bit error rate (BER); and (iii) embedding capacity, calculated by hiding ratio [2, 3].

12.2 Related Work

There are several transform coefficients used for compressed video steganography: discrete cosine transform (DCT), DST, discrete wavelet transform, quantized discrete cosine transform (QDCT), and curvelet transform; they are also used to transfer the input data into frequency domain. These coefficients are used individually or sometimes their combination makes a hybrid approach of transformation.

Since the early 1990s, researchers were dealing with most likely DCT-based video steganography in a compressed domain. Yilmaz et al. [10] has used H.263+ encoder-decoder for intra- as well as inter-frame coding where the secret data was concealed into the even-odd signals produced by DCT of the input video frame. This procedure consists of three steps that must be completed: finding error location in the form of damaged block, preventing error from spreading around the neighboring blocks, and reconstructing damaged block by concealing the error part. In this technique, the binary symmetric channel is used to determine the BER, and the reconstructed quality is evaluated by PSNR. The method was experimented on (Y) luma, or brightness, (U) blue projection, and (V) red projection (YUV) video, and the average peak signal-to-noise ratio (APSNR) was obtained for concealed and damaged video for different BER. The result obtained by this method was notable as the PSNR reached 41.34 dB from 29.07 dB based on the range of bit rate 200 kb/s to 1 mb/s, and the BER is equal to 10^{-5}.

Using DCT for video steganography, Wisam Abed Shukur et al. [11] constructed a carrier object to conceal the secret information in the form of R component of RGB video frame which was then embedded in the movie. He achieved the MSE from 88 to 94 giving the PSNR between 28.3597 dB and 28.6720 dB. Both the parameters do not indicate the significant achievement in quality of vide steganography; rather, in this case, the MSE value is extremely high.

In [12], Ramadhan J. Mstafa et al. suggested a video steganography method for YUV cover video and text-based secret message. He employed the Bose–

Chaudhuri–Hocquenghem (BCH) error correcting code on the encryption of secret messages before concealing into YUV-DCT coefficients. He got the PSNR value up to 42.73 dB with the maximum Sim of 1 and HR of 27.53%. Mstafa et al. [13] enhanced their prior work by improving encryption at two levels by applying Hamming and BCH (7, 4, 1) code. Despite this, the results of this adjustment are nearly equivalent to those previously obtained [12]. He has also given the multi-object tracking and error correcting code-based video steganography using DCT coefficients of RGB cover video [14]. In this method, he preprocessed the secret message by Hamming and BCH code before embedding into DCT coefficients of motion the region of cover video. The maximum PSNR value was obtained as 48.67 dB with HR 3.46%, BER between 0 and 11.7%, and Sim nearer to 1.

It was proposed by Shuyang Liu et al. [9] to use threshold secret sharing to encode the secret message, which was then embedded into a 44 luminance DST block. This method is based on secret sharing and is quite resilient. They achieved the maximum PSNR 46.38 dB along with the BER 20.41%–22.59%, indicating that the video steganography performed well.

The quality of video steganography in associated work is examined based on the quality measurement parameter for imperceptibility being PSNR. A higher value of PSNR indicates good quality of imperceptibility that has been achieved by known approaches, ranging between 28.3597 dB and 48.67 dB, depending on the method used. The existing approaches also accomplish resilience against the compression method of video steganography measured by BER varying 0–22.59%. It indicates the variance in embedded and extracted secret messages. The results achieved by these methods have room for major improvement in both of these areas. We discuss how one very effective DST-based video steganography technique, when applied to the parameters previously listed, can significantly improve video steganography's efficiency in the next sections.

12.3 Proposed Methodology

There are two distinct stages to the suggested compressed video steganography method, known as DST-SBPMRM. At the stage of embedding, a secret message is encrypted into the compressed video, and at the stage of extracting, the secret message is decrypted from the compressed stego video.

12.3.1 Embedding Stage

The inclusive structure of the proposed method DST-SBPMRM's embedding stage is as shown in Figure 12.2.

In this proposed embedding procedure, the stego key is used to select random confidential frames from the compressed RGB video. It also constructs the carrier object from the selected frames that are first extracted from the motion region using the exhaustive search block matching algorithm (EBMA) [15].

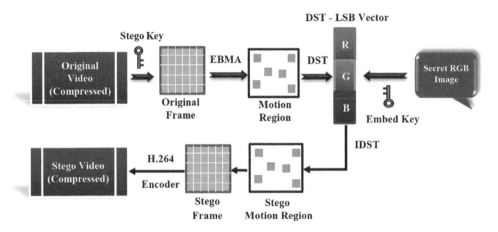

FIGURE 12.2
Proposed DST-SBPMRM embedding stage block diagram.

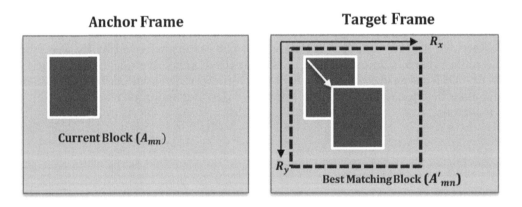

FIGURE 12.3
Exhaustive search block matching algorithm block diagram.

12.3.1.1 Exhaustive Search Block Matching Algorithm

In the EBMA method, using the specified search range, an individual block A_{mn} of anchor frame is compared with different blocks of target frame A'_{mn}. The mean absolute deviation (MAD) is calculated using A_{mn} and A'_{mn}, the minimum error is considered while matching the best block of anchor frame and the target frame.

$$MAD = \frac{1}{mn} \Sigma\Sigma \left| A_{mn} - A'_{mn} \right| \tag{12.1}$$

where m and n indicate the size of the block.

Also, as shown in Figure 12.3, R_x and R_y indicate the search range in EBMA.

The different block size of pixels is used to improve the accuracy of EBMA, with the most commonly used block size of $8 \times 8, 16 \times 16$ pixels. The step size is also essential, while the block displacement is considered through best matching with the blocks. Generally, for searching, the step size is considered as one pixel to get a more accurate search, but sometimes a half-pixel search can give a more precise representation of motion [15].

The collected motion region is translated from spatial to frequency domain using the DST. As a result, utilizing DST, the intensity values of the motion region's red (R), green (G), and blue (B) components will be translated into two forms: integer and fractional.

The two-dimensional (2D) DST is related to the Fourier transform which uses a purely real matrix; it is as calculated in Equation 12.2 [16]:

$$s_{a,b} = \frac{4\epsilon_a\epsilon_b}{MN} \sum_{m=0}^{M-1}\sum_{n=0}^{N-1} x_{m,n} \sin\left[\frac{\pi(2m+1)(a+1)}{2M}\right] \sin\left[\frac{\pi(2n+1)(b+1)}{2N}\right] \quad (12.2)$$

$$a = 0, 1, ..., M-1 \text{ and } b = 0, 1, ..., N-1$$

where $x_{m,n}$ indicates the spatial domain–based pixel value of an image and $s_{a,b}$ represents the pixel's DST-based converted value in transformed domain.

The DST components have both integer and fraction parts from which the integer part is used to conceal the secret information. When using inverse DST (IDST), there is a lower possibility of changing a pixel's original intensity value. The embed key is used to extract the LSB of the integer part of the DST coefficient and embed the binary data of the RGB secret message.

The stego frames will be constructed utilizing the opposite process, employing IDST to obtain the embedded stego motion region. The 2D-IDST is a theoretically determined transform that again transforms the pixel value into the spatial domain. Equation (12.3) [16] represents the mathematical computation of 2D-IDST:

$$x_{m,n} = \sum_{a=0}^{M-1}\sum_{b=0}^{N-1} \epsilon_a\epsilon_b s_{a,b} \sin\left[\frac{\pi(2m+1)(a+1)}{2M}\right] \sin\left[\frac{\pi(2n+1)(b+1)}{2N}\right]$$

$$m = 0, 1, ..., M-1 \text{ and } n = 0, 1, ..., N-1 \quad (12.3)$$

where

$$\epsilon_r = \begin{cases} 1/\sqrt{2}, r = M-1 \text{ or } r = N-1 \\ 1, otherwise. \end{cases}$$

where, $s_{a,b}$ is the pixel's intensity value in the frequency domain, while $x_{m,n}$ is the pixel's spatial domain IDST converted value.

Algorithm 12.1 describes the complete embedding procedure in steps.

Algorithm 12.1: Proposed Embedding Algorithm for DST-SBPMRM

Input: Cover video Ψ ; secret message (RGB image) Ω; cover video frames: M rows, N columns; secret message: m rows, n columns

Output: Compressed stego video $\hat{\Psi}$

1. Begin
    // Stego Key start //
2. T = Total Frames of Ψ
3. I = Number of Cover video frames
4. for each $i = 1\,to\,I$
5. $\quad x(i) = mod(i * 255 + T, 100)$ //frame numbers

    $\quad \alpha = \Psi(x)$ // Anchor Frame
6. $\quad \tau = \Psi(x+1)$ // Target Frame
7. $\quad \beta = [16\,16]$ // Block Size
8. $\quad$ *//Exhaustive search Block Matching Algorithm (EBMA)//*
9. $\quad \lambda = \text{EBMA}\,(\alpha, \tau, \beta)$ $\quad$ // λ = Indices of Motion Pixel, # *EBMA*
10. end for
    // Stego Key end //
11. for each $i = 1\,to\,3$ $\qquad$ // Each R, G, B channel of Ω
12. $\quad \Omega_i = \Omega(:,:,i)$ $\qquad$ //Takes any channel from the RGB planes of Ω .
13. $\quad \Omega_{ip} = (3 * \Omega_i)/I$ $\quad p = 1, 2, \dots I$ $\quad$ // p indicates portion of Ω_i on the basis of I .
14. $\quad$ for each Ω_{ip} and F_i
15. $\quad\quad f_j = F_i(:,:,j),$ $\qquad j = 1,2,3$ $\quad$ //Takes any channel from the RGB planes of F_i
16. $\quad\quad \xi = f_j(\lambda)$ $\quad j = 1,2,3$ // Motion region of frame f_j
17. $\quad\quad$ for each row r of ξ
18. $\quad\quad\quad$ for each column c of ξ
19.

$$\phi(a,b) = \frac{4\epsilon_a\epsilon_b}{RC}\sum_{r=0}^{R-1}\sum_{c=0}^{C-1}\xi_{r,c}\,\sin\left[\frac{\pi(2r+1)(a+1)}{2R}\right]\cdot\sin\left[\frac{\pi(2c+1)(b+1)}{2C}\right]$$

$\quad\quad a = 0,1,\dots,R-1$ *and* $b = 0,1,\dots,C-1$

$\quad\quad \xi$: R Rows, C Columns
$\quad\quad$ // Perform 2D-DST to transforming the motion region ξ from spatial domain to frequency domain
20. $\quad\quad\quad$ end for
21. $\quad\quad$ end for

22. $\phi_{sign} = \pm sign\, of\, \phi$

23. ϕ_{int} = Integer part of $|\phi|$

24. ϕ_{frc} = Fractional part of $|\phi|$

25. $\phi_{LSB} = LSB\, of\, \phi_{int}$

26. $\Omega_{ip} bits = 8 * \Omega_{ip}$ // no. of bits of Ω_{ip}

27.   for each $u = 1\, to\, \Omega_{ip} bits$

28.   for each $v = 1\, to\, (length\, of\, \xi_{LSB}) - 2$

29. $\delta = \left[\phi_{LSB}(v), \phi_{LSB}(v+1)\right]$

30. δ_{DEC} = binary to decimal of δ

31.   if $\delta_{DEC} = 0\, or\, 1$

32. $\phi_{LSB}(v+1) = \Omega_{ip} bits(u)$

33.   end if

34.   end for

35.   end for

36. ϕ_{int} = binary to decimal of ϕ_{LSB}

37. $\phi = \phi_{sign} * \left(\phi_{int} + \phi_{frc}\right)$

38.   for each row a of ϕ

39.   for each column b of ϕ

40.

$$\xi(r,c) = \sum_{a=0}^{R-1}\sum_{b=0}^{C-1} \epsilon_a \epsilon_b \phi_{a,b} \sin\left[\frac{\pi(2r+1)(a+1)}{2R}\right] \cdot \sin\left[\frac{\pi(2c+1)(b+1)}{2C}\right]$$

$$r = 0,1,...,R-1 \quad and \quad c = 0,1,...,C-1$$

$$where\ \epsilon_t = \begin{cases} 1/\sqrt{2}, & t = R-1\, or\, t = C-1 \\ 1, & otherwise. \end{cases}$$

            // Perform 2D-IDST to transforming the stego motion region ϕ from frequency domain to spatial domain.

41.   end for

42.   end for

43. $\hat{f}_j = \xi(\lambda)\ j = 1,2,3$ // Stego Motion region is replaced into f_j

44. $\hat{F}_i$ = Concatenation of $\hat{f}_j$ // Construct RGB Stego frame $\hat{F}_i$

45.   end for

46.   end for

47. $\Psi(x) = \hat{F}_i$ // Replace $\hat{F}_i$ in place of F_i into Ψ

Output: Compose stego video $\hat{\Psi}$ using sequence of frames of Ψ by H.264 codec.

#EBM A

$\lambda = \text{EBMA}(\alpha, \tau, \beta)$ // λ = Indices of Motion Pixels

1. $h = \beta(1),$ // Height of block

2. $w = \beta(2)$ // Width of block

3.   for each row η_1 of α

4. $\eta_1 = 1 : h : M - h + 1$ // M = Rows of α

5. $RS_1 = \eta_1$ // Range start_1

6. $RE_1 = \eta_1 + h$ // Range end_1

7.   for each column η_2 of α

8. $\eta_2 = 1 : w : N - w + 1$ // N = Columns of α

9. $RS_2 = \eta_2$ // Range start_2

10. $RE_2 = \eta_2 + w$ // Range end_2

11. $\vartheta = \alpha(\eta_1 : \eta_1 + h - 1, \eta_2 : \eta_2 + w - 1)$ // ϑ = Anchor block

12. $\epsilon = 255 * h * w * 100$ // ϵ = Error

13.   for each row y of τ

14. $y = RS_1 : RE_1 - h$ // y = Rows of τ

15.   for each column x of τ

16. $x = RS_2 : RE_2 - w$ // x = Columns of τ

17. $\mu = \tau(y : y + h - 1, x : x + w - 1)$ // μ = Target block

18. $\epsilon_{temp} = \sum \sum |\vartheta - \mu|$

19.   if $\epsilon_{temp} < \epsilon$

20. $\lambda = [\eta_1 \, \eta_2]$

21.   end if

22.   end for

23.   end for

24.   end for

25.   end for

12.3.1.2 Extracting Stage

The hidden message is obtained by extracting a compressed stego video. The stego frames are separated from the stego video using the H.264 (AVC) decoder, and the concealed secret data are retrieved from it. Figure 12.4 depicts the extraction step process diagram.

At the receiver end, the compressed stego video is expanded in the sequence of video frame using H.264 video decoder. The stego key is used to separate those stego frames from video frame sequence in which the secret message was embedded during the embedding stage. It also extracts the motion region where the secret message is hidden, using the EBMA method. DST is used to convert the motion area from a spatial to a frequency domain, and the bits of the secret message's red (R), green (G), and blue (B) components are retrieved from the LSB of the DST component. Finally, the secret message known as the extracted secret message is produced by concatenating the RGB components. Algorithm 12.2 describes the steps involved in the extraction process.

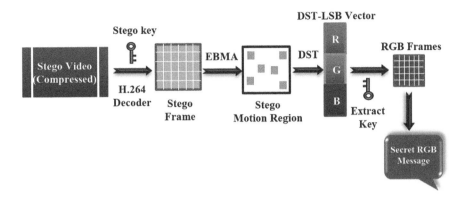

FIGURE 12.4
Proposed DST-SBPMRM extracting stage block diagram.

Algorithm 12.2: Proposed DST-SBPMRM Based Extracting Algorithm

Input: Compressed stego video $\hat{\Psi}$; dimension of secret message [m, n]

Output: Secret message (RGB image) $\hat{\Omega}$

1. Begin
    // Stego Key start //
2. T = Total Frames of $\hat{\Psi}$
3. I = Number of Cover video frames
4. for each $i = 1\,to\,I$
5. $\quad x(i) = mod(i * 255 + T, 100)$ //frame numbers
    $\quad \hat{\alpha} = \hat{\Psi}(x)$ // Stego Anchor Frame
6. $\quad \hat{\tau} = \hat{\Psi}(x+1)$ // Stego Target Frame
7. $\quad \hat{\beta} = [16\,16]$ // Stego Block Size
8. $\quad$ //*Exhaustive search Block Matching Algorithm (EBMA)*//
9. $\quad \hat{\lambda} = $ EBMA $(\hat{\alpha}, \hat{\tau}, \hat{\beta})$ // $\hat{\lambda}$ = Indices of Motion Pixel of Stego Frame, # *EBMA*
10. end for
    // Stego Key end //
11. T = m*n // Total number of pixels of secret message
12. for each $i = 1\,to\,3$ // Each R, G, B channel of $\hat{\Omega}$
13. $\quad T_p = (3 * T) / I$, $p = 1, 2, \dots I$ // p indicates portion of $\hat{\Omega}$ on the basis of I.
14. $\quad$ for each T_p , $\hat{F}_i$ and $\hat{F}_i(\hat{\lambda})$
15. $\quad\quad \hat{f}_j = \hat{F}_i(:,:,j)$, $j = 1, 2, 3$ // Takes any channel from the RGB planes of $\hat{F}_i$
16. $\quad\quad \hat{\xi} = \hat{f}_j(\hat{\lambda})$ $j = 1, 2, 3$ // Motion region of frame $\hat{f}_j$
17. $\quad\quad$ for each row r of $\hat{\xi}$

18.   for each column c of $\hat{\xi}$

19.

$$\hat{\phi}(a,b) = \frac{4\epsilon_a\epsilon_b}{RC}\sum_{r=0}^{R-1}\sum_{c=0}^{C-1}\hat{\xi}_{r,c}\,\sin\left[\frac{\pi(2r+1)(a+1)}{2R}\right]\cdot\sin\left[\frac{\pi(2c+1)(b+1)}{2C}\right]$$

$a = 0,1, ..., R-1$ *and* $b = 0,1, ..., C-1$

$\hat{\xi}$: R Rows, C Columns

// Perform 2D-DST to transforming the motion region $\hat{\xi}$ from spatial domain to frequency domain

20.   end for

21.   end for

22. $\hat{\phi}_{sign} = \pm sign\,of\,\hat{\phi}$

23. $\hat{\phi}_{int} = $ Integer part of $\left|\hat{\phi}\right|$

24. $\hat{\phi}_{frc} = $ Fractional part of $\left|\hat{\phi}\right|$

25. $\phi_{LSB} = LSB\,of\,\phi_{int}$

26.   for each $u = 1\,to\,8*T_p$

27.   for each $v = 1\,to\left(length\,of\,\hat{\xi}_{LSB}\right)-2$

28. $\hat{\delta} = \left[\hat{\phi}_{LSB}(v),\hat{\phi}_{LSB}(v+1)\right]$

29. $\hat{\delta}_{DEC} = $ binary to decimal of $\hat{\delta}$

30.   if $\hat{\delta}_{DEC} = 0$

31. $\hat{\Omega}_{ip}(u) = 0$

32.   else if $\hat{\delta}_{DEC} = 1$

33. $\hat{\Omega}_{ip}(u) = 1$

34.   end if

35.   end for

36.   end for

37. $\hat{\Omega}_{ip} = $ binary to decimal of $\hat{\Omega}_{ip}$

38.   end for

39. $\hat{\Omega}_i = $ Reshape $\hat{\Omega}_{ip}$ to dimension $[m,n]$

40.   end for

Output: Secret message $\hat{\Omega}$ by concatenating the R, G, and B components $\hat{\Omega}_i$, $i = 1,2,3$.

12.4 Experimental Results and Discussion

The suggested DST-SBPMRM for video steganography is experimented over a compressed domain using the MATLAB platform. The cover is represented by a video with various resolutions, and a confidential message is represented by an RGB image. Figure 12.5 shows the many quality assessment factors used to evaluate video steganography performance.

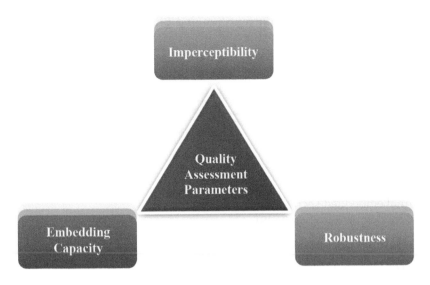

FIGURE 12.5
Quality assessment parameters used for video steganography.

12.4.1 Imperceptibility

Video steganography's major purpose is to safeguard the secret sensitive message behind the cover video, which can possibly have been destroyed due to distortion. It measures the visual quality of stego video based on the original and embedded stego frame. The fundamental parameters for evaluation imperceptibility are MSE and PSNR. The minimum value of MSE leads to maximum PSNR, indicating that higher imperceptibility has been achieved. Equations 12.4 and 12.5 are used to calculate MSE and PSNR, respectively [2, 3, 22–27].

$$MSE = \frac{\sum_{i=1}^{m}\sum_{j=1}^{n}\sum_{k=1}^{h}\left[O(i,j,k)-E(i,j,k)\right]^2}{m \times n \times h} \tag{12.4}$$

$$PSNR = 10 \times Log_{10}\left(\frac{MAX_O^2}{MSE}\right)(dB) \tag{12.5}$$

The original frame is represented as O, and embedded stego frames are represented as E. Resolution of frame is represented by $m \times n$, while the RGB color components are $(k = 1, 2, \text{and } 3)$ represented as h. The highest pixel value in frame O is represented as MAX_O.

12.4.1.1 Robustness

Robustness is used to determine the strength of steganography methods against attacks, as well as to verify that the hidden data is retrieved precisely and without errors. It is evaluated in the form of two parameters: Sim and BER. The high value of Sim and low value of BER indicate the high robustness of video steganography. Equations 12.6 and 12.7 are used to calculate similarity and BER, respectively [2, 3, 22–27]. The robustness analysis for both parameters Sim and BER is mathematically expressed as follows:

$$Sim = \frac{\sum_{i=1}^{y}\sum_{j=1}^{z}\left[R(i,j)\times\hat{R}(i,j)\right]}{\sqrt{\sum_{i=1}^{y}\sum_{j=1}^{z}R(i,j)^2}\times\sqrt{\sum_{i=1}^{y}\sum_{j=1}^{z}\hat{R}(i,j)^2}} \tag{12.6}$$

For an example, the secret image size is considered as 242×150.
    Here,

R = Original embedded secret message (RGB)

$\hat{R}$ = Extracted secret message (RGB)

y = 242 pixels (height of secret image)

z = 150 pixels (width of secret image)

(i,j) indicates the intensity value of a pixel of image.

Therefore,

$$Sim = \frac{\sum_{i=1}^{242}\sum_{j=1}^{150}\left[R(i,j)\times\hat{R}(i,j)\right]}{\sqrt{\sum_{i=1}^{242}\sum_{j=1}^{150}R(i,j)^2}\times\sqrt{\sum_{i=1}^{242}\sum_{j=1}^{150}\hat{R}(i,j)^2}} = 0.9918$$

$$BER = \frac{\sum_{i=1}^{y}\sum_{j=1}^{z}\left[R(i,j)\oplus\hat{R}(i,j)\right]}{y\times z}\times100\% \tag{12.7}$$

$$= \frac{\sum_{i=1}^{242}\sum_{j=1}^{150}\left[R(i,j)\oplus\hat{R}(i,j)\right]}{242\times150}\times100 = 0.0029\%$$

The concealed and extracted hidden data are represented as R and $\hat{R}$, respectively, and the sizes of hidden data are represented as " y " and " z ".

12.4.1.2 Embedding Capacity

The payload/hiding capacity of steganography is also known as embedding capacity. The value of the embedding capacity increases as more secret information is buried in the cover object. Equation 12.8 [2, 3, 22–27] is used to get the hiding ratio (*HR*):

$$HR = \frac{Size\,of\,the\,embedded\,message}{Video\,size}\times100\% \tag{12.8}$$

According to Hanafy et al. [4], steganography techniques with a higher hiding ratio than 0.5% have more embedding capacity.
    The proposed DST-SBPMRM is implemented on a well-known video dataset (*Elecard 2019, Remega Video*) [17–20] with a variety of resolutions, frame rates, and total frames. Furthermore, the RGB color image with various resolutions is used to disguise a sensitive

message. For successful embedding of a secret message, the appropriate size of cover frame is taken into consideration. Generally, the secret message having R, G, and B three different components such that the number of cover video frames are selected is in a multiple of three: 3, 6, 9, . . . etc. If the number of secret cover video frames is three, then the whole RGB component is concealed into a single frame; for six cover video frames, half of the RGB components are concealed into each frame; and in case of nine frames, one-third part of RGB components are concealed into each frame, and so on.

The efficiency of the given method is evaluated based on the previously mentioned quality parameters, and the obtained results are tabulated in Table 12.2.

Table 12.2 displays simulation results of DST-SBPMRM based video steganography on the different well-defined datasets. The AMSE varies from 0.0000 to 0.0076, and the average PSNR is obtained based on AMSE, which varies between 69.304 dB and Inf (infinite). The value Inf of the PSNR shows no variation between the original frame and the embedded stego frame [21]. These results are evidence that the proposed algorithm substantially improved the imperceptibility parameter of video steganography against H.264 video compression.

Furthermore, the Sim value obtained by the proposed method is nearer to 1 which is a clear indication the extracted confidential message is similar to the original message with little BER. To carry the confidential information into the cover object securely, the quality assessment parameter hiding capacity of video steganography plays a vital role. Carrier object versus confidential message is used to measure the hiding ratio. It is calculated using proposed experimentations varying from 0.58353% to 2.69598%, which shows a good embedding capacity.

In the experiment of the suggested algorithm, the stego key selects a varied number of secret frames to conceal the secret information for various scenarios, namely 3, 6, and 9. It is self-evident that increasing the number of frames allows for more carrier object spaces, implying that more bits of secret message can be hidden. As a result, video steganography's concealment capability can be improved.

The size of the secret message versus the increase in the number of secret frames utilized as a cover object improves the imperceptibility. The PSNR value grows as does imperceptibility as an increasing number of cover frames are used for a constant amount of secret data, but on the contrary, it reduces the concealing capacity. Furthermore, an incremental increase in the number of cover video frames increases the processing time at both embedding and extracting stages. The empirical results show that an increasing number of cover video frames also improves the BER and decreases the Sim in the retrieval of secret messages.

12.5 Conclusion and Future Directions

The proposed video steganography technique, dubbed DST-SBPMRM, was developed using the frequency domain in the compressed domain. Based on quality assessment characteristics such as imperceptibility, resilience, and hiding capability, the empirical results acquired through experimentation demonstrate the suggested video steganography method's efficiency. The PSNR value obtained by the reported methods ranged from 28.3597 to 48.67 dB, but the APSNR value obtained by the suggested method ranged from 69.304 dB to Inf (infinite). In the presence of noise, the quality of stego video achieved by

TABLE 12.2

Experimental Results of DST-SBPMRM Based Video Steganography

Serial Number	Name of the Cover Video	Cover Video	Cover Video Size (Height × Width)	Frame Rate	Total Number of Frames	Number of Frames Selected from Cover Video	Secret Message (SM)	Secret Message Size (Height × Width)	Imperceptibility		Robustness		Embedding Capacity
									AMSE	APSNR (dB)	Sim	BER (%)	HR (%)
1	Basketball Drive		1080 × 1920	50	108	3		242 × 150	0.0001	90.358	0.9918	0.0029	0.58353
2	BQ Terrace		1080 × 1920	60	143	3		339 × 210	0.0056	70.676	1.0000	0.0004	1.14439
3	Cactus		1080 × 1920	50	132	6		260 × 420	0.0029	73.581	0.8524	0.0520	0.87770
4	Kristen and Sara		720 × 1280	60	165	6		203 × 328	0.0001	87.709	0.9450	0.0447	1.20414
5	Slide Editing		720 × 1280	30	167	9		236 × 381	0.0000	Inf	0.8060	0.0821	1.08406
6	Traffic		800 × 1280	30	109	3		362 × 224	0.0008	79.304	0.9853	0.0039	2.63958
7	Party Scene		480 × 832	50	228	6		323 × 200	0.0001	89.758	0.8819	0.0552	2.69598
8	Basketball Drill		480 × 832	50	197	3		129 × 208	0.0002	86.157	0.9602	0.0016	2.23958
9	People on Street		800 × 1280	30	150	3		139 × 224	0.0000	Inf	0.9634	0.0036	1.01354
10	China Speed		768 × 1024	30	233	3		125 × 202	0.0076	69.304	1.0000	0.0004	1.07023

the proposed technique is significantly superior to that obtained by the described method. In addition, the BER produced by the reported approach ranges from 0% to 22.59%. The BER achieved using the proposed technique ranged from 0.0004% to 0.0821%, indicating that the error in retrieved secret messages is less when compared to the stated methods. In addition, the suggested technique has significantly improved embedding capacity, with a hiding ratio of better than 0.5% in all cases.

In the future, on extracted features, the video steganography can be performed in the compressed domain. To conceal more confidential information, more cover video frames can be used by maintaining the BER and the hiding ratio. Other frequency transformations, namely, DCT, discrete wavelet transform, discrete wavelet transform, and fast Fourier transform, can also be implemented to increase the imperceptibility and robustness. There is potential to obtain large compression capacity without sacrificing video quality using the current compression technology H.265 (High-Efficiency Video Coding).

References

[1] Yunxia Liu, Shuyang Liu, Yonghao Wang, Hongguo Zhao, and Si Liu, "Video Steganography: A Review", *Neurocomputing* (Accepted Manuscript), Elsevier, November 2018 [DOI: 10.1016/j. neucom.2018.09.091]

[2] Ramadhan J. Mstafa and Khaled M. Elleithy, "Compressed and Raw Video Steganography Techniques: A Comprehensive Survey and Analysis [J]", *Multimedia Tools and Applications*, Volume 76, Issue 20, pp. 21749–21786, Springer, October 2017 [DOI: 10.1007/ s11042-016-4055-1]

[3] Ramadhan J. Mstafa, Khaled M. Elleithy, and Eman Abdelfattah, "Video Steganography Techniques: Taxonomy, Challenges, and Future Directions", *Applications and Technology Conference (LISAT)*, 2017 IEEE Long Island. pp. 1–6, IEEE 2017 [DOI: 10.1109/LISAT.2017.8001965]

[4] Amr A. Hanafy, Gouda I. Salama, and Yahya Z. Mohasseb, "A Secure Covert Communication Model Based on Video Steganography", *2008 IEEE Military Communications Conference*, pp. 1–6, IEEE 2008 [DOI: 10.1109/MILCOM.2008.4753107]

[5] Yeshwanth Srinivasan, Brian Nutter, Sunanda Mitra, Benny Phillips, and Daron Ferris, "Secure Transmission of Medical Records Using High Capacity Steganography", *17th IEEE Symposium on Computer-Based Medical Systems*, IEEE 2004 [DOI: 10.1109/CBMS.2004.1311702]

[6] S. Balu, C. Nelson Kennedy Babu, and K. Amudha, "Secure and Efficient Data Transmission by Video Steganography in Medical Imaging System", *Cluster Computing*, pp. 4057–4063, Springer March 2018 [DOI: 10.1007/s10586-018-2639-4]

[7] A. H. Mohsin, A. A. Zaidan, B. B. Zaidan, Shamsul Arrieya Bin Ariffin, O. S. Albahri, A. S. Albahri, M. A. Alsalem, K. I. Mohammed, and M. Hashim, "Real-Time Medical Systems Based on Human Biometric Steganography: A Systematic Review", *Journal of Medical Systems*, Volume 42, Issue 245, pp. 2–20, Springer October 2018 [DOI: 10.1007/s10916-018-1103-6]

[8] Iain E. Richardson, *The H.264 Advanced Video Compression Standard*, Wiley Publications 2010, ISBN: 978-0-470-51692-8.

[9] Shuyang Liu and Degang Xu, "A Robust Steganography Method for HEVC Based on Secret Sharing", *Cognitive Systems Research*, Volume 59, pp. 207–220, Elsevier January 2020 [DOI: 10.1016/j.cogsys.2019.09.008]

[10] Ayhan Yilmaz and A. Aydin Alatan, "Error Concealment of Video Sequences by Data Hiding", *2003 International Conference on Image Processing*, pp. 679–682, IEEE 2003 [DOI: 10.1109/ ICIP.2003.1246771]

[11] Wisam Abed Shukur, Wathiq Najah Abdullah, and Luheb Kareem Qurban, "Information Hiding in Digital Video Using DCT, DWT and CvT", *Journal of Physics: Conference Series*, Volume 1003, pp. 1–19, Conference 1, 2018 [DOI: 10.1088/1742-6596/1003/1/012035]

[12] Ramadhan J. Mstafa and Khaled M. Elleithy, "A DCT-based Robust Video Steganographic Method Using BCH Error Correcting Codes", *2016 IEEE Long Island Systems, Applications and Technology Conference (LISAT)*, IEEE 2016 [DOI: 10.1109/LISAT.2016.7494111]

[13] Ramadhan J. Mstafa and Khaled M. Elleithy, "A Novel Video Steganography Algorithm in DCT Domain Based on Hamming and BCH Codes", *37th IEEE Sarnoff Symposium*, pp. 208–213, IEEE 2016 [DOI: 10.1109/SARNOF.2016.7846757]

[14] Ramadhan J. Mstafa, Khaled M. Elleithy, and Eman Abdelfattah, "A Robust and Secure Video Steganography Method in DWT-DCT Domains Based on Multiple Object Tracking and ECC", *IEEE Access*, Volume 5, IEEE—Institute of Electrical Electronics Engineers, Inc., ISSN No.: 2169–3536, pp. 5354–5365, 6th April 2017 [DOI: 10.1109/ACCESS.2017.2691581]

[15] Oge Marques, *Digital Video Processing Techniques and Applications*, John Wiley & Sons, ISBN: 978-0-470-04815-3, Chapter 22, pp. 561–589, IEEE Press 2011.

[16] Vladimir Britanak and K. R. Rao, "Two-Dimensional DCT/DST Universal Computational Structure for $2^m \times 2^n$ Block Sizes", *IEEE Transactions on Signal Processing*, pp. 3250–3255, IEEE 2000. [DOI: 10.1109/78.875483]

[17] Video Compression Guru, *Elecard Video*, June 2019, www.elecard.com/videos.

[18] Remega Video Database, November 8, 2017, https://github.com/remega/video_database/tree/master/videos.

[19] Tampere University of Technology, Ultra Video Group, July 15, 2018, http://ultravideo.cs.tut.fi/#testsequences.

[20] Xiph.org Foundation, Derf's Test Media Collection, October 27, 2017, https://media.xiph.org/video/derf/.

[21] Abbas Cheddad, Joan Condell, Kevin Curran, and Paul Mc Kevitt, "Skin Tone Based Steganography in Video Files Exploiting the YCbCr Colour Space", *2008 IEEE International Conference on Multimedia and Expo*, pp. 905–908, IEEE 2008 [DOI: 10.1109/ICME.2008.4607582]

[22] Rachna Patel, Kalpesh Lad, Mukesh Patel, and Madhavi Desai, "A Hybrid DST-SBPNRM Approach for Compressed Video Steganography", *Multimedia Systems Journal*, Volume 27, pp. 417–428, Springer January 2021 [DOI: 10.1007/s00530-020-00735-9]

[23] Rachna Patel, Kalpesh Lad, and Mukesh Patel, "Study and Investigation of Video Steganography Over Uncompressed and Compressed Domain: A Comprehensive Review", *Multimedia Systems Journal*, Volume 27, Issue 5, pp. 985–1024, Springer March 2021 [DOI: 10.1007/s00530-021-00763-z]

[24] Rachna Patel, Kalpesh Lad, Mukesh Patel, and Madhavi Desai, "An Efficient DCT-SBPM Based Video Steganography in Compressed Domain", *International Journal of Information Technology*, Volume 13, pp. 1073–1078, Springer April 2021 [DOI: 10.1007/S41870-021-00648-4]

[25] Rachna Patel, Kalpesh Lad, and Mukesh Patel, "Novel DCT and DST Based Video Steganography Algorithms Over Non-dynamic Region in Compressed Domain: A Comparative Analysis", *International Journal of Information Technology*, pp. 1–9, Springer September 2021. [DOI: 10.1007/s41870-021-00788-7]

[26] Rachna Patel, Kalpesh Lad, and Mukesh Patel, "A Robust Video Steganography Over DCT Components of Motion Region in Compressed Domain", *Soft Computing and Signal Processing*, AISC, Volume 1325, pp. 363–374, Springer May 2021 [DOI: 10.1007/978-981-33-6912-2_33]

[27] Rachna Patel, Kalpesh Lad, and Mukesh Patel, "FFT-Based Robust Video Steganography Over Non-dynamic Region in Compressed Domain", *Applied Information Processing Systems, AISC*, Volume 1354, pp. 201–215, Springer July 2021 [DOI: 10.1007/978-981-16-2008-9_19]

13

Video Matting, Watermarking and Forensics

Dhivyaa C R and Anbukkarasi S

CONTENTS

13.1 Introduction

Of late, there is a tremendous growth in multimedia contents. Image and video play a vital role in many recent applications. Growth in use of smartphones and social media applications creates a vast multimedia content which can be easily accessible through the internet. Image and video contents are shared online and processed online or offline on seconds basis. Video contents involve various processing including matting and watermarking. Video matting is used in video editing software. It is the process of separating the videos into layers as foreground and background, generating opacity estimates known as alpha matte that determines the layer blending. It helps in processing the layers of video individually. Image matting is the predecessor technology for video matting which was established mathematically [1]. The alpha matte is considered as a sequence of images in a digital video. Matte acts as a binary mask that determines which part of the image is visible.

The availability of the excess video contents and editing tools on the internet makes accessing and tampering of video easy. Hence, it is necessary to find a solution which protects the copyright and detects and identifies the tampering. The existing standards for coding, namely, H.263 and H.264, are replaced by High-Efficiency Video Coding (HEVC/H.265). In spite of the high efficiency of HEVC, it suffers to provide reliable functionalities for authorization and trademark applications. The previous video codecs have been implemented with successful watermarking techniques. In order to maintain the efficiency of HEVC, the existing watermarking techniques can be enhanced with copyright protection, authentication,

DOI: 10.1201/9781003218111-13

tampering identification, etc. Fragile/semi-fragile methods can be used for authentication, whereas robust watermarking techniques are meant for copyright protection [2]. The existing watermarking techniques need to be improvised to fit the new features and tools of HEVC [3, 4]. Watermarking techniques can be majorly classified as follows:

- Based on human perception
- Based on the extracting process at the recipient side
- Based on inserting data into video
- Based on domain

Based on human perception, the watermarkings can be made either visible or invisible. For copyright protection, visible watermarking can be used. It could be considered fragile as it is possible to cover, crop or remove the watermarking from the non-significant part of the video. This strength of this technique could be improved by placing the watermark in the various locations of the video randomly, which makes the removal of watermarking difficult [5]. This invisible watermarking technique could be used both for authorization and trademark purposes. Blind tampering of video can be detected with various video forensics techniques. This is one of the emerging fields in video processing as social media gives a platform to the common people to create multimedia content. The approaches for altering the visual data can be done in two ways: inter-frame method and intra-frame method [6]. With these techniques, any video can be tampered by inserting, deleting, repeating and cropping the frames of the video. Inter-frame forgery involves interfering the contents within frames, whereas intra-frames involve individual frames. Techniques such as run-length matrix (RLM), support vector machine (SVM), and discrete cosine transform (DCT) are implemented for detecting video forgeries.

The major contributions of the proposed work are as follows:

- To extract the frequency domain information of the image and to retain the values of the image, the combination of discrete wavelet transform (DWT) and singular value decomposition (SVD) is used.
- To extract the various frequency features from the images, the convolutional neural network (CNN) architecture is employed.
- To combine these two techniques for performing the extraction and embedding process in video watermarking.

In this chapter, we discuss video matting, watermarking/fingerprinting and forensics. Apart from this, we propose a new algorithm for implementing watermarking techniques in videos. This chapter is organized as follows: Section 13.2 describes related works, Section 13.3 specifies methodology and Section 13.4 concludes our proposed work.

13.2 Related Works

13.2.1 Video Watermarking

In a networked multimedia system, the users of the internet are increasing rapidly which introduces various possible attacks during the transmission of multimedia content, especially video files. The attackers distribute the pirated copy of the video files illegally over the internet to the global audience. Hence, the well-known technology known as video watermarking is developed in which additional information is embedded in the original video to avoid digital theft, and the additional information is called a "watermark". For uncompressed domain watermarked videos, the scalable architecture [7] is proposed which performs a single full encoding technique on the original video, and it encodes the watermarked video by reusing the coding information of full encoding in the fast encoders. This architecture provides low computational complexities and is more scalable than the traditional architecture. The multiple watermarking [8] is employed by combining the DCT, DWT and CNN techniques. These techniques are applied on the middle band of the video frame that provides imperceptibility and high robustness against various attacks of the image processing. For each wavelet coefficient, the value of the weight factor is calculated by using the CNN, and for the selected coefficient, the watermark bits are included without affecting the quality of the original image. This multiple watermarking model yields 14% more efficiency than other existing works.

A deep learning–based model [9] is proposed for a watermarking scheme where the trigger set is used as a watermark that contains the features of the watermark and the neural network is used to train the normal training data along with a trigger set to verify the identity of the model. In order to avoid the generalization of the watermarks, the automatic LLing scheme based on chaos is applied for annotation of the trigger set in black box watermarking to save manpower. This model avoids the leakage of keys and possible attacks in the watermarking. Due to the fast growth of mobile usage, when the senders transmit the videos across the network, they recompress the file size to the certain limit on the sender's side and send to the receiver. To avoid the recompression attacks [10], a robust compressed-domain video watermarking algorithm is employed with various quantization parameters in which the texture and motion information of the video is used to identify the optimal location of the watermark embedding. It does not include the location map that includes the security risks for locating the watermark. This algorithm attains great robustness against a recompression attack and also effectively reduces degradation in the quality of the video.

To solve the limitations of video watermarking, a hybrid approach of DCT and DWT [11] is investigated to resist against the various attacks of watermarking like Gaussian filter and sharpen attacks. In this approach, the frames of the videos are selected randomly to apply the DCT algorithm, and then the Arnold algorithm is used to scramble the selected video frame's first column. DWT is applied to transform the reshaped direct current coefficients into four various sub-bands, and the unique matrix transformation is used to enhance the robustness of the watermarking algorithm. To manage the quality loss of video, the integration of SVD, DWT and rail fence methods [12] is developed to embed the watermark in the video file, and also, high-frequency sub-bands are formed from the video frames. This scheme imposes several attacks on the watermarked video files to compute the efficiency and robustness of the techniques that reduce the quality loss of data.

For identifying the malicious consumer of the video file, a novel video watermark approach [13] is designed to include artificial distortion to the video file. This approach makes explicit changes using a single encoder, and it automatically propagates into various forms of implicit distortions which are artifacts and are imperceptible. These implicit distortions represent the watermark in the video files. This approach is robust against the video manipulation of the files. The scale invariant feature transform [14] is employed for the visual system in which low- and high-frequency sub-bands are obtained by decomposing every frame of the video by contourlet transform, and the largest energy value is selected to be embedded into watermarking signals. By altering size ratio between low-frequency sub-band's histograms, the watermarking signals are embedded, further masking threshold is computed based on contourlet domain, and it is embedded in the high energy value as watermarking signals. This model improves transparency and robustness and also resists geometric attacks.

From our investigations, the various kinds of domains known as spatial, transform and compressed are applied to embed a watermark in the video files. The spatial domain watermarking techniques are simple and computationally more efficient than other domain techniques. The transform-based technique is complex, time consuming, increases the computing power and provides imperceptibility and more robustness to the attacks than the other two domain techniques. Over recent decades, the research has been conducted in compressed domain using well-known compression standards such as MPEG-2 and MPEG-4 to embed a watermark in the compressed video files. The next generation of compression standard is H.265/HEVC that can deal with watermarking techniques. In the survey, the existing approaches are not fulfilling the requirements, especially imperceptibility, security and robustness, to the attacks.

13.2.2 Video Matting

Video matting techniques are used to extract the desired moving foreground objects from the video files by removing artifacts such as spatial and temporal. Over the years, the various video matting methods have been proposed in a supervised way and also in an unsupervised way. The effectiveness of the methods is based on the accuracy of the optical flow and special hardware systems. Due to the limitation of binary segmentation, the supervised tri-level segmentation approach [15] is adopted to generate trimaps for each frame of the video by applying the optical flow, and the result of tri-level segmentation is fed into video matting techniques for alpha matte generation. The optical flow–based approaches are different from the special hardware-assisted systems which include some extra information capturing for video matting. For instance, the multi-parameter video camera [16] is used to synchronize the video streams that can share a point of view with various focusing and depth of field to estimate the video trimaps for matting automatically, without user assistance.

The sparse and low-rank representation [17] can be applied to create the non-local structures for the pixels to overcome the problem of video matte caused by feature ambiguity, topology changing and motion variations. The sparse coding is applied to select the best samples for all the pixels in the unknown region, and low-rank representation is used to discover the global structures of the data with similar features. The two representations are combined to generate the video mattes effectively. The well-known machine learning technique [18], namely, SVM is developed to detect the appropriate foreground object from the given input video where it uses two one-class SVMs to be trained at each pixel location for foreground segmentation and also solves boundary matting problems with less user interactions. In the survey, the challenges of extracting the objects from the video are identified, such as big data size, temporal coherence and fast motion.

A fast block matching algorithm based motion estimation method [19] is proposed where it selects the proper key frames from the input video sequence based on the rule, and these frames are segmented into background and foreground with the help of grabcut, and then these segmented frames are propagated to obtain the final alpha matte sequence which enhances the quality of the matting using optical flow. By using edge features [20], the video matting method is applied to detect the background and foreground objects from the given video sequences which is a crucial task of video matting.

To obtain the scribbles, the gradient factor is identified from every RGB color channel using edge features and produces the alpha matte in an efficient manner. The Bayesian approach [21] is employed to estimate the global motions to generate the good mattes by using the information of the image. First, each frame is separated from the sequence into foreground and background, and then usable mattes are extracted by utilizing the global motion.

13.2.3 Video Forensics

In multimedia forensics, forgery detection is essential for protecting visual media from malicious manipulation that causes serious issues in society. Several existing approaches have been developed to predict the copy-move forgery by analyzing the feature correlation between the original frame and duplicate frames created by either inserting or replacing the frame in the digital video files. The features are detected based on the image features of every frame such as pixels, gray values, textures, color and the video features such as motion, compression and coding. The coarse-to-fine detection approach [22] is adopted to identify the frame copy forgery in which coarse detection is used to obtain the suspected tamper point by analyzing the optical flow, and fine detection is applied to find the location of the forgery that includes the pair of duplicated frames depending on the correlation of optical flow. This approach is effective and efficient and is evaluated on three various benchmark datasets such as video trace library, Surrey University Library for Forensic Analysis, and Derf's Test Video Collection to predict the forgery, attacks and also noises present in the video files.

A motion adaptive–based [23] detection method is developed to identify the frame deletion forgery where features based on frame motions are analyzed to find the location of the deletion point of the frame and then a post-processing procedure is applied to remove the interferences like light changes, focus vibration and frame jitter. This method is demonstrated on several datasets with variable length of the motion and attained a 90% true positive rate with a 0.3% false alarm rate. The CNN-based model [24] is proposed to capture information about the video codec which is an asset for the purpose of forensics. Two CNNs are used to locate the temporal splicing for the video sequence created by concatenating the various video segments. To estimate the quality of the video frames, this model is validated on the datasets that contain the videos at various resolutions encoded with different codecs such as MPEG2 and MPEG4 at different qualities.

The forensic video analysis framework [25] is developed to help the forensics investigation by employing the efficient video-enhancing algorithm and deep learning–based tracking algorithm. The contrast limited adaptive histogram equalization is applied to improve the quality of the video taken by closed-circuit television footage for the purpose of forensic investigation. For the analysis of the video, a deep learning–based tracking algorithm is proposed to predict the objects and suspects from the CCTV footages. The new technologies are developed in video forensics to identify the integrity and authenticity of the digital video files. For the video fie containers, the unsupervised analysis [26] is introduced and focused on the two main applications. First, the video integrity is verified depending on the dissimilarity between the reference and the file containers, and then it deals with brand identification based on the structure and content of the containers. The effectiveness of the method is evaluated on the dataset composed of 578 videos taken by smartphones and produced promising results with low computational cost.

13.3 Video Watermarking Techniques

In this work, an improved CNN-based [27] video watermark algorithm is proposed in which the mathematical transformations such as DWT and SVD are employed for embedding and extracting the watermarks in the video. The proposed algorithm consists of the watermark embedding process that embeds the watermark into the input video and the watermark extracting process that extracts the original video from the watermarked video frames, as shown in Figure 13.1.

13.3.1 Video Embedding Process

DWT [8, 11] along with SVD [12] are proposed to improve the robustness of the watermarking model. First, the input video is divided into number of frames, and every frame is converted to YUV frames from RGB frames, where each frame is processed by the DWT, and it is processed by SVD. The two-level DWT is computed for the Y matrix in all the frames to obtain the 16 strips that contains four sub-bands of LL, four sub-bands of LH, four sub-bands of HL and four sub-bands of HH. Then, SVD is applied on the HL sub-band in every frame which is used for the embedding process, and the sub-band coefficient matrix is decomposed into three independent matrices. In addition, an improved CNN is adopted for each pixel of the watermark in the intermediate band that was selected in the zigzag order. The two images are used for watermarking the input videos. The high- and low-frequency CNN features are embedded into the sub-bands of HH, HL and LH, LL, respectively. The inverse DWT is also applied for maintaining the watermark components of the frame, and finally, all the watermarked frames are combined to obtain the watermarked video as shown in Figure 13.2.

13.3.2 Convolution Neural Network

In the field of image analysis and computer vision, CNNs, also known as ConvnetCVPs, play a major role. It is the kind of deep neural network which is used to analyse the features of the image. This network could be used in video recognition, image analysis, image classification and natural language processing (NLP) oriented tasks. Convolution is a mathematical function which performs the linear operation wherein two functions are multiplied together to get a third function which mentions how one function modifies the other function. In CNN, three layers are stacked together to form a CNN architecture: convolutional layer, pooling layer and fully connected layer.

FIGURE 13.1
Video watermarking block diagram.

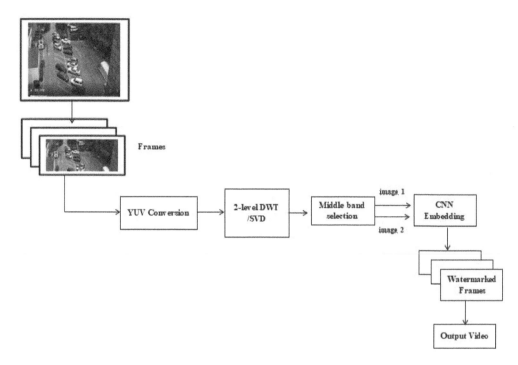

FIGURE 13.2
Embedding process.

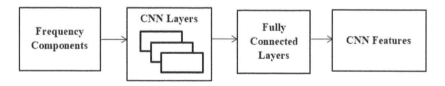

FIGURE 13.3
Architecture of convolutional neural network.

The convolutional layer is responsible for identifying and extracting various features of the given input. The fully connected layer performs the classification of the given input based on the extracted features in the previous step. To reduce the computational layer, the pooling layer decreases the size of the given feature map. Apart from these layers, the CNN network has two important parameters known as dropout and activation functions. To avoid the overfitting of the input, the dropping of few neurons is performed using dropout and hence the size of the model is reduced. The activation function is responsible for passing the required information to the end of the model by adding non-linearity to the model. Some of the activation functions are ReLU, Softmax and sigmoid.

The various hyper-parameters used for the proposed model are discussed in Table 13.1.

TABLE 13.1

Hyper-parameters of the Proposed Model

Parameters	Values
Loss function	Categorical cross-entropy
Optimizer	RMSProp
Activation	Relu
Batch size	64
Epoch	10
Learning rate	0.001

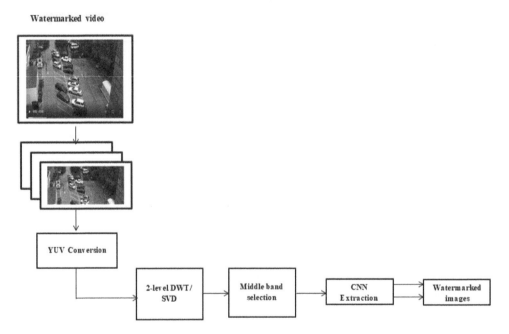

FIGURE 13.4
Extracting process.

13.3.3 Video Extracting Process

In the video extracting process, the watermarked video is divided into the number of watermarked frames, and each frame is converted into YUV frames from the RGB frame format where every frame is processed by DWT and SVD. The two-level DWT [27] is computed for the frames to obtain the sub-bands such as wLH21, wHH21, wLH22, wHH22 and so on. Further, the SVD [12] is applied on wHL sub-band, and the sub-bands coefficient matrix is decomposed into three independent matrices. The embedded watermark is extracted using CNN and compared with the original watermark for reconstructing the original image.

13.3.4 Performance Measures

To analyze the performance of the work, the dataset is created by taking some sample videos from the VIRAT video dataset and also by capturing some real-time videos to execute the proposed model. The performance of the video watermarking techniques is evaluated in terms of mean squared error (MSE) and peak signal-to-noise ratio (PSNR). The average of the squares of error is estimated by the MSE and is measured by

$$MSE = \frac{1}{PQ[\sum\limits_{g=1}^{p}\sum\limits_{h=1}^{Q}(C(g,h)-E(g,h))}$$

(13.1)

where P is height and Q is width of the image; $C(g,h)$ is the cover image's pixel value; and $E(g,h)$ is the embedded image's pixel value.

The degradation of the output image is represented by PSNR and is calculated as follows:

$$PSNR = 10\log 10\left(\frac{P*Q}{MSE}\right)$$

(13.2)

where P is height and Q is width of the image; and MSE is the error between the improved image and the reference image.

The proposed CNN-based watermarking technique is compared with the DWT and DWT-SVD techniques. As compared in Table 13.1, the performance metrics such as PSNR and MSE are calculated for each technique, and the proposed technique yields the better PSNR and MSE values shown in Figure 13.5 and Figure 13.6.

TABLE 13.2

Comparison of the Proposed Watermarking Techniques

Techniques	PSNR in Decibels (dB)	Mean Squared Error
DWT	73.18	0.055
DWT-DCT	73.27	0.053
DWT-SVD	73.44	0.052
CNN-based proposed technique	74.46	0.050

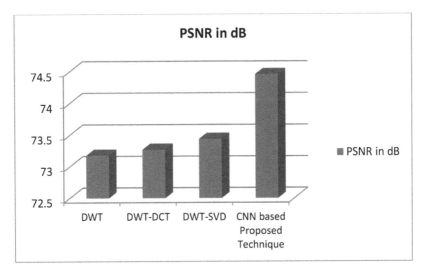

FIGURE 13.5

Comparison on the basis of peak signal-to-noise ratio values.

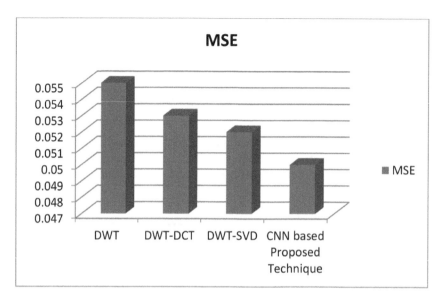

FIGURE 13.6
Comparison on the basis of mean squared error values.

13.4 Conclusion

In this chapter, we discussed various aspects of video processing techniques such as video matting, video forensics and watermarking techniques. The techniques and details of those processing models have been discussed. Apart from that, we introduced a new technique for implementing watermarking technique in the video. The given video is segregated into frames, and we applied DWT and SVD techniques for processing the frames. With these techniques, we applied CNN architecture for embedding and extraction purposes. By implementing this combined feature, we achieved 74 dB PSNR and 0.050 MSE. In the proposed work, the techniques for extracting and embedding the watermarks in video have been discussed, but we did not discuss methods to handle the attacks such as salt and pepper noise, Poisson, speckle noise and additive Gaussian noise. In the future, this approach could be extended for handling more attacks to enrich the performance of the model.

Code snippets for deep learning model

```
uploaded = files.upload()
MY _ TRAIN _ DIR = 'D:/dataset/video/train'
MY _ TEST _ DIR = 'D:/dataset/video/test1'
ISZE = 70
NAME _ MODEL = tamvid-{}-{}.model'.format(LR, '6conv-basic')
```

```
def LB(dgm):
lab1 = dgm split('.')[-3]
if lab1 == 'c1': return [1, 0]
elif lab1 == 'c2': return [0, 1]

def CTR():
TDA = []

for dgm in tqdm(os.listdir(MY _ TRAIN _ DIR)):
LL = LB(img)
path = os.path.join(MY _ TRAIN _ DIR, img)
dgm = lib.imread(path, lib.IMREAD _ GRAYSCALE)
dgm = lib.resize(img, (ISZE, ISZE))
TDA.append([np.array(img), np.array(LL)])
shuffle(TDA)
np.save('TD.npy', TDA)
return TDA

def process _ test _ data():
my _ testing _ data = []
for img in tqdm(os.listdir(MY _ TEST _ DIR)):
path = os.path.join(MY _ TEST _ DIR , img)
number = img.split('.')[0]
img = lib.imread(path, lib.IMREAD _ GRAYSCALE)
img = lib.resize(img, (ISZE, ISZE))
//Shuffeling
numpy.save('test _ data.npy', my _ testing _ data)
return my _ testing _ data
TD = CTR()
test _ data = process _ test _ data()

convnetCVP = input _ data(shape =[None, ISZE, ISZE, 1], name ='input')
convnetCVP = conv _ 2d(convnetCVP, 32, 5, activation ='relu')
convnetCVP = max _ pool _ 2d(convnetCVP, 5)
convnetCVP = conv _ 2d(convnetCVP, 64, 5, activation ='relu')
convnetCVP = max _ pool _ 2d(convnetCVP, 5)
convnetCVP = conv _ 2d(convnetCVP, 128, 5, activation ='relu')
convnetCVP = max _ pool _ 2d(convnetCVP, 5)
convnetCVP = fully _ connected(convnetCVP, 1024, activation ='relu')
convnetCVP = dropout(convnetCVP, 0.8)
convnetCVP = fully _ connected(convnetCVP, 2, activation ='softmax')
convnetCVP = regression(convnetCVP, optimizer ='adam', learning _ rate = LR,
loss ='categorical _ crossentropy', name ='targets')
model = tflearn.DNN(convnetCVP)
train = TD[:-300]
test = TD[-300:]
XX = np.array([i[0] for i in train]).reshape(-1, ISZE, ISZE, 1)
YY = [i[1] for i in train]
TE _ ax = np.array([i[0] for i in test]).reshape(-1, ISZE, ISZE, 1)
TE _ ay = [i[1] for i in test]
model.fit({'input': XX}, {'targets': YY}, n _ epoch = 5,
validation _ set =({'input': TE _ ax }, {'targets': TE _ ay}),
my _ snapshot _ Step = 500, show _ metric = True, run _ id = NAME _ MODEL)
```

References

1. T. Porter and T. Duff, "Compositing Digital Images," *Computer Graphics*, vol. 18, pp. 253–259, 1984.
2. Y. Yu, H. Yao, R. Ni, and Y. Zhao, "Detection of Fake High Definition for HEVC Videos Based on Prediction Mode Feature," *Signal Processing*, vol. 166, p. 107269, 2020.
3. Q. Xu, J. Lu, X. Peng, S. Yuan, and L. Li, "A Video Zero-Watermarking Algorithm Based on Text Detection," in *2015 IEEE 16th International Conference on Communication Technology (ICCT)*. IEEE, 2015, pp. 328–333.
4. M. Z. Konyar, O. Akbulut, and S. Öztürk, "Matrix Encoding-Based High-Capacity and High-Fidelity Reversible Data Hiding in HEVC," *Signal, Image and Video Processing*, vol. 14, no. 5, pp. 897–905, 2020.
5. T. M. Thanh and P. T. Hiep, "Frame Background Influence Based on Invisible Watermarking to Visible Video Watermarking," in *2013 International Conference on Advanced Technologies for communications (ATC 2013)*. IEEE, 2013, pp. 563–568.
6. S. Jaseela and S. G. Nishadha, "Survey on Copy Move Image Forgery Detection Techniques," *International Journal of Computer Science Trends and Technology (IJCST)*, vol. 4, no. 1, pp. 87–91, 2016.
7. H. Mareen, J. De Praeter, G. Van Wallendael, and P. Lambert, "A Scalable Architecture for Uncompressed-Domain Watermarked Videos," *IEEE Transactions on Information Forensics and Security*, vol. 14, no. 6, pp. 1432–1444, June 2019. https://doi.org/10.1109/TIFS.2018.2879301.
8. F. Khan and M. S. Raeen, "Robust and Blind Multiple Image Watermarking Using CNN and DWT in Video," *Smart Moves Journal Ijoscience*, vol. 6, no. 3, pp. 8–13, 2020. https://doi.org/10.24113/ijoscience.v6i3.275.
9. Y.-Q. Zhang, Y.-R. Jia, X. Wang, Q. Niu, and N.-D. Chen, "DeepTrigger: A Watermarking Scheme of Deep Learning Models Based on Chaotic Automatic Data Annotation," *IEEE Access*, vol. 8, pp. 213296–213305, 2020. https://doi.org/10.1109/ACCESS.2020.3039323.
10. H. Ding et al., "A Compressed-Domain Robust Video Watermarking Against Recompression Attack," *IEEE Access*, vol. 9, pp. 35324–35337, 2021. https://doi.org/10.1109/ACCESS.2021.3062468.
11. Jie Sang, Qi Liu, and Chun-Lin Song, "Robust Video Watermarking Using a Hybrid DCT-DWT Approach," *Journal of Electronic Science and Technology*, vol. 18, no. 2, pp. 1–10, June 2020.
12. C. Sharma and A. Bagga, "Video Watermarking Scheme Based on DWT, SVD, Rail Fence for Quality Loss of Data," in *2018 4th International Conference on Computing Sciences (ICCS)*. IEEE, 2018, pp. 84–87. https://doi.org/10.1109/ICCS.2018.00020.
13. H. Mareen, J. De Praeter, G. Van Wallendael, and P. Lambert, "A Novel Video Watermarking Approach Based on Implicit Distortions," *IEEE Transactions on Consumer Electronics*, vol. 64, no. 3, pp. 250–258, August 2018. https://doi.org/10.1109/TCE.2018.2852258.
14. Z. Li, S. Q. Chen, and X. Y. Cheng, "Dual Video Watermarking Algorithm Based on SIFT and HVS in the Contourlet Domain," *IEEE Access*, vol. 7, pp. 84020–84032, 2019. https://doi.org/10.1109/ACCESS.2019.2899378.
15. J. Ju, J. Wang, Y. Liu, H. Wang, and Q. Dai, "A Progressive Tri-level Segmentation Approach for Topology-Change-Aware Video Matting," *CGF*, vol. 32, no. 7, pp. 245–253, 2013.
16. M. McGuire, W. Matusik, H. Pfister, J. F. Hughes, and F. Durand, "Defocus Video Matting," *ACM Transactions on Graphics*, vol. 24, no. 3, pp. 567–576, 2005.
17. D. Zou, X. Chen, G. Cao, and X. Wang, "Unsupervised Video Matting via Sparse and Low-Rank Representation," *IEEE Transactions on Pattern Analysis and Machine Intelligence*, vol. 42, no. 6, pp. 1501–1514, 1 June 2020. https://doi.org/10.1109/TPAMI.2019.2895331.
18. M. Gong, Y. Qian, and L. Cheng, "Integrated Foreground Segmentation and Boundary Matting for Live Videos," *IEEE Transactions on Image Processing*, vol. 24, no. 4, pp. 1356–1370, April 2015. https://doi.org/10.1109/TIP.2015.2401516.
19. J. Zhao and X. Xiang, "A Novel Video Matting Approach Based on Motion Estimation," *2016 9th International Congress on Image and Signal Processing*, BioMedical Engineering and Informatics (CISP-BMEI), 2016, pp. 84–88. https://doi.org/10.1109/CISP-BMEI.2016.7852686.
20. M. Koeshardianto, E. Rahmanita, J. Hammad, F. Kurniawan, J. Santoso, and E. S. Honggara, "The Edge Feature Subtraction for Completing Video Matting," *2021 3rd East Indonesia*

Conference on Computer and Information Technology (EIConCIT). IEEE, 2021, pp. 433–437. https://doi.org/10.1109/EIConCIT50028.2021.9431869.

21. Anil Kokaram, B. Collis, and Sharika Robinson, "Practical Motion Based Video Matting," *The 2nd IEEE European Conference on Visual Media Production*. IEEE, 2006, pp. 130–136.

22. S. Jia, Z. Xu, H. Wang, C. Feng and T. Wang, "Coarse-to-Fine Copy-Move Forgery Detection for Video Forensics," *IEEE Access*, vol. 6, pp. 25323–25335, 2018. http://doi.org/10.1109/ACCESS.2018.2819624.

23. C. Feng, Z. Xu, S. Jia, W. Zhang, and Y. Xu, "Motion-Adaptive Frame Deletion Detection for Digital Video Forensics," *IEEE Transactions on Circuits and Systems for Video Technology*, vol. 27, no. 12, pp. 2543–2554, December 2017. http://doi.org/10.1109/TCSVT.2016.2593612.

24. S. Verde, L. Bondi, P. Bestagini, S. Milani, G. Calvagno, and S. Tubaro, "Video Codec Forensics Based on Convolutional Neural Networks," in *2018 25th IEEE International Conference on Image Processing (ICIP)*. IEEE, 2018, pp. 530–534. http://doi.org/10.1109/ICIP.2018.8451143.

25. J. Xiao, S. Li, and Q. Xu, "Video-Based Evidence Analysis and Extraction in Digital Forensic Investigation," *IEEE Access*, vol. 7, pp. 55432–55442, 2019. http://doi.org/10.1109/ACCESS.2019.2913648.

26. M. Iuliani, D. Shullani, M. Fontani, S. Meucci, and A. Piva, "A Video Forensic Framework for the Unsupervised Analysis of MP4-Like File Container," *IEEE Transactions on Information Forensics and Security*, vol. 14, no. 3, pp. 635–645, March 2019. http://doi.org/10.1109/TIFS.2018.2859760.

27. Farha Khan and M. Sarwar Raeen, "Robust and Blind Multiple Image Watermarking Using CNN and DWT in Video," *Smart Moves Journal Ijoscience*, vol. 6, no. 3, March 2020, https://doi.org/10.24113/ijoscience.v6i3.275.

14

Time Efficient Video Captioning Using GRU, Attention Mechanism and LSTM

Gurdeep Saini and Nagamma Patil

CONTENTS

14.1 Introduction: Video Captioning Is the Product of Combining Two Tasks

- Computer Vision: It is used to extract the features.
- Natural Language Processing: It is used to create the caption at the end of a network [1].

Video captioning is a method of creating a caption for a video that describes the video's events or provides a concise overview of the video. Since a large volume of video material is uploaded to the internet every day, video captions can offer an efficient way of content browsing [2]. It can be used for video summarization [3], navigation by a person who is visually challenged [4], human-robot interaction [5], scene understanding [6, 7], and so on. Initially, researchers used the sentences template to create the caption [8, 9]. It first identifies the semantic elements in the video, such as the noun, object, and scene, and these elements are then made fixed-form sent from those predefined templates.

This approach was not good enough for complex tasks such as video description generation [1, 10]. The sequence model converts a sequence of frames to a sequence of words [11, 12] in which a recurrent neural network (RNN) is used to generate the caption, and these methodologies have shown impressive results. The template pool and encoder-decoder technique have been used in a lot of previous work. The encoder and decoder solution had a lot of success. A fixed size vector is created using visual features from the frames/images in the encoder-decoder approach. Then in the decoder part, RNN is used to generate the caption.

DOI: 10.1201/9781003218111-14

Each word is created using the graphic and text features of a previously generated word. All these approaches are time-consuming even taking more than 12 hours for training only on the Microsoft research video description corpus (MSVD) or similar data set. In this chapter, we improved the accuracy and time taken to train/test the model using the long short-term memory (LSTM) and gated recurrent unit (GRU) so the model can be used in a real-time system. We also reduced model complexity by combining the GRU and attention mechanism in place of LSTM because GRU has a smaller number of gates as compared to LSTM but produced similar accuracy.

The main contribution of our model is as follows:,

- Frames are first transformed from the input videos. The frames are then passed to a VGG16 model that has been pretrained to extract the features [13]. The extracted features are given as input to GRU. GRU is used to deduce information from the frames and it takes less training time as compared to LSTM.

- The output of GRU is given as an input to the Bahdanau attention mechanism to create the context vector C_t. At the end, the context vector along with GRU output is given as input to LSTM to generate long sequences.

- We performed the experiment on the MSVD [14] dataset.

14.2 Related Work: Existing Image and Video Captaining Mechanism Can Be Classified in Two Different Classes

- Template based [8]
- Encoder-decoder approaches [1, 15, 14]

The first step of template-based caption generation is splitting the large sentences into fragments using the rules of respective language grammar for example, subject, verb, and object. Each generated fragment is linked with an attribute or object in the image/video. Now using the predefined template, sentences are generated from the fragments. Therefore, generated sentences are extremely reliant on the template structure. Later, Rohrbach et al. generated a video description after generating the relationship between the video components. For this purpose, Authors learned the conditional random field between the video component [16].

Deep RNN-based researchers recently demonstrated the effectiveness of neural machine translation using deep RNNs. An encoder-decoder based network for image and video captioning was created as a result of this. The image or video is first encoded by a convolutional neural network (CNN), then the extracted features are fed into RNN to produce captions. A multimedia RNN is used to caption images [17]. Using the previously generated word and image feature, it predicts the next word.

Venugopalan et al. used mean pooling across the frame to create an LSTM-based model for video description [18]. A video, unlike an image, contains both spatial and temporal detail. The author used both spatial and temporal knowledge to improve the precision of the sentences. Vinyals et al. [14] proposed the deep neural network using GoogleNet and LSTM. Venugopalan et al. has suggested a model for video encoding and sentence comprehension using the LSTM [1]. Pan et al. proposed a hierarchical RNN encoder. It uses two layers of LSTM to make use of the various time-scale abstractions of temporal information [19]. Using whole sentence semantics and video material, Pan et al. created a model to learn visual-semantic embedding [20].

For natural language descriptions of human behavior, a concept hierarchy of actions was created [8]. For video sentence creation, a video-to-language embedding model was developed [13]. While template-based languages can produce complete sentences, the caption that is generated is very rigid and constrained in certain ways.

The dense video captioning task is proposed by Zhiwang Zhang et al. as a new visual cue–assisted sentence summarization task. For each event proposal, several sentences are created to describe the various visual material. Two LSTM layers are used at the end. The first layer serves as an encoder, while the second serves as a decoder [21].

Xiangpeng Li et al. proposed a methodology for both image and video captioning by using the hierarchical LSTM and attention model. It uses two kinds of attention: temporal and spatial. Temporal attention is being used to select the region inside the frame. Adaptive attention is used to determine whether the next prediction will be based on the visual information on the screen or the previously created sentences. In the end, hierarchical LSTM is used to generate captions that take care of both visual information and previously generated words [22].

Initially, researchers have used template-based captioning (selecting caption from the pool) that was totally inefficient. Later we observed that researchers have used the deep learning model to select the caption from the caption pool. But encoding and decoding mechanisms changed the history of image/video captaining. In the present work, we are extending that research to decrease time taken to train/test the encoder-decoder model and to increase the accuracy.

14.3 Methodology: The Workflow Diagram of Present Work

Figure 14.1 represent the workflow diagram of present work. In the initial phases, frames are generated from the videos, after those visual features are generated using pretrained model VGG16. We have chosen the VGG16 model because it achieved the highest (92.7%) top five accuracies on ImageNet dataset. It produced higher accuracy over AlexNet [23] because it uses a larger kernel size of 3*3. GRU-based RNN is used to make it time efficient, and attention mechanism and LSTM are used to generate the video description.

1. RNN—The feedforward neural network is expanded by including feedback connections to model sequence information to create the RNN. As the number of layers increases, RNN does not produce better accuracy because of its gradient problem. To address this problem, LSTM is used instead of basic RNN.

2. Video caption using RNN—LSTM is the caption generator. The hidden state of the LSTM is determined by combining the previous hidden state H_{t-1} with the input data X_t. Mathematically it is calculated using the formula given in Equation 14.1:

$$H_t = LSTM \ (X_t, H_{t-1}) \tag{14.1}$$

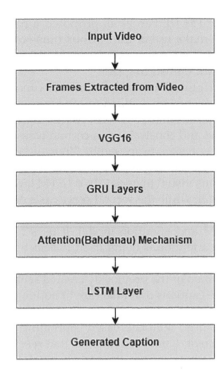

FIGURE 14.1
Workflow diagram.

The dimensionality of the hidden state H_t is fixed. The visual and textual features are used to form input data X_t (Equation 14.2):

$$X_t = [W, V_t, E_{t-1}] \tag{14.2}$$

Here [,] denotes the concatenation operation, V_t denotes the visual feature input given to LSTM in the tth step.

3. Gated RNN—Our present work is to show the performance of the GRU over LSTM on the video captioning. First, we discuss the implementation of these, and then we see results.

   i. LSTM Unit—Researchers have used the RNN in machine translation, speech recognition, image captioning, and video captioning since it was introduced [1, 18]. The feedback connections to the feedforward neural network can be used to build a basic RNN model. Three layers make up a feedback network:

      • Input layer (v)

      • Hidden layer (h)

      • Output layer (y)

      The network weights are updated by using current input and previous hidden state, which is denoted by the following equations:

$$h_t = \varphi(W_h v_t + U_h h_{t-1} + b_h) \tag{14.3}$$
$$y_t = \varphi(U_y h_t + b_y) \tag{14.4}$$

where φ is the activation function, W_x, U_x are weights matrices, and b_x is biases. These parameters will be updated with epochs. But, the main problem with this approach is the vanishing/exploding gradient problem. To address the mentioned problems, LSTM was developed to adaptively select the information by forgetting and updating the previous and current information.

$$i_t = (W_i y_t + U_i h_{t-1} + b_i) \tag{14.5}$$
$$f_t = (W_f y_t + U_f h_{t-1} + b_f) \tag{14.6}$$
$$o_t = (W_o y_t + U_o h_{t-1} + b_o) \tag{14.7}$$
$$g_t = (W_g y_t + U_g h_{t-1} + b_g) \tag{14.8}$$
$$m_t = f_t m_{t-1} + i_t g_t \tag{14.9}$$
$$h_t = O_t \odot \varphi(m_t) \tag{14.10}$$

Here, W *, U*, and b* are the parameters of the weight matrices that must be known; y_t denotes the LSTM unit's input vector at each time phase t; (σ) denotes the nonlinear logistic sigmoid activation function; φ denotes the element-by-element product with the gate value in Equation 14.10; and φ denotes the hyperbolic tangent function. Figure 14.2 represents the LSTM structure [24].

ii. Gated Recurrent Unit—In 2014, Cho [25] proposed the gated recurrent unit, and many researchers started using it in place of LSTM [24]. It enables the recurrent unit to capture the dependencies at different time scales. GRU has gated units similar to LSTM which is used to module the information flow inside the cell.

$$h_t^j = \left(1 - Z_t^j\right) h_{t-1}^j + z_t^j \tilde{h}_t^j \tag{14.11}$$

The interpolation of candidate activation $\tilde{h}_t^j$ (14.11) and prior activation h_{t-1}^j yield current activation at time t. z_t^j (14.12) represents the update gate. This gate determines how much of its content is being updated. The update gate can be calculated by using Equation 14.12:

$$z^j = \sigma(W_z x_t + U_z h_{t1}) \tag{14.12}$$

In both the LSTM and GRU units, the linear sum of the existing state and the new computed state is calculated in the same way. But in case of GRU, it does

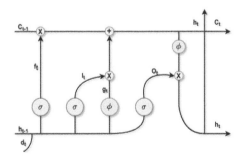

FIGURE 14.2
Long short-term memory.

not have a controlling mechanism from which its state is exposed. The candidate activation unit $\tilde{h}^j$ (14.13) is calculated in the same way as the traditional recurrent unit.

$$\tilde{h}_t^j = tanh\left(W_x t + U\left(r_t \odot \tilde{h}_{t-1}^j\right)\right) \tag{14.13}$$

where $\odot$ is the element-wise multiplication, and r_t is the set of reset gate. Whenever r_t^j (14.14) is equal to zero, then the reset gate forces the model to forget the previously calculated state by acting as if it was reading the initial collection of pixels from the input frame. Reset gate r_t^j in Equation 14.14 can be calculated similar to the update gate.

$$r^j = \sigma(W_r x_t + U_r h_{t-1}) \tag{14.14}$$

A graphical diagram of GRU is described in Figure 14.3.

4. Bahdanau Attention Mechanism—In case of LSTM, GRU, RNN all these focus each part of feature equally. The attention model helps to focus on the relevant part of data from a large bunch of input. It is similar to the real-life analogy, i.e., humans focus on only the relevant part of a visual scene. RNN efficiency decreases as the sequence length increases. The performance of RNN [26] degrades when the length of the series is long, regardless of if it is sequential. But LSTM and GRU help to some extent in Vanilla network [24].

The attention mechanism can solve this problem using an alignment score [25]. It forms the addition attention layer that learns from the past output. This lets the network decide which features it wants to keep. RNNs can learn long sequences using the attention mechanism. To get the output for the current cell, the attention mechanism uses the weighted sum of all states and the last state. Attention weights are used to retain the output for the next cell. It allows which input should be chosen for the next cell from each previous input. So, it allows the network to catch the most important objects for the current cell. The context vector is calculated in Equation 14.15:

$$C_t = \sum_{j=1}^{T} \alpha_{tj} h_j \tag{14.15}$$

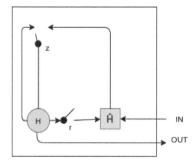

FIGURE 14.3
Gated recurrent unit.

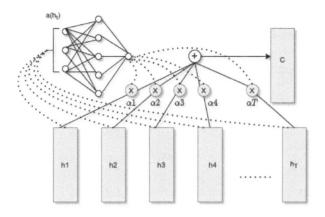

FIGURE 14.4
Bahdanau attention.

where α_{tj} is calculated using Equation 14.17 and state sequence s is calculated by using the context vector C_t, which is determined by the previous state sequence s_{t-1} as well as the model's output at time step $t-1$.

$$e_{tj} = a\ (s_{t-1},\ h_j) \tag{14.16}$$

$$\alpha_{tj} = \frac{exp\Big(score\big(e_{tj}\ h_s\big)\Big)}{\sum_{\{k=1\}}^{T} exp\big(e_{tk},h_s\big)} \tag{14.17}$$

The e_{tj} denotes the attention score, and it is calculated as given in Equation 14.16. The overall model using all the concepts is represented in Figure 14.4. The alignment score is calculated using the Bahdanau mechanism. Alignment score increase the weight of nodes where model have to focus from all hidden layers to generate better result. In other words, we can say that the alignment score tells the model on which pixel we have to focus to predict the next word. Bayesian optimization is used to select the better hyperparameter. To select the learning rate for a neural network, a randomized search is used.

14.4 Experiment

Our MSVD labeled dataset consisted of 1,970 videos downloaded from Microsoft.com [27]. Of those, we used 1,575 for training and 425 for testing. These videos are actually collected from YouTube. Each video duration is between 10 and 25 seconds. Each video roughly has 40 annotations. These videos include activities such as "animal activity", "instruments playing activity", and "kitchen cooking".

If we think about humans, everyone has their own way to generate captions. It means we cannot compare whole sentences, because for the same content more than one sentence is possible. For the caption analysis, many evaluation matrices came into existence. Evaluation matrices are used to figure out how one caption relates to another caption. BLEU score, ROUGE score, and METEOR score are three common evaluation matrices.

1. BLEU Score

The quality of generated text is assessed using BLEU score. BLEU score does not check the syntactic correctness of the sentences, rather it matches each generated text with its respective reference texts that are composed by humans [28].

$$BLEU = \left(1, \frac{G_L}{R_L}\right) \left(\prod_{i=1}^{4} \left(precision_i\right)\right)^{1/4} \tag{14.18}$$

$$Precision = \frac{C_W}{T_W} \tag{14.19}$$

where G_L denotes the length of the generated sentence, R_L denotes the length of the reference sentence/caption, C_W denotes the matched words in the generated captions, and T_W denotes the total length of the generated caption.

Algorithm 14.1: Code snippet to calculate Bleu score of generated captions

1: Calculate Bleu score of each generated caption using Equation 14.18

2: BLEU=0

3: for each sentence bleu score:

4:     BLEU=BLEU+sentence bleu score

5: return BLEU/total generated captions

Table 14.1 shows the BLEU score on test data using Algorithm 14.1. Where BLEU-1 represents the calculated BLEU score using unigram, and BLEU-2 represents the calculated BLEU score using bi-gram, and so on.

2. ROUGE Score

The ROUGE score is also used to evaluate the generated captions's accuracy. The ROUGE score compares human-written captions and generated captions using word-pair and n-grams [29]. Overall, the ROUGE score is calculated using Algorithm 14.2.

TABLE 14.1

BLEU Score on Test Data

Matrix Name	Calculated Value
BLEU Score-1	0.769
BLEU Score-2	0.628
BLEU Score-3	0.521
BLEU Score-4	0.413

Algorithm 14.2: Code snippet to calculate ROUGE score of generated captions

1: Calculate ROUGE score of each generated caption using the methodology presented in Tingting et al. [29]

2: ROUGE=0

3: for each sentence rouge score:

4:   ROUGE=ROUGE+sentence rouge score

5: return ROUGE/total generated captions

3. METEOR Score—It is used to evaluate the similarity between the actual and predicted captions. It takes the weighted harmonic mean of precision and recall. It also takes care of synonymy and stemming matching along with standard word matching. It is designed to fix the error present in BLEU matrix evaluation. At the segment or phrase level, it also produces a good correlation with human judgment [30].

14.5 Results Analysis

1. Result of Evaluation Matrices—Table 14.2 represent the results of evaluation matrices of different similar models developed. We have used the MSVD dataset to calculate the accuracy.

First we developed the model using CNN and LSTM which produced very low accuracy. Then we used GRU in placed of LSTM, and similar results have been observed. The GRU + attention + GRU model and LSTM + attention model produced similar evaluation matrices. But GRU combined with attention mechanism and LSTM produced the highest accuracy. It is because of three reasons. Using GRU, we are able to reduce the training time. Using attention mechanism, we are able to focus on the relevant parts of videos, and using LSTM we are able to catch the long sentences or captions.

TABLE 14.2

Evaluation Matrix

Methodology	Bleu-1	Rouge	Meteor	CIDer
CNN + LSTM	0.696	0.639	0.278	0.45
GRU (Tanh activation) + LSTM	0.703	0.627	0.280	0.47
GRU + Attention + GRU	0.751	0.634	0.291	0.53
LSTM + Attention	0.753	0.641	0.295	0.54
GRU + Attention + LSTM	0.769	0.673	0.312	0.61

2. Comparative Analysis

Table 14.3 represents evaluation matrices results of our model compared to other state-of-the-art models. Venugopalan proposed a sequence-to-sequence model using LSTM and achieved a 29.8 meteor score [1]. Thomson et al. made a factor graph model using entities, activities, and scenes present in the video [31]. Yao et al. generated caption using both local and global temporal structures present in frames [33]. Bin et al. used attention-based bi-direction LSTM [34]. Gao generated sentences from video using hierarchical LSTM and an adaptive attention model [32].

3. Time Taken to Train and Test the Models

Table 14.4 represents time taken in our model with respect to the LSTM-based model. We have trained the model for 2,300 epoch. Time taken has been decreased nearly 30%. GRU works similarly to LSTM but works faster than LSTM.

4. Test Examples

Figure 14.5 represents the screenshots of test video 1. These screenshots have been taken at first and fifth seconds of video.

TABLE 14.3

Comparison Matrices

Model Names	BLEU-4	METEOR
S2VT [1]	—	29.8
FGM [31]	—	29.3
Hierarchical-LSTM [32]	0.36	28.2
GoogleNet + CNN [33]	—	29.6
Bidirectional-LSTM [34]	0.37	29.8
GRU + Attention + LSTM (present work)	0.41	31.2

TABLE 14.4

Time Taken to Train the Model

Model Name	Time Taken
LSTM + Attention	17 hours 36 minutes
GRU + Attention + LSTM	12 hours 32 minutes

FIGURE 14.5A
First screenshot of test video-1.

FIGURE 14.5B
Screenshots of test video-1.

Result analysis for test video 1:

Actual Caption 1: A woman gallops on a horse.

Actual Caption 2: A girl is riding a horse.

Actual Caption 3: A man is jogging on the horse.

Actual Caption 4: A man is riding on a horse.

Generated Caption (LSTM + Attention): A man is riding a horse.

Generated Caption (GRU + Attention + LSTM): A man is riding a horse in a yard.

Figure 14.6 represent the screenshots of test video 2. These screenshots have been taken at the first and fourth seconds of video.

Result analysis for test video-2:

Actual Caption 1: A man is shown playing a wooden flute.

Actual Caption 2: The man is playing the wooden flute.

Actual Caption 3: He is playing the flute.

Actual Caption 4: A boy playing a flute.

Generated Caption (LSTM + Attention): A man is playing a flute.

Generated Caption (GRU + Attention + LSTM): A man is playing a flute.

5. Loss Plot
   - Epoch: Iteration over the whole training data.
   - Loss: This is a scalar value. In model, we try to keep this value as low as possible. As the loss decreases, we are getting closer to the accurate guess.

FIGURE 14.6A
First screenshot of test video-2.

FIGURE 14.6B
Screenshots of test video-2.

As the number of epochs increased, we can see that the loss decreased from 0.006 to 0.0051. We have tried from 1,000 to 2,500 epochs, but after 2,300 epochs, the loss is not decreasing below 0.000505; therefore, we have trained until 2,300 epochs. Figure 14.7 represents how the loss is decreasing in the last 120 epochs.

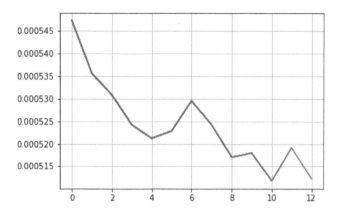

FIGURE 14.7
Loss plot.

14.6 Conclusion

In this work, we have presented a novel video captioning approach. We have optimized the accuracy and time consumed to train the model using GRU, attention mechanism, and LSTM. The present model trained and tested on Google-Colab using the MSVD dataset. In the case of LSTM with attention mechanism, we get a 0.75 BLEU-1 score, and the time taken is 17.5 hours. In the case of GRU with attention mechanism and LSTM, time taken is 12.5 hours, and the BLEU-1 score is 0.769. This shows that a combination of GRU, attention mechanism, and LSTM generated excellent results. Time taken in the case of GRU is much less as compared to the LSTM. GRU maintained the temporal relationships and complementary information in the successive frames. LSTM generated the long caption effectively. Further, we can enhance accuracy using bidirectional LSTM with GRU.

References

[1] Venugopalan, S.; Rohrbach, M.; Donahue, J.; Mooney, R.; Darrell, T.; Saenko, K. Sequence to sequence—Video to text. In *Proc. IEEE Int. Conf. Comput. Vis.* Jun. 2015; pp. 4534–4542; https://ieeexplore.ieee.org/document/7410872.

[2] Tan, X.; Guo, Y.; Chen, Y.; Zhu, W. Accurate inference of user popularity preference. In a large-scale online video streaming system. *Sci. China Inf. Sci.* 2017; vol. 61, no. 1, Art. no. 018101.

[3] Li, X.; Zhao, B.; Lu, X. A general framework for edited video and raw video summarization. *IEEE Trans. Image Process.* 2017; vol. 26, no. 8, pp. 3652–3664.

[4] Li, X.; Zhao, B.; Lu, X. Key frame extraction in the summary space. *IEEE Trans. Cybern.* Jun. 2018; vol. 48, no. 6, pp. 1923–1934.

[5] Fang, H.; Shang, C.; Chen, J. An optimization-based shared control framework with applications in multi-robot systems. *Sci. China Inf. Sci.* 2018; vol. 61, no. 1, Art. no. 014201.

[6] Li, X.; Zhao, B.; Lu, X; Wang, Z. A CNN—RNN architecture for multi-label weather recognition. *Neurocomputing.* Dec. 2018; vol. 322, pp. 47–57.

[7] Wang, Q.; Gao, J.; Lin, W.; Yuan, Y. Learning from synthetic data for crowd counting in the wild. In *Proc. IEEE Conf. Comput. Vis. Pattern Recognition.* 2019; pp. 8198–8207; https://arxiv.org/abs/1903.03303.

[8]   Guadarrama, S., et al. YouTube2Text: Recognizing and describing arbitrary activities using semantic hierarchies and zero-shot recognition In *Proc. IEEE Int. Conf. Comput. Vis.* Dec. 2013; pp. 2712–2719.

[9]   Krishnamoorthy, N.; Malkarnenkar, G.; Mooney, R.J.; Saenko, K.; Guadarama, S. Generating natural-language video descriptions using text-mined knowledge. In *Proc. 27th AAAI Conf. Artif. Intell.* 2013; pp. 541–547.

[10]   Donahue, J., et al. Long-term recurrent convolutional networks for visual recognition and description. *IEEE Trans. Pattern Anal. Mach. Intell.* Apr. 2017; vol. 39, no. 4, pp. 677–691.

[11]   Zeng, K.H.; Chen, T.H.; Niebles, J. C.; Sun, M. Title generation for user generated videos. In *Proc. Eur. Conf. Comput. Vis.* 2016; pp. 609–625; https://link.springer.com/chapter/10.1007/978-3-319-46475-6_38.

[12]   Long, X.; Gan, C.; de Melo, G. Video captioning with multi-faceted attention, *CoRR.* Dec. 2016; vol. abs/1612.00234; https://arxiv.org/abs/1612.00234.

[13]   Simonyan, Karen; Zisserman, Andrew. Very deep convolutional networks for large-scale image recognition. *arXiv,* 2014; https://arxiv.org/abs/1409.1556.

[14]   Vinyals, O.; Toshev, A.; Bengio, S.; Erhan, D. Show and tell: A neural image caption generator. In *Proc. IEEE Conf. Comput. Vis. Pattern Recogn.* 2015; pp. 3156–3164.

[15]   Shetty, R.; Laaksonen, J. Video captioning with recurrent networks based on frame and video level features and visual content classification. *CoRR.* Dec. 2015; vol. abs/1512.02949; https://www.semanticscholar.org/paper/Video-captioning-with-recurrent-networks-based-on-Shetty-Laaksonen/3bcca85ad84806be6d38d3882f7a6aac0ad90253.

[16]   Rohrbach, M.; Qiu, W.; Titov, I., et al. Translating video content to natural language descriptions. In *Proc. IEEE Int. Conf. Comput. Vis.* 2013; pp. 433–440.

[17]   Mao, J.; Xu, W.; Yang, Y., et al. Deep captioning with multimodal recurrent neural networks (M-RNN). *arXiv:1412.6632,* 2014.

[18]   Venugopalan, S.; Xu, H.; Donahue, J.; Rohrbach, M.; Mooney, R.; Saenko, K. Translating videos to natural language using deep recurrent neural networks. *arXiv:1412.4729,* 2014.

[19]   Pan, P.; Xu, Z.; Yang, Y.; Wu, F.; Zhuang, Y. Hierarchical recurrent neural encoder for video representation with application to captioning. In *Proc. IEEE Conf. Comput. Vis. Pattern Recogn.* 2016; pp. 1029–1038.

[20]   Pan, Y.; Mei, T.; Yao, T.; Li, H.; Rui, Y. Jointly modeling embedding and translation to bridge video and language. In *Proc. IEEE Conf. Comput. Vis. Pattern Recogn.* 2016; pp. 4594–4602.

[21]   Zhiwang, Zhang at el. Show, tell and summarize: Dense video captioning using visual cue aided sentence summarization. In *IEEE Transactions on Circuits and Systems for Video Technology.* Aug. 2019; vol 30.

[22]   Song, J.; Li, X.; Gao, L.; Shen, H.T. Hierarchical LSTMs with adaptive attention for visual captioning. In *IEEE Transactions on Pattern Analysis and Machine Intelligence.* Jan. 2019, pp. 1–1.10.1109/TPAMI.2894139.

[23]   Krizhevsky, Alex; Sutskever, Ilya; Hinton, Geoffrey E. ImageNet classification with deep convolutional neural networks. In *Commun. ACM.* 2012; vol. 1, pp. 1097–1105.

[24]   Junyoung, Chung, et al. Empirical Evaluation of Gated Recurrent Neural Networks on Sequence Modeling. In *NIPS Workshop on Deep Learning.* Dec. 2014; https://www.semanticscholar.org/paper/Empirical-Evaluation-of-Gated-Recurrent-Neural-on-Chung-G%C3%BCl%C3%A7ehre/adfcf065e15fd3bc9badf6145034c84dfb08f204.

[25]   Kyunghyun, C., et al. Learning phrase representations using RNN encoder-decoder for statistical machine translation. In *EMNLP 2014,* pp. 1724–1734; https://aclanthology.org/D14-1179/.

[26]   Pengfei, Liu; Qiu, Xipeng; Huan, Xuanjing. Recurrent neural network for text classification with multi-task learning. *Proc. Twenty-Fifth Int. Joint Conf. Artif. Intell.* 2016; pp. 2873–2879.

[27]   Chen, D. L.; Dolan, W. B. Collecting highly parallel data for paraphrase evaluation. In *Proc. 49th Annual Meeting of the Association for Computational Linguistics: Human Language Technologies. Association for Computational Linguistics.* 2011; vol. 1, HLT '11, pp. 190–200.

[28]   Papineni, K.; Roukos, S.; Ward, T.; Jing Zhu, W. Bleu: A method for automatic evaluation of machine translation. In *Proc. 40th Annual Meeting of the Association for Computational Linguistics.* 2002; pp. 311–318.

[29]   Tingting, H.; Jinguang, Chen; Liang, M.; Zhuoming; G.; Fang, L.; Wei Shao; Qian Wang. ROUGE-C: A fully automated evaluation method for multi-document summarization. In *IEEE Int. Conf. Granular Comput.* 2008; pp. 269–274.

[30] Denkowski, M.; Lavie, A. Meteor universal: Language specific translation evaluation for any target language. In *Proc. Ninth Workshop on Statistical Machine Translation*, Baltimore, Maryland, June 2014; pp. 376–380.

[31] Thomason, J., et al. Integrating language and vision to generate natural language descriptions of videos in the wild. In *Proc. 25th Int. Conf. Com- put. Linguistics, Tech. Papers (COLING)*, Dublin, Ireland, Aug. 2014; pp. 1218–1227.

[32] Gao, L.; Li, X.; Song, J.; Shen, H. T. Hierarchical LSTMs with adaptive attention for visual captioning. In *IEEE Journal of Latex Class Files*. Aug. 2015; vol. 14.

[33] Yao, L.; Torabi, A.; Cho, K.; Ballas, N.; Pal, C.; Larochelle, H.; Courville, A. Describing videos by exploiting temporal structure. *arXiv:1502.08029v4*, 2015.

[34] Bin, Y.; Yang, Y.; Shen, F.; Xie, N.; Shen, H. T.; Li, X. Describing video with attention-based bidirectional LSTM. In *IEEE Transactions on Cybernetics*, 2018; https://ieeexplore.ieee.org/document/8365878.

15

Nature-Inspired Computing for Feature Selection and Classification

Rahul Chakre, Dipak V. Patil and M. U. Kharat

CONTENTS

DOI: 10.1201/9781003218111-15

15.1 Introduction

A large amount of medical data gets generated in the modern world in the form of images. For more than a decade, the area of image processing has seen remarkable changes due to the rapid expansion of computational capabilities. A revolution has occurred in space, processing speed, and algorithmic complexity. It has prompted research scholars and scientists worldwide to develop efficient algorithms and ideas in image processing. One such computational model, i.e. nature-inspired computing, was developed in recent years. In current trends, digital image and video processing are regarded as critical study areas. Real-world data contains uncertainties, ambiguities, and partial truth; evaluating and processing this data using traditional algorithms and methodologies is a time-consuming task. The concept of nature-inspired computation could be employed to overcome these problems. It is a fascinating and relatively new topic in which natural principles are used to develop and implement new and improved computing approaches for dealing with uncertainty, ambiguity, and partial truth. The majority of these nature-inspired approaches have already been successfully applied to a variety of problems, including digital image processing, data knowledge discovery, classification, decision-making tasks, pattern recognition, computer security, time-series conjecture, conjunctional optimization, biometrics, machine learning, and many others. Bio-inspired techniques include genetic algorithm (GA), biodegradability forecasts, cellular automata, and artificial neural networks, as well as unnatural life, immune computing systems, and bacterial territories, subsequently, insect organizations such as honeybees, ants, termites, and wasps. The motivation behind this study is the way nature-inspired computing handles different problems in feature selection and classification. Nature-inspired computing efficiently deals with the issues when

- The problem is complicated and nonlinear, with many variables or alternative solutions or several goals.
- Traditional methodologies, such as complicated pattern recognition and classification, are insufficient to solve the problems.
- Traditional ways to find an optimal solution are inadequate, difficult to achieve or guarantee. As discussed earlier, real-world data contains uncertainties, ambiguities, and partial truth, and evaluating and processing these data using traditional algorithms and methodologies is a time-consuming task.

Furthermore, nature-inspired computing utilizes a distributed, bottom-up approach. It often entails establishing a foundation for establishing a collection of a simple set of rules, a simple set of organisms that implement those directives, and a mechanism for applying that simple set of rules iteratively. In computer-aided image analysis, effective feature extraction, feature selection, and classification strategies are also required. These strategies can be implemented by using nature-inspired computing.

The major contribution of this chapter is the study of nature-inspired computing techniques in solving feature selection and classification problems in medical image analysis. Swarm intelligence and immune computing solutions are discussed to address these issues. Effective feature selection is required, which is accomplished via swarm-based intelligence; similarly, immune computing is used to classify images. Swarm intelligence is a computational technique that attempts to make a candidate solution better against a set of standard criteria. On the other hand, immune computing is a collection of adaptive techniques based on the exploratory immune system and actual immune activities, principles, and models used to address issues. Particle swarm optimization, ant colony optimization, and artificial bee colony optimization are three swarm intelligence–based feature selection strategies discussed in this chapter. Later, immune computing algorithms such as the negative selection algorithm, clonal selection algorithm, and dendritic cell algorithm are discussed to carry out the classification task. Hence, the approach will be used for image analysis based on the discussed swarm intelligence and immune computing algorithms.

15.2 Nature-Inspired Computing

Nature is a significant source of inspiration, encouraging many researchers and scientists to work in this broad domain. Most state-of-the-art techniques are currently based on nature with their inspiration from nature. Physics-based computing, biology-based computing, and chemistry-based computing are the three categories of nature-inspired computing. Essentially, it is determined by the degree of depth and information given about the sub-sources. The most significant levels of sources are considered here to comprehend the aim. This chapter focuses on and explains biology-based algorithms. In a broad sense, nature is the source of inspiration, which is why all new algorithms are labelled as "nature inspired." The majority of nature-inspired algorithms include biological-like iterative characteristics. Consequently, biology-based, a.k.a. bio-inspired computing is a large-scale fragment of nature-inspired computing.

Swarm intelligence is now being used to enhance a special class of bio-inspired computing. Swarm intelligence is, in fact, one of the most widely used techniques for addressing a variety of real-world optimization problems. Among these are particle swarm optimization, ant colony optimization, artificial bee colony optimization, and other methods. Artificial immune-based systems are another popular type of bio-inspired computing. Another everyday sort of bio-inspired computing is artificial immune-based systems. Immunocomputing-based approaches are another name for these methods. These were developed with the biological immune system in mind. This method yields a superior result. Negative selection algorithm, clonal selection algorithm, and dendritic cell algorithm are types of immune computing–based techniques. This chapter explains the swarm intelligence and immune computing strategies for feature selection and classification, respectively.

15.3 Feature Selection

Feature selection is essential in all types of processing because it eliminates redundant, irrelevant, and insignificant features, resulting in a more precise output. Consequently, dimensionality is reduced, providing an edge over space and time complexity [1,2]. Filter methods, wrapper methods, and embedded methods are the three main classes of feature selection techniques. The filtering technique prioritizes feature association, relevancy, and redundancy. The accuracy of the classification technique is taken into account in the wrapping technique. Subsequently, the embedded methods obtain the prime divisor [3,4]. Pattern recognition and classification rely heavily on feature selection. Local optima and time complexity plague current feature selection algorithms. As a result, the feature section task is considered a global optimization problem. The swarm intelligence–based techniques for feature selection are utilized to address these issues. Because of its global search capability, these strategies provide the best characteristics. This chapter describes three important swarm intelligence–based feature selection techniques: particle swarm optimization, ant colony optimization, and artificial bee colony optimization.

15.4 Swarm Intelligence

Swarm intelligence is a special class of bio-inspired computing. This technique focuses on the collaborative and emergent behaviour of multiple agents who communicate with one another via simple protocols. They demonstrate the self-organized functioning of a whole system in which many individuals are engaged through grouped or collective intelligent behaviour. Many algorithms are now being developed based on the natural swarm intelligence systems. All swarm-based algorithms are composed among many individuals and are inspired by the cooperative behaviours of ants and bees and other communities such as flocks of birds or schools of fish.

The traditional particle swarm optimization (PSO) algorithm is motivated by bird and fish flocking, while the ant colony optimization (ACO) algorithm is inspired by ant cooperation, the firefly algorithm (FA) was inspired by firefly lighting behaviour, the bat algorithm (BA) was inspired by bat foraging behaviour, the cuckoo search technique was inspired by cuckoo bird brooding dependency, whereas the artificial bee colony (ABC) was inspired by honeybee foraging behaviour. Swarm intelligence–based algorithms are widely employed and famous for addressing a variety of problems for two primary reasons:

- Because these algorithms share information across several persons, they have better self-organization, co-evolution, and learning throughout the iterative process, resulting in increased algorithm efficiency.
- Multiple individuals can work in parallel comfortably, making large-scale optimization more effective and practical from an implementation point of view.

As mentioned earlier, the next section focuses on the three significant swarm intelligence–based techniques: PSO, ACO, and ABC.

15.4.1 Particle Swarm Optimization

PSO is a popular swarm-inspired intelligence method that takes inspiration from nature. It was invented by Kennedy and Eberhart in 1995 and is also known as an evolutionary technique [5]. The very first PSO model was developed by observing and simulating a flock of birds. Later, Shi and Eberhart [6] proposed the standard PSO in 1998, which included new parameter inertia weight. The intelligent foraging behaviour of a group of birds or fish is the focus of this technique. Each potential problem in PSO is represented as a particle flying through a problem space at a specific velocity. In today's era of unlimited data, the capacity to interpret imprecise, unstructured, and inconsistent data and extract the essential features from it has become a critical prerequisite of feature selection. PSO is a crucial technique for feature selection in various real-world issues, particularly numeric challenges. Compared to other evolutionary techniques, such as the GA [6], PSO performs better. The typical PSO, which is utilized in various domains such as text selection, digital image processing, and biomedical research, surprisingly produces better feature selection results.

PSO starts with a population of random solutions and iteratively seeks the optimum one. Essentially, it employs a population in which each particle represents a potential solution. The particles update the fitness function throughout iterations, resulting in particles moving over the problem space with N-dimensions using the present higher-accomplishing particles. Each particle is allowed to calculate its own fitness and the fitness of its neighbours at each step of the optimization. Each particle can maintain its focus on its own solution, resulting in improved fitness and the ability to check the candidate solution for the better performing particle in its vicinity [6]. PSO is a population-based optimization algorithm. The conventional PSO was explained earlier, but the world is not limited to it. PSO is modified on a real-time basis to satisfy the requirements of the problem, which is why it is flexible enough to be used in a variety of contexts. The issue of feature selection is becoming increasingly prevalent, necessitating the development of a practical algorithm for separating data. In PSO, a cluster of particles uses their personal and collective afire to investigate a decision space and obtain superior results [6]. PSO works in the same way as an evolutionary algorithm, starting with an arbitrary population that becomes a possible solution and then updating the population. Every response is referred to as a particle in this technique, and the characteristics of the algorithm are communicated through the particle's information. The particles of this technique are later positioned in the best rank with the slightest error after each iteration, based on their current location information. Later, a group of particles shifted and placed themselves in the best possible position.

15.4.1.1 Feature Selection Using Particle Swarm Optimization

After the feature extraction procedure, some of the features in the set are redundant, irrelevant, or unconnected. The classification rate is affected as a result of these aspects. The main goal of feature selection is to diminish unrelated data and eliminate insignificant features to avoid exploitation. The conventional PSO's flowchart is depicted in Figure 15.1.

To put this another way, find the best features from the extracted features that can discriminate better. As a consequence, the classification performance will increase. The PSO technique is explained here, focusing on the feature selection task. The main characteristic

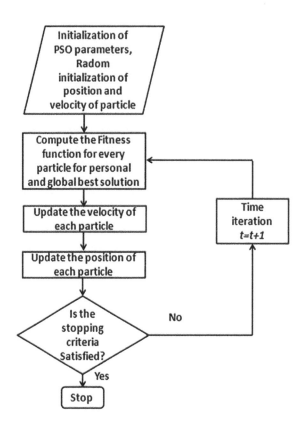

FIGURE 15.1
Flowchart of standard PSO.

of PSO is that it does both global and local searches in the feature space step by step. This technique utilizes a group of arbitrary particles to travel them throughout the problem's solution space. This is accomplished by enhancing the succession, which helps in a better solution. This process will continue until convergence is attained. In this algorithm, as shown in the flowchart, m numbers of the arbitrary particles are given from the feature space. Every particle has some parameters b, which is acquired after the feature extraction step. Those parameters and the random velocity of each particle forms position matrix $Y = [m, b]$. For initial iteration, the threshold for selection of random particles and their respective positions are calculated using the following function:

$$V [i, j] = e (Y [i, j]) \text{ where, } 1 < i < m \text{ and } 1 < j < b \tag{15.1}$$

The velocity and their corresponding locations are described by the $V_i = (v_{i1}, v_{i2}, v_{i3} \ldots v_{ib})$ and $Y = (y_{i1}, y_{i2}, y_{i3} \ldots y_{ib})$, respectively. If the currently calculated velocity is bigger than the value of the threshold, then its position and velocity are chosen in the next iteration. It is anticipated that during every iteration the classification rate of the classification system will be increased with currently chosen new feature from the extracted feature space. Thus, with the help of the objective function, known as the fitness function, it is used to calculate the success rate. It is applied to condense the local and global information about the features. This fitness function is evaluated and compared to its previous best and global best for every particle. After, knowing these best values, particles start updating their locations and velocities with the help of the following equations:

$$V_i(t+1) = w * V_i(t) + c_1 * r_1 * (P_{besti}(t) - Y_i(t)) + c_2 * r_2 * (G_{besti}(t) - Y_i(t)) \tag{15.2}$$

$$Y_i(t+1) = Y_i(t) + V_i(t+1) \tag{15.3}$$

where
$V_i(t)$: Velocity of the particle or individual at a time t.
w: Inertia weight.
c_1, c_2: Weight factors.
r_1, r_2: Random number in between 0 and 1.
$Y_i(t)$: Position of the particle at time t.
$P_{besti}(t)$: Personal best of ith particle at time t.
$G_{besti}(t)$: Global best of ith particle at time t.

The PSO can be summed up by the following steps:

1. Initialization
   - For each particle in population size
     - Initialize the position vector stochastically
     - Initialize the velocity vector stochastically
     - Calculate the fitness rate
     - Initialize the personal best
   - Initialize the global best with prime fitness rate
2. Repeat until convergence
   - For each particle
     - Upgrade the position vector and velocity vector
     - Calculate the fitness rate
     - Update the personal best
     - Update the global best

15.4.2 Ant Colony Optimization

Dorigo et al. [8] presented an ACO, a meta-heuristic algorithm inspired by nature. The algorithm is inspired by the way actual ant colonies obtain food in their natural environment. A chemical molecule called a pheromone is used by real ants to trace their path in search of food. The remaining ants use the same pheromone to track down the food source. It is widely used to address optimization problems, including the travelling salesman problem, job shop problem, and graph colouring problem [9]. The ACO algorithm is composed of adaptability and cooperative mechanisms [10]. The ant-based system is the very initial ACO technique. This algorithm was first introduced in the early 1990s. The update of the pheromone value during each iteration is a significant component of the ant system. Probabilistic combinatorial optimization problems can be efficiently handled with the help of ant systems. Positive response, shared computing, and greedy heuristics are all crucial features of this strategy. Positive feedback increases the chances of finding a solution quickly, shared computing decreases the chance of early convergences, and acquisitive heuristics benefit in finding better solutions [11–13]. The ACO algorithm's overall procedure is depicted in Figure 15.2. It starts with the ant's initialization. These are positioned on the graph in a random order (an arbitrary feature will allocate, i.e., each ant).

Natural ants traverse among the nodes of the graph to determine the shortest path and deposit the pheromone. The real ants use the direction stochastically and follow the higher-density pheromone. The shortest route will have the most pheromone, which the natural ants will eventually select. This procedure will continue until the pheromone levels on other pathways drop [14]. By identifying the path with the minimum cost, the

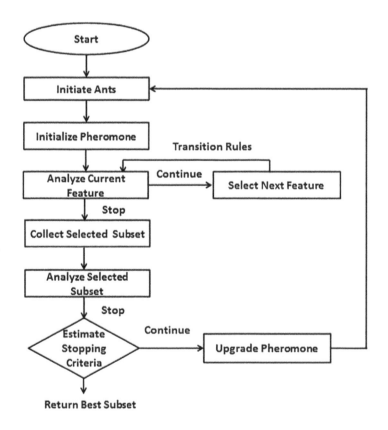

FIGURE 15.2
Flowchart of ant colony optimization.

ACO can be used to solve a problem of selecting the features. In the standard ACO technique, nodes in the network graph represent features, whereas edges represent the next feature [15].

15.4.2.1 Feature Selection Using Ant Colony Optimization

On the graph, the population of ants and the population of feature are equal. Each ant will start building the trail at a different feature. They shift the edge stochastically with the help of these positions until the halting criteria are met. The outputs are put together and then analyzed. If an ideal feature subset is found, the procedure is stopped, and the prime feature subset is delivered. When the method has been run a particular number of times, the process will halt and return the excellent feature subset. If both conditions are met, the pheromone is upgraded again, a new group of ants are formed, and the iteration mechanism begins again.

This section outlines how ACO performs. The graph represents the feature selection problem. The node represents the feature, while the edges represent the next feature choice based on heuristic traversal desirability and edge pheromone rate. It is also known as the probabilistic transition rule. The representation of the probabilistic transition rule for an ant with the feature m selecting to travel to feature n at time t:

$$P_{mn}^k(t) = \frac{[\Phi_{mn}(t)^\beta].[\lambda_{mn}(t)]^\alpha}{\sum_{l=N_m^k}[\Phi_{ml}]^\beta.[[\lambda_{ml}]} \text{ if } n \in N_n^k \tag{15.4}$$

where
k = Total number of ants
λ_{mn} = Heuristic desirability of traversal selecting the feature n when at m
N_m^k = Group of neighbouring nodes which are yet to be visited
β, α = Parameters that decide relative pheromone rate and heuristic information
$\Phi_{mn}(t)$ = Virtual pheromone on edge (m,n)

The pheromone updating formula is given as follows

$$\Phi_{mn}(t+1) = (1-\eta).\Phi_{mn}(t) + \eta.\Delta\Phi_{mn}(t) \tag{15.5}$$

where
η : Decay constant

If the edge between m and n is traversed, the virtual pheromone becomes the 0. Here, the decay constant is used to stimulate the evaporated pheromone.

$$\Phi_{mn}(t) = \sum_{k=1}^{n} \omega(R^k) / \lfloor R^k \rfloor \tag{15.6}$$

where
R^k = Feature set developed by ant k

According to the quality of the feature selected by the ant, the pheromone is updated.

The stepwise procedure is shown, which is as follows:

1. Initialize all the parameters
2. Generate a set of binary bit strings (length equal to the size of the feature set) and allocate them to the ants
3. Individual ant chooses a feature based on the pheromone rate and the heuristic knowledge and produces feature subsets
4. Individual ant upgrades the pheromone rates of the features found on selection
5. Individual ant drives the feature subsets to the classifier for estimation
6. Upgrade the pheromone rates with the help of prime ant and the best feature subset
7. Retain the prime feature subset produced
8. Replicate steps from 3 to 5 for a preplanned number of iterations

15.4.3 Artificial Bee Colony

An artificial bee colony (ABC) is a swarm-based meta-heuristic intelligence system developed by Karaboga in 2005 [16]. This technique has been widely used in various engineering optimization problems [17,18], and the natural functioning of honeybees influences it. Employed bees (Type E), onlooker bees (Type O), and scout bees are the three types of bees in the colony (Type S). The algorithm starts with the generation of food source locations, denoted by the letter N. The number of Type E bees is proportional to the quantity of available food locations. A food site is allocated to each Type E bee. Type E bees use the location of food to communicate nectar amount details to Type O bees. The number of Type E and Type O bees is equal here. The Type O bees use the food location and communicate with their neighbours with the help of details shared by the Type E bees until the food location becomes empty. Type E bees in an empty food location then become Type S bees. Type S bees start looking for new food sources. The standard of the solution accessible from the food site is nectar knowledge. The number of nectar and the chance of selecting a specific food place, as performed by Type O bees, are related to each other [19]. The ABC algorithm is a collective intelligence swarm of honeybees that forage. Each honeybee has a specific job to perform, and they work together to complete it. Each food location indicates a feasible solution in this situation. The employed bees are responsible for finding food and collecting information about its quality. The population of bees' employees and the population of food locations is the same. Unemployed bees are separated into two groups: onlooker bees and scout bees. Employed bees provide the knowledge to the onlooker bees and search for a better-quality food source to inspect the neighbour. Onlooker bees are turned into employed bees in this way. When the food source is depleted, the employed bees transform into scout bees. In particular, the employed bees find out the food location, including better-quality with neighbourhood until convergence is done. The scout bees seek to find a new food location.

15.4.3.1 Initialization

The native algorithm suggests the random food locations as a each probable solution to the problem.

$$y_{ij} = y_j^{\min} + rand(0,1)(y_j^{\max} - y_j^{\min}) \tag{15.7}$$

where $i = 1,\ldots\ldots,N, j = 1,\ldots\ldots D, N$ is the food locations, and D are some optimization parameters.

15.4.3.2 Employee Bee Step (Type E)

Each employed bee searches the food location and stores the information about its quality. The neighbourhood search is stated as

$$u_{ij} = y_{ij} \Phi_{ij} (y_{ij} - y_{kj})$$ (15.8)

For each food location, y_i, a food location u_i is determined with the help of variable optimization j, i.e., y_{ij} is modified, and j and k are the random parameters. Then $k = (1, \ldots N)$ and the value of k is different from the i, $\Phi_{ij} = \{1, -1\}$. Once u_i is obtained, the fitness rate F of the food location can be calculated by

$$F_i = \begin{matrix} 1/1+c_i \ldots\ldots\ldots\ldots if\_c_i \geq 0 \\ 1+abs(c_i)\ldots\ldots\ldots if\_c_i < 0 \end{matrix}$$ (15.9)

where c_i is a cost function. Later, employed bees became the onlooker bees. The likelihood of an onlooker bee to pick up the food location to be searched is related with the fitness rate, i.e.,

$$P_i = \frac{F_i}{\sum\limits_{n=1}^{F} F_i}$$ (15.10)

With the help of values obtained from the search probability, the onlooker bees will choose the food location. Figure 15.3 shows the flowchart of the ABC algorithm from initialization to get the best feature set (food location).

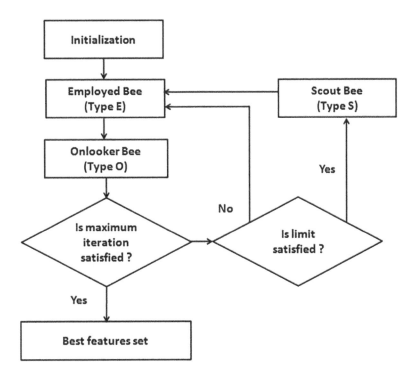

FIGURE 15.3
Flowchart of artificial bee colony.

15.4.3.3 Onlooker Bee Step (Type O)

The onlooker bees use the food locations with superior likelihood for inspection. Later on, they become the employee bees.

15.4.3.4 Scout Bee Step (Type S)

The ABC algorithm checks for the drained food location, which must be rejected. A variable is used to decide the status of the food location, which is upgraded during the search. If the value of that variable is bigger than the maximum limit, then the food location is supposed to be drained, and it is dumped. The dumped food location is replaced by the new food locations discovered by the scout bees.

15.4.3.5 Feature Selection Using Artificial Bee Colony

Representation of the individual is the first step of the ABC algorithm. The individuals are nothing, but the bees or particles termed as X having the M dimensions represented as $Y = (y_1, y_2, y_3, \ldots y_M)$, where M is the number of extracted features and $y_1, y_2, y_3, \ldots y_M$ represents the value of each feature. In the second stage, the search space's initial population is set. The total number of bees, individuals, or particles is denoted by D. Subsequently, the fitness value is computed applying a suitable fitness function. The accuracy of the selected features is evaluated using a confusion matrix. In this process, if convergence occurs, stop and choose the optimum feature set; otherwise, proceed until the desired accuracy is achieved using the maximum number of iterations. When a new optimal feature set is found, the population is updated. New places are randomly assigned to bees or individuals, with the initial and last locations chosen based on the most negligible fitness value. When the algorithm reaches the end of its life cycle, it comes to a halt and provides the smallest number of feature sets possible, resulting in improved classification accuracy.

The stepwise procedure in an ABC is as follows:

1. Initialize all the features
2. Initialize all the parameters
3. Estimate the fitness value of each separate feature
4. Employee bee step
    - i) Create feature subsets stochastically
    - ii) Compute the feature subset fitness
    - iii) Determine the likelihood of the feature subset
5. Onlooker bee step
    - i) Choose the feature depending on the known possibility
    - ii) Find the optimal feature subset using greedy selection
6. Scout bee step
    - i) Calculate the scout bee and the rejected solution
    - ii) Compute the prime feature subset for iterations
    - iii) Retain the prime optimal feature subset
    - iv) Cycle = Cycle + 1
    - v) Until a preplanned number of iterations are reached

15.5 Classification

Classification [20,21] is the procedure of rationalizing the data according to numerous samples and predicting a definitive result developed on the conventional input. Understanding and learning become more accessible due to this, which has various advantages. Several scholars and scientists are working on the classification problem [22,23]. Support vector machines, decision trees, neural networks, expert systems, statistical methods, and other techniques are now available and recommended for classification tasks [24,25].

The training data is utilized as the input for the classification system, and a specific algorithm is employed for the subsequent process of determining the desired class. Each classification algorithm has its own set of merits and demerits. They can also choose the relationship between the input and target values in terms of their characteristics [26]. The classification algorithms discussed in this chapter are based on the artificial immune system, often known as immune computing algorithms or immunocomputing, more specifically, three significant algorithms: negative selection, clonal selection, and dendritic cell algorithms.

15.6 Immune Computing Algorithms

As described in the first section, immune computing algorithms, also known as an artificial immune system or immunocomputing, is a subset of bio-inspired computing based on the biological immune system. Its features, complexity, and working differ from individual to individual. The immune system is employed to defend organisms against pathogens, which are foreign agents that cause diseases. Biological immune systems are adaptable and versatile mechanisms designed to protect humans from pathogens. This task can be performed by using the natural immune system's pattern detection and feedback procedure. It employs a variety of effective response mechanisms for the destruction or neutralization of the pathogen's effect. Antigens are proteins found on the pathogen's surface that are unique to it; they are also known as non-self-elements or non-self-antigens. Antigens, also known as self-elements or self-antigens, can be found in human body tissues. Self-non-self discrimination is the process of distinguishing between self-antigen and non-self-antigen. Thymus and bone marrow are two organs in the biological immune system responsible for initiation and maturation of immune cells known as lymphocytes. These are white blood cells that are accountable for detecting and classifying non-self-antigens. T cells and B cells are lymphocytes generated in the thymus and bone marrow, respectively [27,28]. The primary concept for classifying large-scale classification problems is self and non-self discrimination. The artificial immune system is the newest and most rapidly developing topic of bio-inspired computing, and it is utilized for tasks such as virus detection, functional optimization, and classification. Artificial immune systems have specific impressive characteristics as listed for the classification process:

- The ability of an artificial immune system to learn, remember, extract features, and detect feature patterns is an advantage [29].
- As a result, it is adaptive, highly distributed, and self-assembled for solving conventional computational problems.

Many scientists and researchers are working in this field to solve real-world problems. This chapter concentrates on the classification task performed by immune computing techniques. Three effective techniques, known as the negative selection algorithm, clonal selection algorithm, and dendritic cell algorithm, are thoroughly explained.

15.6.1 Negative Selection Algorithm

The negative selection algorithm (NSA) is developed on the biological immune system's negative selection process. This algorithm is based on the biological system's discriminatory mechanism. The primary goal of the NSA algorithm is to separate the data from the real world into two classes: normal (self) and abnormal (other) (non-self). NSA was first developed to address the problem of computer security, which includes detecting unauthorized computer usage, preserving data privacy, and stopping the spread of computer viruses. It focuses on self-non-self discrimination, which was invented by Forrest et al. in 1994 [30–32]. Here, self includes the authorized users, not corrupted data, and non-self includes unauthorized users and corrupted data. Later, this algorithm was used in various areas, including computer security, network security, and anomaly detection. The negative selection concept can be easily characterized by removing any self-reactive cell [33]. The negative selection algorithm gives a command to the T and B lymphocytes to remove the probable autoreactive cells in the course of evolution. The thymus gland helps in the maturation of T cells, and its negative selection takes place inside it. The T cells do not identify if normal (self) cells survived [34]. For anomaly detection, a novel technique based on NSA is proposed. The proposed approach combines NSA and traditional classification approaches and yields better results [35]. The NSA was improved in 2009, an antibody population was reduced for better training and classification [36]. Later, NSA was simulated without producing the group of antibodies [37]. For both antibodies and samples, an NSA-based technique is developed to optimize the feature space with the neighborhood. This technique starts to upgrade the twinning functions between detectors and samples, leading to enhanced performance for the high dimensions. The NSA algorithm can perform pattern recognition using negative selection of T cells in the thymus [38,39]. Figure 1.4 shows the flowchart of the NSA algorithm.

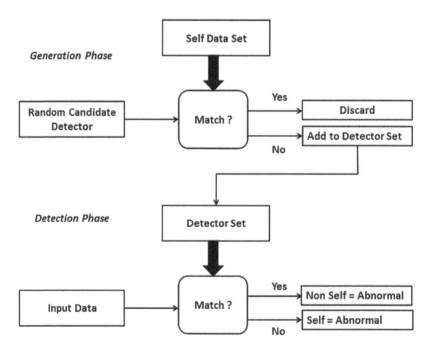

FIGURE 15.4
Negative selection algorithm.

The block diagram of the negative clonal selection is provided to classify the self and non-self elements. The detection and generation phases are the two phases in which this NSA algorithm works. Decides on the self-data set over the countable alphabet during the generation phase: the group to be retained and monitored. Subsequently, the detector set is generated, which does not match any element in the self-data set. This method employs the partial matching law, which says that two input strings match if the strings are having at least r-contagious matching symbols in common. During the detection phase, a continual match of the self-data set to the detector set is performed.

15.6.1.1 Classification Using Negative Selection Algorithm

The three important steps in the NSA for classification are as follows:

- Initialization Phase
- Generation Phase a.k.a. Learning Phase a.k.a. Censoring Phase
- Detection Phase a.k.a. Classification Phase a.k.a. Monitoring Phase

15.6.1.2 Initialization Phase

A set of features is obtained from the feature selection process along with their neighbourhood. This set is the self-data set. Here, a threshold parameter is determined to represent the degree of matching.

15.6.1.3 Generation Phase a.k.a. Learning Phase a.k.a. Censoring Phase

Here, candidate detectors are generated randomly. Affinity evaluation is done with the help of the Euclidean distance among the sensors and each individual in the self-data set. Subsequently, the selection task is completed by using the matching rule. If the randomly generated detectors match with the self-data set, then those detectors are eliminated. Otherwise, the candidate is included in the relevant detector set.

15.6.1.4 Detection Phase a.k.a. Classification Phase a.k.a. Monitoring Phase

Here, a point is selected, and a suitable measure is estimated using the neighbourhood. The algorithm matches the selected point with the appropriate detector set. If the two strings satisfy the r-contagious matching symbols and are similar, the element is classified as a non-self set and is eliminated from the population. Otherwise, the string is classified as the self-set.

15.6.1.5 Next Step in a Negative Selection Algorithm

1. Construct the null set of self-tolerant artificial lymphocytes as C;
2. Resolve the training dataset of self-patterns as S;
   Repeat
   - Stochastically produce artificial lymphocytes, x_i;
   - Evaluate the similarity among x_i and every pattern in S;
   - If the evaluated similarity with minimum one pattern in S is greater than similarity threshold, then decline xi; otherwise, append xi to the set C;
   - Until cardinality of C is equal to the preplanned number.

15.6.2 Clonal Selection Algorithm

The clonal selection principle is one of the most commonly recognized notions in the artificial immune system model proposed by de Castro et al. in 2000. The clonal selection principle imitates B cells to defend the human body against the antigens such as parasites, viruses, and other bacteria and remove the contaminated cells. The complete process of antigen detection, cell proliferation, and cell differentiation is called as clonal selection principle. This principle is used to understand the primary feature of adjustable immune reaction to antigenic boost. Here, the clonal selection principle represents the fundamental characteristics of an immune feedback to an antigenic stimulus. It develops the plan that only cells that identify the antigens they have been subjected to proliferate. The chosen cells are used for the similarity maturation procedure, which enhances the similarity to selective antigens. This powerful computational algorithm focuses on solving critical machine learning problems like pattern classification and multi-objective optimization [40]. The clonal selection and affinity maturation is the prime task of the clonal selection principle, which is homogenous to mutation-based evolutionary algorithms. Darwin's principle "survival of the fittest" applies in the clonal selection principle. The native name of this principle was the clonal selection algorithm (CSA). Later, it was renamed as CLONALG (CLONal Selection ALGorithm) [41]. In this algorithm, antibodies will acknowledge the antigen initiated during the identification procedure and will be used to go through the similarity maturation operation. In 1959, Burnet proposed a clonal selection theory which states that the immune system is excited by the presence of the antigens, and eventually, there is a rise of the antibodies at a specific level. More specifically, when the pathogen captures the body, it will proliferate and demolish the internal cells. To preserve the equilibrium of biological functions, the immune system combats against the pathogen, and proliferates the immune cells. Subsequently, it detects and banishes the pathogen [42].

15.6.2.1 Classification Using Clonal Selection Algorithm

There are several steps in the classification with the help of the clonal selection algorithm, which works on the clonal selection principle. The steps are as follows:

1. Decide the artificial immune system configuration. In this section, the clonal selection algorithm is explained for the task of the classification after obtaining the optimal feature set.
2. Calculate the initial antibody population. The appropriate number of the antibody population is determined. This should not be too large or small. The small number of the antibody population causes the relative input to the optimum solution with many hurdles. A big antibody population will make the system time-consuming.
3. Estimate the initial affinity. The affinity of antibody and antigen is the nothing but similarity measure which is represented by using the spatial distance. More specifically, the Euclidean distance formula is used. The estimation of the initial affinity is represented by using the following formula:

$$R = \sum_{q=1}^{p} \min\{M_{1q}, M_{2q}, M_{3q} \dots M_{cq}\} \tag{15.10}$$

where M is the distance between the antigens, i.e., input data and center of each population, p is the total number of features from the input feature set, q is the sequence number, and n is the number of antibodies in the set.

15.6.2.2 Selection and Divergence

After estimating the affinity of each antibody, based on the screen samples, highest antibodies are chosen and remaining are kept for further selection and differentiation. After the viewing is completed, antibody will allocate the number of clones using the following formula:

$$Z_a = \sum_{l=1}^{s} round\{\frac{\alpha \bullet Z}{l}\} \tag{15.11}$$

where Z_a is the total number of clones, α is the multiplying factor, Z is the total number of antibodies, l is the sequence number, and s is the highest affinity antibody.

15.6.2.3 Mutation

This step is important for the promotion of the individual's affinity. The prime concept of the mutation is the eminent affinity and minimum mutation rate. A suitable type of distribution is used to perform the mutation to obtain the optimum solution.

15.6.2.4 Recalculate the Affinity

This step is used to check better affinity than the previous affinity after completing the mutation step. Figure 1.5 shows the flow flowchart of the clonal selection algorithm. Next steps in the clonal selection algorithm, for the given group of patterns P, CLONALG works as mentioned in the following steps as shown in Figure 1.6 [43].

15.6.3 Dendritic Cell Algorithm

Evolutionary computation is one of the most popular strategies used to resolve a wide range of issues using the principles of biological expansion [44]. The artificial immune system is one of the major subsets of natural a.k.a biological computation inspired by conceptual immunology, known immune functions, fundamentals, and procedures [45]. Many approaches have been used to construct several artificial immune systems for the various applications in digital image processing, classification, pattern identification, clustering, and other similar machine learning domains [46]. In this section, the main focus is on the working of the dendritic cell algorithm which is one of the techniques in artificial immune system for the classification task. The development of the artificial immune system (AIS) techniques for the task of classification is mainly based on the concept of self-non-self discrimination [47]. It is an immunological theory which reveals that the natural immune system is identified by its extraordinary pattern identification ability, which is used to classify among the foreign bodies entering in the human body, identified as non-self elements, and the body's own cells, identified as self elements. The recent immunological theory is named the danger theory [48], also called second theory, and it discovers a detailed explanation about the self-non-self concepts. The danger theory, as the name indicates, looks for danger-causing elements and incidents while discriminating for the self and non-self elements. Due to this additional facility, the danger theory becomes more popular among AIS scientists. The dangers' strategy relies on dendritic cells, which are a

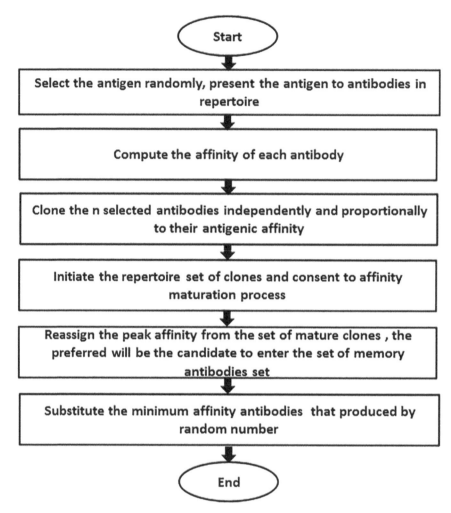

FIGURE 15.5
Flowchart of clonal selection algorithm

special type of immune cell. Innovation from their actions guides the evolution of an immune system-based classification technique called dendritic cell algorithm (DCA) [49].

The AIS-based DCA classifier is efficiently implemented to a variety of real-world problems from various domains. The notable features expressed by this algorithm present many convincing and advantageous characteristics for classification problems. This factor got more attention from many scientists and researchers to study the algorithm in more detail and explore its workings. This guide to variations in DCA for directing at rescripting and enhancing the typical version of the DCA. The following section presents the workflow of the DCA. The DCA is based on an abstract model of dendritic cell biology. The workflow of DCA is categorized into four major tasks: preprocessing and initialization, detection, context assessment, and classification. These tasks are shown in Figure 1.7. In DCA, each agent is represented by a dendritic cell, and it has the ability to collect the data elements named as antigens acting the data to be classified.

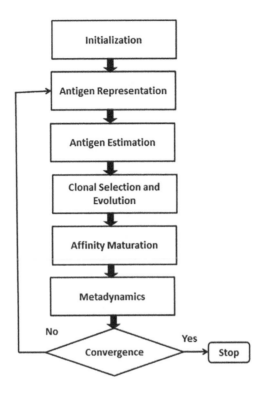

FIGURE 15.6
Workflow of clonal selection algorithm.

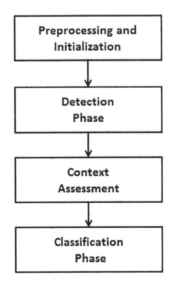

FIGURE 15.7
Block diagram of dendritic cell algorithm.

15.6.3.1 Classification Using the Dendritic Cell Algorithm

The DCA consists of two input types, first signals from all categories and antigens. The vectors of real-valued numbers are represented as signals, and data items IDs are represented as antigens. The binary dendritic cell (BDC) classifier has to categorize the antigen in normal a.k.a. semi-matured cell context or anomalous a.k.a. mature cell context. So, the product of the DCA is the context of antigen that is represented in terms of binary, where 0 state is normal antigen and 1 state is the anomalous antigen.

15.6.3.2 Preprocessing and Initialization Phase

In the use of DCA, the data preprocessing phase is required to adapt the relevant problem domain to the specified search space. The preprocessing consists of two important tasks, namely, feature reduction and signal grouping. From the input training dataset, the DCA selects the important features and allocates each selected feature to its particular signal class which is safe signal denoted as SS, danger signal denoted as DS, or pathogen-associated molecular pattern signal denoted as PAMP. Every feature is depicted as a signal class depending on the immunological fundamentals. The *initialize-DC ( )* function is used for an automated data preprocessing task.

Figure 1.8 shows the flowchart of the DCA [50].

15.6.3.3 Detection Phase

In the detection phase, the principal work of DCA is to produce the signal database combining antigens and input signals. This merging is performed by using both *get-antigens()*

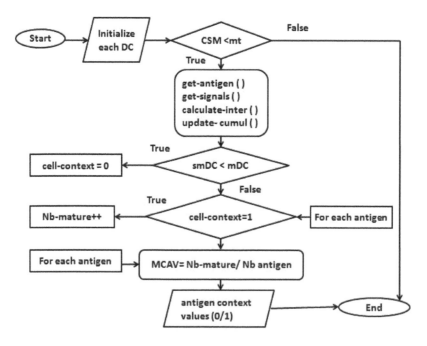

FIGURE 15.8
Flowchart of dendritic cell algorithm.

and *get-signals()* functions. The row in the influenced input signal database represents the antigens that are used to categorize the features into three signals: SS, DS, and PAMP. Formally, the population of artificial DCs was responsible for achieving this combination where the same antigen is sampled by DCs many times. The feature value for every antigen is computed by using the particular process as explained next [50].

Steps for calculation of PAMPs and SSs:

i. Select the appropriate feature.

ii. Calculate the average of all selected feature points across both classes' data.

iii. The feature becomes the safe signal, when the value is greater than the average, otherwise it is PAMP. With the help of the mean, absolute distance is computed and added to SS rate, and the PAMP signal value takes 0 (and vice versa) [50].

Steps for calculation of DSs:

i. For every feature, calculate the mean values with the help of normal class a.k.a. class 1, excluding the abnormal class (class 2) which are the PAMP and safe signals;

ii. Evaluate the absolute distance between the feature values and the estimated means for each attribute value separately;

iii. Use the determined distance values in a subsequent computation to obtain a single estimate for the danger signal. The formula for absolute distance is shown in Equation 15.12:

$$Danger\ Signal = \frac{\sum Absolute\ distance}{Total\ no.\ of\ attributes} \tag{15.12}$$

iv. Repeat this procedure for each of the selected attributes' entries [50].

After generation of the signals, the signal dataset is used as result of the feature vectors. The method processes its input signals using the influenced signal database to generate three results. The results are cumulative output signal values called the costimulatory molecule signal value (CSM), the semi-mature signal value ($smDC$), and the mature signal value (mDC). This process is executed using the *calculate-inter()* function, in which cumulative output signal values are estimated using an equation for signal processing [50] and a collection of weights. DCA uses the following weighted sum equation to create intermediate output signals: $C = C_{[CSM, smDC, mDC]} : [50]$

$$C = \frac{(W_{PAMP} * \sum_i PAMP_i) + (W_{ss} * \sum_i SS_i) + (W_{DS} * \sum_i DS_i)}{(W_{PAMP} + W_{ss} + W_{DS})} * \frac{1 + I}{2} \tag{15.13}$$

Let PAMP*i*, DS$_i$, and SS$_i$ be the values for types PAMP, DS, and SS, respectively. *WPAM P*, *WSS*, and *WDS* represent the weights used for PAMP, SS, and DS, respectively [50]. The inflammation signal is represented as *I*. Each output signal in Equation 15.13 is executed three times to compute CSM, smDC, and mDC output. The values are successively added with reference to time [50]. The weights applied by this algorithm are user-specified values or obtained empirically using the data. The three output signals carry out two functions: to decide whether an antigen is anomalous type and to control the data sampling time. Initially, each dendritic cell in the solution population is allocated a value "mt" (migration threshold). The dendritic cell stops sampling signals and antigens if CSSM is greater than mt. The algorithm persists in computing and updating CSM, mDC, and smDC values by applying *update-cumul ( )* procedure [50].

15.6.3.4 Context Assessment Phase

After the migration and completion of context assessment of every cell, the dendritic cell has the capacity to proceed and gather signals and antigens. To perform the anomaly detection in antigen assessment, the dendritic cell forms a cell context. The cumulative output signals are examined, and the substantial smDC or mDC output signal is developed as cell context. The cell context helps to classify all the antigens gathered by the dendritic cell with the obtained context of 1 or 0. This knowledge is applied in generating an abnormality coefficient that deals in classification phase [50].

15.6.3.5 Classification Phase

After completing the context assessment phase, the mature context antigen value (*MCAV*) is calculated. It is used to estimate the degree of an anomaly of provided antigen value. Its closest value is 1, which gives the greater probability of anomalous antigen. The formula [50] for the *MCAV* is as follows:

$$MCAV = \frac{\text{Count of an antigen appearing in the mature}}{\text{Total number of presentation of that antigen}} \tag{15.14}$$

The classification process begins once the MCAV has been calculated, that is, executed by comparison the MCAV from every antigen the threshold of abnormality. The anomalous threshold might be a user-specified parameter or autocomputed using the data. The potential danger is shown by the distribution of class 1 and class 2 data. The calculation [50] displayed in Equation 15.15 shows this process.

$$Abnormality\ threshold = \frac{\text{Number of abnormal data items}}{\text{Total number of input items}} \tag{15.15}$$

Antigens with MCAVs bigger than the anomalous threshold are categorised as abnormal, while those with MCAVs less than the anomalous threshold are classified as normal [50].

15.7 Analysis of Nature-Inspired Algorithms

References	Algorithm Used	Image Modality	Major Findings
Mohammad Taherdangkoo et al. [51]	Ant colony optimization	Brain MRI	Gives effective segmentation as compared to other algorithms like GA
K. H. Wandrab et al. [52]	SSO-PSO-SVM (Hybrid approach)	UCI image dataset	Gives better classification accuracy than other conventional methods
Gehad Ismil et al. [53]	PSO, ACO, ABC, MA, and SVM	Thermogram breast image	Gives better classification accuracy
Sushmita Mitra et al. [54]	Natural computing algorithms	Brain, breast, liver, and skin images	Gives effective CAD
P Rajesh Kumar et al. [55]	PSO	Mammographic image	Gives better evaluation as compared to conventional DWT and existing GA
Martagalinaska et al. [56]	Swarm intelligence and ACO	3D medical image	Gives better image segmentation
Mahua Bhattacharya et al. [57]	PSO	CT and MR images	Gives automatic image registration
Iztokfister Jr. et al. [58]	Nature-inspired meta-heuristic algorithms	Review papers	
Nazmul Siddique et al. [59]	Nature-inspired meta-heuristic algorithms		
Vamsidhar Enireddy et al. [60]	PSO-cuckoo search	Image dataset	Gives improved classification
Madhubaniaitra et al. [61]	Improved variant of PSO	Image dataset	Overcome the curse of dimensionality and gives better results
Ayan Seal et al. [62]	PSO	Thermal human face image	Effective feature selection
Atiq-ur-rehman et al. [63]	DBPSO, PSO-SVM	MRI brain image	Improved classification accuracy as compared to other methods
Faizal hafiz et al. [64]	2D learning approach for PSO	Image dataset	Gives better feature selection as compared to GA, ACO
Imadzyout et al. [65]	PSO with supervised learning algorithms	Mammographic images	Gives the promising performance for textural features
G. Manga et al. [66]	Artificial immune network	Asymmetric pair of mammographic images	Gives high classification rate
P. Mohankumar et al. [67]	Artificial immune system and PCA	Breast mammographic	An effective detection classification system
S. Valmarthy et al. [68]	DWT and AIS, GA with AIS	Image dataset	Optimize feature selection results in better classification
Stein Keijzers [69]	NSA	Medical image dataset	Gives promising similarity search results
Wenping Ma et al. [70]	Clonal selection algorithms	MRI	Gives the effective medical segmentation with improved computational complexity

(Continued)

(Continued)

References	Algorithm Used	Image Modality	Major Findings
Gabriele Magna et al. [71]	Adaptive AIS	Mammographic breast images	Gives improved classification accuracy
Chuin Muwang et al. [72]	CSA	Brain MRI	Gives feasible and efficient results
ChuinMuwang et al. [73]	EAIS	Brain MRI	Gives improved classification
Ismhenedehache et al. [74]	AIRS	Mammographic breast images	Effective classification accuracy
Wen-Jie Wu et al. [75]	AIS and SVM	Mammographic breast images	An effective CAD system
Ana I. L. Namburete et al. [76]	CNN	Fetal neurosonography images	Gives effective brain localization and segmentation
M. Anousouya Devi et al. [77]	ANN	Cervical cancer cell images	Gives effective classification of normal and abnormal cells
El-sayed Ahmed El-dahshan et al. [78]	DWT, PCA, FPANN, KNN	Brain MRI	Improved classification of brain MRI images

Note: DWT, discrete wavelet transform; PCA, principle component analysis; KNN, K nearest neighbor.

15.8 Other Swarm Intelligence Approaches for Feature Selection

For feature selection, new methods such as ACO and ABC have been developed in addition to methods such as PSO. There are a few more swarm intelligence approaches for the same task which are highlighted in this section.

15.8.1 Grey Wolf Optimization

Grey wolf optimization is a novel evolutionary computing method that imitates the natural leadership structure and hunting technique of grey wolves. The goal of grey wolf optimization is to locate optimal paths in the complex search space by applying population interaction. Grey wolves are an acme predator, which means they hold a peak position in the food chain. Grey wolves choose to be part of a pack. The average pack size is minimum 5 and maximum 12. They follow a rigid social hierarchy. The alphas are a male or a female. Generally, the alpha is in charge of hunting, sleeping arrangements, and waking times, among other things. The pack is told what to do by the alpha. In the grey wolf hierarchy, beta is the second highest rank. The betas help alphas in making important decisions and similar group responsibility. The beta wolf may be female or male, and if one of the alpha wolves dies or becomes old, he or she is the most likely contender to become the alpha wolf. Omega is the grey wolf with the lowest rank. As a scapegoat, the omega is used. At all times, omega wolves must surrender to all other dominant wolves. Subordinate or delta is the fourth classification level. Despite kneeling to alphas and betas, delta wolves command the omega. Elders, sentinels, scouts, caretakers, and hunters comprise this group. Scouts are in charge of monitoring the territory's boundaries and informing the pack if there is any threat. Sentinels guard the pack and ensure its safety. Elders are wolves who have previously served as alpha or beta. Hunters serve the alphas and betas by hunting animals and give food for the pack. The caretakers must care for the pack's weak, injured wolves [79].

15.8.2 Whale Optimization Algorithm

The whale optimization method (WOA) is a population-based meta-heuristic algorithm. To update whale positions, WOA employs a shrinking encircling mechanism, spiral rise, and random learning procedures [80]. WOA [81] is a novel optimization algorithm. It was created to resemble humpback whales' natural behaviour. The survival of these whales is usually dependent on their hunting habits. Although hunting strategies have been used before to solve optimization problems, the whale method is unique in that it can use an arbitrary or prime agent in the search domain to pursue the prey and the capacity to use spirals to imitate the humpback whale's bubble-net attachment mechanisms [81]. This algorithm's modelling incorporates three operators that represent humpback whales' hunt for prey that is the inspecting stage of encircling prey and bubble-net foraging that is the optimization stage.

15.8.3 Moth-Flame Optimization

The moth-flame optimization (MFO) technique is a newly developed swarm-based intelligent optimization technique that imitates moth movements. The suggested approach is used for the feature selection in the domain of machine learning using a wrapper-based feature selection mode to discover the best feature combination. Moths have evolved to fly at night by relying on a navigation procedure called transverse orientation. A moth flies by preserving a steady inclination with the moon [82]. One of the most efficient ways to travel long distances in a straight line is to use this strategy [83]. As the moon is so distant from the moth, this strategy ensures that the moth will fly in a linear way. When moths sense a man-made artificial light, they attempt to fly in a linear way by maintaining a like inclination with light. As this light is in close vicinity to the moon, maintaining a similar angle to the source of light produces a fruitless or dangerous spiral fly route for moths [84]. The moth gradually converges toward the light when exposed to artificial light.

15.8.4 Grasshopper Optimization Algorithm

Saremi et al. [85] introduced the grasshopper optimization algorithm, which is one of the new nature-inspired and population-based algorithms that replicate the natural working of grasshopper swarms. Exploration and exploitation of the search space are two crucial phases of optimization; grasshoppers supply these two phases during the food quest through social interactions. Slow movement and short steps of the grasshoppers are the major characteristics of the swarm in the larval stage. In adulthood, on the other hand, long-range and sudden movement is a necessary element of the swarm.

15.9 Applications

Nature-inspired techniques are applied by the use of various platforms like MATLAB, SCILAB, and OCTAVE, among others. The visual representation of this kind of platforms helps in effective decision-making while performing the classification or regression task.

WEKA is one of the popular and powerful tools for analyzing the various types of swarm-based techniques. It is open-source software written in Java and provides a user-friendly environment for performing various tasks such as classification, regression, clustering, etc.

Nature-inspired computing plays a very important role in analyzing the various types of data. The proposed techniques can be effectively applied in the field of image processing, precisely in medical image analysis. The purpose of image processing is to visualize, sharpen, restore, retrieve, measure the pattern and various objects, and recognize the input image. These methods can be effectively applied to fields like medical image analysis, satellite image analysis, hyperspectral image analysis, remote sensing image analysis, geographic image analysis, morphological image analysis, etc. For diagnosis of diseases, various kinds of imaging tools like X-ray (2D, 3D), ultrasound, magnetic resonance imaging (2D, 3D, 4D), computed tomography (CT), microscopic images, thermographic, mammography, positron emission tomography, etc. are used. The accurate prediction of the medical image plays a very important role which directly affects the patient's life. Classification of the medical image is one of the most important tasks in clinical applications which can be efficiently done by the use of various computational intelligence techniques. The following are some of the medical imaging applications:

- Brain MRI classification: The input brain MRI is categorised into benign and malignant.
- Mammography breast image classification: This is used to classify the input mammographic breast image into three types: normal, benign, and malignant.
- Ultrasound breast image classification: Normal, benign, and malignant.
- Heart disease recognition—To identify heart illness, crucial diagnostic criteria such as size and shape of the heart must be known.
- Lung disease identification—This is used to classify the lung diseases.

15.10 Conclusion and Discussion

An improved optimized feature selection is possible by using swarm-based intelligence. It will help in many applications for effective interpretation of large-scale, multidimensional data, whereas an enhanced classification can be achieved by the use of immune computing algorithms. Due to this, the decision-making process becomes more functional. Swarm intelligence is a global search technique which optimizes the problem, iteratively focusing on the improvement of the candidate solution with respect to quality of measure. These are effective evolutionary algorithms used for obtaining the subset of significant features which leads to the efficient classification rate. The immune computing algorithm provides promising results for the large-scale, multidimensional data. This employs the computationally and algorithmically linear functions which results in empirically light weight in terms of running time; therefore, it gives better and adequate classification outcomes in contrast with other modern classifiers.

Feature selection is a crucial stage in the classification procedure that can diminish the dimensionality of the dataset and enhance the accuracy and performance of the machine learning problem. A subset of features is selected in feature selection which is based on the optimization criteria. Conventional statistical methods are ineffective when the number of observations and the number of attributes linked with each observation increases.

Here, swarm intelligence algorithms which are PSO, ACO, and ABC are discussed for the feature selection. They are efficient in lowering computational time, and providing better knowledge of the input sample leads to improved system performance. Swarm intelligence techniques are a global search approach for optimizing a problem by recursively attempting to enhance an available solution against a set of standard quality criteria. This global search approach iterates through the issue space in search of optimal solutions. PSO, ABC, and ACO are effective evolutionary techniques for finding a subset of minimum features in order to have enough information about the problem and improve the classification algorithm's accuracy. They are more straightforward and effective feature selection techniques. The selected features are passed to a classifier for the classification task. Here, immune computing algorithms which are NSA, CSA, and DCA are discussed as classifiers. The immune computing will give encouraging results through reducing high rates of false positives. It will also enhance the performance when used with both noisy and high-dimensional data. Among the various techniques available for image analysis, the swarm intelligence–based immune computing classifier gives better performance.

References

[1] Cai R, Hao Z, Yang X, Wen W. "An efficient gene selection algorithm based on mutual information", *Neurocomputing*, 72:91–999, 2009.

[2] Saeys Y, Inza I, Larranaga P. "Review of feature selection techniques in bioinformatics", *Bioinformatics*, 23(19):2507–2517, 2007.

[3] Xue B, Zhang M, Browne WN, Yao X. "A survey on evolutionary computation approaches to feature selection", *IEEE Transactions on Evolutionary Computation*, 20(4):606–626, 2016.

[4] Guyon I, Elisseeff A. "An introduction to variable and feature selection", *Journal of Machine Learning Research*, 3:1157–1182, 2003.

[5] Kennedy J, Eberhart R. "Particle swarm optimization", In: *The Proceedings of the 1995 IEEE International Conference on Neural Network*, vol. 4, pp. 1942–1948, 1995, https://doi.org/10.1109/ICNN.1995.488968.

[6] Wang X, Yang J, Teng X, Xia W, Jensen R. "Feature selection based on rough sets and particle swarm optimization". *Pattern Recognition Letters*, 28(4):459–471, 2007, ISSN 0167-8655, https://doi.org/10.1016/j.patrec.2006.09.003.

[7] Kıran MS, Özceylan E, Gündüz M, Paksoy T. "A novel hybrid approach based on particle swarm optimization and ant colony algorithm to forecast energy demand of Turkey", *Energy Conversion and Management*, 53(1):75–83, 2012, ISSN 0196-8904, https://doi.org/10.1016/j.enconman.2011.08.004.

[8] Dorigo M, Gambardella LM. "Ant colony system: A cooperative learning approach to the traveling salesman problem", *IEEE Trans. on Evolutionary Computation*, 1:53–66, 1997.

[9] Blum C. "Ant colony optimization: Introduction and recent trends", *Physics of Life Reviews*, 2:353–373, 2005.

[10] Dorigo M, Birattari M, Stutzle T. "Ant colony optimization", *IEEE Computational Intelligence Magazine*, 1(4):28–39, 2006.

[11] Dorigo M, Maniezzo V, Colorni A. "Positive feedback as a search strategy", *Dipartimento di Elettronica*, Politecnico di Milano, Italy, Tech. Rep. 91–016, 1991.

[12] Dorigo M. "Optimization, learning and natural algorithms (in Italian)", PhD dissertation, Dipartimento di Elettronica, Politecnico di Milano, Italy, 1992.

[13] Dorigo M, Maniezzo V, Colorni A. "Ant System: Optimization by a colony of cooperating agents", *IEEE Transactions on Systems, Man, and Cybernetics—Part B*, 26(1):29–41, 1996.

[14] Al-Ani A. "Ant colony optimization for feature subset selection", *WEC*, 2:35–38, 2005.

[15] Huang CL. "ACO-based hybrid classification system with feature subset selection and model parameters optimization", *Neurocomputing*, 73(1):438–448, 2009.

[16] Karaboga D. "An idea based on honey bee swarm for numerical optimization", *Technical Report-TR06* (Erciyes University, Engineering Faculty, Computer Engineering Department), 2005.

[17] Bao L, Zeng J.-C. "Comparison and analysis of the selection mechanism in the artificial bee colony algorithm", *Proceedings of the IEEE Ninth International Conference on Hybrid Intelligent Systems*, pp. 411–416, 2009, https://doi.org/10.1109/HIS.2009.319.

[18] El-Abd M. "A cooperative approach to the artificial bee colony algorithm", *IEEE Congress on Evolutionary Computation*, pp. 1–5, 2010, https://doi.org/10.1109/CEC.2010.5586007.

[19] Zou W, Zhu Y, Chen H, Zhu Z. "Cooperative approaches to artificial bee colony algorithm", *Proceedings of the IEEE International Conference on Computer Application and System Modeling*, 9:44–48, 2010.

[20] Kumar R, Verma R. "Classification algorithms for data mining: A survey", *International Journal of Innovations in Engineering and Technology (IJIET)*, 1(2), 2012, ISSN: 2319-1058.

[21] Kilany RM. "Efficient classification and prediction algorithms for biomedical information", Unpublished doctoral dissertation, University of Connecticut, USA, 2013.

[22] Fidelis MV, Lopes HS, Freitas AA. "Discovering comprehensible classification rules with a genetic algorithm", *IEEE, Proceedings of the Congress*, 1:805–810, 2000.

[23] Athitsos V, Sclaroff S. "Boosting nearest neighbor classifiers for multiclass recognition", In: *Computer Society Conference on Computer Vision and Pattern Recognition (CVPR'05) - Workshops*, pp. 45–45, 2005, https://doi.org/10.1109/CVPR.2005.424.

[24] Weiss SM, Kulikowski CA. *Computer systems that learn: classification and prediction methods from statistics, neural nets, machine learning, and expert systems*. Morgan Kaufmann Publishers Inc., San Francisco, CA, 1991.

[25] Gonzalez F, Dasgupta D, Kozma R. "Combining negative selection and classification techniques for anomaly detection", In: *Proceedings of the 2002 Congress on Evolutionary Computation, CEC 2002*, vol. 1, pp. 705–710, IEEE, 2002.

[26] Rao KH, Srinivas G, Damodhar A, Krishna MV. "Implementation of anomaly detection technique using machine learning algorithms", *International Journal of Computer Science and Telecommunications*, 2(3):25–31, 2011, ISSN 2047–3338.

[27] Dasgupta D. "Advances in artificial immune systems", *IEEE Computational Intelligence Magazine*, 1:40–49, 2006.

[28] Warner NL. "Membrane immunoglobulins and antigen receptors on B and T lymphocytes", In: *Advances in Immunology*, vol. 19 (Academic Press), 67–216, 1974.

[29] Dasgupta D, Yu S, Nino F. "Recent advances in artificial immune systems: models and applications", *Applied Soft Computing*, 11(2):1574–1587, 2011.

[30] Forrest S, Perelson S, Allen L, Cherukuri R. "Self–non-self-discrimination in a computer", In: *Proceedings of IEEE Symposium on Research in Security and Privacy*, 202–212, 1994.

[31] Ji Z, Dasgupta D. "Revisiting negative selection algorithms, evolutionary computation", *Massachusetts Institute of Technology*, 15(2):223–251, 2007.

[32] Igawa K, Ohashi H. "A negative selection algorithm for classification and reduction of the noise effect", *Journal of Applied Soft Computing, Elsevier Ed*, 9(1):431–438, 2009.

[33] Nino F, Dasgupta D. *Immunological computation: Theory and applications*, Auerbach Publications, 2008.

[34] Timmis J, Knight T, de Castro LN, Hart E. "An overview of artificial immune systems", In: *Computation in Cells and Tissues*. Berlin; Heidelberg: Springer, 51–91, 2004.

[35] Gonzalez F, Dasgupta D, Kozma R. "Combining negative selection and classification techniques for anomaly detection", In: *Proceedings of the 2002 Congress on Evolutionary Computation. CEC'02 (Cat. No.02TH8600)*, pp. 705–710, vol. 1, 2002, https://doi.org/10.1109/CEC.2002.1007012.

[36] Elberfeld M, Textor J. "Efficient algorithms for string-based negative selection", In: *International Conference on Artificial Immune Systems*. Berlin; Heidelberg: Springer, 109–121, 2009.

[37] Lískiewicz M, Textor J. "Negative selection algorithms without generating detectors", In: *Proceedings of the 12th Annual Conference on Genetic and Evolutionary Computation*, ACM, 1047–1054, 2010.

[38] Wang D, Xue Y, Yingfei D. "Anomaly detection using neighborhood negative selection", *Intelligent Automation & Soft Computing*, 17:595–605, 2011.

[39] Textor J. "Efficient negative selection algorithms by sampling and approximate counting", In: *International Conference on Parallel Problem Solving from Nature*. Berlin; Heidelberg: Springer, 32–41, 2012.

[40] De Castro LN, Von Zuben FJ. "The clonal selection algorithm with engineering applications", In: *GeEcco 2002—Workshop Proceedings*, 36–37, 2000.

[41] De Castro LN, Von Zuben FJ. "Learning and optimization using the clonal selection principle. Evolutionary computation", *IEEE Transactions*, 6(3):239–251, 2002.

[42] Silverstein A. "The clonal selection theory: What it really is and why modern challenges are misplaced", *Nature Immunology*, 3:793–796, 2002.

[43] De Castro LN, Timmis JI. *Artificial immune systems: A new computational intelligence approach*, Springer Publication, 2002.

[44] Agoston E, Smith J. *Introduction to evolutionary computing*, Springer Science & Business Media, 2003.

[45] Timmis J. "Artificial immune systems—today and tomorrow", *Nature Computational*, 6:1–18, 2007.

[46] Zheng J, Chen Y, Zhang W. "A survey of artificial immune applications", *Artificial Intelligence Review*, 34:19–34, 2010.

[47] Janeway C. "The immune system evolved to discriminate infectious nonself from noninfectious self immunol", *Immunol Today*, 13:11–16, 1992.

[48] Matzinger P. "The danger model: A renewed sense of self", *Science*, 296:301–304, 2002.

[49] Greensmith J, Aickelin U. "Introducing dendritic cells as a novel immune-inspired algorithm for anomaly detection", In: *Proceedings of the 4th International Conference on Artificial Immune Systems*, ICARIS, 153–167, 2005.

[50] Greensmith J. "The dendritic cell algorithm", Ph.D thesis, University of Nottingham, 2007.

[51] Taherdangkoo, Mohammad, HadiBagheri, Mohammad, Yazdi, Mehran, Andriole, Katherine P. "An effective method for segmentation of MR brain images using the ant colony optimization algorithm", *Journal of Digit Imaging, Society for Imaging Informatics in Medicine*, 1116–1123, 2013.

[52] Gagnani LP, Wandra KH, Chhinkaniwala H. "Classification optimization using PSO-SSO based support vector machine", In: *Proc. of 3rd IEEE International Conference on Computational Intelligence and Communication Technology (CICT)*, pp. 1–4, 2017, https://doi.org/10.1109/CIACT.2017.7977300.

[53] Sayed GI, Soliman M, Hassanien AE. "Bio-inspired swarm techniques for thermogram breast cancer detection", *Medical Imaging in Clinical Applications*, 651:487–506, Springer Cham, 2016.

[54] Mitra S, Shankar BU. "Medical image analysis for cancer management in natural 4 computing framework", *Journal of Information Science: An International Journal Archive*, 306(C):111–131, June 2015.

[55] Kumar PR, Kumar MP. "Image fusion of mammography images using meta heuristic method Particle Swarm Optimization (PSO)", *International Journal of Applied Engineering Research*, 11(9):6254–6258, 2016, ISSN 0973–4562.

[56] Galinska M, Badura P. "Swarm intelligence approach to 3D medical image segmentation", *Advances in Intelligent Systems and Computing*, 471:15–24, Springer Cham, 2016.

[57] Bhattacharya M, Das A. "Registration of multimodality medical imaging of brain using particle swarm optimization", In: *Proceedings of the First International Conference on Intelligent Human Computer Interaction*, Springer, 2009, pp 131–139.

[58] Fister Jr. I, Yang Xin-She, Fister Iztok, Brest Janez, Fister Dusan. "A brief review of nature-inspired algorithms for optimization", *Electrotechnical Review*, 80, July 2013.

[59] Siddique Nazmul, Adeli Hojjat. "Nature inspired computing: An overview and some future directions", *Cognitive Computation*, 7:706–714, Springer, 2015.

[60] Enireddy V, Kumar RK. "Improved cuckoo search with particle swarm optimization for classification of compressed images", *Sadhana*, 40:2271–2285, Part 8, December 2015.

[61] Maitra M, Chatterjee A. "A hybrid cooperative-comprehensive learning based PSO algorithm for image segmentation using multilevel thresholding", *Expert System with Applications*, 34(2):1341–1350, Elsevier, 2008.

[62] Seal A, et al. "Feature selection using particle swarm optimization for thermal face recognition", In: *Applied Computation and Security Systems, Advances in Intelligent Systems and Computing 304*, Springer India 2015.

[63] Rehman A, Khanum A, Shaukat A. "Hybrid feature selection and tumor identification in brain MRI using swarm intelligence", In: *Proc. of 11th International Conference on Frontiers of Information Technology*. IEEE, 2013.

[64] Hafiz F, Swain A, Paola Casti CN. "Two dimensional framework for particle swarm optimization", *Pattern Recognition*, 76:416–433, Elsevier, 2018.

[65] Zyout I, Czajkowska J, Grzegorzek M. "Multi-scale textural feature extraction and particle swarm optimization based model selection for false positive reduction in mammography", *Computerized Medical Imaging and Graphics*, 46(Pt 2):95–107, 2015, https://doi.org/10.1016/j.compmedimag.2015.02.005. Epub 2015 Feb 24. PMID: 25795630.

[66] Magna G, Casti P, Salmeri M. "Identification of mammography anomalies for breast cancer detection by an ensemble of classification models based on artificial immune system", *Knowledge Based Systems*, 60–70, Elsevier, February 2016.

[67] Mohankumar P, Kavetha BV. "An artificial immune system based investigation of the breast cancer classification", *International Journal of Pharmacy & Technology*, 8(4):23097–23107, December 2016.

[68] Valarmathy S, Suthanthira Vanitha N. "Hybrid artificial immune systems for classification on MRI Brain images", *IIOABJ*, 7(9):730–739, December 2016.

[69] Keijzers S, et al. "Image similarity search using a negative selection algorithm", *Artificial Immune, Neural and Endocrine Systems*, ECAL, 2013, https://doi.org/10.7551/978-0-262-31709-2-ch123.

[70] Ma W, Jiao L, Shang R, Zhao F. "Medical image segmentation based on immune clonal optimization", In: *Proceedings of IEEE International Conference on Intelligent Computing and Intelligent Systems*, Shanghai, 2009, pp 377–381.

[71] Magna G, et al. "Adaptive classification model based on artificial immune system for breast cancer detection", In: *Proceedings of XVIII AISEM Annual Conference*, IEEE, 2015.

[72] Wang CM, Kuo CT, Lin CY, Chang GH. "Application of artificial immune system approach in MRI classification", *Journal on Advances in Signal Processing*, Hindawi Publishing Corporation, 2008, 547684, 2008. https://doi.org/10.1155/2008/547684.

[73] Wang C-M, Chu S-W, Su C-Y. "Extension artificial immune system approach in MRI classification", In: *IEEE, World Congress on Intelligent Control and Automation*, pp. 855–859, June 21–25, 2011, https://doi.org/10.1109/WCICA.2011.5970636.

[74] Dehache I, Souici-Meslati L. "Artificial immune recognition system for mammographic mass classification", In: *Proceedings of 3rd Conference on Complex System (WCCS)*, pp. 1–5, November 2015, https://doi.org/10.1109/ICoCS.2015.7483253.

[75] Wu Wen-Jie, Lin Shih-Wei, Moon Woo Kyung. "An artificial immune system based support vector machine approach for classifying ultrasound breast tumor images", *Journal of Digit Imaging*, 28(5):576–585, Springer US, October 2015.

[76] Namburete AIL, et al. "Fully-automated alignment of 3D fetal brain ultrasound to a canonical reference space using multi-task learning", *Medical Image Analysis*, 46:1–14, 2018.

[77] Devi MA, Ravi S, Vaishnavi J, Punitha S. "Classification of cervical cancer using artificial neural networks", *Procedia Computer Science*, 89:465–472, Elsevier 2016.

[78] El-Dahshan El-sayed Ahemd, Hosny Tamer, Salem Abdel M, *Hybrid technique for MRI brain image classification*, ACM Digital Image Processing, vol. 20, issue 2, Academic Press Orlando, FL, March 2010, pp. 433–441.

[79] Emary E, Zawbaa HM, Grosan C, Hassenian AE. "Feature subset selection approach by gray-wolf optimization", In: Abraham A, Krömer P, Snasel V (eds) *Afro-European Conference for Industrial Advancement. Advances in Intelligent Systems and Computing*, vol. 334. Springer, Cham, 2015.

[80] Guo W, et al. "An improved whale optimization algorithm for feature selection", *Computers, Materials & Continua*, 62(1):337–354, 2020.

[81] Seyedali M, Lewis A. "The whale optimization algorithm", *Advances in Engineering Software*, 95:51–67, 2016.

[82] Mirjalili S. "Moth-flame optimization algorithm: A novel nature inspired heuristic paradigm", *Knowledge-Based Systems*, 89:228–249, 2015.

[83] Gaston KJ, Bennie J, Davies TW, Hopkins J. "The ecological impacts of nighttime light pollution: A mechanistic appraisal", *Biological Reviews, Hindawi Publishing Corporation*, 88(1):912–927, 2013.

[84] Frank KD, Rich C, Longcore T. "Effects of artificial night lighting on moths", *Journal of Ecological Consequences of Artificial Night Lighting, Hindawi Publishing Corporation*, 2015(1):305–344, 2006.

[85] Saremi S, Mirjalili S, Lewis A. "Grasshopper optimisation algorithm: Theory and application", *Advances in Engineering Software*, 105:30–47, 2017.

16

Optimized Modified K-Nearest Neighbor Classifier for Pattern Recognition

Priyadarshan Dhabe, Affan Shaikh, Jayanti Runwal, Ashwini Patil and Sneha Shinde

CONTENTS

16.1 Introduction

KNN [1] is an extensively used pattern classification [2] algorithm owning to its simplicity and ease of implementation on any computing platform. It uses the rote learning, that is, it stores all the training patterns in its memory, as it is, without processing them to extract generalized knowledge applicable for each pattern class. When a test pattern is given as input, then KNN computes distance of a given test pattern wrt all the patterns in the training set. KNN then using $k > 0$ (user-defined hyper-parameter) nearest neighbors and voting decides the class label of the applied test pattern. The working of KNN is summarized in Figure 16.1. In this approach, $k > 0$ is the tunable learning hyper-parameter that needs to be decided in training,

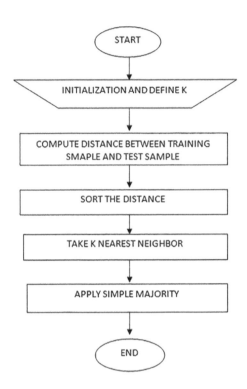

FIGURE 16.1
Flowchart of working of KNN classifier.

Motivation

Even though the KNN is the simplest classifier to understand its working and to implement, it has several limitations. KNN is suitable for the small data sets, since we need to store all the training patterns in the memory. Again, the large number of training patterns needs more time for both computing the distances and finding first k minimum distances, in the recall phase.

Thus, the time and the space requirement of KNN is proportional to the size of the training data and hence becomes, both, compute and memory intensive, for large data sets. These drawbacks of KNN are prime motivations behind this work to reduce memory and recall time and to increase the scope of KNN for larger data sets.

We already tried to eliminate/reduce this drawback by proposing modified KNN (MKNN) [3] at our institute; we will refer to this research by short name MKNN [3]. There are several other methods also proposed for enhancing the KNN classifier. But, in this chapter, we are proposing the modification to MKNN [3] earlier proposed by us.

Literature Review

T.M. Cover proposed the nearest neighbor (NN) classifier in [1], and KNN is an updated version of the NN classifier. KNN is updated by many researchers for efficiency and memory optimization. In Brown and Koplowitz [4], weights are used to improve the classification to the neighbors. Weights are used in the K neighborhood of the testing pattern so as to reduce the effects of outliers. Short and Fukanaga [5,6] describe novel approaches for taking the distances. Methods described in [7] and [8] are favoring generation of a new training set with minimum training samples by removing redundant samples. On the other hand, methods in Hwang and Wen [9] and Pan et al. [10] advocate use of fast methods to calculate the distances for improving efficiency. The proposed approach in Dhabe et al. [3] uses a transformed training set of few training samples, since group prototypes are few in number than the actual training samples, we need less memory and thus less recall time. Group prototypes in MKNN [3] are calculated using a single scalar distance. But the proposed method OMKNN uses a distance vector, with possibly a different distance for each class, so that we can get an optimal number of group prototypes for each class. This thereby reduces the memory cost. This reduced hypothesis also improves reasoning about unseen test patterns according to the *Occam's razor* principle [12].

16.1.1 Brief Discussion of MKNN Classifier

In the MKNN, we planned to reduce the input patterns and thought that instead of using individual patterns, if we use their groups prototypes by grouping them using a simple distance parameter $0 \leq d \leq 1$, that needs to be decided. By using the maximum possible value of d, i.e., with a minimum number of group prototypes, we must get good classification. MKNN is then assumed to be trained at that value of d, and the related number of group prototypes are created for that value of d. The group prototypes are created by creating the pattern groups first. The user defined parameter d is chosen by the user. Then, from the patterns of each class we prepare group prototypes, as shown in Figure 16.2. We find the patterns of class i and decide the groups of patterns within that class. All the patterns which have Euclidean distance $\leq d$ are used to form a group. The group prototype is then the arithmetic mean of all the patterns within that group. Now we have a single group prototype for class $i = 1, 2, ..., m$. Now we need to repeat the same procedure for the remaining patterns of class $i = 1, 2, ..., m$ and prepare the group prototypes. When the group prototypes are created for the patterns of all the classes, then training is assumed to be done, and we need to store the group prototypes in the memory of MKNN for the testing/recognition and classification phase. Figure 16.2 depicts group prototype formation in MKNN. Note that we reduced recall time per pattern, since instead of large number of training patterns per class, only few group prototypes are used for reasoning. In this case, we also have to find the value of k by experimenting with different values, but now, MKNN [3] algorithm will consider k nearest neighbor group prototypes instead of k nearest neighbor patterns. Another big achievement is the amount of memory required, since the group prototypes are very few in numbers as compared to the total number of patterns in the training set, MKNN needs very small memory as compared to the K-NN. Thus, we achieved both reduction in time and memory. As per the time-memory trade-off (also termed as space-time trade-off) [11] in computer science, we can increase the memory and save the time or increase the computational time by decreasing the use of memory. But, achieving both time and memory is the most difficult task that is achieved in MKNN [3].

16.1.2 Overall Idea Behind the Proposed OMKNN

In this chapter, we are proposing further modifications to MKNN for the optimization purpose, and the proposed approach is called OMKNN and is the primary topic of this chapter. The main purpose is to use a $m > 1$ dimensional vector of distance parameters

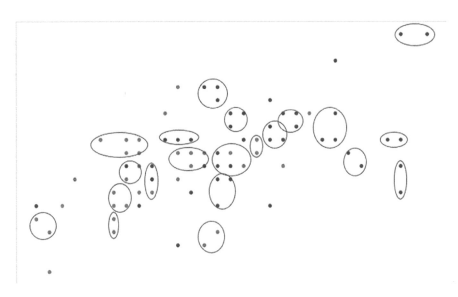

FIGURE 16.2
Formation of group prototypes in MKNN.

for m class training set. Now the distance vector is $\vec{d} = [d_1, d_2, ..., d_m]$, ($\vec{d}$ is a vector) where d_i is the distance parameter applicable for the patterns of class $i = 1, 2, ..., m$ such that d_i and d_j can be different for $i \neq j$ for $i, j = 1, 2, ..., m$. The proposed OMKNN approach is expected to further reduce the group prototypes, since now we can have a highly opti-mized distance parameter d_i (possibly) unique and finely tuned for the patterns of each of the specific classes $i = 1, 2, ..., m$. The distance parameters d_i are selected in such a way that they must generate the fewest group prototypes with good classification accuracy for that class. Thus, we can say that OMKNN is the generalization of MKNN where the user-defined, scalar distance parameter $0 \leq d \leq 1$ is changed to the vector $\vec{d} = [d_1, d_2, ..., d_m]$.

16.1.3 Basic Philosophy Used in MKNN and OMKNN

We like to mention here that we proposed both MKNN and OMKNN by using the *Occam's Razor Principle* [12]. This principle can be stated in many ways, but the ultimate interpreta-tion is that if we have multiple ways of solving the problem, then always prefer the simple/short hypothesis. The hypothesis chosen by the regular K-NN [1] is very long, since it uses all the patterns in the training set. By preparing group prototypes, we are making hypotheses short and simple. And in OMKN, we are making hypotheses extremely short. According to the *Occam's Razor Principle* [12], simple and short hypotheses are applicable in more situations than the long hypotheses. It means that a short hypothesis provides you a better recognition rate in the classifiers. This fact is also experimentally verified and proven in MKNN [3] and the proposed OMKNN.

The remaining part of this chapter is organized as follows: Section 16.2 describes the proposed algorithm of OMKNN, experimentation is done in Section 16.3, conclusions are given in Section 16.4, and references are cited at the end.

16.2 Algorithm of Proposed OMKNN

Let $m > 1$ be the number of pattern classes in the training set. Let $0 < \delta <<< 1$ (i.e. δ is greater than zero and far less than 1) be the increment (e.g., $\delta = 0.05$) suggested in one or more elements of the distance vector $\vec{d} = [d_1, d_2, ..., d_m]$, as defined in Section 16.1.2. Let $\%C_f$ be the percentage classification obtained. Then, the algorithm of OMKNN can be summarized as follows:

Algorithm OMKNN

Step 1: Train MKNN and find the distance parameter

$0 < d < 1$ and for neighborhood size $k > 1$.

Step 2: Optimize MKNN

Step 2.1: Prepare distance vector $\vec{d} = [d_1, d_2, ..., d_m]$ by initializing $d_i = d$ for

$i = 1, 2, ..., m$, where d is calculated in Step 1.

Step 2.2: Optimize each $d_i \in \vec{d}$ for $i = 1, 2, ..., m$

for i = 1 to m
    old_value = d_i, Flag = 0;
    do{
        a. *new_value = old_value* $+ \delta$;
        b. Prepare group prototypes in MKNN using *new_value*
           for patterns of ith class.
        c. Compute $\%C_f$ using MKNN classification algorithm using
           whole training set and using new group prototypes computed in
           step b for i^{th} class.
        d. *If* $(\%C_f < 100)$
                Then set *new_value = old_value;*
                Flag = 1;
      end
    } *whille*(Flag $\neq$ 1)
  end

In the OMKNN algorithm, in Step 2.2, we are increasing continuously the element of distance parameter vector $d_i \in \vec{d}$ by the small increment δ for the ith pattern class to its maximum such that still it must provide 100% or acceptable classification. This increase in element of distance parameter vector generates bigger pattern groups and hence a lesser number of group prototypes. The lesser number of group prototypes provides a shorter hypothesis and thus satisfies Occam's Razor Principle [12] and thus is expected to give a better recognition rate and reduce the recall time per pattern.

We are also providing the algorithm of MKNN for immediate context.

Algorithm MKNN [3]

Step 1: Initialize user-defined distance parameter $0 < d < 1$. If $d = 0$, MKNN will be collapsed to KNN

Step 2: Find the Euclidean distance between the patterns of the same class

Step 3: Form the groups of these instances with Euclidean distances $\leq d$ and compute the group prototypes

Step 4: Now give these group prototypes as input to the original KNN classifier with appropriate neighborhood value k for classification and recognition purposes.

16.3 Experimental Results

The experimental analysis was done on *Iris Dataset* [13] and *Indian Liver Patient data set* [14].

16.3.1 Data Set Description

16.3.1.1 Iris Data Set

This is the data set composed of 150 patterns of 3 classes viz. Iris Setosa, Versicolor, and Verginica. This data set is about the classification of plants with the four attributes named *sepal length, sepal width, petal length,* and *petal width* in centimeters.

16.3.1.2 Indian Liver Patient Data Set

This data set is collected from UCI repository [14] and is used to classify the patients of abnormal liver. It consists of 583 instances, with 441 samples of males and 142 instances of females. Each sample is described with 10 features as *Age, Gender, Total Bilirubin, Direct Bilirubin, Alkaline Phosphatase, Sgpt Alamine Aminotransferase, Sgot Aspartate Aminotransferase, Total Proteins, Albumin,* and *A/G Ratio Albumin and Globulin Ratio.*

16.3.2 Experimentation with Iris Data Set

In this subsection, we will do the experimentation with Iris data set using KNN, MKNN, and the proposed OMKNN and will compare the results. We used randomly selected 120 patterns as training set, i.e. 40 patterns per class and the remaining 30 patterns as the testing set for knowing the recognition accuracy.

16.3.2.1 Experimentation with K-NN Classifier

Table 16.1 shows the percentage classification (%C_f) for various neighborhood size k. From Table 16.1, one can conclude that the best classification accuracy is obtained at $k = 5$ as indicated by the bold row. Thus, we can use $k = 5$ for MKNN.

16.3.2.2 Experimentation with MKNN Classifier

Table 16.2 shows the result of MKNN classifier for $k = 5$. We have calculated the number of group prototypes, percentage classification %C_f, and the time required for the MKNN classifier. We achieved the highest percentage classification of 97% using distance parameter $d = 0.3$, and MKNN has created 86 group prototypes here. If we further increase the distance parameter d, MKNN creates less group prototypes and thus classification accuracy decreases slowly. We also noted, and it is obvious from Table 16.2, that if we use less group prototypes, then the time required for classification also reduces. We decided to use $d = 0.3$ for experimentation with proposed OMKNN, since we got the highest classification accuracy there.

TABLE 16.1

Classification Accuracy for Various Values of k

K	%C_f	Time Required (in seconds)
2	97.49%	0.089
3	96.67%	0.100
4	95.83%	0.082
5	**97.5%**	**0.092**
6	95.83%	0.0899
7	96.67%	0.0911
8	97.5%	0.0932
9	95.8%	0.0931

TABLE 16.2

Classification Accuracy for Various Values of d and for $k = 5$

d	Number of Group Prototypes	%C_f	Time Required (in seconds)
0.3	86	97.00	0.091104
0.35	73	95.00	0.089121
0.4	68	96.67	0.08889
0.45	61	95.80	0.08652
0.5	54	96.67	0.0827
0.55	48	95.00	0.08095

16.3.2.3 Experimentation with OMKNN Classifier

In the experimentation with proposed OMKNN, we initialized each element of the distance vector to $d = 0.3$, i.e. $\vec{d} = [0.3, 0.3, 0.3]$ and the increment $\delta = 0.05$. Parameter vector $\vec{d}$ has three elements, since there are three classes in the Iris data set. Table 16.3 shows the distance parameter vector, number of group prototypes created, and classification accuracy and time required for classification.

From Table 6.3, we can see that for $\vec{d} = [0.3, 0.35, 0.3]$, we obtained the highest classification accuracy with creation of a minimum number of group prototypes.

Table 16.4 compares performance of KNN, MKNN, and OMKNN for the Iris data set. As per the observation of Table 16.4, OMKNN provides the same classification accuracy as KNN by using only 80 group prototypes, where KNN needs 120 patterns and MKNN needs 86 group prototypes to exhibit the same performance. Again, OMKNN requires less time for recognition than KNN and MKNN. The main achievement of OKMNN is that it works very well for unseen patterns as its recognition accuracy is maximum 96.66% as compared to KNN and MKN. This fact is highlighted in Table 16.4. Thus, Table 16.4 proves that we can create shorter hypotheses in machine learning that require less recall time and provide better recognition accuracy.

16.3.4 Experimentation with Indian Liver Patient Data Set

We did the experimentation with the Indian Liver Patient data set using KNN, MKNN, and OMKNN, and the results are discussed as follows. We used randomly selected 80% patterns as training set and remaining 20% as testing set. Preprocessing is done using [15] and [16].

TABLE 16.3

Time and Classification Accuracy of OMKNN for Various Distance Vectors

$\vec{d}$	Number of Group Prototypes	$\%C_f$	Time Required (in seconds)
d[0.3,0.35,0.3]	80	97.5%	0.1154
d[0.3,0.4,0.3]	78	96.67%	0.1144
d[0.3,0.35,0.35]	78	95.83%	0.1095
d[0.3,0.3,0.35]	84	95%	0.0999
d[0.3,0.45,0.55]	67	96.67%	0.0917

TABLE 16.4

Performance Comparison of KNN, MKNN, and OMKNN for Iris Data Set

	KNN	MKNN	OMKNN
Number of group prototypes/patterns used	120	86	80
$\%C_f$	97.50%	97.00%	97.50%
Recognition accuracy	95.55%	95.83%	96.66%
Time required (in seconds)	0.092000	0.091104	0.0906

16.3.4.1 Experimentation with K-NN Classifier

We conducted an experiment to find the value of neighborhood k where maximum classification accuracy can be obtained. Table 16.5 shows this experiment. As per the highlighted row of Table 16.5, one can conclude that the maximum classification accuracy of 100% is achieved for $k = 2$ (since we cannot take $k = 1$ as otherwise it will collapse to the nearest neighbor classifier). Thus, we set $k = 2$ in the experimentation with MKNN.

16.3.4.2 Experimentation with MKNN Classifier

Table 16.6 shows the result of MKNN classifier for $k = 2$. We have calculated the number of group prototypes, classification accuracy for various values of distance parameter d. As per the highlighted row of Table 16.6, the maximum classification accuracy of 100% is obtained at $d = 0.3$ using 442 group prototypes. Thus, we set $d = 0.3$ for OMKNN and worked on further experimentation.

16.3.4.3 Experimentation with OMKNN Classifier

Table 16.7 shows the result of OMKNN classifier for $k = 2$ and the initial distance vector of $\vec{d} = [0.3, 0.3]$. We calculated the number of group prototypes and classification accuracy for different distance parameter vectors $\vec{d}$, and the results are tabulated in Table 16.7. As per the highlighted row of Table 16.7, we can conclude that for $\vec{d} = [0.4, 0.3]$, we obtained

TABLE 16.5

Classification for Various Values of k Using KNN and Indian Liver Patient Data Set

Serial Number	k	$\%C_f$
1	1	100
2	**2**	**100**
3	3	100
4	4	100
5	5	100
6	6	100
7	7	100

TABLE 16.6

Classification Obtained Using MKNN and Indian Liver Patient Data Set

Serial Number	d	Number of Group Prototypes	$\%C_f$
1	0.1	457	100
2	0.2	454	100
3	**0.3**	**442**	**100**
4	0.4	420	99.78
5	0.5	372	98.06
6	0.6	339	95.06
7	0.7	292	92.06

TABLE 16.7

Classification Obtained Using OMKNN and Indian Liver Patient Data Set

Serial Number	$\vec{d}$	Number of Group Prototypes	%C_f
1	[0.25,0.3]	447	100.00
2	[0.35,0.3]	438	100.00
3	**[0.4,0.3]**	**435**	**100.00**
4	[0.45,0.3]	429	99.78
5	[0.25,0.35]	440	99.78
6	[0.375,0.325]	431	99.78
7	[0.4,0.325]	430	99.78
8	[0.4,0.275]	437	100.00
9	[0.4,0.25]	438	100.00
10	[0.42,0.25]	437	100.00
11	[0.425,0.325]	427	99.78
12	[0.425,0.275]	433	99.78
13	[0.425,0.3]	441	99.58

TABLE 16.8

Performance Comparison of KNN, MKNN, and OMKNN for Indian Liver Patient Data Set

Criterion of Comparison	KNN	MKNN	OMKNN
Number of group prototypes/patterns	466	442	**435**
%C_f	100%	100%	**100%**
Percentage recognition accuracy	64.95%	64.95%	**65.81%**
Time required (in microseconds)	3996.84	3996.37	**3994.94**

maximum classification accuracy of 100%, with the minimum number of group prototype of 435. Hence, we did further experimentation on OMKNN using these settings.

The performance comparison of KNN, MKNN, and OMKNN for the Indian Liver Patient data set is presented in Table 16.8.

From Table 16.8, one can conclude that the proposed OMKNN prepares less group prototypes and provides better accuracy for unseen patterns as compared to KNN and MKNN. The proposed OMKNN also requires less recall time than KNN and MKNN. We can also expect at least similar or better results from the bigger data sets using OMKNN. The classification accuracy of 100% using MKNN and OMKNN indicates that group prototypes created indeed captured peculiarity of all the pattern classes. The reduction in group prototypes also leads to increase in the recognition accuracy (although small close to 1%), but for larger data sets we can expect better improvement.

16.4 Conclusions

By observing experimentation with the Iris data set given in Table 16.4, one can conclude that MKNN achieves 28% better reduction in memory than KNN, and OMKNN obtained a 33% reduction in prototypes as compared to the number of patterns need to be stored in memory for KNN. It is also noted that OMKNN got a 5% reduction in group prototypes than MKNN for Iris data set. Similarly, for Indian Liver Patient data set, Table 16.8, we can say that MKNN obtained 5.15% reduction in number of group prototypes than the number of training patterns used in KNN. OMKNN requires 2% less group prototypes than MKNN, in this case. We also observed that the recall time required for OMKNN is smaller than both MKNN and KNN, as expected. The accuracy of OMKNN for unseen patterns is better in OMKNN than MKNN and KNN. We achieved reduction in memory, reduction in recall time, with increase in recognition accuracy using OMKNN.

References

[1] T.M. Cover and P.E. Hart, "Nearest Neighbor Pattern Classification," *IEEE Transactions on Information Theory*, 13 (1), pp. 21–27, 1967.

[2] R.O. Duda, P.E. Hart, and D.G. Stork, *Pattern Classification*. New York: John Wiley & Sons, 2001.

[3] P.S. Dhabe, S.G. Lade, Snehal Pingale, Rachana Prakash, and M.L. Dhore, "Modified K- Nearest Neighbor Classifier Using Group Prototypes and Its Application to Fault Diagnosis," *CIIT Journal of Data Mining and Knowledge Engineering*, 2 (5), pp. 82–85, 2010.

[4] T.A. Brown and J. Koplowitz, "The Weighted Nearest Neighbor Rule for Class Dependent Sample Sizes," *IEEE Transactions on Information Theory*, IT-25, pp. 617–619, Sept. 1979.

[5] R. Short and K. Fukanaga, "A New Nearest Neighbor Distance Measure," *Proceedings of the Fifth IEEE International Conference*. Pattern Recognition, pp. 81–86, 1980.

[6] R. Short and K. Fukanaga, "The Optimal Distance Measure for Nearest Neighbor Classification," *IEEE Transactions on Information Theory*, 27 (5), pp. 622–627, 1981.

[7] P.E. Har, "The Condensed Nearest Neighbor Rule," *IEEE Transactions on Information Theory*, IT-14 (3), pp. 515–516, 1968.

[8] R. Li and Y. Hu, "KNN Text Classifier Training Sample Crop Method Based on Density," *Journal of Computer Research and Development*, 41 (4), pp. 539–546, 2004.

[9] W.J. Hwang and K.W. Wen, "Fast KNN Classification Algorithm Based on Partial Distance Search [J]," *Electron Let*, 34 (21), pp. 2062–2063, 1998.

[10] J.S. Pan, Y.L. Qiao, and S.H. Sun, "Neighbors Classification Algorithm [J]," *IEICE Transactions on Fundamentals*, E87-A (4), pp. 961–961, 2004.

[11] Time-Memory-Trade-Off, available online https://en.wikipedia.org/wiki/Space%E2%80%93time_tradeoff

[12] T.M. Mitchell, *Machine Learning*. New York: McGraw-Hill, 1997.

[14] D. Dua and C. Graff, *UCI Machine Learning Repository*. Irvine, CA: University of California, School of Information and Computer Science, 2019, http://archive.ics.uci.edu/ml.

[15] https://towardsdatascience.com/introduction-to-data-preprocessing-in-machine-learning-a9fa83a5dc9d

[16] www.statisticshowto.datasciencecentral.com/normalized/

[17] https://scikit-learn.org/stable/modules/generated/sklearn.preprocessing.StandardScaler.html

Appendix A

A generic function in Python which takes class value as input and generates all prototypes for that class is as shown [17].

```python
def OMKNN (class_value:int):
    """
    OMKNN is a generic function which takes a class_value and developes group prototypes for that class.
    """
    global number_of_previous_class,current_prototype

    number_of_instances_class=y_train_df[y_train_df.Species==class_value].shape[0]

    d_class=d[class_value]

    for i in range(number_of_previous_class,number_of_previous_class+number_of_instances_class):

        if(prototypes_assigned[i]==-1):

            prototypes_assigned[i]=current_prototype
            for j in range(number_of_previous_class,number_of_previous_class+number_of_instances_class):

                d_instance=distance.euclidean(x_train[i],x_train[j])
                if(d_instance<d_class and prototypes_assigned[j]==-1):
                    prototypes_assigned[j]=current_prototype

            current_prototype+=1

    number_of_previous_class+=number_of_instances_class
```

17

Role of Multi-objective Optimization in Image Segmentation and Classification

Ujwala Bharambe, Ujwala Bhangale and Chhaya Narvekar

CONTENTS

17.1 Introduction

The technique of image segmentation is an essential part of image processing that identifies the regions of an image. The segmentation of images is a key component of every computer vision system, minimum in preprocessing, if not in the final image processing or

DOI: 10.1201/9781003218111-17

in applications where segmentation is critical, such as object detection, traffic monitoring, biomedical imaging, and video surveillance. In order to segment an image, it is necessary to divide it into a number of distinct regions. Two characteristics of intensity values are considered: discontinuities and similarity. A method using abrupt changes in intensity values (edge detection) is part of a method that recognizes images based on discontinuities in intensity values (FredyGustavo et al., 2020). The alternative technique combines groupings of pixels with similar values (homogeneous regions) into a single class. Thresholding and region-growing algorithms are examples of this type of technique.

Segmentation is basically a process of finding a similar region in an image that represents various objects. Multiple objectives can be explored in order to reach this goal. Different objectives for a problem, on the other hand, are inherently conflicting in this process. As a result, optimizing all objectives at the same time is extremely challenging. In most real-world problems, there are distinct objectives to be achieved. As an example, minimize intra-cluster distance, maximize feature similarity index, maximize inter-cluster distance, and minimize feature count. It is a challenging issue to optimize these images since there are many types and modalities of information. Hence, multi-objective solutions are very useful in determining segmentation based on the optimization of various objective functions. Metaheuristic algorithms are typically used in conjunction with multi-objective optimization. Metaheuristics seem particularly suitable to solve multi-objective optimization problems, because (i) metaheuristic algorithms are good at balancing exploration and diversification, (ii) handle large computational complexity, (iii) require very few parameters, and (iv) have the ability to converge to global minimum.

This research aims to show that there has been a recent literature review on this topic. Section 17.2 describes image segmentation as a problem with many objectives and contexts. The section also identifies several goals linked to image segmentation. The current image segmentation approaches, such as clustering and classification, are discussed in Section 17.3 using multi-objective optimization. The application of multi-objective optimization methods is discussed in greater detail in Section 17.4. In Section 17.5, we concentrate on metaheuristic techniques for image segmentation, classification, and multi-objective optimization. Our discussion of metaheuristics for image segmentation and classification, as well as multi-objective optimization, appears in Section 17.5. Section 17.6 discusses image segmentation and multi-objective optimization trends and future directions.

17.2 Background

The purpose of image segmentation is to represent an image meaningfully in order to make analysis easier. In this process, each pixel is assigned a label where each pixel is associated with a certain characteristic. It is also capable of locating objects and boundaries in images, such as curves and lines. Image segmentation produces various segments that can cover the entire image. The process is very computationally intensive, and the input image contains no prior knowledge about the object or boundary. This makes this process difficult to converge to certain objects or labels. In order to address these problems and extract quality information from images, multi-objective optimization methods are put forth in literature. For example, Nakib et al. (2008) proposed multi-objective optimization for image segmentation for two objectives, first within-class variance and other one overall probability of error. This section provides an introduction to image segmentation and classification. Moreover, it introduces multi-objective optimization as an optimization problem.

17.2.1 Introduction to Image Segmentation and Classification

Segmentation is primarily concerned with dividing an image into meaningful parts that can be used in specific applications. Image segmentation can be classified into basic types: (i) histogram thresholding, (ii) clustering, (iii) region based, (iv) edge based, etc.

17.2.1.1 Histogram Thresholding

Grey-level images are most often segmented using histogram thresholding. When we assume that colour is a constant attribute of every object's surface in an image and map each pixel into a certain colour space, there is a high likelihood that various items will appear as clusters in the image. Due to shading effects and noise from the acquisition device, the dispersion of these points within each cluster is determined by colour differences. By constructing certain ad hoc histograms based on colour attributes, such as hue, instead of mapping pixels into colour spaces, it is likely that objects will appear as peaks.

17.2.1.2 Split-and-Merge Techniques

Usually, split-and-merge techniques start with an initial homogeneous partition of the image, and they keep performing splitting until homogeneous partitions are obtained. Quadtree is used to implement this procedure. Following the splitting phase, there are frequently many little and fragmented regions that must be united in some way. Before using the region adjacency graph (RAG) to build maximally connected segments, the merging step achieves this goal by combining neighbouring regions and verifying that homogeneity conditions are met.

17.2.1.3 Region-Growing Techniques

A homogeneous region of an image can be created using a growth process that begins with a preselected seed and gradually increases with points around it that satisfy a homogeneity condition. When no more points can be added to the region, the growth process comes to an end. Single regions are processed using region growth procedures. However, by combining different and subsequent growth processes, all of the points of an image can be collected in regions, resulting in its segmentation. Following a region-growing method, there may be some very small regions or two or more neighbouring regions with comparable properties that were created at separate times. Following that, post-processing is essentially a merging phase in which alimentation is accomplished by creating larger zones.

17.2.1.4 Edge-Based Techniques

Image segmentation can also be performed by detecting the edges among regions. This method has been extensively examined for grey-level images. Several techniques for detecting discontinuities in colour images have also been proposed. Edges in grey-level images can be identified using functions that approximate gradients or Laplacians of images, which are, of course, scalar functions.

17.2.1.5 Clustering

The process of clustering is the unsupervised classification of objects, without any prior knowledge. Clustering follows the principle that objects in one category have a high degree of similarity while across different categories they should have low similarity. A very popular clustering for image segmentation is adaptive k-means clustering. It requires a separate classification for a group of segmentation algorithms that combine the idea of k-means clustering with the desirable characteristics of local colour adaptation and spatial continuity. By averaging them over a sliding window whose size gradually decreases, this class of algorithms can be considered intermediate to feature-space-based strategies. As a result, the algorithm starts with global estimates and gradually adapts to each region's local characteristics.

17.2.2 Multi-objective Optimization

In computability theory, solvable problems are categorized as counting; decision and optimization. A single-objective problem can be classified into a multi-objective problem as illustrated in Figure 17.1.

The multi-objective optimization problem can then be defined as the problem of finding the following:

> Decision variables that satisfy constraints and optimize a vector function of variable elements that represents the objective functions. In mathematics, these functions represent criteria that often conflict with one another. Thus, to "optimize" entails finding a solution that presents acceptable values for each objective function to the decision maker.

> *(Coello et al., 2007: 5)*

Multi-objective optimization problems require computing two or more objectives simultaneously. Moreover, these objectives are always contradictory, and it is extremely challenging to find a solution that meets all of them. A solution good for one function may not be so good for another function. In the real world, most problems have multi-objectives. Due to their difficulty to solve, multi-objective problems are usually turned into single-objective problems. As suggested by Deb (2007), there are three fundamental differences among them: (i) they have two goals instead of one, (ii) they deal with two search spaces simultaneously, and (iii) no artificial fix up is possible for them.

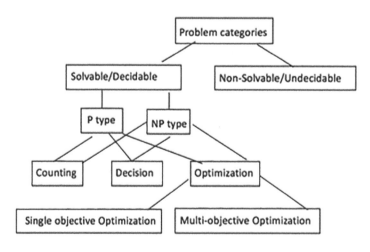

FIGURE 17.1
Problem classification.

Mathematical model for multi-objective optimization:

$$\max\{f(x)\} \Leftrightarrow \min\{-f(x)\}$$

$$y = F(x) = \left[f_1(x), f_2 \right] \cdots f_m(x) \ T \tag{17.1}$$

$$s.t g_j(x) \leq 0 (j = 1, 2, \ldots p)$$

$$x_i^{min} \leq x_i \leq x_i^{max} (i = 1, 2, \ldots n)$$

$$x = [x_1, \ldots x_n] t \in$$

$$y = [y_1, \ldots y_n] t \in$$

where m is the number of optimized objective functions, Θ is a n-dimensional search space, and decision variables $x = [x_1, \ldots x_n]t$; Ψ is the m-dimensional vector space of objective functions and is determined by Θ and the objective function $f_1(x), f_2 \cdots f_m(x)$, p constraints.

Problems with multi-objective optimization are those for which two or more objectives are measured in distinctly different units and can never be combined into one usable result. Multi-objective optimization aims at finding a set of Pareto optimal solutions and selecting the best one, with the decision maker's preferences largely determining the choice (Chen et al., 2010). Pareto optimization is based on the concept of dominance as a key idea. Dominance is defined as (Domination): Given two solutions x, y, we say that $x = (x, x \ldots x)$ dominates $y = (y, y \ldots y)$ if and only if $F(x)$ is partially less than $F(y)$ if and only if $f(x) \leq f(y) \forall i = 1 \ldots q$ and $\exists \ i \in \{1 \ldots q\}$ with $f(x) \leq f(y)$. The solutions provided by Pareto optimization can be classified into dominated solutions and non-dominated solutions. As in Figure 17.2, each point represents one solution in the objective space for two objectives (bi-objective representation). When no other feasible solution dominates a Pareto optimal solution, it is called a Pareto optimal solution.

A bi-objective representation is illustrated in Figure 17.2, where each point represents one solution in the optimization process. The Pareto optimal solution is one that is not dominated by any other possible solution. For any two solutions $x$and, $x$is said to dominate $x$if the following criteria are satisfied: (1) $x$is not inferior to$x$in all objectives and (2) $x$is superior to than $x$in at least one objective.

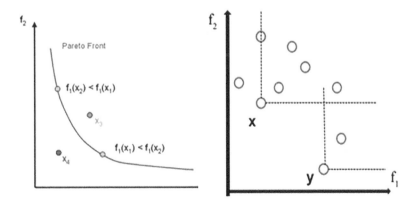

FIGURE 17.2
Illustration for bi-objective minimization problem: (a) Pareto front, (b) for example, x dominates five other individuals, and y dominates two individuals.

It is usually extremely difficult to identify a single solution that outperforms all other alternatives in a multi-optimization problem. There are more likely to be numerous Pareto optimal solutions, which will form a Pareto front (PF). According to the Pareto optimal solution of the Pareto front, every increase in one objective is almost certain to result in a decrease in one or more other objectives. This multi-objective optimization function aims to produce a number of plausible solutions that are closer to the Pareto front, so that the best solution can be selected.

17.2.2.1 Classification Multi-objective Optimization

Multi-objective optimization techniques can be classified in many ways. They can be classified based on two stages:

- Optimization of multiple objective functions
- Making decisions about which "trade-offs" to make is the decision-making process from the perspective of a decision maker

As a starting point, Cohon and Marks (1975) provide a popular classification based on following two stages: (i) Generating method (a posteriori articulation of preferences). (ii) Method which relies on the prior articulation of preferences (non-interactive methods). (iii) Method relies on progressive articulation of preferences (interaction with the decision-maker). Several classifications are based on these classifications. In this work, we have used the classification provided by Cui et al. (2017).

A priori methods: In a priori approaches, the decision maker's preferences are first elicited, and then the solution that best satisfies these preferences is determined. However, it is quite challenging to ask the decision maker what kind of solution they want, and to understand the type of preference information. The decision maker also needs to have prior understanding of his own preferences, the interdependencies of the objectives, or the feasible objective values. Examples of a priori methods include ε-constraint method, weighted sum, objective programming method, etc.

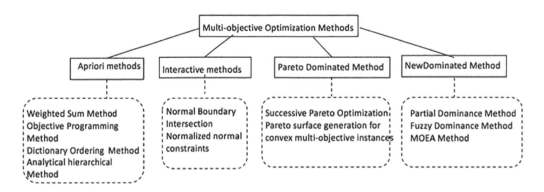

FIGURE 17.3
The multi-objective optimization classification used in this work. Influenced by Cui et al. (2017), we have classified a priori method, interactive method, Pareto-dominated method, and new dominated method.

The advantages of a priori methods include the following:

- The solution found is Pareto optimal for all possible preferences
- The decision maker's preferences can be precisely modelled in the chosen way
- Each Pareto optimal solution can be found with some preference

And the disadvantages are as follows:

- It is not easy for the decision maker to tell exactly how he wants the solution and spending time for it.
- Also, the decision maker has to understand his own preferences.

Interactive methods: Interactive methods were developed in order to utilize decision makers' expertise and experience, including interactive weighting, the NIMBUS method, and Light Beam Search Tchebycheff (Miettinen et al., 2008). During the optimization process, the interactive approaches incorporate decision makers' preferences for each objective. Interactive techniques, as is customary, use an achievement scalarization function to provide Pareto optimal options. Advantages of the interactive method are as follows:

- As the decision maker may guide the search, only Pareto optimal solutions that are interesting to him are computed.
- The burden to the decision maker gets lighter, as the decision maker only evaluates a few solutions at a time.

Pareto-dominated method: There are many methods that can be used to solve multi-objective optimization problems, and this method is popular. It consists of two steps: the first is the generation of a set of all Pareto optimal solutions; the second is the selection of the best solution or using heuristics. When the non-dominated sorting genetic algorithm (NSGA) was first applied to attain the Pareto front for the multi-objective optimization problem in 1994, a series of intelligent optimization techniques based on Pareto-dominated approaches began to emerge. Most Pareto-dominated methods fall into two classes: "classical methods" are dominated by solving multiple single-objective optimization problems simultaneously and evolve into a representative set of Pareto optimal solutions. Evolutionary algorithms mimic natural selection and evolve a "population of solutions" simultaneously. Using evolutionary algorithms to solve problems of this type is motivated in part by their population-based nature, which allows them to generate several components of the Pareto optimal set at once. Further, some multi-objective optimization problems (MOPs) may be too complex to implement conventional OR MOP-solving techniques (e.g., noise, disjoint Pareto curves, uncertainty, very large search spaces, etc.).

New dominance methods: It is important to recognize that Pareto domination methods have some disadvantages. Further, the true convergence behaviour of non-dominated solutions within the Pareto optimal set remains unclear despite the poor performance of MOPs with complex Pareto fronts. Laumanns et al. (2002) propose multiple methods to address this issue proposed. One is ε-dominance mechanism and another is μ-domination principle.

17.3 Metaheuristics Algorithms

When classical methods are too slow, or when the exact solution cannot be found, a heuristic is a way to solve problems faster or to find an approximate solution. Heuristic approaches have the following characteristics in general (Bandaru et al., 2016): (i) they are computationally fast because they do not explore every possible solution in the search space before arriving at the final solution, (ii) they look for an approximate solution, (iii) they do not require a mathematical convergence proof, and (iv) they look for an approximate proposed solution.

Metaheuristics methods are commonly utilized to solve optimization problems. It refers to a technique that employs one or more heuristics. The metaheuristic method

- Aims to identify a near-optimal solution rather than attempting to determine the exact ideal solution
- Shows there is no proof of convergence to the optimal solution
- Is frequently more computationally efficient than exhaustive search

The majority of these methods are iterative in design, and they frequently use stochastic processes to change one or more initial populations during their search process. Due to the intrinsic complexity of many real-world optimization problems, classical optimization techniques may not always be applicable or reasonable in solving such problems in a pragmatic manner. In the recent past, metaheuristic algorithms are considered to be reasonable and acceptable solutions for a variety of complex practical problems (Bandaru et al., 2016).

Natural, physical, or biological principles are the basis of most metaheuristic methods, and they attempt to duplicate them at their most fundamental level. Metaheuristic techniques fall into three categories: evolutionary algorithms, swarm intelligence algorithms, and physical phenomena-based algorithms (Figure 17.4). Swarm intelligence algorithms replicate the behaviors or interactions of both living and non-living animals (such as ants, birds, bees, fireflies, glow worms, bacteria, fishes, white blood cells, and so on) (like river systems, water drops, masses under gravity, etc.).

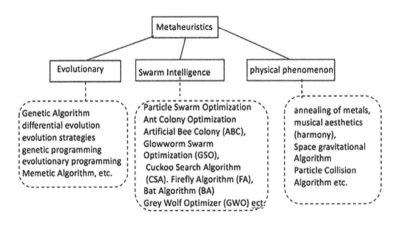

FIGURE 17.4
Metaheuristic algorithm classification.

Various features of evolution in nature, such as survival of the fittest, reproduction, and genetic mutation, are mimicked by evolutionary algorithms (such as genetic algorithms, differential evolution, evolution strategies, genetic programming, evolutionary programming, and so on). The remaining metaheuristics are modeled after physical phenomena such as metal annealing, musical aesthetics (harmony), and so on.

Due to these characteristics, metaheuristics approaches are more advantageous in the context of recovering from local optima and also provide an opportunity for handling multiple objectives compared to classical optimization approaches such as hill climbing, simplex method, etc. Table 17.1 demonstrates the difference between metaheuristic optimization and classical optimization approaches.

A common theme among all metaheuristic approaches is to balance between exploration and exploitation. The exploration process can also be understood informally as the ability of the algorithm to search globally. In contrast, the exploitation process is the act of visiting regions of the search space that are adjacent to previously visited points, resulting from local searches. Balancing exploration and exploitation is connected to maintaining population diversity. When population diversity is high, the algorithm is explorative; when it is low, the behaviour is exploitative. Multiple ways exist for achieving this balance, e.g., fitness sharing, crowding density operators, etc. Multi-objective optimization for mainlining diversity using the niching method is a widely used method in the literature. Pareto optimal solutions are produced by multi-objective optimization problems and must be further processed to reach the preferred solution. A metaheuristic method can find many non-dominated solutions in a single simulation run by using population in iteration. Because trade-offs can be observed between objectives, this technique becomes quite natural to use. The most frequent choice for addressing multi-objective problems is to use evolutionary algorithms and swarm intelligence for the following properties of metaheuristic techniques: (i) global search ability, (ii) ease of implementation, (iii) robustness and reliability, (iv) implied parallelism, (v) approximate and non-deterministic, and (vi) effective ability to explore search spaces.

TABLE 17.1

Metaheuristic Optimization versus Classical Optimization

Type of Problem	Handle Input Complexity	Handle Problem Computational Complexity	Characteristics
Metaheuristics optimization	Large	High (P type and NPhard: Exact algorithm not known)	Advantages: (i) Metaheuristics require no gradient information, (ii) do not require prior gradient information, (iii) can recover from local optima, (iv) can handle multiple objectives Disadvantage: Slower than classical optimization
Classical optimization	Small, medium	Low (P type problem: Exact algorithm is known)	Advantages: Fast and always terminate Disadvantages: (i) Not able to generate good enough solutions, (ii) require prior gradient information, (iii) cannot recover from local optima, (iv) cannot handle multiple objectives

17.3.1 Multi-objective Evolutionary Algorithm

The use of multi-objective optimization in evolutionary algorithms was first suggested by Rosenberg in 1960. In 1984, David Schaffer introduced the vector evaluation genetic algorithm (VEGA), which was the first implementation of MOEA. Evolutionary algorithms are suitable because they can take into account a large number of solutions simultaneously.

By using this method, it becomes easy to discover many members of the Pareto optimal set in one single "run" as opposed to numerous iterations as in traditional mathematical programming. In addition, evolutionary algorithms can cope with discontinuous or concave Pareto fronts more easily (e.g., they can cope with a discontinuous or concave Pareto front), whereas both of these issues are real concerns for mathematical programming techniques. A multi-objective evolutionary algorithm's main purpose is (i) to generate solutions that are as close to the Pareto optimal front as possible, (ii) to extract with a diverse variety of solutions, and (iii) to create a set of satisfying solutions that reflect the decision maker's preferences, where satisfying refers to a decision-making method that aims to meet adequacy requirements rather than finding the best option.

In general, multi-objective optimization algorithms have the following steps:

- First phase is initialization in which N individuals are generated in the population and evaluate fitness.
- The next phase is Pareto ranking based on dominance relation. The objective of ranking is to remove Pareto-dominated individuals from populations.
- In the next phase, again population is reduced based on density estimation techniques such as niching, sharing, and crowding.
- Create new individuals by recombination, mutation, etc., using appropriate parameter values.
- After evolutionary operations, individuals are selected for next generations. Various techniques can be utilised for selection for example elitism, binary tournament selection, etc.
- When a termination condition, for example, maximum number of generations or convergence criteria, is not met.
- Either remove Pareto-dominated and infeasible individuals or make infeasible individuals viable.
- Maintain a list of non-dominated and feasible individuals.
- Local search operations can also provide good performance in hybrid or memetic MOEAs by only focusing on the Pareto front, i.e., moving to specific regions towards the limit of the objective space.

MOEAs generally start with a population of individuals and then use evolutionary analysis operators (selection, recombination, and mutation) to generate generations of solutions, ranking individuals and preserving non-dominated solutions in a repository.

17.3.2 Image Segmentation and Classification

Segmentation is a basic task used in image analysis. A segmentation algorithm is generally used in preprocessing of computer vision-based applications, specifically useful for object extraction while ignoring the rest of the scene. Essentially, image segmentation is partitioning an image into several regions. Given an image $I(u, v)$ and R its whole area, based on segmentation, we can say R contains n sub-regions R_i, i 1, 2, . . . , n such that the following is true:

- Each pixel of an image must be included in a sub-region, which means segmentation must be complete.
- The pixels present in R_i share a common property.
- The resultant segment must be disjoint, i.e., $R_i \cap R_j$ for all i, j where i, j are sub-regions.
- Sub-regions should not be empty.

The goal of metaheuristics is to avoid getting stuck on local optimal points and find a global solution through a competitive selection of individuals within a population. This will enhance greatly the quality of segmented image and algorithm performance. Additionally to genetic algorithms, artificial bee colonies (ABC), cuckoo search (CS), and harmony search (HS) algorithms are among the other metaheuristic methods used for segmentation. Most previous metaheuristic methods maximize or minimize a single-objective function.

17.3.3 Image Segmentation as Optimization Problem

Segmentation of an image can be modelled as an optimization based upon its application. It also depends upon why it is required in that particular setting. It can be used in supervised and unsupervised settings. This section described the different ways to model image segmentation problems as multi-objective optimization.

Figure 17.5 represented multi-objective settings for image segmentation where image is input and then several objectives are defined to get a segmented image using multi-objective optimization. Commonly, image segmentation problems are designed as unsupervised learning problems in literature. Different approaches have utilised different objectives to achieve the clustering. For example, proposals by Mukhopadhyay et al. (2006) utilized two objectives: the first is used for maximizing the separation among clusters and the second is to minimize the variance of clusters. Qian et al. (2008) defined two objectives for achieving clustering for segmentation: the first one is based on compactness which is basically intra-cluster consistency and the other is based on connectedness of clusters which is similarity of neighbouring points. Table 17.2 demonstrates various image segmentations and objectives adopted from Mesejo et al. (2016) and Ezugwu et al. (2020).

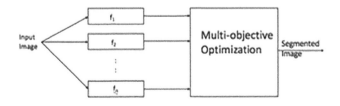

FIGURE 17.5
Multi-objective optimization for image segmentation.

TABLE 17.2

Comparison of Popular Metaheuristic Algorithms Used in Image Segmentation

Name of Algorithm	Proposed by	Approach	Pros	Cons
Improved cuckoo search (ICS)	Jiao et al. (2021)	Parasitic brood of Cuckoo with Levy flight search	Optimization problem is solved quite efficiently by simulating the brood of species of cuckoo, for performance improvement of algorithm, Levy flight search mechanism used	Accuracy of the image after segmentation is not considered that is a limitation of the algorithm.
Swarm optimization and multilevel histogram thresholding	Boldaji and Semnani (2021)	Combines Kapur's entropy and Otsu's method with MOPSO	Multi-objective optimizers keep the algorithm out of local optima and speed up the optimization process	Because Kapur's entropy and Otsu's approach are complementary, combining them could yield superior results.
Automatic clustering using multi-objective Emperor Penguin optimizer (ACMOEPO)	Kumar et al. (2019)	Inspired by entanglement in quantum mechanics	When compared to other clustering approaches, ACMOEPO produces well-separated optimum clusters	Novel concept introduced for computation weighted cluster centroid and setting dynamic threshold as well.
Multiverse optimization algorithm (MVO) based on Levy flight	Jia et al. (2019b)	Based on the multiverse theory of physics	Increases population diversity to avoid premature convergence	The MVO is likely to become caught in the local optima during the iterations of the process.
Grasshopper optimization algorithm with minimum cross-entropy and differential evolution	Jia et al. (2019a)	Inspired by the swarming behavior of grasshoppers in nature	Optimization capabilities of this hybrid model were increased without increasing the computational complexity	Due to the disadvantages of GOA, like uneven exploration-exploitation, sluggish speed of convergence, and population diversity is less, DE was used to improve search efficiency.
Covariance matrix adaptation evolution strategy (CMA-ES)	Debakla et al. (2019)	Developed by Nikolaus Hansen	ES algorithm ensures that there is a global optimum; ES also recommended for real-number function optimization	Time complexity is high.
Bat algorithm (BA)	Yang and He (2013)	Echolocation behavior of microbat is the inspiration	BA can automatically zoom into areas with good solutions by using frequency tuning to boost population diversity; instead of using a fixed parameter, BA uses parameter control to vary the values of its parameters over time	It quickly converges. It is not easy to conduct a mathematical study of the parameters employed and the rate of convergence. The best value for a real-world application is unclear.

Name of Algorithm	Proposed by	Approach	Pros	Cons
Artificial bee colony algorithm (ABC)	Karaboga (2010)	Foraging behavior of honeybees is the principle here	ABC method is extremely reliable, converges quickly, has a small number of parameters, and is adaptable	In the later stages of its search, the ABC algorithm exhibits premature convergence, at the same time classification accuracy of its best achieved value may not be good.
Cuckoo search (CS)	Yang et al. (2010)	Reproduction process of cuckoo is the inspiration	Capable of achieving a truly global optimum Can perform both local and global searches Employs Levy flying as a global search approach	CS produces low classification accuracy. CS has a low convergence rate.
Firefly algorithm (FA)	Yang and He (2013)	Flashing phenomena of firefly is the inspiration	Has the potential to divide a population into multiple groups automatically, which is useful for variation	FFA performance, like that of several metaheuristic algorithms, is dependent on proper parameter adjustment. Diversification in the FFA can result in a slower rate of convergence.
Harmony search	Zong Woo Geem et al. (2001)	Inspired by improvisation process of music players	Simple implementation, fewer parameters to change, and quick convergence	Algorithm is incapable of striking a good balance between global and local searches.
Ant colony optimisation	Dorigo and Di Caro (1999)	Based on foraging behaviour of ant	—Ant produces solutions independently and simultaneously, hence the construction process for ACO is naturally parallel. —ACO's distributed computation prevents premature convergence. Its adaptable nature makes it an excellent choice for dynamic applications.	—ACO distribution of probability changes with iteration. —Even though it is guaranteed convergence, time for convergence cannot be defined. —ACO's behaviour is challenging to analyze theoretically since it is built on a series of random decisions made by distinct artificial ants.
Differential evolution algorithm (DEA)	Storn (1995)	Inspired by evolutionary theory	—DEA excels at diversity and exploration —DEA capable of handling non-differentiable, multimodal, and nonlinear cost functions —DEA is capable of handling high-complexity cost functions —DEA is capable of achieving the global minimum	—DEA is not stable for convergence. —DEA stuck in regional optimum. —DEA parameter tuning is necessary.

(Continued)

TABLE 17.2

(Continued)

Name of Algorithm	Proposed by	Approach	Pros	Cons
Genetic algorithm (GA)	Holland (1992)	Mimic the process of natural selection	—GA is easy to implement —GA can deal with a variety of objectives and restrictions; may handle issues with high computational complexity —GA can be used to solve problems with nonlinear or discontinuous constraints and goal functions	—GA may suffer from premature convergence thus losing the population diversity. —There's no certainty the global maxima is discovered. It has a significant chance of becoming stuck in local maxima.
Particle swarm optimization	Reynold (1987)	Based on bird gathering	—Calculation in PSO is simple —Many engineering research problems can be easily modelled using PSO	—In PSO, due to solutions converging prematurely, population diversity is lost. —PSO has a problem with partial optimism.

17.4 Metaheuristics Approaches and Multi-Objective Optimization for Image Segmentation and Classification

A metaheuristic is a high-level process or heuristic used in computer science to find or pick a heuristic that can help solve an optimization problem. Simulated annealing, genetic algorithms, particle swarm optimization, tabu search, and ant colony optimization are some of the most popular metaheuristics algorithms. Multi-objective systems are commonly employed in metaheuristic techniques. It is specifically used in the evolutionary process' selection mechanism for contradictory criteria. In order to address this issue, there are several publications for image segmentation and classification using metaheuristics with multi-objective configuration (Ma, 2017). Table 17.3 explores various metaheuristic approaches with multi-objective optimization for image segmentation and classification.

17.4.1 Review of Image Classification Techniques

There are three main types of image classification techniques: (i) supervised classification, (ii) unsupervised classification, and (iii) semi-supervised classification. A supervised classification involves labeling data points and training an unknown group of pixels. In unsupervised classification, no labeled data are used, and random data can be used whenever trained pixels are not available, or in simpler terms, there is no training to be performed. Semi-supervised classification combines the benefits of both supervised and unsupervised classification, and instead of highly interacting domain experts, unlabeled data points are used, reducing the likelihood of bias since the data is poorly represented. With the help of different mathematical techniques, an image classifier identifies the features in an image. The image classification process works in a structured manner where different tasks are

TABLE 17.3

Comparison of Various Metaheuristic and Multi-objective Optimization in Image Segmentation and Classification

Author	Type of Metaheuristic Algorithm	Multi-objective/ Single	Settings (Ua/S)	Utility	Application
Gao Xiao-Zhi1 et al. (2021)	Classification-Hybrid cat SO, CSO	Multi-objective	S	IS	Using hybrid cat swarm optimization, multi-objective feature selection optimization was achieved.
Mohamed Abdelaziz et al. (2021)	Multi-objective whale optimization	Multi-objective	S	FS	Content-based image retrieval is achieved using whale optimization
Takano et al. (2021)	MOGA, NSGA-II	Multi-objective	S	FS	Block detection as a multi-objective optimization problem that makes use of both geometric and aesthetic qualities.
Shouvik Chakraborty et al. (2018)	PSO	Multi-objective	S	FS	In classification, a PSO-based multi-objective multi-label feature selection method is used.
Dey and Ashour (2018)	CS, PSO, GA, FA	Multi-objective	U	IS	A review of metaheuristic algorithms in medical image segmentation.
Yong Zhang et al. (2017)	Nakibs MOBJ, NEW_MOBJ	Multi-objective	U	IS	Tsallis and Rényi entropies were used to fund multi-objective optimization for viewpoint picture segmentation.
Couceiro and Ghamisi (2016)	Particle swarm optimization	Single objective	U	IS	Fractional-order Darwinian PSO for multilevel image segmentation
El Joumani et al. (2017)	WSM used on Gabor filter response	Multi-objective	U	IS	Gabor filters and thresholding based on multi-objective optimization are used to automatically segment coronary arteries.
Sag and Çunkaş (2015)	Bee colony optimization	Multi-objective	U	IS	Artificial bee colony optimization is used for colour image segmentation.
Hsieh and Hu (2014)	PSO with SVM	Multi-objective	S	IC	For fingerprint classification, a multi-objective optimised SVM algorithm was applied.
Cruz-Aceves et al. (2013)	PSO, FCM, ACO	Multi-objective	U	IS IC	Techniques for picture segmentation that are multi-objective and inspired by nature.
Chin-Wei and Rajeswari (2010)	Summary of 18 papers MO algorithms used such as GA, PESA, NSGA-II, and so on	Multi-objective	S/U	IS	Multi-objective optimization-based image histogram thresholding.
Shirakawa and Nagao (2009)	Strength Pareto Evolutionary Algorithm2 (SPEA2)	Multi-objective	U	IS	Image segmentation based on multi-objective clustering.
Nakib et al. (2007)	Nakibs MOBJ1 and MOBJ2	Multi-objective	U	IS IC	Multi-objective optimization based image histogram thresholding.
Bhanu et al. (1995)	Genetic algorithm	Multi-objective	S	IS	To address adaptive picture segmentation challenges, use GA with a linear combination of weights.

Note: FS, feature selection for image segmentation; IC, image classification; IS, image segmentation; S, supervised; U, unsupervised; GA, genetic algorithm; MO, multi-objective; PESA, Pareto envelope-based selection algorithm; (NSGA-II), fast elitist non-dominated sorting in genetic algorithms (NSGA-II); PSO, particle swarm optimization algorithm; FCM, fuzzy c-means; ACO, ant colony optimization.

FIGURE 17.6
Image classification process.

performed in order to achieve the desired results and classify the image accurately. The steps for implementing the image classification process are as follows (Figure 17.6):

- Image preprocessing: This step removes distortions and enhances important features of the image to benefit the models from the enhanced data. This includes reading an image, resizing the image, and data augmentation if necessary.
- Detection of an object: This step segments the image and identifies the object in the image.
- Feature extraction and training: This step involves identifying the patterns and features in the image that might be specific to a particular class, which later determines how the model will distinguish one class from another. The features of the model are derived from the dataset during this process of model training.
- Classification of the object: At this step, detected objects are classified into predefined classes by comparing the image patterns to those of the target.

17.4.2 Role of Multi-Objective Optimization in Image Segmentation and Classification

Image segmentation is recently formulated as multiple objectives in its decision-making process. The main challenge for multiple objectives is that they do not always align with each other, as a matter of fact, they are conflicting with each other. Multiple objectives exist for real-world image segmentation problems, including minimization of features or minimization of error rates, reduction of cluster spread (internal cluster connectivity), and maximization of the number of nodes in the cluster.

In the real world, segmentation is about minimizing the number of features or error rates, minimizing deviation (intercluster spread of data), and maximizing connectivity (intercluster connectivity). As a result, this process utilizes multi-objective optimization. In this section, we describe how images are segmented and classified today.

As mentioned earlier, image segmentation problems actually have multiple objectives: some need minimization, while others need maximization, such as minimizing overall deviation, enhancing connectivity, etc. Due to this, image segmentation problems can be modelled as a multi-objective optimization problem (Liu et al., 2021). Segmentation and classification of shape are based on optimization of multiple heterogeneous objectives that have application-specific different criteria. In multi-objective optimization objectives usually contradict each other. A multi-objective segmentation algorithm such as quantum computing, K-means clustering, multi-objective clustering, strength Pareto evolutionary algorithm, and PSO, these algorithms are used to optimize multiple objectives simultaneously.

Multi-objective optimization algorithms are also used as multiple features fusion strategy for segmentation, author combined texture and colour features. Multiple segmentation criteria can be optimized simultaneously, which will increase the quality of partitioning solutions and the robustness of the solutions towards different data properties. Image segmentation is one of the multi-objective optimization problems that can be solved with metaheuristics algorithms. Multi-objective approaches combining cluster validity measures or their variants with genetic algorithms (GA) were described by Mukhopadhyay et al. (2006) The advantage of these methods is that they can automatically alter the number of clusters and regions. Saha and Bandyopadhyay (2010) presented an algorithm that simultaneously optimizes two cluster validity indices for segmentation of magnetic resonance brain images using archived multi-objective simulated annealing (AMOSA). A MOPSO algorithm was used by Benaichouche et al. (2016) to optimize two complementary criteria based on fuzzy C mean clustering (FCA). This is an example of a clustering of pixels problem in brain tissue segmentation. An important challenge for image segmentation is to choose appropriate criteria that produce good results.

The role of multi-objective optimization in segmentation can be approached from multiple perspectives. In recent research on image segmentation, the application of multiple objectives in problem formulation has been gaining attention (Nakib et al., 2008; Ganesan et al., 2013).

When using multi-objective optimization, objective functions are generally conflicting and prevent concurrent optimization. Image segmentation is a real-life application of multiple objectives. The main goal of multi-objective optimization in the clustering process is (i) to minimize overall intra-cluster data deviation and maximize the intercluster connectivity (Datta et al., 2018); (ii) minimize the intra-distance between pixels and their cluster means; and (iii) maximize the inter-distance between any two clusters, and minimize the quantization error. These multi-objective optimizations are carried out to obtain the optimal clusters required during the segmentation process.

Multi-objective optimization is also used with classification models for maximizing the sensitivity and specificity, simultaneously and improving various classifiers ensemble approaches. Here, it is used for minimizing the overall error on the training dataset of classification and also minimizing complexity and maximizing diversity measures. In turn, this reduces the error rate of the classifiers. As a result, there is a disconnect between the characteristics of segmentation problems and the solutions to realistic problems. Multi-objective optimization is a suitable scheme for this situation (Saha and Bandyopadhyay, 2010; Lin et al., 2017).

17.4.3 Multi-Objective Optimization in Remote Sensing Image Segmentation and Classification

The multi-objective optimization plays an important role in remote sensing image analysis, spatially for clustering or segmentation and classification purposes. The state-of-the-art methods discussed earlier are used widely for multi-objective optimization in remote sensing images.

The nature of remote sensing imagery is complex; it involves spectral and spatial components, as a single pixel in the image may consist of multiple objects. For example, part of the pixel consists of land, and part of it will be a water body. Applying classification or clustering for such types of fuzzy pixels requires multi-objective optimization. It is used mainly for identifying the pixel purity for object classification. Further, the need for automated processes for clustering or segmenting the pixels orients it as optimization problems that usually have multiple objectives.

In remote sensing imagery analysis, multi-objective optimization is applied in many applications, such as minimizing soil erosion and maximizing the yield, minimizing the number of classes by grouping the classes which are quite similar depending upon the object of interests, for example ponds, lakes to consider as water bodies, trees, farms and forest to consider as Greenland, etc., maximizing the accuracy of the classification process with the selected classes. It is also very beneficial for land use planning for agriculture, industry, transportation, forests, etc. to maximize the economic returns, minimize pollution, etc. to get the non-dominant solutions in the remote sensing and GIS domain.

Further, it is used for minimizing the number of features from the geographical entities such as Geo/Bio physical variables and maximizing the robustness and reliability of the results obtained (Pasolli et al., 2012).

Multi-objective optimization is also used in remote sensing image fusion operations considering both spectral and spatial properties of the remotely sensed data captured by different sensors, where the objective is to minimize the loss or error while fusing the images and maximizing the quality index of the fused image (Azarang and Kehtarnavaz, 2020).

Rajagopal et al. (2020) introduced a new multi-objective particle swarm optimization model (MOPSO) with deep convolutional neural networks (CNNs) for scene classification captured by unmanned aerial vehicles (UAV). They observed 97.88% accuracy compared to other CNN models such as AlexNet, VGG-F, VGG-M, VGG-VD19, PlacesNet, etc.

Ma et al. (2021) have proposed the multi-objective neural evolution model SceneNet which provides competitive Parato optimal solution for remotely sensed image classification using evolutionary algorithm based on neural architecture search (NAS).

Genetic algorithms based Non-dominated Sorting Genetic Algorithm-II (NSGA-II) is used by Bandyopadhyay et al. (2007), Saha and Bandyopadhyay (2010), and Zhong et al. (2013) for pixel classification. The selection of objective functions is of prime importance in the optimization process. Objective functions need to be optimised simultaneously. Xie-Beni (XB) index and Fuzzy C Mean (FCM) algorithm are used as objective functions by Bandyopadhyay et al. (2007) for landcover classification; the FCM measure is used for minimizing the within-cluster variance, and the XB index is used as a minimization function with a cluster separation parameter as a denominator, hence maximizing the separation across the different clusters that eventually minimizes the XB index. Shaygan et al. (2013) have also used NSGA-II to evaluate the land use patterns for natural resource management. They have used goal attainment-multi-objective land allocation (GoA-MOLA) for comparison purposes.

17.4.4 Multi -Objective Optimization in Medical Image Segmentation and Classification

Clinical images are analyzed in medical image analysis in order to detect and diagnose diseases affecting body organs or to determine normal physiological processes. Analyses can be conducted on images derived from ultrasounds, radiologies, magnetic resonance imaging, etc. As the leading cause of death among women, breast cancer is a disease that relies heavily on image analysis methodology (Ghosh, 2010). With the help of this methodology, doctors are able to perform an accurate cancer diagnosis. In general, when diagnosing and classifying breast cancer images, the physician considers a number of factors such as tumour size, form, homogeneity, and so on. To aid radiologists in categorizing tumour images, computer-based image analysis algorithms can be developed. The quality of segmentation is critical to the success of a medical image analysis system. It can be found in a variety of real-life applications, such as congenital brain abnormalities or perinatal brain injury, post-traumatic syndrome, neurodegenerative diseases like dementia, and movement disorders like Parkinson's disease and Parkinson-associated dystonia. It is generally the case that input magnetic resonance brain images containing complex structures are noisy and distorted by intensity nonuniformity (INU) artifacts due to a variety of factors, such as variations in illumination or radiofrequency coils in imaging devices. It is therefore challenging to automatically and accurately segment magnetic resonance images into different tissue classes, particularly grey matter (GM), cerebrospinal fluid (CSF), and white matter (WM). The literature contains a variety of segmentation techniques developed over the years to create accurate segmented results. They categorize data processing based on specific goals and factors involved. Image segmentation can be effective with methods like fuzzy clustering and region-based active contours. Each approach treats the image segmentation problem as a non-convex and non-unique energy-fitting problem, but each allows for multiple local minima. In addition to dealing with noise, these approaches suffer from difficulties in avoiding being trapped in the first local minimum they encounter when using gradient descent. Many advanced methods have been developed to address these challenges. For instance, Maulik (2009) uses a genetic algorithm, Ghosh et al. (2016) also used a genetic algorithm for medical images. Ait-Aoudia et al. (2014) used particle swarm optimization (PSO) and corrected bias field information in kernelization by taking into account local partial information. Medical image analysis has extensively used region-based active contour methods.

17.5 Current Trends in Image Segmentation and Classification

Due to the huge popularity of machine learning approaches, recently there is the trend of applying deep learning to image segmentation and classification. Included are convolutional neural network, support vector machine, transfer learning, K-nearest neighbour, random forest, etc. The most popular trend in machine learning is the use of deep learning. Table 17.4 demonstrates the comparison of deep learning and multi-objective metaheuristic algorithms. A common trend is to generate semantic segmentation. In pixel-level classification, objects are grouped together by categories defined within the image. Segmenting an image by semantic features is also known as semantic segmentation. As an example, a street scene might have "pedestrians," "signboards," "vehicles," "roadside," "signs," and so on. Semantic segmentation can then be viewed as a refinement of instance segmentation. A category called "vehicles" is split into "cars," "motorcycles," "buses," etc.— instance segmentation identifies the instances of each category. Multiple objects within the same category are treated as a single unit by semantic segmentation. On the other hand, instance segmentation recognizes specific objects within these categories. Semantic segmentation has many real-world applications such as self-driving cars, medical image processing, satellite image processing, and e-commerce clothing. Following, we mention upcoming areas in image segmentations: (i) semantic segmentation, (ii) three-dimensional point cloud segmentation, (iii) beneration of benchmark for image segmentation, and (iv) neuroevolution for images segmentation.

TABLE 17.4

Comparison of Deep Learning and Metaheuristic and Multi-objective Optimization in Image Segmentation and Classification

Application	Algorithm Used in Recent Literature	Advantages	Disadvantages	Applications
Deep learning based image segmentation and classification	CNN and FCN, RNN, R-CNN, dilated CNN, attention-based models, generative and adversarial models	—Remarkable performance improvements —Often achieving the highest accuracy rates —Generally modelled supervised learning problem —Suitable for high dimensional data —Suitable for large data	—DL model are black box —It is quite difficult to interpret the model —Not a good performer when modelled as weakly supervised and unsupervised learning —Not promising results in real-time setting due to lack of adaptability — Very sensitive to noise and outlier — Nto ot able handle multiple objectives simultaneously — Long training time required	Applied to segment satellite images in the field of remote sensing, including techniques for urban planning or precision agriculture DL-based segmentation techniques in biology and evaluation of construction materials
Metaheuristic algorithm based ISC	GA, ACO.PSO, FA, etc.	complex real-world problems in reasonable time as compared to classical methods. -Generally modelled as unsupportive learning problem —Not very sensitive to noise and outlier -Good for handling multiple objectives	—Computational complexity is comparatively high —Not suitable for large data compare DL model. —If data is high dimensional and number of objective are large then Multi-objective evolutional algorithm give poor results.	Evolutionary robotics, Medical Image analysis, Satellite images

17.6 Current Trends in Multi-Objective Optimization

Over the past two decades, multi-objective optimization has dominated research in evolutionary computation, and it remains a major research area. Traditionally, multi-objective optimization is utilized with clustering and classification approaches for image segmentation and classification. However, there is a recent trend to use MOP in ensemble approaches, evaluation approaches for diversity analysis. Following is some of the latest research in multi-objective evolutionary algorithms: (i) in order to accelerate the solution process, use of surrogate models (exact objectives are converted into surrogate objectives) for dynamic systems (Peitz and Dellnitz, 2018); (ii) achieving multi-objective optimal control using feedback control mechanism (Peitz and Dellnitz, 2018); (iii) reduction techniques for many-objective optimization problems (Peitz and Dellnitz, 2018) (Vachhani et al., 2015); (iv) investigation into how decision makers' preferences are incorporated into the process of evolutionary decision-making, which is called interactive MOEA (Vachhani et al., 2015); (v) consideration of multi-objective dynamic and noisy models that can be optimized but that have some fundamental issues to consider that have not been examined in depth; and (vi) importance of studying quantum evolutionary algorithms in the context of multi-objective, constrained optimization (Vachhani et al., 2015).

17.7 Conclusion

An overview of multi-objective metaheuristic evolutionary algorithms is presented in this chapter for image segmentation and classification. The topic describes the mathematical model of multi-objective optimization, describes the current state of research on MOEA and its four classifications, explores the advantages and disadvantages of different algorithms, and summarizes the application areas. The image is segmented as per the requirement of application domains. Although image segmentation is not new, multiple objectives such as homogeneity, spatial compactness, continuity, and psycho-visual perception to be satisfied make it a challenging research area. In this chapter, several comparative analyses are presented where MOEA algorithms are used, however, the quality of a segmentation result is influenced by the number of competing objectives. Simultaneous optimization of multiple objectives increases the quality of solutions and increases their robustness. Further, this work also covers the wide use of multi-objective optimization techniques in remote sensing and medical image processing domains to serve purposes such as minimizing the overall processing overhead and maximising the accuracy. MOEA in classification and segmentation will have tremendous scope in the near future as computer vision and robotic vision become a part of daily life.

References

AbdelAziz, A. M., Soliman, T., Ghany, K. K. A., & Sewisy, A. (2021). A hybrid multi-objective whale optimization algorithm for analyzing microarray data based on Apache Spark. *PeerJ Computer Science, 7*, e416.

Ait-Aoudia, S., Guerrout, E. H., & Mahiou, R. (2014, July). Medical image segmentation using particle swarm optimization. In *2014 18th international conference on information visualisation* (pp. 287–291). IEEE.

Azarang, A., & Kehtarnavaz, N. (2020). Image fusion in remote sensing by multi-objective deep learning. *International Journal of Remote Sensing, 41*(24), 95079524. http://doi.org/10.1080/014311 61.2020.1800126

Bandaru, S., & Deb, K. (2016). Metaheuristic techniques. *Decision Sciences*, 693–750.

Bandyopadhyay, S., Maulik, U., & Mukhopadhyay, A. (2007). Multiobjective genetic clustering for pixel classification in remote sensing imagery. *IEEE Transactions on Geoscience and Remote Sensing, 45*(5), 1506–1511.

Benaichouche, A. N., Oulhadj, H., & Siarry, P. (2016). Multiobjective improved spatial fuzzy C-means clustering for image segmentation combining Pareto-optimal clusters. *Journal of Heuristics, 22*(4), 383–404.

Bhanu, B., Lee, S., & Ming, J. (1995). Adaptive image segmentation using a genetic algorithm. *IEEE Transactions on Systems, Man, and Cybernetics, 25*(12), 1543–1567.

Boldaji, M. N., & Semnani, S. H. (2021). Color image segmentation using multi-objective swarm optimizer and multi-level histogram thresholding. *arXiv preprint arXiv:2110.09217*.

Chakraborty, S., & Mali, K. (2018). Application of multiobjective optimization techniques in biomedical image segmentation—A study. In *Multi-objective optimization* (pp. 181–194). Singapore: Springer.

Chen, W., Yan, J., Chen, M., & Li, X. (2010). Diversity of Pareto front: A multiobjective genetic algorithm based on dominating information. *Journal of Control Theory and Applications, 8*(2), 222–228.

Chin-Wei, B., & Rajeswari, M. (2010). Multiobjective optimization approaches in image segmentation—The directions and challenges. *International Journal of Advances in Soft Computing and Its Applications, 2*(1), 40–64.

Coello, C. A. C., Lamont, G. B., & Van Veldhuizen, D. A. (2007). *Evolutionary algorithms for solving multi-objective problems* (Vol. 5, pp. 79–104). New York: Springer.

Cohon, J. L., & Marks, D. H. (1975). A review and evaluation of multiobjective programing techniques. *Water Resources Research, 11*(2), 208–220.

Couceiro, M., & Ghamisi, P. (2016). Particle swarm optimization. In *Fractional order Darwinian particle swarm optimization* (pp. 1–10). Cham: Springer.

Cruz-Aceves, I., Avina-Cervantes, J. G., Lopez-Hernandez, J. M., Rostro-Gonzalez, H., Garcia-Capulin, C. H., Torres-Cisneros, M., & Guzman-Cabrera, R. (2013). Multiple active contours guided by differential evolution for medical image segmentation. *Computational and Mathematical Methods in Medicine, 2013*.

Cui, Y., Geng, Z., Zhu, Q., & Han, Y. (2017). Multi-objective optimization methods and application in energy saving. *Energy, 125*, 681–704.

Datta, N. S., Dutta, H. S., Majumder, K., Chatterjee, S., & Wasim, N. A. (2018). A survey on the application of multi-objective optimization methods in image segmentation. In *Multi-objective optimization* (pp. 269–278). Singapore: Springer.

Deb, K. (2007). Current trends in evolutionary multi-objective optimization. *International Journal for Simulation and Multidisciplinary Design Optimization, 1*(1), 1–8.

Debakla, M., Salem, M., Bouiadjra, R. B., & Rebbah, M. (2019). CMA-ES based fuzzy clustering approach for MRI images segmentation. *International Journal of Computers and Applications*, 1–7.

Dey, N., & Ashour, A. S. (2018). Meta-heuristic algorithms in medical image segmentation: A review. *Advancements in Applied Metaheuristic Computing*, 185–203.

Dorigo, M., & Di Caro, G. (1999, July). Ant colony optimization: A new meta-heuristic. In *Proceedings of the 1999 congress on evolutionary computation-CEC99 (Cat. No. 99TH8406)* (Vol. 2, pp. 1470–1477). IEEE.

El Joumani, S., Mechkouri, S. E., Zennouhi, R., El Kadmiri, O., & Masmoudi, L. (2017). Segmentation method based on multiobjective optimization for very high spatial resolution satellite images. *EURASIP Journal on Image and Video Processing, 2017*(1), 1–9.

Ezugwu, A. E., Adeleke, O. J., Akinyelu, A. A., & Viriri, S. (2020). A conceptual comparison of several metaheuristic algorithms on continuous optimisation problems. *Neural Computing and Applications, 32*(10), 6207–6251.

FredyGustavo, R. S., Quintana Rojas, R. L., Vazquez Noguera, J. L., Ayala, H. L., & Pinto-Roa, D. P. (2020, January). Image segmentation based on multi-objective evolutionary algorithms. *Paper presented at the conference of computational interdisciplinary science*.

Ganesan, T., Elamvazuthi, I., Shaari, K. Z. K., & Vasant, P. (2013). Swarm intelligence and gravitational search algorithm for multi-objective optimization of synthesis gas production. *Applied Energy, 103*, 368–374.

Gao, X. Z., Nalluri, M. S. R., Kannan, K., & Sinharoy, D. (2021). Multi-objective optimization of feature selection using hybrid cat swarm optimization. *Science China Technological Sciences, 64*(3), 508–520.

Geem, Z. W., Kim, J. H., & Loganathan, G. V. (2001). A new heuristic optimization algorithm: Harmony search. *Simulation, 76*(2), 60–68.

Ghosh, P. (2010). *Medical image segmentation using a genetic algorithm.* Portland State University. Dissertations and Theses. Paper 25. https://doi.org/10.15760/etd.25.

Ghosh, P., Mitchell, M., Tanyi, J. A., & Hung, A. Y. (2016). Incorporating priors for medical image segmentation using a genetic algorithm. *Neurocomputing, 195,* 181–194.

Holland, J. H. (1992). *Adaptation in natural and artificial systems: An introductory analysis with applications to biology, control, and artificial intelligence.* Cambridge, MA: MIT Press.

Hsieh, C. T., & Hu, C. S. (2014). Fingerprint recognition by multi-objective optimization PSO hybrid with SVM. *Journal of Applied Research and Technology, 12*(6), 1014–1024.

Jia, H., Lang, C., Oliva, D., Song, W., & Peng, X. (2019a). Hybrid grasshopper optimization algorithm and differential evolution for multilevel satellite image segmentation. *Remote Sensing, 11*(9), 1134.

Jia, H., Peng, X., Song, W., Lang, C., Xing, Z., & Sun, K. (2019b). Multiverse optimization algorithm based on Lévy flight improvement for multithreshold color image segmentation. *IEEE Access, 7,* 32805–32844.

Jiao, W., Chen, W., & Zhang, J. (2021). An improved cuckoo search algorithm for multithreshold image segmentation. *Security and Communication Networks,* 2021.

Karaboga, D. (2010). Artificial bee colony algorithm. *Scholarpedia, 5*(3), 6915.

Kumar, D., Kumar, V., & Kumari, R. (2019). Automatic clustering using quantum-based multi-objective emperor penguin optimizer and its applications to image segmentation. *Modern Physics Letters A, 34*(24), 1950193.

Laumanns, M., Thiele, L., Deb, K., & Zitzler, E. (2002). Combining convergence and diversity in evolutionary multiobjective optimization. *Evolutionary Computation, 10*(3), 263–282.

Lin, Q., Jin, G., Ma, Y., Wong, K. C., Coello, C. A. C., Li, J., Chen, J., & Zhang, J. (2017). A diversity-enhanced resource allocation strategy for decomposition-based multiobjective evolutionary algorithm. *IEEE Transactions on Cybernetics, 48*(8), 2388–2401.

Liu, C., Bian, T., & Zhou, A. (2021). Multiobjective multiple features fusion: A case study in image segmentation. *Swarm and Evolutionary Computation, 60,* 100792.

Ma, A., Wan, Y., Zhong, Y., Wang, J., & Zhang, L. (2021). SceneNet: Remote sensing scene classification deep learning network using multi-objective neural evolution architecture search. *ISPRS Journal of Photogrammetry and Remote Sensing, 172,* 171–188.

Ma, J. (2017, December). A multi-objective evolutionary algorithm for color image segmentation. In *Mining intelligence and knowledge exploration: 5th international conference, MIKE 2017, Hyderabad, India, December 13–15, 2017, Proceedings* (Vol. 10682, p. 168). New York: Springer.

Maulik, U. (2009). Medical image segmentation using genetic algorithms. *IEEE Transactions on Information Technology in Biomedicine, 13*(2), 166–173.

Mesejo, P., Ibáñez, O., Cordón, O., & Cagnoni, S. (2016). A survey on image segmentation using metaheuristic-based deformable models: State of the art and critical analysis. *Applied Soft Computing, 44,* 1–29.

Miettinen, K., Ruiz, F., & Wierzbicki, A. P. (2008). Introduction to multiobjective optimization: interactive approaches. In *Multiobjective optimization* (pp. 27–57). Berlin and Heidelberg: Springer.

Mukhopadhyay, A., Bandyopadhyay, S., & Maulik, U. (2006, October). Clustering using multi-objective genetic algorithm and its application to image segmentation. In *2006 IEEE international conference on systems, man and cybernetics* (Vol. 3, pp. 2678–2683). IEEE.

Nakib, A., Oulhadj, H., & Siarry, P. (2007). Image histogram thresholding based on multiobjective optimization. *Signal Processing, 87*(11), 2516–2534.

Nakib, A., Oulhadj, H., & Siarry, P. (2008). Non-supervised image segmentation based on multiobjective optimization. *Pattern Recognition Letters, 29*(2), 161–172.

Pasolli, L., Notarnicola, C., & Bruzzone, L. (2012). Multi-objective parameter optimization in support vector regression: General formulation and application to the retrieval of soil moisture from remote sensing data. *IEEE Journal of Selected Topics in Applied Earth Observations and Remote Sensing, 5*(5), 1495–1508.

Peitz, S., & Dellnitz, M. (2018). A survey of recent trends in multiobjective optimal control—Surrogate models, feedback control and objective reduction. *Mathematical and Computational Applications*, 23(2), 30.

Qian, X., Zhang, X., Jiao, L., & Ma, W. (2008, June). Unsupervised texture image segmentation using multiobjective evolutionary clustering ensemble algorithm. In *2008 IEEE congress on evolutionary computation (IEEE World Congress on Computational Intelligence)* (pp. 3561–3567). IEEE.

Rajagopal, A., Joshi, G. P., Ramachandran, A., Subhalakshmi, R. T., Khari, M., Jha, S., & You, J. (2020). A deep learning model based on multi-objective particle swarm optimization for scene classification in unmanned aerial vehicles. *IEEE Access*, 8, 135383–135393.

Reynolds, C. W. (1987, August). Flocks, herds and schools: A distributed behavioral model. In *Proceedings of the 14th annual conference on Computer graphics and interactive techniques* (pp. 25–34). ACM Press, ISBN: 0897912276.

Sag, T., & Çunkaş, M. (2015). Color image segmentation based on multiobjective artificial bee colony optimization. *Applied Soft Computing*, 34, 389–401.

Saha, S., & Bandyopadhyay, S. (2010). Use of different forms of symmetry and multi-objective optimization for automatic pixel classification in remote-sensing satellite imagery. *International Journal of Remote Sensing*, 31(22), 5751–5775.

Shaygan, M., Alimohammadi, A., Mansourian, A., Govara, Z. S., & Kalami, S. M. (2013). Spatial multi-objective optimization approach for land use allocation using NSGA-II. *IEEE Journal of Selected Topics in Applied Earth Observations and Remote Sensing*, 7(3), 906–916.

Shirakawa, S., & Nagao, T. (2009, May). Evolutionary image segmentation based on multiobjective clustering. In *2009 IEEE congress on evolutionary computation* (pp. 2466–2473). IEEE.

Storn, R. (1995). Differential evolution-a simple and efficient adaptive scheme for global optimization over continuous spaces. *Technical Report, International Computer Science Institute*, 11.

Takano, T., Nakane, T., Akashi, T., & Zhang, C. (2021). Braille block detection via multi-objective optimization from an egocentric viewpoint. *Sensors*, 21(8), 2775.

Vachhani, V. L., Dabhi, V. K., & Prajapati, H. B. (2015, March). Survey of multi objective evolutionary algorithms. In *2015 international conference on circuits, power and computing technologies [ICCPCT-2015]* (pp. 1–9). IEEE.

Yang, X. S. (2010). Firefly algorithm, stochastic test functions and design optimisation. *International Journal of Bio-Inspired Computation*, 2(2), 78–84.

Yang, X. S., & Deb, S. (2009, December). Cuckoo search via Lévy flights. In *2009 World congress on nature & biologically inspired computing (NaBIC)* (pp. 210–214). IEEE.

Yang, X. S., & He, X. (2013). Bat algorithm: Literature review and applications. *International Journal of Bio-Inspired Computation*, 5(3), 141–149.

Zhang, Y., Gong, D. W., Sun, X. Y., & Guo, Y. N. (2017). A PSO-based multi-objective multi-label feature selection method in classification. *Scientific Reports*, 7(1), 1–12.

Zhong, Y., Zhang, S., & Zhang, L. (2013). Automatic fuzzy clustering based on adaptive multi-objective differential evolution for remote sensing imagery. *IEEE Journal of Selected Topics in Applied Earth Observations and Remote Sensing*, 6(5), 2290–2301.

Index